The Scientific Analysis of Personality

The Scientific Analysis of Personality

Raymond B. Cattell

AldineTransaction
A Division of Transaction Publishers
New Brunswick (U.S.A.) and London (U.K.)

First paperback printing 2008

Library of Congress Catalog Number: 2006051149
ISBN: 978-0-202-30915-6
Printed in the United States of America

Library of Congress Cataloging-in-Publication Data

Rodgers, Barbara N.
  The scientific analysis of personality / Raymond B. Cattell.
     p. cm.
  Originally published: Chicago : Aldine Pub. Co., 1996.
  Includes bibliographical references and indexes.
  ISBN 0-202-30915-0 (alk. paper)
    1. Personality I. Title.

BF698.C36 2007
155.2—dc22   2006051149

CONTENTS

4 Further Traits, and their Integration

5 The Techniques of Objective Personality Measurement

6 Finer Issues in Personality Measurement: States, Instruments, Roles

7 The Main Features of Our Dynamic Structure

8 The Clinical Measurement of Conflict and Maladjustment

9 Analysis of the Concept of Integration of Personality

The Scientific Analysis of
Personality

CHAPTER ONE

By What Methods Can Personality Be Studied?

THE BOUNDARIES OF PSYCHOLOGICAL SCIENCE

Personalities react differently even to the study of personality. To the scientifically minded it is the supreme scientific challenge, promising formulae of fantastic and intriguing complexity. To others the notion that we will measure and predict in the field of human personality is a sacrilege and a threat. Yet in an age when we are investigating everything, how can we shut our eyes to the possibilities of scientifically studying personality?

The man who objects on principle to studying, measuring, and using predictive laws about personality because it must be 'for ever unpredictable' is on shaky ground. For his own wife can probably predict with considerable accuracy what he will do when presented with various stimuli and situations. And, as usual, the ability to predict brings to her the ability to control! Psychology thrusts no new moral dilemmas upon us. At most, by increasing possibilities of prediction and control, it demands that we attend more seriously to the solution of old moral and philosophical dilemmas.

For example, the old philosophical debate on free will-*vs*-determinism rears afresh its enigmatic head. Is man a machine, albeit a very wonderful machine, which reacts completely according to causal laws, so that all our decisions are predetermined? Why should one object to making decisions like a chemical balance, which tells us faithfully which weight is heavier? Do we really like an unreliable man, whose erratic decisions spoil our plans? More likely, we call him a madman. Most of us basically prefer an orderliness in our own sensations and feelings, as well as a rationality, i.e. predictive dependability, in the behaviour of those about us. And yet we paradoxically hope that there is some final citadel in each of us in which the unpredictable may happen.

This hope may not be merely vanity, nor is it as unreasonable from the context of science as a Victorian physicist would have asserted. Modern scientists already are compelled to accept the Heisenberg indeterminacy principle which admits that in observing the smallest particles the usual predictive principles break down. Surely it is not altogether unlikely that the psychologist will similarly come to frontiers where laws which hold over large, familiar domains ultimately misfire. But the young science of psychology has scarcely reached such frontiers and, unless and until proof is given to the contrary, psychologists will continue to believe in orderly cause and effect in the mental as in the general physical realm.

The modest but indubitable increase in the power to understand and predict human behaviour which has occurred in the last half-century of psychological research thus really leaves the philosophical issue untouched. But it has aggravated moral issues in regard to legal responsibility for crime, the dangers of political brain-washing, some trespasses by the psychiatrist upon the grounds of the priest, and with questions as to how far advertising should use new and powerful psychological techniques of influence. Our concern in this book is with the science itself. Mostly we must leave these issues of valuation to the reader and his moral leaders.

All science rests upon and begins with accurate description and measurement. Mental phenomena may seem too intangible for measurement. But the faith of the psychologist was simply and cogently stated a generation ago by E. L. Thorndike (1874–1949), at Columbia University, New York, in the dictum that: 'Whatever exists, exists in some quantity and can (in principle) be measured.' Note, however, that he and other psychologists are talking about behaviour, not consciousness. Earlier psychologists and philosophers, e.g. Bertrand Russell, Titchener, and Ward (whose article in the 11th Edition of the *Encyclopedia Britannica* is considered a classic) considered that psychology should be a science of consciousness. But there we cannot measure because no two people can check the same observation. Consequently, the exact connexion of consciousness with behaviour, as talked about in 'the riddle of mind and matter', remains an issue, like free will-*vs*-determinism, which our present methods are incapable of encompassing. In our behaviouristic psychology we may sometimes, for economy of language, use a term dealing apparently with consciousness, like 'pleasure', or 'anger', but to the strictly behaviouristic psychologist this has to be defined by changes in behaviour, physiology, or other measurable manifestations.

Incidentally, one should avoid confusing 'behaviourism' with 'reflexology', which is a special 'model' within psychology, and not a very adequate one at that. Behaviouristic psychology is simply a science based on observing behaviour, and claiming no short-cuts through personal consciousness.

THE THREE HISTORICAL STAGES IN PERSONALITY STUDY

Personality study is only one of several sections into which psychology is sub-divided. Others are perception, comparative (animal) psychology, learning, abnormal psychology, physiological psychology, social psychology, and so on. But it is a very central speciality in that most of the others may be considered abstracted *facets* of the total, unitary personality (or organism) in action. Pursued too narrowly, they easily degenerate into the play without Hamlet.

The systematizing of human knowledge about personality has fallen broadly into three historical phases:

1. The literary and philosophical phase, a game of personal insight and conventional beliefs extending from the first thoughtful caveman to the most recent novelist and playwright.

2. The stage of organized observation and theorizing, which we may call the proto-clinical phase. This grew up through the attempts of medicine to cope with abnormal, 'sick' behaviour. It had its centre in the psychiatric generalizations of men like Kraepelin, the father of medical psychology in Germany, Janet, his counterpart in France, and Freud, whom everyone knows. But it also included philosophers or academic men specializing in personality, like William James in America, Ward, and Klages. All this theory flowered not only in the work of Freud, but also of Kretschmer, McDougall, Jung, Adler, and others who wrote of fascinating, if not always soundly-based notions concerning

personality, from late in the last century until well into this one.

3. The quantitative and experimental phase, which did not begin (as far as personality, rather than other aspects of psychology, is concerned) until just before the turn of this century, and is only beginning to show its fruits in the last decade.

As to the first, the literary or prescientific phase, doubtless it contains insights which still surpass in refinement those depended upon by many psychiatrists or experimental psychologists today. But who knows, among the many brilliant ideas offered, which are true ones? Some will claim that the statements about human nature by Dostoyevsky or Shakespeare constitute the zenith of human understanding of the subject. But if others favour the views of Goethe, or Dumas, or Conrad, or Somerset Maugham, the literary 'method' offers no objective way of sorting out the truth. It is certain, from psychological observations of readers' reactions, that most are quite ready to accept with conviction, as marvels of literary insight, manikins and plots deliberately put together with psychologically false mechanisms. Conversely, literary critics are also ready to reject, as too strange for fiction, a playwright's character who, though unusual, exhibits known psychological mechanisms. Undoubtedly there *are* gems of scientific truth about personality, lying available in this literary approach, but there is no way – except through the fresh start of scientific research – to separate the living truths from the pasteboard shams. Probably we do best to enjoy literature as an aesthetic product, in which scientific hypotheses of some vitality may exist, but not proven scientific discoveries.

Although both of the two following historical phases may, by contrast, be called 'scientific in intention' and general method, their differences today strike us as greater than their similarities. The first defect of the middle, 'clinical' development, relative to the final scientific phase, is that, as the name indicates, it began with the study of the insane and the neurotic. When science still lacks fine instruments, it is good – and, indeed, necessary – strategy to try to understand the normal by looking at the gross exaggerations of its mechanisms in the abnormal magnification. Physiology went through the same phase, as an adjunct of medicine, before it became an experimental science. Most ideas up to the Renaissance came largely from the pathology seen in medical practice. But in the end, a price is paid for this magnification. One may begin to believe that what are essentially special disease processes describe normal functioning. For example, psychiatrists have seen so many neurotic symptoms begin with guilt from the pressure of the super-ego or conscience that for many of them conscience is almost an evil thing! They whittle away at it, and the 'success' they achieve is to begin with a neurotic and end with an 'acting out' disorder – a social nuisance. Only by study of the vaster number of normal people does one come to see that it was not necessarily any excessive development of conscience which created these neurotics, but rather an abnormality and instability in the way in which they reacted to the demands of their super-egos.

The second major shortcoming of the clinical phase was that it did not use and even despised quantitative methods. There is not a single measurement in the work of Pierre Janet, Sigmund Freud, Alfred Adler, and Carl Jung – and very little in that of Emil Kraepelin. When Jung tells that patient X became more and more out of touch with his 'archetypal unconscious', no measurements are offered to demonstrate it, such as we would require if a doctor argued that a patient's illness arose from a continual elevation of his blood sugar. These writers gained a huge popular following, in an audience extending from playwrights to anthropologists and medical men, with theories often based on description of a single case and where the very description failed to agree with that by others.

Of course, there are phases in every science which must be more descriptive than quantitative. Many quite sound developments occurred in botany, physiology, geology, etc., before measurement came into use, and one can point to Darwin's creation of the theory of evolution as a masterpiece which seemed to rest on qualitative description. Measurement, however, was implicit in Darwin's laws and generalizations and was not missing from his notebooks. Moreover, at the physical level we find far less disagreement and misunderstanding among observers than when different psychologists set out to describe the same set of 'facts'. If Darwin said that snails in Patagonia are twice as big as in England, few who travelled would have any doubts on this, but if one psychologist says the level of anxiety among Italians is higher than among Frenchmen, there is usually another ready to assert the opposite with equal confidence, and, what is more, to erect an elaborate theory on his observation!

THE LIMITATIONS OF CLINICAL STUDY

It is not surprising that the intrinsically intriguing and intellectually promising clinical phase of inquiry quickly became a luxuriant jungle of conflicting theoretical growths. Despite its scientific 'intention', its actual methodological kinship to the first or literary phase is shown, among other ways, by the enthusiasm with which writers, from good novelists to Hollywood script-writers, adopted its concepts and its jargon to give 'depth' and 'insight' to their stories. 'Complex', 'repression', 'defence', 'introversion', 'inferiority complex', 'super-ego', 'erotic fixation', etc., became first literary and then newspaper terms. Of course, science lives by conflicting theories, but what were accepted as 'theories' even by many professional psychologists and psychiatrists were very poor imitations of what physical scientists call a theory. These verbally clever elaborations could provide a mystically exciting and rewardingly esoteric conversation for two psychiatrists, but they differed from true scientific theories in that they could neither be proved nor disproved, because they were never thought through with a precision which would permit their being brought into contact with quantitative checks or experiments. Indeed, one of the leading British clinical researchers, Eysenck, has recently thrown a refreshing dash of cold water on these super-heated contestants by pointing out that there is even no proof at the pragmatic level. He points out that there is no proof that therapies based on these theories really perform their intended function – of doing the patient, as distinct from the psychiatrist, some demonstrable good.

History written a generation hence will probably size up the situation by pointing out that although this second phase had its quota of men of great genius, like Jung and Freud, it nevertheless amounted scientifically almost to a disaster in that the impressive façade of pseudo-knowledge took away the incentive to make those more modest experiments on which the advance of science depends. In retrospect, except for something vaguely known as 'free association' – letting the mind wander – it developed no methods to prove what it asserted. Even the father of psychoanalysis, Freud, based his generalizations on so few cases that a statistician can only blush for him, while critics can assert that the conflicts he described were peculiar to middle-class Viennese in a *fin-de-siècle* culture. It is not surprising, therefore, that the clinical contribution finished in a kind of intellectual shouting match, such as one might expect if a crowd of newspaper men invaded the affairs of a laboratory. No one can deny a man the right to believe that he is a genius, so it was inevitable that the insights of men like Freud were soon 'improved', 'modified', or simply called old-fashioned, by several thousand clinicians quite as convinced of their personal genius as was Freud of his.

By contrast, the scientific study of personality which got slowly into motion at the turn of this century has based its theories on actual behavioural measurements. Different laboratories can repeat them and statistical and mathematical treatments of these measurements can be applied by anyone who wishes to check. If a theory asserts that breast-fed babies are more optimistic in temperament as adults than those who are not, the experimenter applies measures of optimism of attitudes to a hundred of each. If it is suspected that anxiety rises in adolescence, then anxiety measures can be given to persons at each of a dozen age levels, and curves plotted. A generalization that introverts more easily become neurotic can be examined by measuring children leaving school on introversion–extraversion scales and keeping clinical records for ensuing years, and so on. It is a harder task, but a more rewarding one, when different scientists can cross-examine the evidence and reach agreement, and when the pieces of the jigsaw puzzle of psychology begin solidly to fit together.

At first there was some tendency to put new wine in old bottles, in that many of the new experimentalists tended, sometimes unconsciously, to take the theories to be experimentally tested exclusively from the second or clinical phase of observation. But increasingly they are finding ideas – ideas of greater precision and complexity – directly from laws and regularities observable in their own more exact data. Even though one believes that the distinction in methodological rigour between the scientific and the proto-clinical is a vital one for science, in which no sloppy compromise can be tolerated, yet it is not necessary to combine new methods with complete rejection of old theories, or to indulge the scientific snobbery of denying our ideational ancestry. There are valuable adumbrations of new and useful concepts to be found in the sensitive intuitions of clinical men. For that reason the present writer has carried on, in his own experimental work, the actual psychoanalytic terminology, wherever recent experiment confirms and sharpens the earlier concept (though not without criticism from some experimentalist colleagues!). On the other hand, personality psychologists have no need to depend for more than a fraction of their hypotheses on second-hand clinical concepts. As the following pages may show, the new methods have produced directly a fascinating array of new notions – notions which, moreover, are immediately in terms and operations fit for continuing experiment.

THE MULTIVARIATE AND UNIVARIATE EXPERIMENTAL METHODS

Possibly the reader is beginning to feel that he has now served a sufficient apprenticeship to historical perspectives and talk about methods, and is ready to be rewarded with some factual discoveries. In physical science, at least until recently, the layman could go a long way in understanding the essentials with little disciplining in method. But psychology is a more tricky field, in which even outstanding authorities have been known to run in circles 'describing things which everyone knows in language which no one understands'. Quite a number of statistical concepts, for example, are essential to understanding what experimental psychology is saying that is different from older notions. Indeed, the student making a profession of psychology is now accustomed to taking about a year simply to get sophisticated about methods, statistics, and the pitfalls which caught earlier generations, and into which he is otherwise all too likely to fall. Consequently we must devote another page or two to defining methods and approaches before we are ready to look at findings.

On scrutinizing the third – quantitative and experimental – historical phase of personality study, we recognize that in fact it splits into two distinct streams. On the one side we see a powerful current of behavioural experiment which began in Russia with Ivan Pavlov and has centred on the conditioned reflex and learning theory. Occasionally writers have miscalled this 'behaviourism', as pointed out in the above introduction. This is a misnomer, for the earlier German experimental work by Wundt and others was often equally behaviouristic, and so also is the second and very distinct main stream we have now to consider. The Russian development of psychology out of physiology, by Ivan Pavlov (1849–1936) and his followers is properly called the *reflexological* development because it takes a reflex (initially an actual nerve reflex arc) from stimulus to response as its 'model'. Actually it is a sub-section of that larger, controlled, laboratory, 'brass instrument' methodology, which includes the work of Wilhelm Wundt (1832–1920) and many others, and which for reasons soon to be explained we shall call the *univariate experimental* approach (or sometimes the 'bivariate', because there is one variable manipulated and one variable watched).

The successes of classical 'univariate' experiments in building a clear-cut body of theory and experiment have been very great, notably in perception and learning, though the repeated attempts to bring it fruitfully into contact with personality and psychotherapy have not been considered so successful – except in Russia. There the tradition fits political assumptions, e.g. of materialistic, physiological emphasis, and the notion that heredity is unimportant compared to environmental conditioning. It may become evident as we study the complexity of personality why this univariate approach – this concentration on a single stimulus with a single response – has had only limited success in dealing with individual differences and the behaviour of the functionally unitary organism. Yet personality and learning theory must be brought together.

The second main confluent stream, which has been called

multivariate experiment (experiment handling many variables at once) had a very different beginning. Sir Francis Galton (1822–1911), a cousin of Darwin, an African explorer, and the discoverer of the cyclone–anticyclone structure in meteorology, was also an indefatigable and very resourceful student of human nature. In connexion with his studies of abilities, he invented (with Karl Pearson, a rather austere mathematical statistician of London University) the correlation coefficient and began to show how the structure and development of individual personality differences could be elucidated by statistical analyses of natural behaviour outside the laboratory, as well as in it. Close to the laboratory which he founded at University College, London, Charles Spearman (1863–1945) and Sir Cyril Burt continued his multivariate development, and the ball was soon picked up abroad by Thurstone, of whom we shall hear more.

Whereas the univariate method follows the older sciences in bringing the man into the laboratory chair, surrounded by brass instruments, the multivariate method says that with sufficient analytical subtlety we can tease out the connexions from the behaviour of the man in his actual life situation – without the false situation of controlling and manipulating. (Multivariate experiment *can* control but it has no *need* to do so.) Consequently, whereas the Wundt–Pavlov methods and interests took their beginnings close to physiology – indeed Pavlov was researching on stomach physiology when he noticed the conditioned reflex, and many of the German psychologists were investigating the physiology of the special senses – the Galton–Spearman developments began broadly with life behaviour as such and especially social behaviour.

Sir Francis Galton gathered statistics on personality and ability wherever it was available, but principally in regard to high cultural performance, while Karl Pearson was especially interested in what the *average* man is like, anthropologically and psychologically. In its break from the classical univariate experiment theirs was a more bold and imaginative step in studying human psychology than Wundt's, and it has led to tremendous developments in mathematical statistical use of the electronic computer in analysing human behaviour. Wundt's clinging more closely to established sciences may have been oriented to giving to the new science of psychology more standing, whereas Galton had the sublime indifference to appearances which one sees in a fox terrier with his nose in a rabbit burrow.

When Spearman, from 1900 to 1930, followed up this early quantitative study of individual differences by setting up controlled 'tests', his approach was still not that of 'taking a bit of a man into the laboratory' but rather of studying the whole man in virtually natural surroundings, and finding out by statistical analysis how various kinds of behaviour are connected. Notably Spearman asked the question, 'Is there one general ability, which we may call general intelligence, or are people's minds made up of *a lot of distinct and independent* abilities?' To answer this, he took a few hundred people and gave them thirty to forty different kinds of test. He then, by a precise computation of correlation coefficients (see Chapter 2), found out if people tended to keep the same rank order in different tests. In answering his question (Yes, there *is* a single general intelligence structure), he gave birth to the method of factor analysis which we shall describe in the next chapter.

One can get a more sympathetic understanding of many disagreements over theory, and a wider view of why personality study is developing the way it is, if one keeps in mind the difference between these two traditions, which we have called the univariate and the multivariate. They still remain to some extent distinct, though equally important parts of the true science of experimental psychology now going forward so vigorously in this century. The persisting feature of the Galton–Spearman approach is that it is multivariate, i.e. it studies many measurements on the same person, instead of only one variable or process at a time, as in the Wundt–Pavlov tradition, and that it studies behaviour with less artificial control or interference. The univariate, laboratory method, with its isolation of the single process, has worked well in the older sciences, but where total organisms have to be studied, the theoretical possibility must be faced that one can sometimes hope to find a law only if *the total organism* is included in the observations and experiences – not just a bit of its behaviour. In this respect, the emphasis on 'wholeness' in the multivariate method is actually the same as in the clinical method, but it is quantitative and follows explicit calculations of laws and general conclusions. For the clinician appraises the total pattern 'by eye', and tries to make generalizations from a good memory, whereas the multivariate experimenter actually *measures* all the variables and may then set an electronic computer to abstract the regularities which exist, instead of depending on human powers of memory and generalization. The clinical approach to personality is thus really that of a multivariate experimenter without benefit of apparatus – and has had the additional drawback that it produces its personality theories from data gathered from abnormal, diseased processes rather than normal ranges.

There is one other respect in which the psychologist studying personality by multivariate methods has advantages over the classical univariate experimenter who clamps his subject in place in the laboratory. The fact that he can study behaviour in its natural setting means that he can deal with emotionally important matters and real personality learning. Neither our ethics, nor the self-protectiveness of people themselves, will stand for psychologists giving subjects major emotional shocks or altering their whole personalities for a laboratory thesis!

An experimenter exactly following the classical experimental design, but who happened to be a moral imbecile, might with cold logic and force of habit set out to find the effect upon the personality of a mother of losing a child. Furthermore, he would need to 'out-Herod Herod' by removing the child in half the cases, and continuing with the child in the other half of his 'controlled experiment'. Since life itself inevitably makes these tragic 'experiments', a researcher in the tradition of the Galton–Spearman statistical tradition will simply compare mothers who have and have not suffered such bereavement and make his analysis of the results 'balancing' for the things he cannot manipulate. In short, the method everywhere seeks to get out by subtle statistical analysis of natural data what in the physical sciences would be done by manipulative control.

To follow the classical univariate controlled experiment in personality study would, therefore, mean to be confined to emotionally trivial, superficial matters or else to be forced to experiment on animals – where major frustration and emotional upsets can be applied. But then one encounters the defect that the 'personality' of an animal is pretty remote from human personality and culture. On the other hand, the development of beautiful and complex mathematico-statistical methods like factor analysis has enabled us to take natural data, much as the clinician has long done – except that normals are now included – and to find laws and build sound theories about the structure and functioning of personality.

THE AIM OF THE PRESENT ACCOUNT

From the above outline of the springs of interest and method in personality study the reader will appreciate that we are setting out, in the spirit of the third historical impulse, towards that scientific analysis of personality indicated by the title of this book. This discipline does not mean that we narrow our subject matter. Dreams, slips of the tongue, neuroses, hypnotism, the conflicts of adolescence, humour, and the clash of cultures come within our scope just as much as they do into psychoanalysis, and the clinical theories of the last generation. And we are prepared to accept, at the level of probability of knowledge on which many everyday human decisions are made, that dreams express suppressed sexual wishes, that humour may show a 'death wish', or that a slip of the tongue may express the same conflict as underlies a neurosis. But these have all to be established again, at any truly scientific level of certainty, by the more objective disciplines we are describing.

Necessarily, we shall not get so far by these newer methods, for they are more difficult and time-consuming. The older stories have considerable advantages for the popularizer of 'psychology' in that they are more colourful, gossipy, and dogmatically complete. We shall spend no time in specifically describing them for they must be known to the reader through hundreds of books, Hollywood, and the Sunday Press.

In the strictly scientific treatment the balance of fact and theory is very different. Here there are only restricted patches of firm order in a mysterious unknown. Indeed, we stand at a tantalizing point where brilliant progress has been made in the initial task of describing and measuring personality, but there has not yet been time for the new instruments to be used over developmental periods, over therapy and learning experiences by clinicians, or in much laboratory experiment, for example, of a physiological kind.

However, what it lacks in terms of such a false completeness, it makes up in terms of practical effectiveness on the one hand, and intricate mathematical beauty of method and theory on the other. It has wedded psychology to 'the queen of the sciences', mathematics, and though the progeny are not yet numerous, they are very promising.

*

READING

Flugel, J. C., *A Hundred Years of Psychology*. (Latest edition) Duckworth, 1951.

Freud, S., *A General Introduction to Psychoanalysis*. Garden City Publishing Co., New York, 1943.

CHAPTER TWO

The Formation of Personality by Environment and Heredity

SITUATIONS AND TRAITS

Personality may be defined as that which tells what a man will do when placed in a given situation. This statement can be formulated:

$$R = f(S.P)$$

which says that R, the nature and magnitude of a person's behavioural response, i.e. what he says, thinks, or does, is some function of the S, the stimulus situation in which he is placed and of P, the nature of his personality. For the moment, we do not attempt to say more precisely what f, the function, is. That is something to be found by research. Nor shall we bother too much at this stage about how the stimulus is to be measured. But we can be reasonably certain that we shall want to describe and measure the personality by a number of *traits*, and perhaps also by mood states at the time.

For example, the situation could be a pretty girl sitting on the next seat in a bus. The response of the young man in whose personality we are interested might be to take surreptitious sidelong glances, or to speak to her, or perhaps to attempt to kiss her. If we know even one trait in his personality, namely, his degree of shyness, we might make a tolerable prediction of how long he would remain silent before attempting conversation. If we watched fifty young men in this situation, we might even find a numerical value for f, which relates the score on shyness (say on a ten-point scale) to the length of time in seconds (measured on a stop watch) before he thinks of something to say. Perhaps it would be:

$$\text{Response Time} = 23 \cdot 5 \times Ps$$

where P_S is the shyness score in personality. It will be noticed that

S, the situation, is left out here, because it is a constant, the same for everyone, but essentially we are using the formula $R = f(S.P)$.

Naturally, one thinks of other traits which will determine how long he takes to say something, such as fertility of imagination in thinking of a good thing to say, so P would have several trait terms in it. Indeed, if he goes to the further response of trying to kiss her, we might infer that he has a trait of being slightly crazy – at least if it is in the first five minutes! It will be seen that there is a mutual inference system here: from behaviour we may infer personality, whereas if we already know the personality traits, we can infer, to some degree of accuracy, the probable behavioural response.

Just how those inferences can be put in effective form, and how mathematically we can combine the various traits in the term P, is something for the next chapter. In this chapter we make only the common-sense assumption that persons have traits and ask what framework of assumptions we employ regarding the formation of such traits. There is admittedly some jumping ahead of our story here, for the fact is that until we have described what traits exist, and by what devices we measure them, it is not possible to find out how they are formed.

But although we wait on measurement research to plot the curve of natural inner maturation for some specific trait, such as kindness, sexual interest, or pugnacity, or to show what experiences lead to acquiring poise or reducing anxiety, yet in a general way we can recognize the influences in personality formation and how they work. Just as an artist 'blocks in' a picture in outline before he gets to detail, so in this chapter we can define the general framework of assumptions about personality within which ensuing chapters will go to greater precision.

PERSONALITY, MOOD, AND ROLE

By holding the situation constant – an averagely pretty girl – we were able to make inferences from traits to behaviour. But in life the situation rarely remains constant! A glance at our very simple equation will show that if we stick to the same man, instead of observing fifty, we should expect *his* response to vary with the strength of the stimulus. With a plain and forbidding young woman, his attempts to join conversation might be minimal, whereas with a beautiful siren making obvious overtures, lively interaction might soon follow.

Lack of allowance for the situation is one of the main causes of misjudging personality. A committee considering the appointment of a young executive were inclined to reject him because a committee member reported that he had shouted in an impolite and excitable manner over the telephone. Inquiry revealed that this happened when his office was on fire. One should divide the response magnitude by the stimulus magnitude (or whatever mathematical relation our equation may settle upon) to arrive at a fair figure for the trait, thus:

$$\frac{R}{S} = f(P)$$

After that, one encounters the question of the effect of transient mood. Psychological state, as distinct from trait, is obviously very important in determining behaviour. Many men have proposed to unsuitable wives in a fit of romantic excitement or killed themselves in a temporary mood of depression. Instability of mood is a trait, but having a particular mood at a particular time is not a trait, yet it determines behaviour. Consequently, our first simple formula must be refined to say 'Personality is what determines behaviour in a defined situation and a defined mood.'

If this is all, however, why does father, in a given mood, and a given situation – a child throwing rolls at the dinner-table – speak sharply to his son but not to his son's friend, the visitor? And why does McCarthy, who merely looked surprised an hour ago when someone went through a red traffic light, now, changed into his police uniform, speak to the current culprit in devastating terms? Obviously, the role of a host, of a policeman, of a father, etc., makes the person behave as if his personality had changed. Has it really changed? To some extent, as we shall see in Chapter 6, this is a semantic matter, depending on where we choose to draw the line between personality and other things. It is probably simpler to say that role is part of personality in the broader sense, for to react in a role the person has had to acquire what it takes to do so. But, regardless of the line, the effect of role must be taken into account just as much as mood in drawing conclusions from behaviour about the more general, basic traits of a personality.

By a trait, therefore, we obviously mean some relatively permanent and broad reaction tendency. Traits are generally divided into three modalities: *abilities, temperament traits,* and *dynamic traits.* An ability is shown in the manner of response to the complexity of a situation, when the individual is clear on what goals he wants to achieve in that situation. A temperament or general personality trait is usually stylistic, in the sense that it deals with tempo, form, persistence, etc., covering a large variety of specific responses. For example, a person may be temperamentally slow, or easy-going, or irritable, or bold. A dynamic trait has to do with motivations and interests. One is speaking of dynamic traits in describing an individual as amorous, or ambitious, or interested in athletics, or having an anti-authority attitude.

Among traits we should also recognize (*a*) common traits – such as intelligence, gregariousness, introversion – which have much the same form for everyone, but of which one person may have more than another, and (*b*) unique traits, which are so specific to an individual that no one else could be scored on the same. The latter are usually either abilities or dynamic traits, e.g. ability to find one's way up Mount X (which only one person knows), degree of friendship for Man Friday.

This brief sketch of trait categories and structures will be given more experimental foundation in Chapter 3, but one can see that one way of describing a personality would be to assign scores on a spectrum of traits.

THE RISE OF TRAITS BY LEARNING

How do we conceive that traits reach the values which they do in different persons? To say that they become what they are either through environment or through the genes might seem prosaic, were it not that some psychologists are for ever omitting one or the other, or introducing some *tertium quid.* Perhaps it would help if one bears in mind that environment means both physical and mental environment and that it begins in the womb. For example, when people read that roughly 20 per cent of the variability in intelligence is found due to environment, they often assume this means schooling differences. But blows on the head, encephalitis, and atherosclerosis probably account for as much of the non-genetic differences in intelligence as do differences of schooling.

Because of the weight of evidence, in studies on animal learning as well as from human clinical material, that the first few years of life are especially potent in learning effects, it is reasonable to conclude that much of the basic formation of personality occurs before, say, six or seven years. On the other hand, it is clear that the irruption of the sex drive in adolescence gives fuel for new learning, and that, combined with independence from the parental roof, it may produce substantial readjustments. Furthermore, personality learning can go on throughout life to old age, as witness King Lear. Age plots of the ego strength factor (see page 285 below) show that this capacity to handle emotional problems and subordinate impulse to more remote satisfactions increases steadily over the whole measured age range.

As in cognitive learning, so in emotional learning, *conditioning* plays an appreciable role. The classical conditioning laws, due to Pavlov, Watson, Hall, Tolman, and others explain the origin, particularly, of some of our irrational fears and prejudices. Watson showed that if the 'conditioned stimulus' – a rabbit in this case – is presented to a child simultaneously with (actually *slightly preceding*) the *unconditioned stimulus* – in this case a frightening loud sound – the young child will soon react by fear, cringing, and crying when the rabbit alone appears.

By subsequently presenting the conditioned stimulus many times with nothing unpleasant happening, or with some positively pleasant association, the fear of the rabbit can be experimentally 'extinguished'. This extinction of conditioned emotional responses has become the basis for what is called *behavioural therapy*, an approach to the cure of neurosis and the mentally ill which is very different from psychoanalysis on the one hand, or chemotherapy – treatment by drugs – on the other.

Change of personality also occurs by a second procedure, different from classical conditioning. In an attempt to squeeze it into the penny-in-the-slot conditioning model it is sometimes called 'operant conditioning', but a better term is *reward learning*. It is most easily illustrated by a rat running a maze when hungry. The passageways which end in food reward become somehow stamped into his habit system, whereas those which do not become forgotten.

With the human child, reward learning obviously plays a powerful role, but the rewards are often so subtle that we cannot immediately understand what happens. In the first place, the human, and also some higher mammals, have drives like self-assertiveness, curiosity, etc. (see Chapter 7 below), which can be as powerful as hunger, sex, and fear in the lower animals. A child may acquire the trait of physical courage through the self-assertive reward (self-regard or pride) of being more like father. Furthermore, there are rewards to the self-sentiment (based on the self concept, Chapter 7) which can more than offset direct losses to a basic drive. When a child is punished by being sent to bed supperless for striking his sister, he suffers not only the loss of hunger-drive satisfactions, by which we teach lower animals, but also a blow to self-regard – a dynamic loss to the self-senti-ment.

Through the endless applications of rewards and punishments (deprivations) by the family, the school, and the peer group, certain patterns of personality response – traits – are gradually built up, fitted to the social culture. Some of this learning involves a third principle, different both from conditioning and the rewards of behaviour on the way to the goal satisfactions of a single drive. This is *integration learning*, the learning of a hierarchy or com-bination of responses which will give the greatest satisfaction *to the personality as a whole*, not just to a single drive. Much of what distinguishes human from animal behaviour is this restraint and subordination of one drive to the satisfactions of many drives – the control of impulse in the interests of a greater long-distance satisfaction of the whole person. There is evidence that integra-tion learning is particularly associated with the development of the frontal lobes of the brain, and, of course, a good intelligence level also often helps in perceiving rewarding integration.

About the role of intelligence in personality learning there is still much doubt. It has a negligible role in conditioning, but both in reward learning and in integration learning it is not necessary that one stumble by trial and error, unconsciously, on the most rewarding adjustment. It can often be perceived by intelligent insight, and this may explain why neurosis and mental disorder tend to be slightly but significantly less common at higher intelligence levels. Intelligent people do not get themselves, on an average, into quite such tangles of frustration. Nevertheless, to see the rewarding thing to do is not the same thing as doing it. It merely helps and, indeed, as St Augustine and other religious leaders have said, high intelligence may even be used to evade emotional learning. Every now and then one is impressed by finding a fundamentally better character, learned in patience, fortitude, and unselfish renunciation, in a borderline mental defective than in some spoilt intellectual *prima donna*.

Intelligence cannot help that part of the learning of emotional attitudes and personality adjustments which is subconscious. And a great deal of our learning of traits is unconscious. One of the gains from the psychoanalytic couch which is least questionable is the realization, in reconstructing the past, of how one came to acquire certain attitudes and ways of responding. The philosopher's ideal, 'Know thyself', is a possible foundation for relearning. However, the clinicians have found that this relearning is not easy, and have been puzzled by an apparent breakdown of the second law of learning in that people will often go on repeating responses which bring punishment rather than reward. This is generally explicable by the third law, in that the personality has become so integrated – perversely in such a case – that obscure rewards, commonly unconscious, have become tied up with the irrationally punishing behaviour.

The sequence of personality learning has been systematized in concepts of 'choice points' or dynamic crossroads, which the reader interested in learning as such may pursue in Chapter 10 and more fully elsewhere (Cattell and Scheier, 1961). Here we have space only to recognize the three main ways in which trait structures may arise through the influence of the environment, principally the human culture. In the next chapter evidence is given for the existence of certain broad traits, like introversion, conscience, desurgency (inhibition), optimism, etc., which show considerable generalization of behaviour. For example, a person who is self-controlled in one situation tends to be self-controlled in another, and a person optimistic in one response tends to optimism in other situations. Psychologists have not yet given adequate explanation of how this might occur through learning. Do conditionings to a lot of specific fears amount to or produce a general fearfulness? Is pessimism of temperament just the average effect of all the misfortunes one has encountered? Or are there constitutional unitary influences? And are there constitutional limits to the amount of integration of drives a person can maintain no matter how he is taught?

The vehemence of argument on the relative importance of heredity and environment might sometimes make one suspect that some people believe environment determines everything, and some heredity. But most debaters are sane enough to recognize that everything is partly environmental and partly hereditary in origin, and the only issue is a quantitative one of *how much* each contributes.

At this point, therefore, let us turn from our brief survey of the environmental, learning influences in personality to the hereditary, genetic influences.

PRINCIPLES AND ILLUSTRATIONS OF EVALUATING HEREDITY AND ENVIRONMENTAL INFLUENCE

It might seem most logical, in any case, to begin with heredity when studying personality because this defines the beginning of the person. However, the influences of heredity do not always come at birth, as witness the appearance of the sex drive at puberty, or of some special hereditary form of deafness or palsy to a middle-aged man. As we actually observe a developing personality it is often quite impossible to distinguish an externally initiated process of learning from an internally determined process of maturation. Yet, as we shall see, there are ways of at least saying *how much* of some total change or difference is due respectively to learning and maturation.

Geneticists seek to boil down the truths and lawful relations of heredity mainly in two ways: (1) in terms of Mendelian laws stating that such and such a trait is determined by one, two, or more genes, that one of a pair of contrasting characters is dominant to another, and a second recessive, and so on; (2) in terms of what the statistician calls variance analysis, directed to stating the fraction of the observed variability (strictly the square of the standard deviation) contributed respectively by heredity and environment. For example, one can conclude that roughly four fifths of the differences we measure on intelligence tests would disappear if people were all of identical heredity, whereas two thirds of the variance on extraversion–introversion would vanish if all people were brought up identically.

With respect to physical traits, e.g. eye colour, number of fingers (for some people *do* vary), shape of head, blood proteins, much progress has been made in accounting for differences by Mendelian methods, but in the psychological world knowledge of such mechanisms is rare, mainly because few mental traits are of the all-or-nothing kind which observers of a family over two or three generations would notice. Nevertheless, there are several clear-cut instances of Mendelian unit inheritance in psychology, such as colour blindness, the inability to taste a urea derivative, Huntington's chorea (a degenerative disorder of behaviour which comes on in middle age), phenyl-pyruvic mental defect, and Kallman's 'process' schizophrenia. The fact that these are mainly defects is no reflection on the beneficence of heredity, but simply due to the tendency of medicine to keep records only of illnesses! The nightmare view of heredity as some inescapable fate, which misses both its flexibility and its beneficent protectiveness, derives largely from these pathological case histories. To be born of an exceptionally intelligent, unusually long-lived family, on the other hand, is to appreciate also the beneficence of hereditary action.

The knowledge that any psychological characteristic fits a simple Mendelian law and unit mechanism enables us to predict when a trait may skip a generation (Huntington's chorea, for instance, is a dominant and does not), where it may be passed down on the female side without being recognized (as in colour blindness) and so on. Naturally, things that are recognized as being passed on by a single gene characteristically do not seem to be much affected by the normal ranges of environmental difference – else we should not recognize them so easily. Nevertheless, even in instances where some Mendelian plan is relatively clear (as in Kallman's data on schizophrenia) there is still room for environmental intervention. Thus, instances are known of one of a pair of identical twins being schizophrenic and not the other, though this is uncommon. And biochemists find ways of altering the body chemistry which, in the form of mental defect mentioned above, is known to be responsible for the mental defect. In this connexion one should keep in mind the stages and

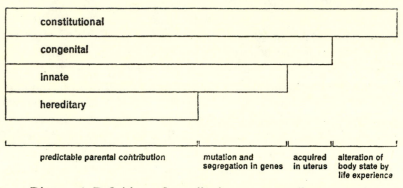

Diagram 1. Definitions of contributions to personality commonly considered 'non-environmental'

places in the chain of causation at which the essential hereditary contribution can be modified. As Diagram 1 briefly shows, all that is *innate*, i.e. in the genes, need not be inherited, because there are possible mutations between parent and child. For example, the haemophilia which affected several descendants of Queen Victoria apparently appeared as a mutation, and was not demonstrably inherited by her from forebears. Again, what is *congenital* (if we use that term to mean 'present at birth') need not be *innate*, since post-genetic effects may occur in the womb. Finally, when people talk of constitutional, they usually allow that 'constitution' is a general physiological basis which may suffer some modifications since birth.

When traits vary in a graded way, presumably due to the

cumulative effects of many genes, however, we generally also find that some part of the observed variance is due to environment, presumably in the form of many such environmental changes. The most powerful method yet developed for discovering how much influence is due to each has been called the Multiple Abstract Variance Analysis (or M.A.V.A.) Method. Although it is complex mathematically, it is simple enough in principle for anyone with a high-school knowledge of simultaneous equations to follow.

If two brothers are brought up in the same family, they will differ due to the usual difference of *environment* within any family for two people in it. This difference we will call d_{we} (*we* standing for within-family environment). It is a difference due to difference of family position, favouritism, the changing age of parents at the infancy of the different children, etc. The brothers will also differ somewhat in heredity. This sometimes surprises people, but it is due to the differing segregation of the parental genes from child to child. His average within-family hereditary difference we will symbolize by d_{wh}. Thus, (a) *Within-families:*

$$d_{BT} = d_{we} + d_{wh}$$

where d_{BT} stands for the actual measured difference of *b*rothers raised *t*ogether, and the quantities may have signs in either direction.

(b) *Between families* we may represent the average hereditary and environment differences as d_{bh} and d_{be}. It is possible to get various combinations of these unknowns by taking pairs of boys from various situations. For example, the average measured difference of two brothers raised in different families, d_{BA} (for *b*rothers *a*part) will be:

$$d_{BA} = d_{we} + d_{wh} + d_{be}$$

and for identical twins raised in different families (d_{TA}) it will be:

$$d_{TA} = d_{we} + d_{be}$$

i.e. with no term for hereditary differences at all ($_{TA}$ = twins apart).

For simplicity these equations are expressed in differences, but the statistician would work in 'variances' which avoid the difficulty about signs. However, this simpler layout will suffice to show the general idea, namely, that by juggling with simultaneous equations like the three given above, which can be extended to all sorts of additional family relations, one can solve for all four unknowns and thus get an evaluation of how much, on an average, the observed differences – measured by psychological tests – are accounted for by hereditary and environmental sources. In search of different family relations, researchers found that in data from certain less strict cultures than our own it proved possible to obtain a sample of children of the same age from different mothers and the same father raised with either family!

Until recently most psychological studies on heredity used the twin method, but the M.A.V.A. method (which *includes* twins as part of its wider scope) is superior in the information it supplies. The comparison only of two kinds of twins tells us mainly *whether heredity has any significant action at all* – for identical twins will then be more alike than fraternal twins, who are merely as alike as brothers, but happen to be born at the same time. But the M.A.V.A. method tells us *how much* of the environmental influence on a trait is typically due to differences in treatment within the family and how much to social differences between families. Similarly, it tells us the typical magnitude of the hereditary difference within families and between families.

Finally, this newer method enables us to attack a problem which has long bothered investigators, namely, that hereditary and environmental influences may be *correlated*. For example, it is possible that an individual who is innately inclined to be more introverted may tend to receive less encouragement from people around to join in social life, thus magnifying the initial effect of heredity, or that an intelligent child will generally receive more schooling, thus confounding the difference, from the researcher's point of view.

Complexities of this kind have led some writers to say offhandedly that heredity and environment are so intermixed that it makes no sense to talk of separating them. This is a defeatist view to find in a scientist, though similar expert views were expressed about separating isotopes when they were first surmised in chemistry. The fact is that the M.A.V.A. method has given us evidence already of the nature–nurture (heredity–environment) influences on a couple of dozen different personality factors and in some cases on the correlations too. Regarding the latter, speculative theorists confidently argued that a positive relation would be found between the hereditary and environmental influences on intelligence, but the findings so far have shown an inverse relation! And this is not so surprising when one reflects that classroom organization necessarily involves giving more attention to bringing up the rearguard while the bright mark time, and that children are rarely reacted to appropriately for their real differences in intelligence.

Of course, at this early stage, with only a handful of researches available on well-measured personality traits, as in those by Blewett, Beloff, Burt, Cattell, Eysenck, Freeman, Gottesman, Holzinger, Hundleby, Prell, Vandenberg, and others in Britain and America especially, we still do not know the detailed manner in which heredity and environment interact. Even the statistical estimates of the relative contributions must be considered rough ones. For intelligence, as stated above, the studies centre on an 80 to 20 per cent ratio, though when Culture-Fair intelligence tests are used the environmental contribution falls still lower. For the temperament trait of Parmia-*vs*-Threctia (Boldness-*vs*-Susceptibility to Threat) discussed in the next chapter, which shows itself in toughness and 'thick-skinnedness' as opposed to shyness and sensitivity, the hereditary determination is almost as high as for intelligence. This ratio fits the finding that this trait has physiological and bodily correlates such as reactivity of the heart to startle. Appreciable, but not predominant genetic determination (around 30–40 per cent) has been shown also for neuroticism, or, at least, the Ego weakness, factor *C*. This finding turns up in American data by the present writer and English samples by Eysenck and Prell. The fact that heredity is unmentioned by the great majority of psychoanalytic writings 'explaining' neuroticism is one more illustration of how the modern experimental approach is guided more in its theories by factual findings which are not lost sight of because they fail to fit the first simple views.

Incidentally, it does not follow from findings such as this that constructive eugenics ought to take action to help eliminate hereditary proneness to neuroticism. Conceivably some sensitivities of great importance to civilization go along with the ego-weakness. tendency, which we call C factor. Hereditary determination is also high on what we shall describe in the next chapter as the cyclothyme–schizothyme dimension of temperament – roughly, that between easy-going sociability at one pole and aloof self-sufficiency at the other. Here no unprejudiced person could call one pole 'good' and the other 'bad'. There are good and bad features about each. For example, the highly sociable 'cyclothyme' persons make good salesmen and club managers, while the schizothymes (or *sizothymes*, if we use the term for the normal range) at the other pole turn out to be more dependable and gifted in such performances as computing and type-setting. Perhaps 'the world' on the whole prefers the cyclothymes in its leisure time, as actors, salesmen, and good mixers, but good house electricians and top scientific researchers turn out to be well to the sizothyme side (see Diagram 31, page 244 below).

Natural selection is continually at work upon individuals and upon nations. Presumably the present central tendency and range in any inherited temperament trait appearing as a continuum, such as extraversion–introversion, represent the result of a continual search for an optimum balance. Complex societies *need* a wide variety of natural temperaments and abilities, of which we are reminded by the saying that 'it takes all kinds to make a world'. Consequently, communities which get too narrow may fail in the struggle to survive. However, the statement that all sorts are needed exaggerates a little, for it is possible for the central value to go too far one way, or for the fringes to go off into sheer abnormalities. The extreme cyclothyme (roughly, extravert) temperament is apt to develop into the superbly sociable, emotionally lively, plausible but quite undependable individual, who, with slight deficiencies in character traits added, becomes the psychopathic swindler and 'con' man. The sizothyme temperament at the opposite extreme is apt to become so shut in and rigid that he fits in nowhere. But the optimum central hereditary constitution may well differ from one culture to another.

SOME SOCIAL AND CLINICAL ASPECTS OF PERSONALITY INHERITANCE

Since the practical and community-responsible man naturally thinks ahead quickly to social implications, it may be good to pause and clarify some of these before proceeding to further technical aspects of personality inheritance. The human lot can be improved by man in two ways: by improving environment and by improving the genetic make-up of man. Naturally, in either there is some disagreement as to what constitutes improvement!

In the psychological as in the medical field, eugenics has a clear view and few difficulties where the avoidance of actual hereditary diseases is concerned. Inherited neurological diseases like Huntington's chorea could be greatly reduced in a single generation by attention to eugenically planned parenthood. And in more normal dimensions, as we have seen, though many are equally good, as far as we yet know in their extremes towards either pole, there are some on which most societies would agree that one direction is less desirable than another. For example, on the intelligence dimension, low intelligence is less desirable for the individual or society and probably a democratic vote of sociologists would lead to the same conclusion on poor emotional balance, and a deficiency of whatever genetic components go into the making of a sensitive conscience. Against the view that it is safest to do nothing about human selection, we must recognize that in the last resort societies, like individuals, have to be adventurous. If they are to get ahead, they have to make wise guesses, before a thing is proved up to the hilt. Most medical advances, for instance, are rightly applied before their full consequences can be known, and when a shrewd evaluation shows the likelihood of ten times as much good as ill from their application.

In this sense there is little doubt that the cultural, economic, and political life will become richer and saner in those communities which first succeed in encouraging a higher birth-rate in their more than in their less intelligent families. The unintelligent individual costs roughly twice as much to educate (because of special classes, etc.), and even then achieves and contributes far

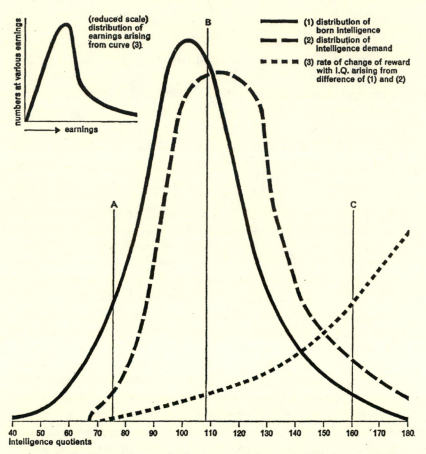

A at I. Q. 75 supply greatly in excess of demand, therefore negligible earning power.

B at I. Q. 108 supply equal demand, therefore normal earning power.

C at I. Q. 160 demand greatly in excess of supply, therefore disproportionate earning.

Diagram 2. Psychology and economics: relation of mental capacity supply and demand to income

less than a child of good average intelligence. He is more prone to become a delinquent and is politically a danger by being a ready prey to the sly slogans of demagogues. As Sir Cyril Burt and the present writer pointed out thirty years ago, in independent studies of intelligence levels in various occupations and the unemployed, chronic unemployment occurs largely at the lower intelligence levels. If we take the rate of earnings as a natural index of the ratio of supply and demand, i.e. of society's *needs* for various intelligence levels and the birth-rate *supply* of various levels, then we have a situation which can be summarized as in Diagram 2.

Where Greece and Rome depended on slaves, and eighteenth-century society upon economic slaves for the most mechanical, repetitive work, the nineteenth century began to substitute machines. The process accelerates as automation is more widely introduced and the demand for those educable only to the level of unskilled work diminishes. It does so even while the birth-rate at these levels, in some countries, increases. Society has needs at all levels of ability, and all are equally worthy, but in a progressive society the birth-rate obviously needs to be encouraged in a way to produce adjustment rather than dislocation between occupations and the necessary talents for occupations. More social conscience in attending to this thirty years ago, when the results shown in Diagram 3 were first revealed, might have saved society from the heavy load of unemployed it now complains of at this level, and supplied it with more brilliant political leaders, scientists, and artists.

Is it possible that the already existing evidence of inheritance in personality suggests that here also the fate of society may be strongly affected by balances of breeding and natural selection? It is the pride of some societies to breed temperamental artists and of others to produce the sober personalities of philosophers. Values vary from country to country, but on one thing most countries are agreed: that they do not want an excess of vicious, anti-social criminal types. If every form of behaviour is partly environmentally determined and partly genetically, then, in spite of the obvious environmental causes of crime, there is likely to be some temperamental endowment which predisposes one person to crime under stresses which another would tolerate. It was fashionable a generation ago to pooh-pooh the assertion of the Italian psychiatrist Lombroso that crime had constitutional associations. Doubtless, in his pioneer researches he exaggerated, but the evidence piles up. It rests largely on the twin method, but also more recently on the M.A.V.A. method. The twin method,

so far described only very briefly, requires that we collect cases
of the two kinds of twins – *identical* or single-egg, and *fraternal*
or two-egg. The former have identical heredity whereas the latter
differ as much as brothers and sisters usually do. They are sibs

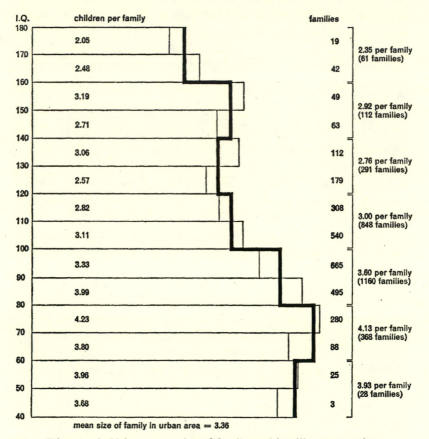

I.Q.	children per family	families	
180			
	2.05	19	2.35 per family (61 families)
170			
	2.48	42	
160			
	3.19	49	2.92 per family (112 families)
150			
	2.71	63	
140			
	3.06	112	2.76 per family (291 families)
130			
	2.57	179	
120			
	2.82	308	3.00 per family (848 families)
110			
	3.11	540	
100			
	3.33	665	3.60 per family (1160 families)
90			
	3.99	495	
80			
	4.23	280	4.13 per family (368 families)
70			
	3.80	88	
60			
	3.96	25	3.93 per family (28 families)
50			
	3.68	3	
40			

mean size of family in urban area = 3.36

Diagram 3. Urban area: size of family and intelligence quotient

who happen to have been born at the same time. The differences
between identical twins must be due only to the within-family
difference of environment, whereas those between fraternals are
due both to this ordinary family environment range *and* to the
normal within-family difference in heredity. Consequently, if
fraternals differ *more* on any trait in later life than do identicals,

we must infer that heredity plays a significant role in determining that trait.

Some years ago, an investigator called Lange began locating criminals in prison who happened to have a twin. He then began to see if the other twin also had a criminal record. To the surprise of many, he found a substantially greater 'concurrence', i.e. agreement in having criminal record, when the second twin was identical than when fraternal. The results have been checked now in several repeat investigations as shown in Table 1, converging on rather more than twice the frequency of concurrence for identical than fraternal twins.

TABLE 1

Percentage of cases in which both twins were criminals

Investigator	Number of cases	Monozygotic twins	Number of cases	Dizygotic but of same sex
Lange	13	76·9	17	11·8
Legras	4	100·0	5	0·0
Rosanoff	37	67·6	28	17·9
Stumpfle	18	72·2	19	36·8
Kranz	31	64·4	43	53·5
Mean	—	69·9	—	33·0

It is widely recognized that sociologists (who unlike psychologists, do not spread from physiology on one flank to social science on the other) have tended in this generation (with a few admirable exceptions) to explain behaviour almost exclusively by social causes. It has seemed intrinsically absurd to many sociologists that anything so culturally relative as crime can have hereditary determination. However, what is more culturally acquired than the ability to spell? Yet the twin studies of Louis and Thelma Thurstone show more hereditary determination of spelling ability than almost any ability they investigated! An individual with this innate 'spelling' disability (which, incidentally is practically ⌐nconnected with intelligence) will be a bad speller in French, English, or Hindi according to the culture into which he happens to be born. (As most writers can painfully testify, a secretary with natural spelling ability generally remains distinctly superior to one with a dictionary and the highest determination to succeed!)

Regardless of theories – sociological or other – in this more serious matter of delinquency, the brute facts remain. In his classical study, *The Young Delinquent*, Burt found the same facts, and tentatively put forward some realistic psychological theories, notably that both low intelligence and low emotional stability (the ego weakness, or *C* factor as the next chapter describes the latter) have appreciable inheritance and mediate the connexion. The rules which are broken by a delinquent are admittedly cultural relatives and will vary from country to country and crime to crime. But a greater difficulty in adjusting to *any* set of rules in a complex society is likely to be experienced by the person of lower intelligence and higher temperamental impulsiveness.

Quite recently some additional evidence has appeared on inheritance of personality factors which helps indicate one cause which may contribute to the above twin finding. A pattern which has been indexed as U.I. 20 and called Comention (meaning to think with the group and be group-dependent, see Chapter 4) was found in a study of 500 relatives by Cattell, Stice, and Kristy by the M.A.V.A. method to show the highest inheritance of any factor except intelligence. Recently, Knapp, in the study of military offenders, and Howard, in studying Chicago street gangs, have shown that delinquents, particularly of the gang type, score significantly higher on this factor.

Crime is a complex event, with sociological, economic, and several known distinct psychological contributors associated with it. For example, America has a crime-rate of an order many times that of, say, Britain or Switzerland, and the coloured population there constitutes one tenth of the population but is responsible for one third of the total crime. No one would or should, without further evidence, conclude that such differences as these are due to hereditary differences. Economic causes are primary in one difference, sociological in another, and so on. For example a sociologist, Wolfgang, has recently concluded that 'under comparable circumstances to those given whites, the Negro crime rate would not be substantially different'. But regarding individual differences in crime truly within the same culture, the fact remains that in some sense (as the psychiatrist's present views on 'the psychopath' and the lobotomized also argue) the capacity to acquire a strong conscience and good emotional balance must be in part genetically determined. Theoretically, the hope exists, therefore, that eugenics can in time breed a society which is not only more intelligent but more responsible and altruistic.

THE EVIDENCE OF PERSONALITY INHERITANCE FROM ANIMAL AND PHYSIOLOGICAL RESEARCH

Despite sex being such a preoccupation of humanity, the fact remains that the human species breeds too slowly to provide an investigator with much evidence on family inheritances measurable within his own lifetime. Consequently many psychologists have turned to the breeding of animals, notably, of the convenient rat. The results are in one respect clear-cut: by inbreeding with respect to certain traits, either of an ability or of a temperament nature, strains can be produced which are quite different in behaviour from others.

Rundquist separated rats according to the amount of spontaneous activity they preferred on the revolving drum, and, after breeding from the most and the least active, obtained two subraces so distinct that the least active of one was more active than the most active of the other. Tyron did the same with ability to learn mazes, obtaining in ten generations two strains which no longer even overlapped in maze-learning ability. Similar studies have shown the inheritance of emotionality and of wildness and tameness (toleration of human handling).

Such findings come as no surprise to the pedigree-animal breeder, who frequently has found segregation of particular kinds of *behaviour* even when he was selecting primarily for particular *physical* characteristics. For example, only the Dalmatian dog breed will learn readily to run behind a horse under a carriage, and only a sheepdog breed can be trained, without considerable frustration for all concerned, to round up sheep in a systematic manner – and so on.

More analytical understanding of such inheritance was gained by the studies of Stockard, who showed that slender, e.g. whippet, body-build as compared with thick-set, e.g. bulldog, physique is systematically associated with higher anxiety (as we may now infer) levels and with more rapid conditioning of reflexes. Pavlov, in Russia, had similarly noticed higher excitement in conflict in some dogs and greater inhibition in others.

Although these findings from animal experiment are in these respects clear and definite, they present us with difficulties in translating to human personality. An alternative approach is the corresponding one of trying to tie mental characteristics to physical characteristics. This has taken many forms. Some of these, like phrenology, have proved quite futile. Others like William McDougall's attempt, from statistics differentiating northern and southern French types, to associate introversion and alcoholism with Nordic physical type and Mediterranean physical type with extraversion, have never been followed up. Perhaps the most promising, judged by its recurrent checking by psychologists such as Kretschmer and Sheldon, has been the association of cyclothyme temperament with round, broad body build and sizothyme (shut in, steady) temperament with lean and leptosomatic (long-narrow) body build.

This began in the clinical phase of research with studies on the inheritance of insanity. There it was soon found that manic-depressive or cyclic disorder – in which there may be enormous mood swings from manic excitement to months of melancholic depression – has a high degree of inheritance, almost like a simple Mendelian dominant. Similarly from Kallman's studies of hundreds of schizophrenic families it was concluded that at least certain forms of schizophrenia are highly inheritable. However, it must be added, with caution, that these studies often failed to use the 'raised together–raised apart' comparisons used in the M.A.V.A. method developed for normal personality ranges, which alone can reliably separate hereditary from environmental influences. How do we know that being raised by an intermittently schizophrenic mother may not be itself enough to make a child with non-schizophrenic inheritance prone to become schizophrenic? The finding that among children of manic-depressives there is a somewhat higher percentage of schizo-phrenics than in the general population *could* be explained by an emotionally unbalanced atmosphere contributing to schizo-phrenia. A summary of Kallman's earlier results is given in Diagram 4.

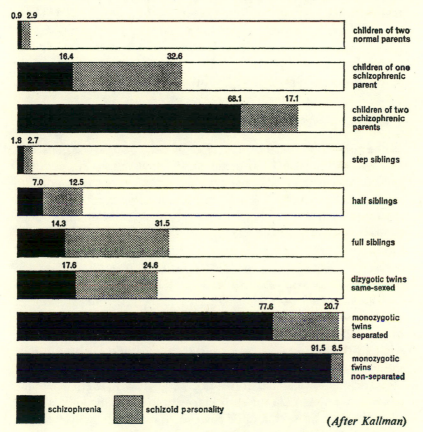

(After Kallman)

Diagram 4. The frequency of schizophrenia and schizoid personality among the relatives of schizophrenics

We shall not explore here the complexities of the Mendelian laws believed to be operative, or sort the volumes of complex medical evidence, but we may conclude that these two distinct forms of mental disorder have significant but by no means in-fallible inheritance, and that each tends to be inherited in its own form. Furthermore, we recognize that Kretschmer found statistically clear evidence of the round body build going with the cyclic disposition, as described above, and of schizophrenia with the slim build, as well as with what he called the athletic type. Sheldon checked this with ratings on normals, and, though he used three body types, found essentially the same trend. These associations, however, are not close, i.e. the physique does not show a high degree of determination of temperament, and it would be true to say that so far nothing more than moderate associations have been found between physique and personality.

THE INTERACTIONS OF HEREDITY AND ENVIRONMENT

In the normal or near-normal range of behaviour some degree of real inheritance has been established for a surprising array of special traits, e.g. stammering, hypertension, perseveration, enuresis, etc. Among the normal personality dimensions to be discussed in the next chapter, important degrees of inheritance (under conditions which cancel out direct effects of family environment) have been shown to exist for the Threctia (tendency to shyness-*vs*-boldness) dimension, for ego weakness which predisposes to neurotic traits, for dominance–submissiveness (which is also sex-correlated) and, of course, for intelligence.

Regarding the manner in which heredity and environment interact some important generalizations have been made above – e.g. that their effects can become systematically correlated. First, the experiments on what is called 'imprinting' in animals, by Hess, Schneirla, Lorenz, and Tinbergen, show that environment is far more powerful in the early stages of life. For instance, young geese brought up with a child instead of a mother goose will remain firmly attached to the child later, even when a mother goose is provided, but this does not happen if the young geese are beyond a certain stage of development. This imprinting effect is indeed not only a matter of the sheer earliness of influence, but also of timeliness in relation to a naturally maturing process. Some instances of sex perversion are traceable to a strong environmental influence of the wrong kind coming at the time of natural irruption of the sex interest.

When psychologists fail to find sufficient environmental cause for a trait in later life, and trace it back and say that it must be due to some environmental effects of quite early infancy, one should always be ready to suspect the possibility that it is actually an innate tendency. An environmentalist who fails to find any environmental association in the life period is not averse to concluding that the effect must be due to environment at the moment of birth (birth trauma) or in the uterus. Freud, unlike most of his followers, *did* recognize an inherited predisposition to neurosis in what he called a 'psychosexual disposition'. But individual differences alleged to be due to individual differences in birth trauma, and difference in super-ego development due to vague happenings alleged in the first or second year of life may well go back farther still than these theorists suppose!

The interaction with environment often goes by fits and starts, showing, at least in the ability field, what the present writer has called 'aids'. It can be seen from the work of Piaget, for example, that a young child may quite suddenly perceive the meaning and use of a new intellectual tool, e.g. the meaning of an analogy, the idea of a mirror image, the notion of 'flow' of water and other fluids or of temporal sequence. When he applies this novelty vigorously, the plot of his general power to cope with the environment shows a distinct spurt. It may be that if he had acquired this 'aid' a year earlier his whole development in the intelligence field would have experienced a lift, with some permanent consequences to his position relative to others. It is of such stuff that the 20 per cent environmental contribution to individual differences in intelligence may be made. Precisely similar emotional learning effects produce similar aids occurring in social and personality development.

To the laws of interaction of heredity and environment which are seen at work in 'imprinting', and the episodic action of 'aids', one can add a third law deriving from the discovered correlations of hereditary and environmental 'variance contributions' mentioned above. When the correlations for over a dozen different personality factors were assembled, it was found that they are predominantly *negative*. What does this mean? To illustrate by the trait of dominance-*vs*-submissiveness, it means that the naturally more dominant have met more environmental influences pushing towards submissiveness, while the naturally more submissive appear to have been encouraged to show more self-assertion. This *law of coercion to the bio-social mean* probably operates because what is biologically and socially the existential mode tends also to become the ideal. In some traits, such as intelligence and conscientiousness, one might expect that the ideal would lie to one side of the average, but what evidence exists suggests that at least in regard to intelligence the environmental stimulus to intelligence development remains greater for those of lower ability. If one has less, one needs to use it more, in classroom and life, and if one has more than average, one needs (competition-wise) to use it less – except for a few scientists and others challenged by something beyond society's demands.

A fourth generalization, less a law than a reminder for the proper sorting out of environmental and hereditary effects, is that the effects of environment often determine the *area* in which a trait is displayed, whereas heredity more often governs its *amount*. Virtually all our skills are acquired, and whether we become good at Latin or ski-ing or mending clocks will depend on environment. But, as with the instance of spelling described above, or playing the violin, or tennis, the *level* we reach may be much determined by heredity. And herein lies a paradox: that the more uniform and extensive society makes its schooling, the greater will be the contribution to ultimate individual differences from heredity. For the nature–nurture ratios discussed above state the relative contribution to existing, observable, final individual differences of (*a*) differences in schooling and (*b*) differences in natural aptitude. If (*a*) is reduced, (*b*) will stand out more. This is an important reminder that the nature–nurture ratios are not fixed and immutable laws, but statements which may change with culture patterns and the ranges of racial, genetic difference within the given population.

Finally, in correctly perceiving the relative roles of heredity and environment, we should observe the distinction between broad general traits (intelligence, dominance, sizothymia) on the one hand, and specific attachments on the other. This difference is particularly noteworthy with respect to dynamic traits (Chapter

7 below) where everyone has, say, a general level of self-assertive drive, for example, or of sex drive. This level may prove to be partly hereditarily determined. But the *particular attachments* in sex, and the *particular areas* of expression of assertive ambition, are obviously almost entirely environmentally determined. Sometimes even a *broad* behaviour pattern is largely environmentally determined, for the personality dimensions we call premsia–harria (emotional sensitivity) and surgency–desurgency (debonairness) in the following chapter yield ratios lying largely to the environmental side. The first is a dependence and sensitivity which seems due to being brought up in well-protected and indulgent homes. The second is a general carefreeness and impulsive enthusiasm as contrasted with sober and cautious behaviour, and one's level seems largely determined by the level of the punishing, demanding, and restricting qualities of one's earlier environment.

An area of environmental–hereditary interaction of particular interest to the psychologist is that observed in the clinic. That insanity has appreciable heredity, and neurosis some, is less important from a constructive viewpoint than the nature of the *particular* resources of an individual which are to be treated as constitutional 'givens'. In the early nineteenth century, Séguin, the 'apostle of the idiots', believed that mental exercise would convert imbeciles into normals. The wooden 'forms boards' which he constructed survive as intelligence tests. But, apart from wasted effort, much harm was probably done to the disposition and personality of the unfortunate child of low intelligence by coercing him to do the impossible.

The carpenter adjusts his construction to the grain and quality of the wood, and the architect to the shape of the land. So too the clinician, if he knew more about which traits are largely innately given and which are susceptible to therapeutic change, would go about his business more cleverly, not wasting effort attempting to change biological limitations and taking full advantage of the resources of firm leverage in the personality. What these are can only be properly investigated when experimental research has revealed more about personality structure and measurement, as in the following chapters.

Obviously, the practical uses of knowledge about the nature–nurture ratios are numerous. Heredity is not 'fate' any more than that the element copper should have the properties of copper is 'fate'. It is a knowledge of properties useful in making the best of every individual. To individuals of more far-reaching social conscience, knowledge of heredity also has eugenic importance; to the psychologist it brings ways of studying how maturation and learning processes interact; to the student seeking his best self-expression it means choosing lines of work and occupational expression that are fruitful rather than frustrating; to the educator it means taking the natural strengths and weaknesses of personality into account early; and to the clinician it means rectifying failures to take account of natural strengths and weaknesses, by readjusting the individual's dynamics in proper relation to his resources.

*

READING

Scheinfeldt, A., *New You and Heredity*. Lippincott, New York, 1950; Chatto and Windus, 1952.

Fuller, J. L., and Thompson, W. R., *Behaviour Genetics*. Wiley, 1960.

CHAPTER THREE

Personality Structure: The Larger Dimensions

THE USE OF TYPES AND TRAITS IN DESCRIBING PERSONALITY

A sketch has just been given of the way in which the psychologist sees the personality building up from the hereditary raw material interacting with the learning processes imposed by environment. That it is no more than a sketch is partly due to limited space but largely to the fact that psychologists have only recently begun to measure personality traits with an accuracy which permits specific and precise conclusions to be drawn.

Accordingly, we turn now to see what progress has been made in that defining of 'the individual at a given moment' upon which all research depends. For, as the introduction pointed out, every science has had to develop through a stage of accurate measurement, of ability to describe the dimensions of an event. Psychology is also somewhat belatedly developing its taxonomic (classificatory) and descriptive technique. To get some 'practical' psychologists and psychiatrists to face the difficult theoretical issues of measurement, it has been necessary to reiterate that dependable laws about how personality grows, changes, and operates are to be found only after we can accurately refer to this 'given personality at a given moment'. Similarly, we are able to see the dynamic movement of people in a movie film only because the instantaneous 'frames' which rush through at sixteen a second are themselves each descriptively exact.

In the previous chapter we accepted, as a first approximation to description, the use of 'traits' (but also moods and roles) as popularly understood. The novelist, for example, uses nouns to indicate particular traits, and then becomes implicitly quantitative by introducing adjectives to indicate more or less of each trait. In this implicit quantifying, fortunately for his peace of mind, he does not have to 'test' his measurements, for he can, and frequently does, make his characters do impossibly inconsistent things – even in the most valued literature. The literary tradition of personality description also uses types, as when Hamlet calls his uncle a villain. What is a villain? He, and every other type, is a *whole pattern of traits* which are uniquely combined and which are seen to repeat themselves often enough to justify the utility of a label.

Description by trait and description by type are therefore not opposed systems. Traits are conceived through abstracting from experience of\many types, as the colour brown is abstracted from our experience of many diverse brown objects. Reciprocally, types can be and must be fixed in terms of traits, as when we describe an 'adolescent type' as having unusual enthusiasm, naïveté, impulsiveness, altruism, shyness, etc. The description of personality has long made use of types. For example, as early as the reign of Edward I in England a distinction was made between the 'born fool' and the lunatic who 'by grief or other cause hath lost his reason'. Psychologists and psychiatrists have oscillated in their techniques between use of traits and use of types. For example, at one time psychiatrists were satisfied if they could pigeon-hole any given patient under a type rubric such as an hysteric, a manic depressive, a schizophrenic, etc. But later they had doubts, consequent upon disagreements between one hospital and another (about one quarter of one psychiatrist's classifications are changed by the next). Obviously, there are intermediate cases, and although intermediates can be handled by types ('He is three quarters fool and one quarter rascal'), they can be more easily handled by traits, duly quantified.

Indeed, the term type, at least in the precise notion of 'species type' (as in the distinct species of animals) also implies *discontinuity*. There is nothing – if we set aside the myth of centaurs – existing half-way between a man and a horse. But types are not particularly apt for most personality description because the great majority of human traits appear to be continuous. In intelligence, for example, our population represents every gradation from the level of genius to that of idiocy. For this and other reasons the basic techniques for description and measurement of personality have developed more around *trait* concepts. Types, where they exist, have later been defined as *patterns of trait measures*, any one such type being singled out because it occurs in our populations with some peculiar, useful frequency.

THE INVENTION OF CORRELATION AND FACTOR ANALYSIS

However, the trouble with measuring traits is that there are too many of them! Allport and Odbert, at Harvard, searched the dictionary and found over 3,000 trait words for describing personality. The tendency in the past has been for a psychologist to fancy some particular trait, such as 'authoritarianism', 'extraversion', 'flexibility-*vs*-rigidity', 'intolerance of ambiguity', etc., and to concentrate on its relations to all kinds of things. Even such devotion or addiction does not solve the problem. Thousands of traits are still neglected and the prejudices and preferences of individual psychologists lead to a system which tries to handle at least as many traits as there are psychologists! For example, when Scheier and the present writer began their researches on anxiety they found over 400 published researches on anxiety. The studies showed almost as many different shades of meaning and ways of measuring it, so that the studies could not be integrated. What a tower of Babel would arise in chemistry if every chemist had a different test for the presence of, say, chlorine, and, indeed, no really common conception of what chlorine is!

The answer to this problem, though it has technical complications which are still not fully straightened out by many of its users, is a statistical method called *factor analysis*. Prior to factor analysis some psychologists reached such a stage of desperation that they were ready to fix traits if necessary by fiat, by setting up a commission to say what the important traits are and how they should be defined. Factor analysis, on the other hand, believes that there are natural, unitary structures in personality and that it is these traits, rather than the endless labels in the dictionary, on which we should concentrate. In other words, if there are natural elements in the form of functional unities, logically equivalent to an element in the physical world, then it would be far better to begin our studies – our comparisons and developmental understandings – on measures of such traits.

The problem which baffled psychologists for many years was to find a method which would tease out these functionally unitary influences in the chaotic jungle of human behaviour. But let us ask how, in the literal tropical jungle, the hunter decides whether the dark blobs which he sees are two or three rotting logs or a single alligator? He watches for movement. If they move together – come and disappear together – he infers a single structure. Just so, as John Stuart Mill pointed out in his philosophy of science, the scientist should look for 'concomitant variation' in seeking unitary concepts.

When it came to putting this philosophical notion into practice, psychologists were for a while baffled, until the statisticians came to their help. For it is rare for two manifestations literally to go together *every* time they are observed. They become 'by chance or nature's changing course untrimmed'. How *much* observed going together does there have to be for us to conclude that, but for other interfering circumstances, these two (or more) behavioural manifestations would always constitute a single trait?

The answer to this appeared in the form of the correlation coefficient, which Sir Francis Galton conceived when he was sheltering, on his daily walk, from a passing shower. The English statistician Pearson and the French mathematician Bravais polished it up, and it became known as the Bravais–Pearson correlation coefficient. The way it works can be seen by looking at Diagram 5.

If a school teacher asks whether skill in English and in arithmetic are quite different traits or expressions of a single trait of general intelligence, he would administer tests of both to, say, a hundred children and plot the results as shown opposite. Each point represents a person, his position being defined by his score on the English axis and his score on the arithmetic axis. If there is a tendency for abilities to 'go together', the persons will scatter in a long ellipse as shown at (*a*), i.e. when a person's score on English is above average his arithmetic score will tend to be above average, and vice versa. On the other hand, if they are unrelated a random circular mass will appear as at (*b*). If they are

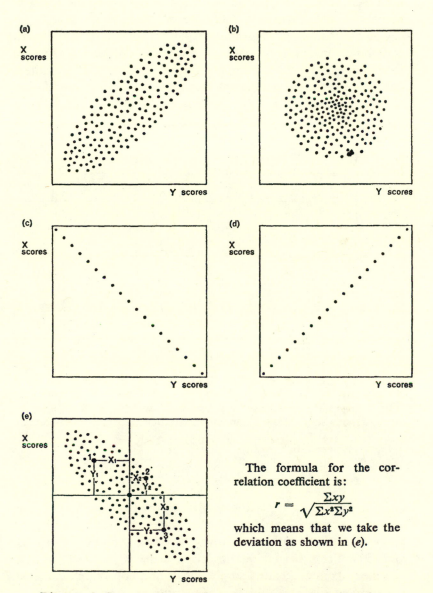

The formula for the correlation coefficient is:

$$r = \frac{\Sigma xy}{\sqrt{\Sigma x^2 \Sigma y^2}}$$

which means that we take the deviation as shown in (e).

Diagram 5. Correspondences of measurement on people in various sizes of correlation coefficient

negatively related the ellipse will slope backwards as in (*c*). The correlation coefficient is a value derived from these plots, by a calculation shown in Diagram 5 but which we shall not stop to elaborate. The result is that the correlation coefficient, r, varies from + 1·0 when the two are perfectly related, as at (*d*), through 0·0 when there is no relation, as at (*e*), to — 1·0 when the relation as in (*c*) becomes so narrow an ellipse that it is a line, i.e. English and arithmetic would be perfectly *inversely* related.

	a	b	c	d	e	f	g
a		+.7	+.8	+.8·	—.1	.0	.0
b			+.9	+.7	.1	.2	.0
c				+.8	—.2	—.1·	—.1
d					.0	—.1	.2
e						.6	.7
f							.7
g							

The lower left would, of course, be an image of the upper right and is not entered.

By adding together the scores on a, b, c, and d, we could get an estimate of the underlying source trait X, and similarly, but not quite so reliably, of Y from e, f, and g.

Trait X covers a, b, c, and d.

Trait Y covers e, f, and g.

Diagram 6. Correlation matrix

From the basic correlation coefficient the beginnings of factor analysis were developed by Charles Spearman, reader and professor in psychology at the University of London between 1907 and 1931. From his interest in giving a better basis to the I.Q. he asked, 'Is intelligence a single power or a collection of several independent powers, that is, is it a unitary trait?' Instead of taking behavioural measures two at a time, as had hitherto been done with the correlation coefficient, he took a very large number of supposed manifestations of mental ability and intercorrelated them in every possible way, as shown in what is called a correlation matrix in Diagram 6.

Here it will be seen that manifestations *a*, *b*, *c*, and *d* 'go together' in every possible way, having substantial correlations (above 0·7) of *a* with *b*, *b* with *c*, *a* with *c*, etc. They make a single functional unity. Similarly, *e*, *f*, and *g* go together in a single cluster, but *e*, *f*, and *g* are practically uncorrelated (no connexion being above 0·2) with *a*, *b*, *c*, and *d*. Thus among these seven behaviours we can say there are really only two underlying functional unities, which we can call *X* and *Y*. A matrix is thus a condensed means of showing all the possible relations among a set of behaviour – or, for that matter, any other kinds of measurement made over a sample of cases or occasions.

Factor analysis is actually a very complex mathematical technique, and goes beyond the mere recognition of clusters as in the above example, but this shows its essence. The factor *X* is said to 'load' *a*, *b*, *c*, and *d*, and *Y* to load *e*, *f*, and *g*. From the nature of these loadings we can begin to infer what the underlying influences *X* and *Y* really are. Conversely, if we know how much of *X* or *Y* a person has, we can make an estimate from the loadings of what *a*, *b*, *c*, etc., would be. Thus, from the above, approximately:

$$c_i = 0 \cdot 9 X_i$$

where c_i is the standard score of individual i on behaviour *c*, and X_i is his endowment in the factor trait *X*.

For example, Spearman found that a factor which covered most 'intelligent' performances (and, therefore, constituted some kind of general ability) loaded most highly such tasks as completing verbal analogies, perceiving the nature of arithmetical series, and so on. From this he concluded that intelligence is the 'capacity to perceive relationships' and he was able to make up tests which measured this particular *X* factor with increasing reliability and validity. No longer was there any excuse for different intelligence test constructors to make up arbitrary definitions or to disagree about the relative validity of different kinds. For on factoring a lot of ability measures, all investigators would finish with the same general factor and the relative loading or correlation of any two competing tests with this general capacity could be found experimentally. Thurstone (1887–1940), an American psychologist who independently made great contributions to factor analysis, entering ability research with more specific, 'narrow' measures, showed several 'primary abilities' were also involved, such as numerical, spatial, verbal, and logical abilities. But these were only, as it were, 'branches' of the truly general intelligence factor underlying all of them. (The terms 'first order' and 'second order' factor will later be used in our account to describe this kind of narrower and broader factor relation.)

Factor analysis was extensively applied to clearing up the structure of human abilities from 1905 onwards, but it was not until about 1930 that any very systematic application began with respect to personality structure. People were at first much too easily satisfied with clinical guesses about structure, or their own colourful intuitions, to feel the need for the more objective methods which ultimately had to come. Indeed, only as insoluble differences of opinion arose among these confident clinical assertions did it become evident that scientific psychology had to use trait concepts different from those long used in popular, literary, or clinical naming.

THE THREE DATA BASES OF PSYCHOMETRY

To get correlations we have to start with measures of the two things that have to be correlated (or the many that enter a correlation matrix). As recognized in the Introduction, some people object to the idea that the mind can be measured, and we have replied that whatever exists must exist in some degree. Nevertheless, the demonstrating of this degree and the development of principles for measuring traits can become extremely complex. Indeed, a whole science has grown up, as a special branch of psychology, called *psychometry*.

The psychometrist of personality, if he is to get an unbiased picture of the whole, must have some concept of the totality of human behaviour, which we shall call the *personality sphere*. This may be roughly defined as what people do over a sample twenty-four-hour period, and it will vary somewhat with different ages and culture. Such behaviour we can observe and record broadly in three ways: (1) By ratings made by observers on the frequency and intensity with which specific kinds of behaviour occur in the people they observe. (2) By questionnaires which are answered by the person himself, from his own self-observation and introspection. (3) By *objective* tests, i.e. miniature situations set up for a person to react to, in which he does not really know on what aspect of his behaviour he is being scored (hence 'objective').

Technically the first is called '*L*-data' or 'life-record' because it deals with behaviour in the actual, everyday-life situation. Ideally it would include behaviour which can be scored without employing the intervening judgement of a rater, and such specific behaviours can be found, for example, in 'number of automobile accidents over twenty years', 'frequency of engagements', 'number of societies to which the person belongs', 'marks in school', and so on. However, such 'hard data' is difficult to get and the psychologist commonly takes his life-record data 'second-hand' in the form of a rating by someone who knows the person well. Thus a person may be rated on a 1 to 10 scale by two or three observers on such trait elements as 'sociability in school', 'emotional stability on the playing field', 'conscientiousness in performing duties', and so on, with reliabilities we shall discuss later.

The second source of data for personality calculations – that offered by questionnaires – has been called *Q*-data. Information offered in the medical, psychiatric consulting-room has essentially the same properties. It depends on introspection and is liable to distortion by imperfect self knowledge, delusions about the self, or an intention deliberately to 'fake'. Although a questionnaire looks like a simple series of questions to which a person underlines a brief answer, such as 'yes', 'no', 'generally', etc., actually a great deal of art enters into the psychologist's choice of words, the direction of the question, the use of adjectives to ensure that all alternatives are well used, and so on. These, and related questions of reliability, mode of scoring, etc., will be discussed in a later chapter on questionnaires as such.

The third type of evidence used for getting at personality structure lies in *objective tests*, called *T*-data for short. Occasionally questionnaires are called objective by teachers who are used to the essay type of examination, but the only thing objective about them is the scoring. That is to say, the scoring is done by a key, not by the subjective judgement of the psychologist. This degree of dependability in scoring is possible only if the tests have what is called 'closed end', or multiple choice answers, i.e. given answers between which the subject chooses. If he were free to *write down* any answer he liked in an open-ended or inventive answer test, obviously different psychologists would be likely to score each response differently. The multiple choice questionnaire type of test is better called *conspective* than *objective*. Conspective means 'seeing together', since two examiners are guaranteed to see the same answer and assign the same score when they have a key and a selective rather than inventive answer form. By contrast, the objective test in the sense of a behavioural miniature situation is truly objective, in that the subject is not being asked to evaluate himself, but is simply behaving in a standard situation, and his behaviour is being objectively observed and measured. The principles for designing such truly objective tests are so specialized that the whole matter must be deferred to a later chapter, and in this chapter we shall continue with the discussion of life record (or behaviour rating) and questionnaire data only.

PERSONALITY FACTOR A: THE CYCLOTHYME–SIZOTHYME TEMPERAMENT DIMENSION

A few more technical points about rating and questionnaire procedures with which the reader should become familiar will be postponed to the next chapter. For it is time to make contact with actual trait discoveries, without which these technical points are not too meaningful. If one takes two or three hundred young men or women and arranges for them to be rated by people who know them well, on each of, say, sixty different trait elements, such as the ten shown in Table 2 below, a basis is obtained for calculating a correlation matrix, as shown above in Diagram 5.

A correlation is calculated between every possible pair of trait elements, e.g. the rating for quarrelsomeness and shyness, showing in each case the degree to which the rank orders of the 200 people on the two traits agree.

TABLE 2
List of ten rating traits

1. *Adaptable*: flexible; accepts *vs* *Rigid*: insists that things be done changes of plan easily; satisfied with compromises; is not upset, surprised, baffled, or irritated if things are different from what he expected.
   Rigid: insists that things be done the way he has always done them; does not adapt his habits and ways of thinking to those of the group; nonplussed if his routine is upset.

2. *Emotional*: excitable; cries a lot *vs* *Calm*: stable, shows few signs of (children), laughs a lot, shows affection, anger, all emotions, to excess.
   Calm: stable, shows few signs of emotional excitement of any kind; remains calm, even under-reacts, in dispute, danger, social hilarity, etc.

3. *Conscientious*: honest; knows *vs* *Unconscientious*: somewhat un-what is right and generally does it, even if no one is watching him; does not tell lies or attempt to deceive others; respects others' property.
   Unconscientious: somewhat unscrupulous; not too careful about standards of right and wrong where personal desires are concerned; tells lies and is given to little deceits; does not respect others' property.

4. *Conventional*: conforms to ac- *vs* *Unconventional, eccentric*: acts cepted standards, ways of act-ing, thinking, dressing, etc.; does the 'proper' thing; seems dis-tressed if he finds he is being different.
   Unconventional, eccentric: acts differently from others: not con-cerned about wearing the same clothes or doing the same things as others; has somewhat eccen-tric interests, attitudes, and ways of behaving; goes his own rather peculiar way.

5. *Prone to jealousy*: begrudges the *vs* *Not jealous*: likes people even if achievement of others; upset when others get attention, and demands more for himself; re-sentful when attention is given to others.
   Not jealous: likes people even if they do better than he does; is not upset when others get atten-tion, but joins in praise.

TABLE 2 (*contd*)

List of ten rating traits

6. *Considerate, polite*: deferential to needs of others; considers others' feelings; allows them before him in line, gives them the biggest share, etc. vs *Inconsiderate, rude*: insolent, defiant, and 'saucy' to elders (in children); ignores feelings of others; gives impression that he goes out of his way to be rude.

7. *Quitting*: gives up before he has thoroughly finished a job; slipshod; works in fits and starts; easily distracted, led away from main purposes by stray impulses or external difficulties. vs *Determined, persevering*: sees a job through in spite of difficulties or temptations; strong-willed; painstaking and thorough; sticks at anything until he achieves his goal.

8. *Tender*: governed by sentiment; intuitive, empathetic, sympathetic; sensitive to the feelings of others; cannot do things if they offend his feelings. vs *Tough, hard*: governed by fact and necessity rather than sentiment; unsympathetic; does not mind upsetting others if that is what has to be done.

9. *Self-effacing*: blames himself (or nobody) if things go wrong; reluctant to take credit for achievements; does not seem to think of himself as very important or worthwhile. vs *Egotistical*: blames others whenever there is conflict or things go wrong; often brags; quick to take credit when things go right; has a very good opinion of himself.

10. *Languid, fatigued, slow*: lacks vigour; vague and slow in speech; dawdles, is slow in getting things done. vs *Energetic, alert, active*: quick, forceful, active, decisive, full of pep, vigorous, spirited.

When such a set (matrix) of correlations (covering the whole personality sphere, by perhaps fifty bipolar elements, not just a sample ten as in Table 2) is factor analysed as discussed in Section 2 of this chapter, the result is usually that one gets evidence that between twelve and twenty independent factors or source influences must be at work. Furthermore, one gets recognizably the same factors from repeating the process at different age levels, except that a few of the differentiating dimensions which exist at the adult level are found not to have much contribution at earlier levels. Since it is most desirable to look at these new patterns without prejudice from earlier clinical notions or traditional popular terms, the first investigators in the 1930s and 1940s decided simply to symbolize the dimensions by letters of the alphabet. The investigators of vitamins did just the same, in a parallel situation, where the entities could be identified and partially described for some years by their *effects* before truly interpretive chemical labels could be attached to them. In the present area the letter *A* was given to the factor of greatest contribution to the totality of individual differences (the 'variance' of all ratings) and so down the alphabet to smaller factors.

As it happened, the largest factor turned out to be a dimension for differentiating individuals which had already been recognized as very important by the German psychiatrists Kraepelin and Kretschmer, and the Swiss, Bleuler, in their studies of mental hospital cases half a century earlier. Kraepelin first defined *dementia praecox* (now called schizophrenia) as a special 'withdrawn' pattern of behaviour. Following this Bleuler had pointed out that functional insanities, i.e. those not due to observable brain damage, fall into two exclusive and to some extent opposed types, called the cyclic insanities and schizophrenia. The former are characterized by a gross disturbance of emotional mood, towards extreme depression, on the one hand, or manic elation on the other, with some tendency to swing between the two. The latter show no marked abnormality of mood, except for a certain dullness and inaccessibility, but manifest a disconnexion of thoughts and feelings, a general silliness and inaptness of emotional expression, and commonly an obstinate seclusiveness. (This 'splitting' gave rise to the use of 'schizophrenia', from *schizo*, to split or cut.) Schizophrenia is somewhat more likely to strike people for the first time around adolescence, whereas manic-depressive, cyclic insanity is more frequent around middle age and more frequently clears up naturally, at least for a time.

Kretschmer, around 1920, pointed out that the types recognized by Bleuler also existed in less extreme forms in normals and he called them the cyclothyme and schizothyme temperaments. (Thus insanity might strike anyone, but the form which it would take was expected to depend on the individual's prior temperament.) He added that this temperament had some relation to body build and that schizothymes tended to be thin and slight in build whereas cyclothymes were stocky and rounded. Table 3 shows the ratings most strongly affected by (loaded in) factor *A* and a comparison of these with those clinically described by Kretschmer shows a striking agreement. In Table 3 each trait element is given in bipolar opposites, as the axis of the earth might be fixed by north and south poles, and the rater spreads people out from those high in the trait (on the left-hand side) to those showing mostly the trait on the right. Consequently the factor which derives from these must also be considered bipolar, the positive or high score corresponding to the label on the left-hand side here. However, the reader should recognize from the outset that no value judgement is implied by calling cyclothymia 'positive' and schizothymia 'negative'. Each has its good uses and its bad consequences and the direction of scoring is purely arbitrary.

In connexion with this naming, in spite of Kretschmer's using *schizothyme* to distinguish the normal temperament from the schizophrenic, the general public continues to regard 'schizo' as

TABLE 3

Source trait A. Affectothymia-vs-sizothymia in ratings

A+ (Positively Loaded)		*A*− (Negatively Loaded)
Good-natured, easy-going	vs	Critical, grasping
Cooperative	vs	Obstructive
Attentive to people	vs	Cool, aloof
Soft-hearted	vs	Hard, precise
Trustful	vs	Suspicious
Adaptable	vs	Rigid

indicating abnormality. And since the tests we shall describe for this factor are likely to be recorded for schoolchildren and discussed with parents, it has seemed best to avoid misunderstandings by using finally the new title for it now adopted, namely *sizothymia*, instead of schizothymia, for *sizo*, deriving from the same root as 'size' in painting, means 'flat' and refers to what psychiatrists call the 'flatness of affect', i.e. the absence of lively and vibrant emotion, in the sizothyme. And it is this coldness and aloofness which, more than anything else, characterize the *normal A* (minus), i.e. the sizothyme person. Henceforth, with normal behaviour, we shall therefore characterize this basic division, so central in all personality differences, as sizothymia. Perhaps it will also recommend itself to psychologists to refer to the cyclothyme, when normal, as an *affectothyme*, because the primary characteristic is affect or emotion, not merely the cyclical ups and downs of elation and depression which occur in the abnormal, cyclically insane person.

If one runs one's eye over the group of trait elements which come together at this normal, 'lower' sizothyme pole, one sees a detached, shut-in, emotionally inexpressive type, which is quite healthy and normal in itself; however, if such an individual became abnormal, e.g. by having hallucinations and losing control, it is easy to see that he would behave as in schizophrenia. Similarly, as Kretschmer has pointed out, the warm-hearted, gentle, full emotionality of the affectothyme could develop, under unusual stress and exhaustion, that loss of mood control, and that abnormal domination of thought by elation or of pervasive depression which one sees in the 'affective' psychoses (insanities).

THE MEASUREMENT OF SOURCE TRAIT A BY QUESTIONNAIRE

What comes out by the statistical calculations of factor analysis, as a unitary dimension or factor, is best characterized psychologically as a *source trait*. For it operates as an underlying source of observed behaviour. However, not all observed behaviour which correlates together can be identified with a source trait. Sometimes things go together by reason of overlap of several influences. Then we speak of a *surface trait* or *syndrome* (if it is abnormal). Thus a bunch of behaviour elements cluster together to constitute neuroticism, e.g. anxiety, indecision, inability to concentrate, irrational fears, etc., but neuroticism is due to a conjunction of several factors, not one. Or again, among men in the street there is a correlation cluster or surface trait among such things as larger vocabulary, some understanding of mathematics, of history, etc. We recognize that a person high in this surface trait is likely (*a*) to have had longer education, (*b*) to be naturally more intelligent, and (*c*) to have a studious temperament. Here three distinct factors of personality and personal history combine to give a single pattern.

It is important to distinguish source traits from surface traits. Right in the present area of behaviour there exists what some psychologists consider a broad surface trait – extraversion–introversion. We have reason to believe it is a 'second-order factor' (see page 117), but regardless, it should not be confused with the primary source trait of 'affectothymia-*vs*-sizothymia' which we are now recognizing. The term extraversion–introversion, due to the Swiss psychiatrist Jung, is now so battered by popular usage that it may mean anything from sociability to good emotional adjustment, depending on the background of the user. If we accept, however, the unique definition by the second-order factor above, in which case we may prefer more precisely to call it 'exvia-*vs*-invia', then the statistical analysis shows that affectothymia-*vs*-sizothymia is only one component (along with the factors below labelled *F* and *H*) in this total exvia–invia temperament difference.

With this rejection of a possible false identification, let us note that a good deal more is now known about source trait *A*. First, as seen in Chapter 2, it has quite an appreciable hereditary determination and some relation to broad and thin body-build difference. Second, it is significantly higher in women than men, which accounts for some of the more expressive emotionality and tenderness of women, and is connected with the known higher rate of manic-depressive disorders of women and of schizophrenic disorders in men. Thirdly, there are marked differences of level between occupations: teachers and social workers are higher than average (affectothyme) and electricians and engineers, among others, lower (sizothyme).

It has been stated as one of the aims of modern scientific psychology to proceed to measurement in terms of natural functional unities in personality, not of arbitrary, artificial scales. Having discovered such a unity, and one contributing much to total personality differences, in affectothymia–sizothymia, describable in terms of behaviour ratings made on real life behaviours, we want to measure it. However, of the three 'media' of observation discussed above, only two of them – *Q*-data and

T-data – are strictly *test* media. Behaviour rating is in one sense the *criterion* – the real behaviour – which the test has to predict. In any case, it is scarcely useful as a test, defined as 'a portable measuring device' because one cannot cart around the *same* judges from group to group. And unless we have the same judges, with the same standards, equal score figures on two people do not mean the same thing.

The first attempt at measuring personality was made in the questionnaire medium, which was well in use by 1920, in a number of 'scales'. However, it needs no great shrewdness to realize that self-evaluation, e.g. in responding to the question, 'Are you a worrying person?' is beset by systematic errors. The respondent does not *know* accurately where he stands relative to other people, not having been another person, and, if he did, he might not tell you when, for example, he wants to make a good impression in applying for a job. Also, people in different cultures show differing readiness to express private evaluations publicly. The French have a saying that words are given to us to disguise our feelings. And Freud has stressed that the barrier to the unconscious mind prevents our really knowing our desires and interests.

In spite of these shortcomings which can be commented upon systematically later, the questionnaire has worked tolerably well, when intelligently designed. The usual procedure is to present several 'items', generally from five to forty for *each* factor scale one wishes to measure. A person's score is the number out of the total array of questions, which he answers in the keyed way. Usually, to get rid of effects from response sets, for example, tendency to say yes, or to choose the left answer, the items have to be balanced, i.e. made so that as many 'yes' or 'no' answers contribute to a positive score.

But how are the original question items chosen? In the construction of the Sixteen Personality Factor Questionnaire by Eber and the present writer, and of the corresponding Child Personality Questionnaires by Coan, Porter, and others, the dimensions found in ratings constituted the main framework. That is to say, the psychologist formed a conception of the unitary source traits in the normal personality *from the factor patterns of ratings*, as in affectothymia above, and made up the most potent questions he could to hit this target. But the patterns found in ratings were considered still only as *hypotheses*, not as guaranteed to reproduce themselves also in questionnaires. The structure of factors in questionnaire item responses had to be established independently, on its own merits. (If only for the reason that few psychologists can make up a question the answer to which will indeed correlate with that to other questions in the manner in which they intend it to do!) The difficulties which here mock intuition and blunt understanding are largely introduced by the need to construct questions so indirect that they gain some immunity to faking.

So the psychologist, though he is guided by hunches from rating factors, also adds many other items. In fact, he is guided by the original personality sphere notion – to represent as much of the totality of human behaviour as possible. Thus the procedure is to present hundreds – in the long run thousands – of carefully chosen items to large groups of normal persons. Each item is then correlated with every other to see which sets 'go together'. Factor analysis, usually pursued with the help of electronic computers, shows how many independent dimensions are required to account for the discovered connexions, and gives an

TABLE 4

Factor A in questionnaire responses

(1) I would rather work as:
      (a) an engineer   (b) *a social science teacher*
(2) I could stand being a hermit?
      (a) True   (b) *False*
(3) I am careful to turn up when someone expects me
      (a) *True*   (b) False
(4) I would prefer to marry someone who is:
      (a) a thoughtful companion   (b) *effective in a social group*
(5) I would prefer to read a book on:
      (a) *national social service*   (b) new scientific weapons
(6) I trust strangers:
      (a) sometimes   (b) *practically always*

A person who answers all of the above in the indicated direction (*italic answers*) has a highly affectothyme temperament, but most will answer roughly a half.

indication of what these are, in terms of which items are loaded – just as we saw with rated trait elements. Actually, there quickly emerges a factor which seems to be a 'mental interior': a self view, corresponding to the affectothymia–sizothymia rating pattern seen above. The question items which it loads most highly are given in Table 4.

The warm sociability at one pole and the aloofness and unconcern with people at the other are as evident here as in the observers' ratings.

THE SOURCE TRAIT C OF EGO STRENGTH

The striking – and encouraging – finding in these Q-data experiments is that despite different random samples of questions being used, one seems to get (*a*) approximately the same number of factors for 'mental interiors' as for 'behavioural exteriors', and (*b*) a very good alignment, in total meaning, of the two series of factors. This supports up to a point a theory of 'indifference of indicator'. That is to say, we seem to see the same 'shapes' despite the difference in the 'dress' (i.e. the form of expression or observation device), as a microscopist might expect to locate largely the same true objects, somewhat modified in appearance, despite using different wave lengths of light or different dyes.

There are some differences, to be sure, notably in that some factors like radicalism-*vs*-conservatism (Q_1), and internal self-sufficiency (Q_2), show up much more readily in the questionnaire than in gross behaviour. There are also some differences of emphasis, as when the sizothyme person describes himself in Q-data as slow and reserved, whereas people tend to see him rather (in ratings) as cold and arrogant. Similarly, high surgent individuals (page 92 below) describe themselves as gay and happy-go-lucky, whereas observers consider them as casual or even defective in conscience. But the failure of 'measures' on the same factor through two different media to correlate perfectly is now understood in terms of what are called 'instrument factors', that is, error intruding into one measure from a 'rating instrument' factor and into its 'twin' from a 'questionnaire instrument' factor, while a true common factor continues to exist.

In this connexion, one can see that it is a mistake to assume that all or most of the error is in the questionnaire, as some do, and that the behaviour rating is *the* 'criterion', i.e. that by which the questionnaire measure is to be validated. There are advantages and disadvantages on both sides. The interview, which is a form of rating – aided by a standard, if brief, situation – has been proved again and again by psychological experiment to be most unreliable, though interviewers will continue to fancy their talents. A major shortcoming of rating, as a technique, is that judges see subjects usually only in one place, e.g. the classroom, or the office, for a special part of the day, and from the position of a person in a particular role. Each of these three is an additional source of error. The questionnaire respondent, however, is *always* with himself, and sees a day and night sample of behaviour. On the other hand, especially in those things, e.g. worry, self-confidence, contempt, which people do not fully show openly, an individual, even if wishing to be truthful, lacks any firm standards of comparison from the inner life of others. For example, it is a commonplace that in social situations young people usually mistakenly believe other young people are more self-confident and less shy than they are themselves.

For these 'instrument factor' reasons, correlations of 'self-rated' and 'other-rated' estimates of what appears to be a factor identical in meaning in both tend to run numerically lower than would be expected – except where great care is taken to watch statistical and other conditions, as discussed elsewhere.

However, in the second largest source trait in ratings (which by its position is labelled *B*), there is no real difficulty. This looks like nothing less than general intelligence, and correlates well with actual test results. Although differences in the intelligence factor do tend to involve personality expressions, we must, since our concern is the main personality factors, skip *B* and pass on to the third factor, *C*, which is shown in Table 5 first in its rating and secondly in its questionnaire form. The meaning of this source trait seems to support the psychoanalytic concept of Ego Strength. Further, its demonstrated persistent negative correlation with neuroticism and anxiety, in various experimental groups in America and Britain, supports this interpretation. However, it will be noted that there are some 'viewpoint' differences in that the rater stresses emotionality, lack of responsibility, and evasiveness of reality, whereas the *Q*-data stresses a little more of a sense of worthlessness, emotional fatigue, and inability to cope with reality.

TABLE 5

Source trait C. Ego strength-vs-emotionality and neuroticism, in L- and Q-data

Behaviour ratings by observer on these elements:

C+		C−
Mature	*vs*	Unable to tolerate frustration
Steady, persistent	*vs*	Changeable
Emotionally calm	*vs*	Impulsively emotional
Realistic about problems	*vs*	Evasive, avoids necessary decisions
Absence of neurotic fatigue	*vs*	Neurotically fatigued (with no real effort)

Questionnaire responses on these items:

Do you find it difficult to take no for an answer even when what you want to do is obviously impossible?
  (a) yes   (b) *no*
If you had your life to live over again, would you
  (a) *want it to be essentially the same?* (b) plan it very differently?
Do you often have really disturbing dreams?
  (a) yes   (b) *no*
Do your moods sometimes make you seem unreasonable even to yourself?
  (a) yes   (b) *no*
Do you feel tired when you've done nothing to justify it?
  (a) *rarely*   (b) often
Can you change old habits, without relapse, when you decide to?
  (a) *yes*   (b) no

This source trait is obviously one of the most important things for the clinician to measure, when he is attempting to size up the severity of a neurotic condition. But it also has importance in vocational guidance, in understanding school failures, and in many other ways. The essence of *C* factor appears to be an inability to control one's emotions and impulses, especially by finding for them some satisfactory realistic expression. Looked at from the opposite or positive pole, it sharpens and gives scientific substance to the psychoanalytic concept of 'ego strength', which it has come to be called. Measurements with the 16 P.F. (Sixteen Personality Factor Questionnaire) and the H.S.P.Q. (High School Personality Questionnaire) show that almost all forms of neurotics, as well as alcoholics, narcotic addicts, and delinquents are abnormally low on this ego-strength factor. This also helps in its identification, for we would expect on dynamic grounds that the most widespread inadequacy among such a wide range of distinct abnormalities would be ego weakness. Occupationally, the scores are higher in persons belonging to callings requiring control and decision, as in airline pilots and firemen, and lower in such more sheltered occupations as clerical workers and janitors. Furthermore, there is evidence suggesting that ego-strength development is lower in clinical cases subjected to prolonged anxiety or given to excessive guilt proneness. This fits the psychoanalytic theory that excessive early demands by conscience can so add to the difficulties of finding suitable expression for emotional needs that the ego's capacity to handle impulses rationally is impaired.

As pointed out above, the mathematical nature of a factor is such that we should expect it to correspond to a single, scientific concept or influence, of which the elements listed, for example, in Tables 4 and 5 are expressions. The nature of this underlying power in C can be seen dynamically, as the self or ego, organized to give expression to the drives in a well-balanced way. But in other factors it may not be so easy. For example, how can we interpret the nature of the source trait underlying the A pattern? Much of the behaviour at the negative, sizothyme pole suggests a coldness and disillusionment about humanity. The natural warmth has been disciplined to a detached objectivity, an unwillingness to get much involved with people, and accompanied even by some degree of hostility. However, so far no one has found much evidence of $A-$ (henceforth, we will represent high and low on A by $A+$ and $A-$, and similarly for other factors) individuals having any more unfortunate experiences than others; while the body build and other evidence points to some appreciable constitutional determination. The constitutional influence could either be a lower emotionality – a greater natural detachment and disinclination to react, as is suggested by the term sizothyme (flatness of emotional life) – or some natural obstinacy of self-direction which begets frustration when people expect the individual to conform. This latter concept is not easy to develop in a short space, but if we suppose that some constitutional, temperamental, physiological condition makes some people's drives naturally more persistent and unchanging, this might account simultaneously for the greater natural emotional steadiness of the sizothyme and also for his greater sense of frustration, hostility, and withdrawal (since to have greater perseverance is also to experience greater thwarting) from an ordinarily unaccommodating environment. And what can be more unaccommodating and puzzling than people?

Regardless of the particular interpretation we adopt, it will be evident that a source trait as discovered by factor analysis is some kind of unitary influence in personality which affects a whole structure of responses. Even if psychology cannot immediately trace and interpret the nature of this unitary influence, we do well to represent it by a *symbol* and use it until interpretation is gained. For there is an immediate gain in economy alone in that by measuring a certain number of basic source traits we automatically describe a larger area of personality than if we measured the same number of arbitrary variables at random. What is perhaps even more important is that such traits are likely to have a functional unity and comparative independence in development, and in action, which makes them the most useful concepts around which to develop personality theory and experiment.

Since from this point on the reader will increasingly encounter technical terms, it is hoped that it will prove helpful to him to make use of the glossary which has been provided *at the end of the book*. It may function also to refresh the meaning of terms re-encountered after an interval.

*

READING

Thomson, G. H., *The Factorial Analysis of Human Ability.* Houghton-Mifflin, Boston, 1951; University of London Press, 1951.

Cattell, R. B., *Personality and Motivation Structure and Measurement.* Harcourt, Brace and World, New York, 1957; Harrap, 1958.

CHAPTER FOUR

Further Traits, and Their Integration

THE MEANING OF THE SPECIFICATION EQUATION

As we have seen in studying the affectothyme and ego strength source traits, the implication of the factor analytic method is that each factor covers a whole set of 'behaviours' which spring from some single source. It is not always immediately possible to say what the source is, and, indeed, psychological theory may debate for many years after the discovery of a factor which of several rival hypotheses is correct. Thus the affectothymia-sizothymia dimension, A, points to some as yet unisolated physiological influence on temperament difference, which makes for high tenacity and therefore for a higher sense of frustration in the person possessing it than would occur to an affectothyme in the same environment. The ego strength, C, source trait seems by contrast to be a partly acquired general dynamic trait producing an ability to mediate successfully between impulse and the opportunities of the external world.

Just the same periods and kinds of uncertainty, while ideas stand in a descriptive limbo, occur in other sciences. Typically, the discovery of a new vitamin, a new galaxy or a new sub-atomic particle has to be followed by a long inquiry in which the scientist knows *where* or *who* the entity is, but not *what* it is. Psychiatrists and psychologists, because of their infancy in the glib clinical school, like to have their explorations all at once. Consequently, theory is only slowly adjusting to the scientific discipline of entertaining these real but only partially explained patterns.

Before we fully understand the nature of each source trait, it is nevertheless possible to depend upon the work with certain general properties common to all of them. Chief among these is our ability to determine what is called the *concept* (or construct) *validity*, and the *reliability*, of tests proposed to measure them.

Further, even without fuller knowledge of their inner nature we can discover the principles by which they combine to produce the behaviour of the integrated personality. Let us study these two possibilities while introducing some further important source traits.

It has sometimes been critically remarked about the trait approach that it takes the personality to pieces into recognizable unitary sources but that, like the small boy with the parts of the grandfather clock, it is unable to assemble them again. This has been true of some verbal dialectics, but not of the factor analytic approach, which presents a 'mathematical model' – that is to say a set of precise rules for handling and combining the measurements involved. Any such model in science is the very heart of a theory. By it the theory is tested quantitatively, and on the 'fit' of the experimental results to the quantities predicted the theory stands or falls. By this test the factor theory of personality does very well, which is not to say, however, that like the Newtonian model for the solar system it may not later need smaller adjustments, based on more comprehensive theory.

To illustrate the integration of traits by the three source traits A, B, and C so far described let us consider people playing tennis. Imagine fifty young people placed in order of effectiveness as the result of a long series of matches. Obviously, general intelligence, B, will enter into success because intelligent planning is necessary in match tennis. Possibly also trait A will produce effects because the easy-going affectothymes will not follow up with the tenacity and precision of the sizothymes. Finally, ego strength, C, will also play a part because a low C person, who loses his temper easily or easily becomes discouraged, will not use his abilities to best advantage.

Presumably, by adding each person's scores on these three traits (A and C negatively) we should obtain a first approximation to the relative goodness of each, thus:

$$R_i = -A_i + B_i - C_i$$

where R_i is the tennis 'response' or performance of any individual and the others are his trait scores. However, probably intelligence is decidedly more important than sizothymia, and in fact we can find this out by working out the correlation between the performance rank, R, and A, B, etc. If intelligence is in fact involved more it will have a higher correlation with tennis success. By putting in these correlation 'weights', which might be as follows, we get a better estimate, thus:

$$R_i = -0 \cdot 1A_i + 0 \cdot 6B_i - 0 \cdot 4C_i$$

These values ($-0 \cdot 1$, $+0 \cdot 6$, and $-0 \cdot 4$) are also called *loadings*, showing the degree of involvement of each source trait in the given performance, and they can be alternatively reached by the factor analytic process itself.

At this point it will occur to the common-sense observer that the sheer amount of practice each person has had at tennis is also important, and we ought to add a term T for tennis practice to this, the weight for which can also be found by correlation. Then we should have:

$$R_i = -0 \cdot 1A_i + 0 \cdot 6B_i - 0 \cdot 4C_i + 0 \cdot 7T$$

Traits A, B, and C are called *common* traits, because they enter and are common to a lot of things besides tennis. But T is called a specific, because it is a set of dexterities quite specific to practice in this one thing, tennis.

The equation just set out is a very important one with many implications for personality testing, and it is called the *specification equation*, because it specifies the way in which traits are to be combined to predict and understand any particular performance or response. For instance, having obtained the correlations on our fifty tennis players we could take a fifty-first person, whose play has never been seen, and, from his scores on traits A, B, and C, and the specific, T, weighted and added as in the equation, we might get a pretty good estimate of how well he will actually perform.

Normally, of course, one would consider more than three source traits, and the specification equation can be put in perfectly general form up to any number (K) of factors

$$R_{ij} = b_{jA}A_i + b_{jB}B_i + \dots\ b_{jK}K_i + b_{jS}S_j$$

where j is *any* behavioural response, S_j is the specific to it, and the b's are weights, peculiar to j and to each factor. These b's are mathematically weights but are best psychologically called *situational indices*, or *behavioural situation indices* (hence '*b*'), because they show how much each personality factor is involved in the situation *j*. To the geometrically inclined, it may be helpful to see these *b*'s as tangents, showing how rapidly the performance R_j increases as endowment in the given personality factor increases.

At this point the reader may feel like the modern philosopher who, looking at the work of the physicists, has said, 'If you follow their analysis of matter you will not get anything like common sense has always supposed matter to be. You will get mathematics.' Perhaps the best thing would be to go to arithmetic examples and show, in known persons, that if you insert their 'standard scores' (a device to bring all factors to the same units) on traits you in fact get good predictions from these weights. Such illustration is best deferred, however, to the 'applied' Chapter 11. Here we are concerned only with the principle of combining, and it will be noticed that we have used the simplest way of integrating, namely *adding* (or subtracting) the effect of one trait to that of another. One can imagine that traits might get together in some more complex way, such as by one multiplying the effect of another, or by one catalysing another, and in advanced work these possibilities are being investigated. But science starts with the simplest hypothesis or model and gives it up only if and when some less likely arrangement is required by new facts. At present the additive action of traits in the specification equation fits the data quite well.

If one thinks back now to our general behaviour equation

$$R_{ij} = f(S_j P_i)$$

and the occasion when we put a numerical weight for the situation *S*, he will recognize that we have at last settled on a form for the function *f*. We are now saying that the situation S_j is represented by a lot of situational indices, b_{jA}, b_{jB}, etc., thus:

$$(1) \quad S_j = b_{jA}, b_{jB} \ldots b_{jK}$$

and that the person, P_i, is represented by a lot of dimensions thus:

$$(2) \quad P_i = A_i, B_i \ldots K_i$$

When we link these into a single equation we have:

$$(3)\ R_{ij} = b_{jA}A_i + b_{jB}B_i\ \ldots\ +b_{jK}K_i, \text{etc.}$$

A multidimensional person comes into contact with a multidimensional situation, and the result is a response of magnitude peculiar to that individual *i*.

PRACTICAL PERSONALITY TESTING: SOURCE TRAIT AND SPECIAL PURPOSE TESTS

The meaning of the above will become further evident if we take a first brief incursion into the field of practical testing.

The advantages of using source traits in practical psychological measurements by means of the above 'specification equation' are many – some obvious, some subtle. If the psychologist does *not* use source trait measures his main alternative is to make up what are called 'special purpose tests'. This amounts to making up a special test for each job or clinical diagnosis, or school subject achievement prediction, which will combine the source trait ingredients in the particular combinations required in the actual special purpose test. This was a common method in the past, and it often amounted to making up a test which simulated the very performances in the job. For example, a bus driver's test would set the subject among car controls before a film of traffic, a lathe operator's test would be a performance-recording machine made like a lathe, and a secretarial efficiency test would deal with spelling and filing.

The disadvantages of these special purpose tests, whether based on mere 'face validity' or on evidence of actual correlational testing of predictive validity, are several. First, the combination of traits which worked in one kind of group may not work in another, e.g. veterans and students of the subject. For instance, if one is seeking statistical clerks from among university students the weight given to intelligence will be less than for the general population, because a certain base level of intelligence can be assumed among students. Second, the specific factor is given too much weight. The person who has worked for the last three months on a lathe does better than one who hasn't, though potentially the latter may be *going* to be a better operator. Thirdly, one does not *understand* when one merely has a single score from a conglomerate test, which 'somehow' succeeds in predicting. On the other hand, when one knows what source traits are operative, and why, i.e. what the prediction is based upon, the amount of control is greatly increased. For example, some source traits, like intelligence and ego strength, naturally increase with age. Surgency (see below), on the other hand, is a source trait which steadily decreases with age. Other source traits change with particular experiences, while some are so constitutional that little change is to be expected. Obviously, if one is predicting for success in an occupation some years ahead, this psychological knowledge will increase accuracy beyond that obtainable with mere statistical prediction from a psychologically blind special purpose test.

Furthermore, the specification equation makes it clear that the same level of success (or the same R score in, say, the sense of equal manifestation of a neurotic symptom) *is reached by different people for different reasons.* To return to our tennis match, when two people play to a draw, one may be high on persistence and low on intelligence and the other may make up by intelligent tactics what he lacks in persistence. When we speak of two people performing anywhere, e.g. in music, in debate, in essay writing, with equal goodness but different *quality*, we mean that their source trait profiles are different but that the *s* weightings happen to make the two equivalent. The reader can test this by substituting different score* numbers for different traits in the equation above to try to give the same end result.

A negative b (situational index) value means, of course, that experiment has shown that this source trait actively *interferes* with good performance on the given criterion. Thus the affectothymia temperament score, A, above, though positively loaded in 'success as a salesman', has a negative b value in 'accuracy in computing'. And C, ego strength, has a positive situational index

* Incidentally, the standard scores for traits will normally range from $-2 \cdot 5$ to $+2 \cdot 5$ and the b or situational index values will range from -1 to $+1$.

for acceptance as an air pilot, but a negative one for likelihood of turning up at a clinic as an anxiety neurotic.

Incidentally, the *b* values hold the key to giving the necessary basis for a psychological classification of situations, e.g. jobs. In fact the present writer has suggested, on this basis, the 'two file system' for personnel work in large companies, military organizations, etc. Therein a profile is kept for every person, constituted by the dozen or more personality and ability factor scores, in one file. This is the part P_i in the above formula (page 80). Then in another file a situational index file is kept for every job speciality. This is the part S_j in the above formula. The advantage is that these *b* values in the job profile could be obtained once and for all in an experiment including personality test scores and criteria, i.e. job performance scores, in a study correlating one with the other. With the two files available it becomes possible, as each new position becomes vacant to match objectively individual profiles with job profiles among the available candidates and positions. The process would naturally be followed by an interview check up but it permits the fairest and most comprehensive coverage of personality and ability source trait information on the one hand and job specialities on the other.

Although this is mathematical, and could even be handled by a computer, it is the very antithesis and repudiation of the charge that the analytical psychologist can take a person to pieces all right, in terms of underlying traits, but cannot put him together again. Admittedly, the 'special purpose' *ad hoc* or patent psychological gadget test or arbitrary set of scales is often such that from its scores all the king's horses and all the king's men would not put Humpty Dumpty together again. But by the very nature of factor analytic theory source traits reconstitute the totality of the individual. In fact, the specification equation explicitly states that the *whole* of personality enters into any specific act. For *every* source trait receives a weight in the final result, a weight which differs according to the nature of the act.

The scientific advantage of basing personality measurement on source traits rather than *ad hoc* 'scales' made up to each experimenter's predilections should need no further illustration. Psychology suffered so painfully in public prestige during the period when intelligence tests were made up according to the individual recipes of diverse psychologists, teachers, and industrial personnel managers that no one would want to go back and repeat this sad story in relation to personality traits. Source traits can be uniquely defined by experiments which, if properly technically conducted, will agree from laboratory to laboratory. They can be recognized across different age levels and cultures with minor modifications (see Chapter 12). Finally, they constitute concepts in psychology of basic theoretical importance, like affectothymia, intelligence, ego strength, surgency, and super-ego strength, around which the science of personality development is increasingly being built (see Chapter 10).

Accordingly, a good deal of effort has been given to building up valid test measures of these source traits and, before proceeding farther, we should ask how the validity and reliability of these and other tests are to be evaluated.

THE RELIABILITY AND VALIDITY OF PSYCHOLOGICAL TESTS

The general public is entitled to entertain a certain healthy suspicion of the psychological tests which, from occasion to occasion, in school, job, clinic, and military draft examinations, affect our lives. How can we ascertain how well the psychologist and his tests do what they are supposed to do? Psychologists and psychometrists have naturally given a lot of attention to this matter, mainly under the heading of test *validity* and test *consistency* (which includes what are technically called reliability and homogeneity). Let us scrutinize these.

When a test itself comes up for testing a very important question is its validity, measurable as *the extent to which it measures what it is supposed to measure*. Incidentally, British, American, and Swedish psychologists, to name but three, have progressed far in these fields but when the present writer visited some central European laboratories after the war he found, as many have since commented, that they had fallen behind somewhat during the period of isolation. To the question, 'How do you know that this test measures what you say it does?' he was there often surprised by the answer, 'Because I made it up to do so.' The days are now gone (also in central Europe where psychology has moved ahead strongly) when such an answer could be accepted.

Test constructors generally test validity against what is called a *criterion*. They evaluate the test by seeing how high the correlation is between test and criterion, i.e. how far the test puts a set of, say, two or three hundred people in the same order as the criterion. An ideal test would correlate $+1\cdot0$ with the criterion while the correlation coefficient for a test that is no good at all would yield a value close to zero. If the criterion is a concrete performance, e.g. the number of words a typist types per minute, we speak of a *concrete validity*, whereas if it is a concept, like intelligence or anxiety, we speak of a construct or *concept validity*. Since any concept has to be tied down in a set of operations or pattern of behavioural scores before we can validate a test measurement against it, concept validity commonly turns out to be factor validity.

Now the thoughtful reader will have noticed that one implication of the specification equation is that a whole factor is rarely to be accurately represented by any *single*, concrete piece of behaviour. Any quite specific behaviour is usually the result, as we have seen, of *several* factors acting together. It follows that to get a good estimate of a source trait we must, reciprocally, add together the scores of *several* concrete performances (chosen for their discovered substantial loadings with the factor) to get the single factor score.

For example, the source trait *B*, general intelligence, is found to load such concrete performances as choosing exact synonyms, solving logical problems, choosing right completions for a number series, choosing analogies, and so on. By adding the scores of several of these sub-tests into a single pool we get the best estimate of what is common to them – the intelligence source trait. This procedure both piles up the contribution to the wanted general factor and tends to wipe out any undue contribution from any one specific, concrete skill. We 'sample' intelligence, so to speak, from many of its areas of expression and thus get a relatively unbiased score.

The alternatives to this dependence on discovered loadings are either to take some non-factorial conceptual criterion, for example the ability to learn, or else to use a specific concrete criterion. However, the ability to learn turns out according to factor analysis to cover several factors, not one, depending on the field of learning, so one has to ask 'To learn what?' On closer examination most of these loose and rather grandiose concepts like 'abstract thinking', 'insight', 'success in life', which have been proposed as non-factorial conceptual criteria need a lot more done on them to make them operational and realistic. And the alternate search for a single concrete criterion fails because psychologists cannot get even social agreement on any such criterion. One man says 'ability to do mathematics' is intelligence but others say this is not their idea of general ability. Another says 'academic or scholastic success', but broader-minded scientists think this has already been allowed to influence intelligence tests too much and favour perhaps 'life success'. But what is this? Admittedly it cannot be scored simply as the size of salary after X years. Actually the statistical factor uniquely fixed by the factor analytic process happens to run through most intellectual performances and also satisfies the content demanded by most *a priori* theories. When such a broad functional unity is located it is really unimportant whether we attach to it the traditional term intelligence, or call it general mental capacity, or something else. The important thing is that there exists a functional unity operating across most concrete intellectual performances, and this source is now measurable and known to have certain properties, for example, of increasing with age, decreasing with brain damage, contributing so much to success in mathematics, and so forth. The *validity* of any particular test of 'intelligence' (or at least of B factor or Spearman's 'g') thus ceases to be a matter for personal opinion. We can validate the given test by finding its correlation with the sum total of scores which best estimate this factor.

Similarly in personality factors, it becomes no longer a matter of personal judgement by the psychologist as to whether a particular questionnaire scale (or any other type of test) is measuring a particular source trait. The degree to which it is doing so can be calculated in what has been described above as the validity coefficient. For example, in the case of the 16 P.F. (the sixteen Personality Factor) questionnaire, the measures for factors *A, B,* and *C,* so far discussed above, have coefficients of correlation of the test score with the pure factor which run, for all three, between $+0.7$ and $+0.9$. An *r* (we will henceforth represent the correlation coefficient by the symbol *r*) of 0.8 can be considered very satisfactory for a length of only twenty or so items. The concept validities of some of the later source trait scales, such as *J, M, N,* however, run lower than this.

Although the aim of seeking what has been defined above as a *concrete,* particular validity for any general personality factor becomes rather absurd for any broad trait, such as intelligence and ego strength, this does not mean that the trait measurement should not correlate with various concrete performances, else the factor which it represents must be written off as of no practical relevance for much of our daily life. The 16 P.F. and H.S.P.Q. (High School Personality Questionnaire) questionnaire factor scales mentioned above all have such practical relevances. For example, source trait *A* (affectothymia) correlates about 0.5 with salary as a salesman, *B* about 0.6 with success in school, and *C* (ego strength) about -0.4 with severity of neuroticism. (A negative correlation is, of course, equally valuable for prediction; it simply predicts inversely.) However, such coefficients should strictly be called factor *relevances,* not validities, as is sometimes mistakenly done. Concrete relevances are important, but it is scarcely logical to use them as estimates of a concrete validity, for their purpose is not purely to estimate that concrete performance. The conceptual validity of a test is its important property.

Tests are examined commonly not only for validity but also for *consistency,* i.e. the extent to which the test continues simply to give results consistent with itself regardless of how valid it is. *Consistency* covers three things: (1) *Reliability,* i.e. the extent to which a second administration of the test gives the same results; (2) *Homogeneity,* i.e. the extent to which different parts of the test measure the same thing; and (3) *Transferability,* i.e. the extent to which the test continues to measure the same thing when applied to groups of a different age, educational status, etc. As a gross illustration of the last, the American Stanford Binet or the Wechsler Adult Intelligence Test or the W.I.S.C. in such widespread use today would fail completely in transferability if administered to Chinese or even Italian subjects, whereas the I.P.A.T. Culture Fair Intelligence Test has shown almost perfect transferability across these cultures.

Homogeneity should not exceed a certain point in a good test, else transferability and validity suffer. A test functions *as a whole*, like a well-made watch, and it is often good for the total functioning that its parts should be different. Reliability, on the other hand, should be high. A test can scarcely hope to agree with *anything* – that is, to have validity – if it cannot be true to itself when twice administered. Incidentally, it is partly on account of their low reliability that psychologists deny the validity of the interview and of the essay type of examination. Instances are on record where the same essay has been given every mark from 0 to 10 by different examiners. The late Dr Ballard reported an instance where he himself wrote a model answer, as a standard for grading. This was accidentally included in the papers sent to the second examiner of the essays, who, without looking at the name, gave him a 'fail' grade! The reliability of interview evaluations by two different interviewers commonly runs no better than $+0.3$ or $+0.4$, and the scoring of essays by two different examiners little higher.

Psychological tests, whether of abilities or personality, commonly have very good reliabilities, partly because they are 'selective answer', 'multiple choice' in design, and can be scored by tireless machines. On the other hand, it would be no exaggeration to say that half of those on the test market are grievously defective in concept validity. And though reliability is valuable, it is not as important as validity. Indeed, there are technical reasons – the existence of function fluctuation (Chapter 6) in traits – why one must suspect a test which shows too high a realiability. After all, people vary from day to day.

Not much variation has yet been demonstrated for intelligence (though everyone subjectively feels more stupid on some days than others!) but there is demonstrated variability of *C*, ego strength, and it can be shown to be related to environmental demands, illness, and anxiety. Such real variation is called *function fluctuation* (see Chapter 5 below) and by reason thereof one would suspect a test with reliability of above, say 0·95, because people on Monday simply do not fall into exactly the same rank order of ego strength as, say, on the preceding Saturday. The real unitary function changes still more in growing children, and a test which is really measuring it should show appreciable test–retest change. For example, a retest of a large group on the I.P.A.T. Anxiety Scale shows a 0·88 reliability over two days, but only 0·40 when people are retested after two years, and this latter is no reflection on the test but an indication of how much people can change in this unitary trait.

In comparing the reliability coefficients given for tests one should also note that reliability is a comparatively simple function of test *length*, and that the great majority of tests can be brought to any reliability desired by appropriately increasing their length. Validity cannot be bought so easily!

THE SOURCE TRAITS OF EXCITABILITY, DOMINANCE, AND SURGENCY–DESURGENCY

With this account of how the main properties, *validity* and *consistency*, of tests are assessed we can profitably return to continue the description of the main structural source traits in personality which are the true objects of test measurement. It will be remembered that the assignment of alphabetical symbols to source traits follows the order of importance, in the sense that *A* and *B* affect *more* of a random sample of behaviours from the personality sphere than do, say, source traits *M*, *N*, and *O*. It is of historical interest that the larger source traits found by factor analysis are also those already recognized by popular and clinical approaches. Thus, as mentioned above, the affecto–sizothyme factor may be said to have been recognized by Kraepelin and Bleuler, when they generalized about the broad breakdown of mental disorders into cyclic and schizoid forms. Similarly, the general public has long recognized our *B* factor, intelligence, as important in affecting a whole lot of behaviours, while *C*−, as 'neurotic tendency' and ego weakness, has received much attention from the psychoanalysts.

The *D* factor, next in order, is one which is most prominent in children, and bears the label *excitability*. It is so well known that we shall not set out a table of loaded variables. However, one should point out that it is not the same as the emotionality and impulsiveness of $C-$, which manifest a moody, unstable quality, not simply a high excitement level. The analysis shows that there exists a kind of excitability fundamentally distinct, with tenseness, restlessness, and attention-getting. It would be easy to theorize that this springs from affectional insecurity, as many clinicians normally explain it. But if so the level of need for security must be distinctly hereditarily determined. For the M.A.V.A. nature–nurture studies show appreciable hereditary association for the D factor. There is also some indication that it enters the schizophrenic constitution and shows itself again in what the psychiatrist calls catatonic excitement.

Source trait E is one with which we are all familiar for it shows the following loadings of ratings and questionnaire responses.

TABLE 6

Source trait E. Dominance-vs-submissiveness

$E+$		$E-$
Self-assertive, confident	vs	Submissive, unsure
Boastful, conceited	vs	Modest, retiring
Aggressive, pugnacious	vs	Complaisant
Extra-punitive	vs	Impunitive, intropunitive
Vigorous, forceful	vs	Meek, quiet
Wilful, egotistic	vs	Obedient

Source trait E in questionnaires

1. Do you tend to keep in the background on social occasions?

    No.

2. Do you feel not yet well adjusted to life and that very little works out the way it should?

    No.

3. If you saw the following headlines of equal size in your newspaper, which would you read?
    (a) Threat to constitutional government in foreign country by dictator.
    (b) Physicists make important discovery concerning the electron.

    (*a*).

Dominance is so well recognized as a dynamic 'disposition' in personality that little interpretation of the above patterns seems to be needed. Since there was a hue and cry among social psychologists a decade or so ago over the notion of an 'authoritarian personality' (to which the less scientific assigned all kinds of personal value judgements!), it is perhaps necessary to state that this is certainly not that hypothesized pattern. Indeed, the authoritarian and authority allergic personality concept has no claim to be a unitary concept, for it proves to be a conglomerate of at least four personality factors – and possibly of as many cultures and still more 'stereotypes'. One clear difference is that whereas some writers' conceptions of the authoritarian personality describe a dominant person who kicks those beneath and bows to those above, the high dispositional dominant individual as revealed by the *E* factor leads those below and kicks those above him! He expects a high level of individual independence for everyone. In group dynamics experiments Stice and Cattell found that if all members of a group have a high dominance score they establish a more democratic and free society perhaps because of this need for autonomy in everyone. Another finding which scarcely fits the assignment of anti-social values to leadership is that creative scientists and artists tend to score high on dominance. Presumably their need (on intellectual grounds) to break with convention is here sustained by their 'tough' disposition. Like almost all source traits it has good and bad aspects at *either* pole, and the loadings reveal a pattern which is more subtle than popular stereotypes – like 'authoritarian' – usually are.

Initially, in research, the questionnaire items in these source trait investigations were deliberately selected for having 'face validity'. The examples here given are also chosen for such face validity, in addition to having experimentally demonstrated *concept validity*, in order to disclose to the reader more clearly the nature of the trait. But as test construction proceeds more concept-valid items are developed which lack obvious belonging (face validity) to reduce vulnerability to faking. In this case a couple of such items have deliberately been selected from the 16 P.F. questionnaire to illustrate what can be done to prevent faking. Few people who are told to 'fake dominant' know which way to answer questions 2 and 3 in Table 6 for this purpose.

Dominance–submissiveness scores have shown some interesting

criterion relations besides that just mentioned with creativity. Men and boys score significantly higher than women and girls. Sociopaths (confidence tricksters, incorrigible criminals, etc.) score very high. Compulsive neurotics (compelled to go through meaningless rituals) score below the population average. Firemen, air pilots, and Olympic champions score high. Neurotics improving under psychotherapy show a rise in E, and so on. Though it is definitely affected by environment, being fed by social success (and therefore higher in higher social status persons), it also has a fairly strong constitutional component. Apparently it is the same as a pattern also clear in chimpanzees, rats, and other animals, and in these it responds to the level of male hormone, in either sex.

The next largest source trait in adults – and the largest of all in children – is known as surgency-*vs*-desurgency, and shows itself by the loading pattern in Table 7.

TABLE 7
*Source trait F. Surgency-*vs*-desurgency*

$F+$		$F-$
Cheerful, joyous	vs	Depressed, pessimistic
Sociable, responsive	vs	Seclusive, retiring
Energetic	vs	Subdued, languid
Humorous, witty	vs	Dull, phlegmatic
Talkative	vs	Taciturn, introspective
Placid	vs	Worrying, unable to relax, obsessional

Source trait F in questionnaires

Do you prefer the type of job that offers constant change, travel, and variety, in spite of other drawbacks?

Yes.

Are you well described as a happy-go-lucky, carefree, nonchalant individual?

Yes.

Do you enjoy being at parties and large gatherings?

Yes.

In some ways this may look like a *state* of elation-*vs*-depression, rather than a *trait*. The separation of state and trait is treated in Chapter 6, but it can be said here and now that this is more than a state, and that the evidence points to its representing a steadily enduring individual difference. It seems that the level on this trait reflects in large part the level of inhibition imposed on the individual in upbringing. The inhibition may be partly from relatively punishing and restricting conditions, as evidenced by greater desurgency in lower than upper middle-class homes. It may be partly from more family cultural restraint, as shown by leading scientists being more desurgent than the general population. The reader may theorize for himself whether either or both of these connexions accounts for Warburton's finding that Americans score significantly higher on surgency than Britons!

Sometimes the general reader asks why psychology uses neologisms, like surgency, for its source traits (see also the technical terms for A, H, and I factors), when, as in this case, he might be inclined to suggest that 'sociable' would adequately describe the factor, and be immediately meaningful to everyone. The answer is that popular terms like 'sociable' are vague and almost always describe specific 'behaviour elements' rather than the broad factors which make source traits. If the reader will refer to the specification equation on page 79, he will realize that since source traits A and F are about equally involved in a person's score on sociability, this specific 'readiness to meet people' is likely to be predicted by:

Sociability score $= 0 \cdot 5A + 0 \cdot 5F + \ldots + 0 \cdot 5G$ (super-ego, and other lesser factors).

The *quality* of a person's sociability will differ according as the predominant source is A or F. The 'sociability' we see from affectothyme temperament is a warm-hearted, gentle 'liking to be around people', in which active conversational participation, except in sympathy, is not particularly prominent. That from surgency, on the other hand, is the 'life and soul of the party' sort of sociability, with wit, some exhibitionism perhaps, and even a slap-stick practical joking verging on the callous side. Neither of these sociability components should be confused with the social concern and conscience which comes from the super-ego component G.

THE SOURCE TRAITS OF SUPER-EGO STRENGTH, PARMIA, AND PREMSIA

Just as the experimental and statistical phase of scientific psychology has brought considerable support, by finding the *C* factor, to the concept of some real functional unity behind the various clinical sketches of an 'ego strength' factor, so also it has given definiteness of outline to the notion of super-ego strength. Although further research has proved necessary, and is now in progress, to clear up certain subtleties, the factor first found some fifteen years ago continues to be replicated as follows.

TABLE 8

Source trait G. Positive Super-Ego character-vs-dependent character

G+		G—
Persevering, determined	*vs*	Quitting, fickle
Responsible	*vs*	Frivolous, immature
Insistently ordered	*vs*	Relaxed, indolent
Attentive to people	*vs*	Neglectful of social chores
Emotionally stable	*vs*	Changeable

Source trait G in questionnaires

Are you a person who is scrupulously correct in manners and social obligations and likes others to be the same?

Yes

Are you cautious and considerate that you do not hurt people's feelings by unconsidered conversational remarks?

Yes.

Do you usually keep emotions under good control?

Yes.

This pattern needs no elaboration. It is obviously not just a rational politeness or conformity but a somewhat fierce 'categorical imperative' (to use Kant's description) of the kind exemplified at its strongest by the biblical saints. It is not wholly responsible for determining persistence and perseveration, since these may arise also in the service of personal ambition, but it has much to do with persistence in super-personal goals and ideals, and with attempts to exercise powerful self-control. It measures low in sociopaths (persons psychopathically addicted to crime) and high in face-to-face group elected leaders, probably because (as polls show) fair-mindedness in a leader is one of the prime demands of followers. There are indications that it is higher at lower middle-class socio-economic levels than in the upper classes and the 'intelligentsia' – which may explain why Christ chose fishermen for disciples!

A factor pattern which turns up in different groups with infallible regularity is that which comes as *H* in the series. The nature–nurture studies show *H* to have the highest degree of inheritance found among personality source traits, and this is supported by physiological findings, notably that electric heart records (E.K.G.) show a 'stout-heartedness' and smaller and slower reaction to startle in *H+* individuals. For this reason, on the hypothesis that the *para*sympathetic nervous system predominates in these individuals over the sympathetic, it has been called for short *Parmia* or the parmic temperament. The opposite pole has been called *Threctia*, because its essence is a high susceptibility to threat.

TABLE 9

Source trait H. Parmia-vs-*Threctia*

H+		*H−*
Adventurous, likes meeting people	*vs*	Shy, timid, withdrawn
Shows strong interest in opposite sex	*vs*	Little interest in opposite sex
Gregarious, genial, responsive	*vs*	Aloof, cold, self-contained

Source trait H in questionnaires

When coming to a new place, are you painfully slow at making new friendships?

No.

Are you a talkative person who enjoys any opportunity for verbal expression?

Yes.

Do you find it difficult to get up and address or recite before a large group?

No.

The central feature of the threctic temperament is clearly what is commonly called shyness. The proof of high inheritance here suggests that education directly trying to obliterate shyness may be less successful than giving the individual social skills and mechanisms which accept an underlying shyness. However, age plots of scores for the average person show that $H-$ declines steadily with age, that is shyness of an excessive kind tends naturally to cure itself. Source trait H is sometimes, in relatively clumsy rating procedures, confused with dominance, but a comparison of the loaded elements here with those in E will show the distinction. High H is found in delinquents, manic-depressives, and sociopaths, and it is negatively associated with scholastic achievement (but not achievement generally). There are clear indications of greater coronary heart disease rates in high H individuals, presumably due to their more vigorous emotional activity.

The last source trait we shall describe here is one which gives experimental support to the notion of a tender-minded-*vs*-tough-minded continuum, as discussed by the Harvard psychologist William James half a century ago, and by many others. At first sight the pattern may seem to contain some apparently contradictory elements as follows:

TABLE 10

Source trait I. Premsia (tender-mindedness)-vs-harria (tough-mindedness)

$I+$		$I-$
Demanding, impatient	vs	Emotionally mature
Dependent, immature	vs	Independent-minded
Gentle, sentimental	vs	Hard, realistic
Expresses fastidious feelings	vs	Overrules feelings
Enjoys imaginative fancies	vs	Not fanciful
Easily anxious	vs	Does not show anxiety
Likes to be with people	vs	Self-sufficient

Source trait I in questionnaires

Are you brought to tears by discouraging circumstances?
 (a) *yes*   (b) no
Would you rather be:
 (a) *a bishop*   (b) a colonel
Do you have good physical endurance?
 (a) yes   (b) *no*
Would you rather work:
 (a) *as a guidance worker for young*   (b) as a manager in a technical
  people seeking careers   manufacturing concern
Do your friends regard you as:
 (a) practical   (b) *soft-hearted*

The nature–nurture evidence shows that this is largely a culturally-determined pattern, not a temperament difference. Furthermore, there is evidence that its level is largely an expression of the degree of overprotection or indulgence exercised by parents. The average score is quite significantly higher for girls than boys, which may largely reflect the greater degree of protection and indulgence which our culture exercises over girls. Curiously enough (to first thoughts) it is not related systematically to social status, so it is not a matter of material endowment; indeed, many upper-class families demand more Spartan qualities and responsibility from their children than lower-class families (a matter often commented on in the army). By an acronym this trait has been given the name *premsia*, from *pro*tected *em*otional *s*ensitivity (with harria, from *ha*rd *re*alism, as the opposite).

It has long been realized that intellectual beliefs and socio-political philosophies are as much the expression of personality needs as of rational, logical premises. Personality is, in fact, a 'hidden premise'. This truth is illustrated in the finding (Cattell, 1946, Eysenck, 1953, and others) that premsia expresses itself in a tender-*vs*-tough pattern of beliefs in measured social and political attitudes. The $I+$ persons are against capital punishment, and compulsory vaccination, and against 'tough realism' generally. In view of what is beginning to be understood about the source of this source trait, the term 'tough–tender' is misleading, since tenderness in common speech suggests affection, whereas the central feature of the $I+$ pattern is a certain imaginative escapism or even an undisciplined mind, which reminds one of Tolstoy's sketch of the countess weeping over tender happenings in the theatre while her coachman is freezing to death outside.

On the other hand, some imaginative products of civilization grow only in a protected hot-house, and creativity proves to be positively associated with $I+$. In the clinical field premsia has clearly been shown to be strongly associated with proneness to neuroticism, probably because the anxious sensitivity and lack of realism combine to place the person in emotionally stressful situations. Observations in 'group dynamics' experiments (with small groups) show that a significantly greater number of complaints are made about premsic than harric persons in terms of 'getting off the subject', 'preventing the group's coming to a decision', etc. There are apparently differences between whole cultures in premsia level, older cultures tending to be more premsic and pioneer societies, e.g. U.S.A., Australia, more harric.

THE STABILITY OF SOURCE TRAIT MEASURES ACROSS AGES AND CULTURES

Since no fewer than twenty to twenty-five common source traits are now known, we have obviously been able to deal only with the more important – as defined by the practical criterion of how much general behaviour one can predict from measures of them. Some others will be discussed under moods and states in Chapter 6; but the reader must be referred to larger textbooks for the rest. Some of them, like *M*, autia (proneness to see and believe things in accord with one's wishes), which is so powerful in predicting accident-proneness, and, *O*, guilt, which falls higher in both the neurotic and the delinquent, are especially worthy of study.

Personality psychologists have always been rightly much concerned with personality *development* (see Chapter 10), because this is so important in clinic and school. But, as was pointed out in the opening chapter, real research on development can proceed only when graphs can be plotted for 'organic' functional unities, measurable across different age levels. At this point, therefore, one asks 'Are these source traits recognizable and measurable at various ages?' and 'Can they be demonstrated as concepts applicable in different cultures?'

The source traits described here have been shown to be present, by cross-sectional correlation studies, at most ages, as in the rating work of Digman, in Hawaii, Koch, in the Chicago nursery schools, Howarth in Canada, Hundleby in America, and Pawlik in Vienna on the middle age ranges, Lorr, Huffman, Wittenborn with mental hospital populations, and many others.

Rating studies by teachers, parents, and others have been carefully made by Peterson and Quay at Illinois, Norman and Tupes at Michigan, Eysenck in London, over a wide age range, and except for some differences on finer technical issues they have come out with much the same results. The actual source trait structure is very consistent over age. Some psychologists insisted that at, say, 5, personality structure would be much 'simpler'. It *may* be in some ways, notably in dynamic outlets, but it has not proved so in the sense of needing far fewer factors. A reduction from roughly 16–20 to 12–14 factors occurs. For example, the limitations of children's experience cause a failure to generate clearly such dimensions as 'radicalism-*vs*-conservatism', despite Gilbert's line that each is 'born alive, a liberal or a conservative'. But every four-year-old shows at any rate his temperament as an affectothyme or sizothyme, a dominant or a submissive, and as an individual with a measurable degree of ego strength.

Since ratings are clumsy and poorly comparable in research, questionnaire factorings have been carried up and down the age range from 4 to 70 years, so that the 16 P.F. for adults has been followed by the (14 factor) High School Personality Factor Questionnaire, the (12 factor) Child Personality Questionnaire for ages 8–12, by Dr Rutherford Porter, and the Early School Personality Questionnaire (E.S.P.Q.), for 6–8 years, due to the researches of Professors Richard Coan and Warner Schaie.

In the last, the questions are, of course, read out to the child, and the same is true of the P.S.P.Q. (Pre-School Personality Questionnaire) for ages 4 to 6 now in progress under Dreger, in the U.S.A. and Choynowski in Poland. It is found that the sheer reliability (in the sense defined above) of single items decreases as we go to younger children. Consequently the investigator has to recognize certain limitations in this technique, residing in the fact that younger children need longer questionnaires to give reliability, yet their span of attention is such that they can only be tested for short periods! This is overcome by having more, and shorter, 'equivalent forms', but it can be overcome in a more radical way by shifting to the objective tests described in the next chapter, which actually work better with young children than adults!

This constancy of factor patterns over age gives additional confidence in the reality of the functionally unitary source traits. But perhaps still greater conviction comes from the findings now accumulating that when the hundreds of items in these questionnaires are translated into foreign languages, correlated, and analysed the same general source traits emerge. For example, the factoring of the French, Italian, and Japanese 16 P.F. question-naires clearly yield the affectothyme–sizothyme, the dominant, submissive, the ego strength, and indeed the usual sixteen or more source traits. Table 11 shows the results on four items (taken from results on the French 16 P.F. by Professor Pichot in Paris) two of which contribute to the ego–strength factor, C, and two to the parmia–temperament factor H. It will be seen that their correlation with these factors follows essentially the same pattern. (A curiosity is item 4, which, although intended for H and loading H in both countries, has a subsidiary loading, in the opposite direction on C. Until more research is done this should not be taken too seriously, but it suggests that ego strength encourages a Frenchman to speak up and an American to hold his tongue!)

TABLE 11

Similarity of contribution of source traits to items in American and French population sample

	American Patterns of Loadings		French Patterns of Loadings	
Population samples	C	H	C	H
1. Do you on the whole admire your parents?	+42	+18	+44	+05
2. Is your health unpredictable, forcing you frequently to change your plans?	−49	+18	−56	+10
3. Does your natural reserve stand in your way when you want to approach an attractive stranger of the opposite sex?	−04	−66	−05	−72
4. Would you describe yourself as a sociable, talkative person?	−29	+86	+32	+53

(All affirmative responses load positively) C = Ego Strength-*vs*-Ego Weakness
H = Parmia-*vs*-Threctic

Such findings again suggest that we are dealing with basic traits of general human importance, not just artefacts of a particular culture. Perhaps it should not surprise us that there are say, affectothyme and sizothyme individuals among Japanese, since the syndromes of mental disorders believed to be related to these have similarly been recognized for some time to be the same. At most it has been said that culture intrudes to the extent that the manic-depressive and schizophrenic expressions are somewhat more polite in Japan! Actually, refined analysis does show some small differences of factor patterns across cultures; thus the dominance source trait among Italians perhaps has more authoritarian associations, while the above reversal of expression of ego strength (Table 11) illustrates minor changes which typically occur. But the big fact for the personality analyst is that the *same* major source traits can be recognized and that they can be measured by similar techniques.

Because the number of source traits is large – at least twenty-five, though only sixteen are perhaps large enough in influence to be put into test instrument scales – some practitioners have suggested that we work, alternatively, with second order factors, which are fewer. Thus Eysenck's M.P.I. (not to be confused with the M.M.P.I., a questionnaire which measures syndromes – surface traits – for pathological work, not personality source traits) measures just two or three such factors, and some of the Guilford–Zimmerman questionnaire factors may also be second orders. One treads on complex technical matters here but, in a few words, it may be said that although primary personality factors are distinct, they are not mutually uncorrelated. (In human beings age, sex, and weight are distinct concepts or 'traits', but they are not uncorrelated.) Consequently, one can make a correlation matrix among them as in Table 2 (page 63) and find factors among factors. These will be very broad influences, each extending itself over several primaries. When this is done with the questionnaire factors, as in the 16 P.F., one finds six second order factors, one of which is general anxiety level (see Chapter 5, and, for clinical applications, Chapter 8), and another extraversion to introversion (or exvia to invia, as explained above).

Thus the 16 P.F. is designed to score on six factors instead of sixteen, if we wish. But this scoring, or the ordinary scoring of the M.P.I., will not give us as much prediction of criteria as will sixteen factors. Similarly, if you try to predict world affairs by recognizing only continents and neglecting what you know about individual countries, your conclusions will be more approximate. If nature is complex we do not gain anything from closing our eyes to real complexities. Yet such is the liking of the human mind for easy formulations that oversimplifications are often popular. In a different sense psychoanalysis oversimplified, for it talked largely in terms of three primary factors – ego, super-ego, and id – whereas the multivariate experimental approach shows sixteen to twenty-five. No clinician, or any other human, can keep a patient's individuality on all these dimensions in mind, but an electronic computer can. And Paul Meehl, at Minnesota, and others, have shown that when you feed information to a clinician he benefits from the accumulation of up to six or seven items of information: after that his prediction of a criterion gets no better. On the other hand, when the specification equation for a criterion is known on the 16 P.F. one continues, with a computer, to get as much additional improvement of prediction from the last personality factor measures added as from the first. In many fields of human endeavour, from war games to space travel and clinical psychology, we have perhaps to get used to the idea of helping out the limited memories which underlie our judgements by electronic aids, and when this is more widespread the idea that sixteen is a burdensome lot of things to think about will vanish.

*

READING

Dreger, R. M., *Fundamentals of Personality*. Lippincott & Co., Philadelphia, 1962.

Cattell, R. B., and Pierson, G., *Functional Psychological Testing Practice*. (In press.)

CHAPTER FIVE

The Techniques of Objective Personality Measurement

WHAT IS AN OBJECTIVE TEST?

The fact that the questionnaire (opinionnaire or self-inventory) is objective *at least about its scoring* entitles it, as we have seen, to the title of a *conspective* test – one in which two different psychologists will 'see together', and give the person tested the same score. This achievement in technique is no minor one, for school examiners never obtained it in the last 500 years and in psychology such 'open-ended' tests as the Thematic Apperception Test, and some Rorschach tests, still cannot claim conspective scoring. But in the broader and truer sense the questionnaire is *not* objective, because as admitted above, self-evaluation is subject to distortions ranging from sources such as ignorance of self to deliberate faking.

One reaction to this disability has been an attempt by more conservative psychologists to buttress the questionnaire with corrective devices. For example, the Minnesota Multiphasic Psychological Inventory (M.M.P.I.) has what is called a *K* scale, which claims to show when the subject is being defensive and misrepresenting himself. Since this only tells us when we cannot trust the results it amounts to locking the stable door after the horse is stolen. In recent years the names of Berg, Edwards, Messick, and Wiggins have become associated with attempts to understand the motivational distortion in questionnaires from 'response sets' towards socially desirable responses. More broadly the present writer has experimented on corrections conceived in the framework of 'adoption of roles' described in Chapter 6, supposing not a single direction of faking but several, and a Motivational Distortion Scale has been appended to the 16 P.F. to correct each factor score according to the evidence of how far a given individual is 'giving himself airs' in responding to the questions.

Nevertheless, when this defect is beaten there remain others, due simply to the individual's ignorance of his real status, e.g. through comparing himself with his family instead of the world at large, and through what are called 'instrument factors' – the varying reaction of individuals to particular test media. Instead of patching up the questionnaire with various corrective devices a number of psychologists have set out in the last thirty years on the bolder and more imaginative course of making what may be called fully objective tests. In these the subject is placed in a miniature situation and simply acts, while his responses are observed and measured. His cooperation is required to the extent that he agrees to be tested, but the objectivity in this type of test may be defined by the criterion that the *subject does not know on what aspect of his behaviour he is really being evaluated.*

Early examples of objective personality tests were the rigidity tests, fluency tests and perceptual measures used by Stephenson, Cattell, Hargreaves, and others in Spearman's laboratory around 1930, the Downey and T.A.T. tests in America, the Rorschach test in Switzerland, and various handwriting and 'stylistic' tests in Germany. While this work has developed, the questionnaire has continued to retain its popularity because of its convenience since objective tests require more skilled psychological help in administration, as well as a certain amount of apparatus, and they take perhaps three or four hours where the questionnaire takes only one.

Moreover, unless objective tests are to be employed merely as *ad hoc* special purpose tests unrelated to knowledge of personality structure and function, it is necessary to start again at the beginning here and discover the personality factors in the whole realm of objective behavioural response. Naturally one would expect that much the same personality dimensions would appear as in the rating and questionnaire medium, merely expressing themselves in new kinds of reactions. But this cannot be taken for granted, though the concepts from the older fields have guided the construction of experimental tests. It is not surprising, in view of the large number of tests (over 500) which needed to be invented to cover the expected dimensions, and the technical complexities of organizing many interlocking factor analytic experiments, that it was not until 1955 that the first objective test battery – the O.-A., or *Objective-Analytic Personality Battery* – became available, for measuring eighteen known source traits.

The variety of devices and principles used in objective personality tests is very great indeed, so that no simple classification is possible and the best way to obtain some understanding of them is to sample them as widely as we can in the remainder of this chapter.

THE NATURE OF THE GENERAL INHIBITION SOURCE TRAIT

It soon became evident that when a great variety of objective tests is given to some hundreds of people and the results are correlated one obtains evidence of distinct source traits, just as in ratings and questionnaire items. The interpretation and identification of these factors, however, is a more difficult and intriguing mental exercise than in the former situation because the evidence is not in familiar verbal terms, such as 'I feel frightened', but in some such measure as the change of reaction time when one is threatened by an electric shock – which permits of several explanations. Consequently, since some years may elapse between the research confirmation of a source trait pattern as a pattern, and its ultimate interpretation through experiments on its origin and consequences, the practice has arisen of identifying these mysterious shapes by Universal Index, or U.I. numbers, as reference indices whereby to hang on to them during the period of lacking a final interpretive label.

Such a pattern is that first confirmed as U.I. 17, though now recognized to be what psychologists have long called General Inhibition, and set out in Table 12.

These tests will suffice to mark the source trait, for they are the 'highest loaded'. If this were written for professional journals we should include also detailed particulars of administration and scoring for the miniature situation, but this complication can be dropped here. Further, the list is curtailed, for there are at least a dozen additional, significantly loaded tests which could be added to the above table. These would add to its meaning and aid interpretation though they would make the battery for *measuring* general inhibition too long for most practical uses. For the scores of all the tests listed would be added into a single pool to give the factor score.

TABLE 12

U.I. 17. General Inhibition

Objective test	Factor loading
Large average psychogalvanic response to threat	+32
Suppression of questionable reading preferences	+58
Severe reduction of finger-maze exploration by shock	+30
Slow speed of closure in Gestalt completion	−34
Much slowing of reaction time by complex instructions	+22
Perception of many threatening objects in unstructured drawings	+38

Let us describe these tests briefly. The psychogalvanometer or galvanic skin reflex apparatus passes a small current between conducting pads on the front and back of the hand. An Austrian engineer, nearly a century ago, noticed that when a person responds to a threatening stimulus the electrical resistance drops, and the magnitude of this drop can be read on a galvanometer. At first it was regarded as a measure of emotional expression, but Cattell showed in 1929 that its magnitude is proportional to the *effort or restraint* exercised (which, it is true, will be *partly* a function of the emotionality to be restrained). Persons high on U.I. 17 give big deflexions on the galvanometer to a standard set of threatening phrases, pictures, physical threats, etc. They react with high restraint.

The reading preferences test mixes, in a single list, book titles of a blood and thunder' type along with others. Subjects are asked to check what books they would like to read, and it turns out that the person higher on the electrical deflexion just mentioned tends to avoid in his reading choices the violent type of book.

In the finger maze test, S (by which brief symbol we shall in the future refer to 'the subject' taking the test) puts his finger in a grooved maze, hidden by a curtain, and tries to get as far as possible towards the end of the maze. He thus proceeds 'in the dark' once in ordinary conditions and once with instructions that he will receive an electric shock whenever he enters a blind alley. The *reduction* in the measured amount of exploratory behaviour

Diagram 7. Example of Gestalt Completion Test

when shock is introduced correlates significantly with the U.I. 17 factor.

Two of the tests, it will be noted, are of a 'perceptual' nature. In the Gestalt Completion Test, S is asked to say what the figures, as in Diagram 7, would be when completed. His speed of responding is slower if he is higher on U.I. 17 presumably because he is more cautious than low U.I. 17 persons in coming to a conclusion. In the second perceptual test S is given an 'unstructured drawing', as in Diagram 8, and asked to say what objects he sees in it. The high U.I. 17 individual sees a higher proportion of objects which can be called threatening, e.g. daggers, lightning, tornadoes, pistols.

Finally, in the reaction time experiment, S is first asked to lift his hand from a telegraph key as rapidly as possible when he sees a light go on. Then he is given more complex instructions, e.g. react only when the light is red *and* is preceded by a buzzer.

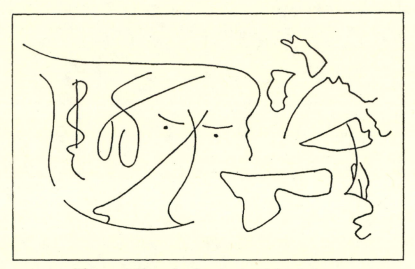

Diagram 8. Example of unstructured drawings test

The difference between the time required with the simple and the complex instruction is greater for the high U.I. 17 individual: he does not like to make mistakes.

What can we infer about the nature of U.I. 17 from these six distinct manifestations? Despite some being pencil-and-paper, group-administrable tests and others apparatus tests, needing an individual testing situation; despite some being 'perceptual' and others 'motor', and so on, *all* have the character of showing *a degree of restraint* or inhibition. For example, the galvanic reflex is known to show restraint, the completion test shows a person waiting longer before he risks a decision, the book list shows a more restrained choice of book, the unstructured drawings test shows greater awareness of dangerous, inhibiting possibilities, and the slower reaction time when instructions are complicated shows an inhibition against making mistakes.

From these experiments we infer the existence in humans of a 'general inhibition' factor akin to that which the Russian psychologist Pavlov observed in dogs. To stand as a source trait, the factor must have highly general manifestations. It would not be sound for us to call this a general inhibition factor if its manifestations were only in the perceptual field, or in choice of books and pictures, or in dexterities and motor performances. It must run across the lot, and this the U.I. 17 pattern is clearly found to do.

It is not surprising to find that this factor runs higher in individuals with a history apparently of more restrained and disciplined family upbringing. It was significantly and conspicuously below normal in a group of sociopaths, in a big State Hospital, that is, in individuals who have been confidence tricksters, irresponsibles, drug addicts, and social nuisances generally, while it runs significantly, but less strongly *above* normal in neurotics. In other words, the normal stands between the over-inhibited neurotic and the happy-go-lucky criminal on this dimension, though there is no proof or suggestion that high inhibition levels are *invariably* or necessarily neurotic.

THE NATURE OF THE MOBILIZATION-*vs*-REGRESSION SOURCE TRAIT, U.I. 23

Another pattern of considerable practical importance was found independently by Cattell at the University of Illinois laboratory and Eysenck at the Maudsley Hospital, London, around 1946. The latter showed that it sharply distinguishes between normals and neurotics, and called it 'the neuroticism factor'; but the former, although confirming its capacity to separate neurotics from normals, found no fewer than six *more* source traits (out of the score of objective test factors now known and listed) which were also just as significantly different for normals and neurotics. Consequently, the factor has now been called (in its 'negative' direction) 'regression', for reasons which will become evident,

BACKWARD WRITING

1. When you hear the signal to start, write the sentence, 'The sky is deep blue' as *often* and as *fast* as you can until time is called. Keep your writing *clear* and controlled.

The sky is deep blue.

2. Now *print* the sentence, 'The sky is deep blue,' in *capital letters* as *often* and as *fast* as you can. Write clearly, but write as fast as you can.

THE SKY IS DEEP BLUE.

3. This time write the same sentence as fast as you can at the go signal *alternating block capital letters and small written letters* as in the example. Correct any errors before going on.

THE aKy la DeEp BlUe.

4. Now write the sentence again with every letter *doubled* in every word as in the example. Write the sentence as often and as fast as you can at the go signal and continue until time is called.

Tthhee sskkyy iss ddeepp bblluuee.

5. Now write your own first and last name *backwards* as often and as fast as you can within the time limit. The arrows in the example 'John Smith' show you how it is written, namely, starting at the letter 'h' and ending at the letter 'J'. Start on the *right* side of the first line at the signal to go.

Write your own name *backwards*, e.g.: ←John ← Smith ← Begin here

Diagram 9

and regarded as only *one* component or source of neuroticism, among several contributors.

Some of the chief objective tests found loaded in it are as follows.

TABLE 13

U.I. 23. High mobilization-vs-Regressive debility (or regression)

Objective test	Factor loading
Lower rigidity (perceptual motor)	−50
Less body-sway suggestibility	−41
Higher ratio of accuracy to speed	+49
Better two-hand coordination	+38
More preference for colour over form in picture preference	−08
Less excess of aspiration over achievement in coding	−41

Rigidity, i.e. the inability to change old habits in the interests of a more flexible, adaptive, and successful response has been much studied by psychologists. Many things which look like rigidity and have often been so labelled turn out on factoring to be something else, such as low intelligence, and we have now to recognize that no fewer than four distinct personality factors contribute to actual behavioural rigidity. However, the correlation of the latter with U.I. 23 is higher than with the other three and high enough to make it a fine contributory measure to this particular source trait. In this test, S writes sentences, his name, etc., rapidly, as he is used to doing, and is then asked to write them in a new way, e.g. beginning at the last letter and working back, doubling each letter, etc. The ratio of number of letters done in impeded to unimpeded conditions gives the score on rigidity.

Capacity to integrate is measured, in a spatial example, by asking S what figure (in Diagram 10) would stand at the intersection of lines drawn from *A* to *B* and *C* to *D*. At speed some people are able to integrate this complex totality really well, whereas others blunder badly.

Two Hand Coordination is a test due to Leon Thurstone, a giant in his contribution to psychometry. In principle it is as old as the child's game of 'rub your head while you pat your stomach'. First S shows how fast he can make patterns with his left hand (an electric stylus permits counting as he taps a pattern over four metal plates). He next, with his right hand, does a different pattern. Then he does both together. A ratio of the last to the two initial performances gives his score. Like the 'capacity to integrate' test, it produces some amusing errors!

Sway suggestibility is also an old test to psychologists, being used by Clark Hull of Yale, and others, in testing suggestibility.

Where do the lines cross?

Instructions:

Your job in this test is to decide just where two lines cross. The lines are not drawn in for you; you are just given end points of the line. Let us try an example. In the following example, where do lines AB and CD cross?

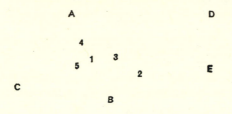

The lines cross at point 1, not at point 2. Therefore, writing down 1 gives you a correct answer. To the question CE-DB, 2 would be the correct answer.

Diagram 10. Example of a 'capacity to integrate' test

S stands with his back to a wall, with closed eyes, while a record suggests: 'You are falling slowly forward. You are falling forward . . . , etc.' A mechanism measures how far he sways. A few neurotics actually have to be caught before they fall!

The next test correlating well with U.I. 23 can be derived from almost any steady measurable performance, but cancelling e's in a page of print is frequently used. As people are told to go faster and faster they make more errors (both by missing e's and cancelling other letters). The rate of increase of errors with speed is greater in the more regressed – U.I. 23(—) – person.

The psychogalvanometer has already been described. In its use for U.I. 23 one presents S with pictures and phrases which evoke conflict or embarrassment, e.g. a sexually suggestive picture, a phrase 'murder father', and also with actual physical dangers, e.g. an electric shock, a hammer blow falling near the fingers. A higher response to the *symbolic* threats (to ego defence) relative to the *physical* 'real' threats is characteristic of the more neurotically regressed person.

It will be noted that the test titles in Table 13 are written out in the U.I. 23 *plus*, or non-neurotic direction of scoring. But it is a little easier to conceptualize the pattern from the negative or 'regression' pole. The discovery of U.I. 23 presents a difficult challenge to both clinical and ability theory. In the first place, many of the tests look like ability measures and might be thought to represent general intelligence if the latter were not already shown in these experiments to be present as a distinct factor. Closer consideration shows, however, that these U.I. 23 behaviours are not so much manifestations of skilled habits of judgement as such as of capacity to *mobilize or apply* the repertory of skills one already possesses. This is particularly clear in the perceptual-motor rigidity and the 'capacity to integrate' tests above. It is as if the individual has the capacities but is not able to pull himself together and bring his energies to bear. It is for this reason it has been called a dimension of *regression*. It might also be called a general fatigue; but if so it is quite different from ordinary daily fatigue, for it does not disappear with sleep. The notion of regression connotes that instinctual energies and interests have in some way *retreated* from their investment in the cognitive, external world.

Score on capacity to mobilize is abnormally low for both neurotics and schizophrenics. It has appreciable hereditary determination. Yet, as Dr Ivan Scheier has shown, the level on this source trait tends to rise if the individual is challenged by practical difficulties. This might suggest that the shock method of treating certain kinds of neurotic depression, e.g. the medieval ducking stool, or the modern electric shock treatment, operate by changing the mobilization level. These somewhat upsetting conclusions, seeming to justify some ancient empiricism, show the need for clinical psychology to research further with these measures.

MEASURING ANXIETY LEVEL

Anxiety is both a state and a trait. That is to say, we all experience higher and lower states with changing circumstances, but there is also evidence that some people vary about levels which are typically different for them from the central tendency in others. We then speak of 'characterological anxiety', i.e. a trait.

Until about ten years ago the measurement of anxiety was scientifically in a very unsatisfactory state, because 'tests' had been constructed without asking such fundamental questions as, 'Is there one entity or are there several distinct kinds of anxiety?' and 'Is anxiety the same as stress reaction, or the adrenal response, or is it different?' Psychiatrists, for example, spoke of 'free' and 'bound' anxiety, as traits which could be at different levels in the same person and have different sets of manifestations. By-passing the crucial issue of one or many anxieties, and ignoring the 'face' and 'bound' distinction, fluent clinical writers and learning theorists had erected rather elaborate and ostentatious theories about anxiety as a unitary entity. They varied from viewing anxiety as the main source of human motivation, to, contrariwise, the view that it is the chief disorganizer of motivation. Some described it as a form of fear, diluted by remoteness and uncertainty of danger, while Freud argued that it consisted of sexual drive 'transformed' in the 'transference neurosis'.

The experimental approach, with which Scheier's ten years of work is particularly associated, undertook to measure together a great variety of commonly accepted manifestations of anxiety, together with behaviour theoretically expected to be different, notably stress response and various dynamic drives, such as sex, fear, assertion, etc. Factor analysis gave a clear verdict that there *is* a single anxiety factor, but different from the effort stress response and from well-known drives. It loads the tests and measures shown in Table 14, among many others.

It will be noted that this pattern contains both objective and physiological tests. It spans, in the longer list elsewhere, all the manifestations commonly ascribed to the notion of anxiety, and shows that it is correct to measure a single dimension here, though research is still faced with certain difficulties in separating anxiety as a trait from anxiety as a state. Nevertheless, the Anxiety Battery derived from present factor analytic research has already been extremely useful in clinical psychology and in evaluating the potency of tranquillizing drugs, etc.

TABLE 14

U.I. 24. Anxiety-vs-good adjustment

Objective test	Factor loading
More common frailties admitted	+48
More tendency to agree	+56
More over-all susceptibility to annoyance	+62
Less confident assumption of skill in untried performance	−38
Higher critical severity (hard-headed cynicism)	+33
More emotionality of comment	+25
Lower average handwriting pressure	−20

The objective Anxiety Battery now exists in eight parallel forms so that the patient can be tested again and again in the course of diagnosis and therapy. Items from the tests in Table 14 above, of the kind appearing in the I.P.A.T. Anxiety Battery, are illustrated by the following:

Annoyances

Indicate whether the following annoy you a little, averagely, or much, by checking one of three spaces.

	Little	Averagely	Much
1. Dishes with smuts on, in restaurants	——	——	——
2. The emphasis on Hollywood domestic troubles in newspapers	——	——	——
3. Shoe laces that go in knots	——	——	——

Comment

Consider the following as newspaper headings and the three statements beneath as possible comments. Check that which comes closest to being your preferred personal comment.

    1. The Y Party wins the Election.

       a. Many people will welcome this.

       b. A d — d good thing!

       c. Now we'll see a change.

2. The tax rate is going up.
   a. They'll want our blood next.
   b. It's necessary, but tough.
   c. A pretty unpopular idea.

The first test above is one of the irritability measures which correlates with anxiety. The 'much' response, of course, gives the highest score. The 'Comments' test is the 'emotionality of comment' test listed in Table 14, and the responses in order of increasing anxiety are *a, c, b* in (1), and *b, c, a* in (2). (Needless to say, no one should evaluate himself on two items per test, and the actual tests are much longer.)

The Critical Severity of Judgement test presents a number of performances, e.g. a drawing, an essay opening, etc., by persons of defined age and circumstances, and S is asked to rate them as adequate to poor on a point scale. More anxious persons, on the total battery score, tend to judge the performances more severely. In the Tendency to Agree test a list of varied attitudes to be checked 'agree' or 'disagree' are presented twice, the statements being made in the opposite direction the second time. The score is the number marked 'agree' in both directions.

The cold pressor test is one in which the individual plunges his bare forearm into a bucket of water with ice floating in it. There is an increase of pulse-rate in response to this, and it has been found that the acceleration is greater in more anxious persons.

Surprise is sometimes expressed that handwriting pressure, as measured by an electrical device in the pen stylus, is *lower* in more anxious people. For a popular view of anxiety, aided by certain adverts, is that anxiety is accompanied by greater muscle tension. An anxious person may certainly have that feeling, and some muscle relaxants do simultaneously appear to lower anxiety, yet the measures by what is called the electromyograph do *not* show general muscle tension in anxiety. Instead, there is only tension in restricted groups of muscles at the back of the neck and shoulder and a few other places, and this is evidently accompanied by lesser pressure on the paper in writing. Muscular efficiency is actually, in general, significantly lower in the more anxious person. Incidentally, part of the debate about muscle tension and anxiety may spring from the confusion of effort stress with anxiety, to be discussed in Chapter 6.

The last of the anxiety measures to be considered is a purely physiological one. It is justified by the discovery by Roy Grinker and his co-workers during the war that parachute jumpers excrete certain substances in the urine in markedly increased concentrations. This is not a very practicable test except where physiological laboratory facilities are available. But in accordance with the principle that any factor or source trait is much better estimated psychometrically from a *wide range* of manifestations, the inclusion of such measures increases validity.

By this point the reader may well be wondering what the relation is between the source traits measured in objective tests of this chapter and those in the questionnaires. Anxiety offers an interesting case by which to illustrate the relations of trait structures as found in the different media. However, discussion of this point requires that we refresh our recollections of what was said above about 'second order factors'. Correlational treatment of experimental measurement of many quite 'specific behaviour variables' yields, in almost any field, a number of those independent 'primary factors' which we have mainly illustrated and which are the influences at work causing the observed correlations. Such factors are 'ego strength', 'surgency', etc., as described in the Q-data chapter, or U.I. 17; 23, etc., as described here. However, once we have achieved good scales or batteries to measure these primary factors, each with a single score, it is possible in turn to discover the correlations among primary factors. The correlations found among factors show, for example, that there is a tendency for persons higher on affectothymia (A factor) also to be higher on surgency (F factor), while a negative correlation is persistently found between ego strength (C) and ergic tension (Q_4).

Now, as pointed out earlier, the correlations among primary factors can be factor analysed just as those among specific behaviours were, and when we do this we obtain what are called *higher-order factors*. These are typical 'organizers of primary factors' just as primary factors are in turn organizers of specific pieces of behaviour. Naturally, these second- or higher-order factors are broader in their influence than primary factors. They are analogous to higher executives in a hierarchy in that they do not have immediate, intimate effect on the lowest operators but act on them indirectly only through their direct influence on the intermediate controllers. Diagram 11 illustrates the theory of second-order factors, operating at a different stratum, by this questionnaire example. The second order in Q-data is identical, however, with a first order (primary) in objective tests, as discussed in the text.

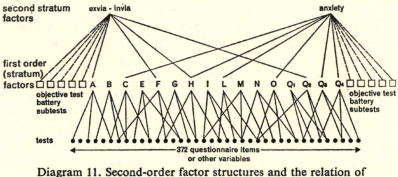

Diagram 11. Second-order factor structures and the relation of questionnaire and objective test factors

When such an analysis is made on results from giving the 16 P.F. or the H.S.P.Q. to normal adults and children, some six second-order factors are found operating among the sixteen primaries, of which we have already mentioned the two largest – anxiety and extraversion. Let us now examine them more closely, with reference to the summary in Diagram 11. The questionnaire second-order which was tentatively called *anxiety* has repeatedly been found to load $C(-)$, ego weakness, O, guilt proneness, Q_4, ergic tension, and also L, $H(-)$ and $Q_3(-)$. The immediately interesting finding here is that it confirms very strikingly the psychoanalytic theory that anxiety is caused partly by undischarged drive tensions, Q_4 (particularly of a sexual and aggressive nature, in our society), and partly by weakness of the ego structure, C-, which causes any internal explosive impulse to be felt as more of a threat than it would if the ego control were strong. From a combination of these anxiety-related primary question-

naire scales a single best weighted composite forty-item questionnaire scale for anxiety, known as the I.P.A.T. Anxiety Scale, has
been built up, one for adults and one for children, for use in
schools and clinical settings.

Now the question becomes crucial, 'Is the source trait we are
measuring by the questionnaire scale the same thing as that which
we are measuring by the objective test battery just described for
U.I. 24?' For our whole measurement theory supposes that these
source trait structures are inherent structures in the personality
itself, and that it is a matter of comparative indifference – indeed,
a mere issue of convenience – whether we measure them by questionnaire or objective test methods. This theory was put to the test
by technical procedures in 'joint factor rotation' too complex to be
described here, but the outcome of such experiments has shown
very clearly that the two approaches are measuring the same thing.

Except for some recognizable slight contribution specific to
each medium, due to what are called instrument factors, the
verbal anxiety measurement correlates highly with the objective
test measurement. However, *the second-order factor in the questionnaire medium lines up with the first order in the objective tests*,
as shown in Diagram 11. The same holds for the measurement of
exvia–invia, as mentioned below and shown in Diagram 11.
How does this difference of 'strata' come about? Presumably
because the questionnaire items are, as it were, smaller particles
than the sub-tests in an objective test battery. The questionnaire
is like a higher-powered microscope. This same difference in the
'level' of the unities perceived exists between an optical microscope, in which cells may be the recognized units, and the electron
microscope, in which large molecules can be perceived. It is not
that one is true and the other false: they are just views of unities
at different levels of organization. In practice, as measuring
anxiety, one can therefore use questionnaire or objective test
according to circumstance. If one has no reason to expect faking –
and patients in clinics feel the need for help too strongly to indulge in much deliberate faking, though applicants for a job
may do so – then the shorter, forty-item questionnaire would be
chosen, whereas in other circumstances, and in basic research,
the objective battery would be better.

The above anxiety batteries have confirmed some theories about anxiety and disproved others. For example, as Diagram 12 shows, the scales confirm that neurotics are much more anxious than normals and that persons psychiatrically diagnosed as 'anxiety hysterics' (or as showing 'anxiety reaction') indeed score very highly. Some of the major psychotic groups, on the other hand, are *not* higher than normals. They also show that certain tranquillizing drugs, such as meprobamate, tend to reduce the anxiety level. On the other hand, when university students are tested at intervals, they are found to be higher three weeks before an important examination than during the examination itself. At the actual time of examination the anxiety falls and the stress response goes up (the differentiation of the stress response is discussed on p. 114). One is reminded of the poet's insights on the greater examination of battle; where Grenfell writes: 'And when

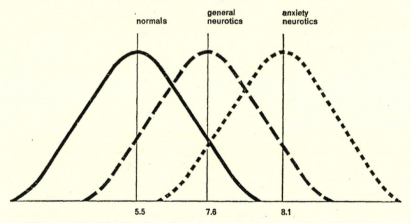

Diagram 12. Distribution of anxiety scores in normals and neurotics

the burning moment breaks, and all things else are out of mind, and only joy of battle takes him by the throat, and makes him blind.'

Another interesting finding concerns the much debated age trend in anxiety. Consistent with the view, expressed by observers from Goethe to Stanley Hall (in his monumental *Adolescence*), that adolescence is a period of stormy maladjustment, we find anxiety high in adolescence and declining as the individual settles his problems of occupational adjustment, marriage, and social setting. However, as Diagram 13 shows, there is also a tendency for anxiety to rise again somewhat in middle age, particularly in housewives. There are complex cultural issues here, but the use of definite measurement instruments applied to different groups offers a means of disentangling the anxiety-creating effects of loss of social function, physical disablement, economic insecurity, and the imminence of death, in this unfortunate modern departure from 'that unhoped serene, which men call age'.

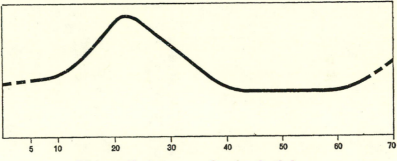

Diagram 13. Age curve of anxiety level changes

That cultural differences, of the kind remarked upon by cultural anthropologists, have a powerful effect on individual anxiety levels, was demonstrated when exact translations of the I.P.A.T. Anxiety scale, as used in different countries, had their norms compared. Compared with the usual range of individual differences some surprisingly large differences between countries are revealed, as shown in Diagram 14. Data also exists showing countries on the difficult border areas between free enterprise and communist zones to be unusually high on anxiety, but to avoid political pressures on scientists these results have not been quoted in Diagram 14. Broadly, one can perhaps generalize that anxiety is determined more by economic status and the fanaticism of political disagreements than by differences in family upbringing or the infantile weaning, etc., trauma about which clinicians have woven fascinating theories. However, let us be tentative and recognize that social psychologists will be able to give more exact answers to such questions only when a larger number of countries have been reliably sampled with standard anxiety scales.

Yet another area where anxiety measurements have proved valuable has been in the introduction of such brief anxiety measures as the I.P.A.T. scale to act as a sort of clinical thermometer in watching and guiding the course of psychotherapy. It has been shown, for example, that clinical treatment *does* typically produce a significant reduction of score on the anxiety scale, and that this measurement is greater where the treatment evidences other signs

The numbers by each country indicate the size of sample gathered

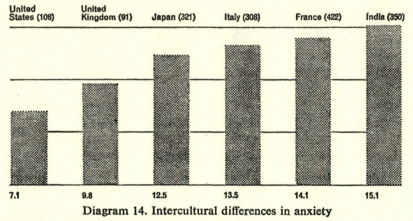

United States (108)	United Kingdom (91)	Japan (321)	Italy (308)	France (422)	India (350)
7.1	9.8	12.5	13.5	14.1	15.1

Diagram 14. Intercultural differences in anxiety

of being more successful. The experienced psychotherapist, moreover, is likely to get additional control from watching the shifts of anxiety level in relation to the specific topics dealt with in the course of analysis and the resistance overcome.

MEASURING EXTRAVERSION-*vs*-INTROVERSION

The introductory discussion described Jung's notions of extraversion and introversion put forward as instances of species 'types'; but we know now that there is a continuous and normal distribution from the extreme introvert to the extreme extravert. For many years this 'dimension' nevertheless remained defined only at the level of a surface trait – a mere conglomerate of attributes which anyone could add to or subtract from as his fancy shaped itself. The first indication that it could be precisely located as a structure came when it appeared as a second-order factor in questionnaire measures. The same correlation of primary factors, and their second-order analysis, which yielded the general anxiety factor, yields also evidence of some general influence which simultaneously connects with liking for people in the sense of affectothymia (A), with talkativeness and cheery optimism in surgency (F), with adventurous boldness of parmia, H, and with the as yet undescribed Q_2 primary which defines a tendency to live with the group as opposed to self-sufficiency and individualism. This second-order extraversion-*vs*-introversion source traits also has some correlation with dominance (E factor), and of freedom from paranoid suspicion (L factor).

The original Jungian clinical idea of extraversion, and its somewhat battered popular meaning, do, therefore, find an underlying core of reality in measurement, deriving from the statistical treatment of ratings and questionnaire responses. On this basis we see the extravert as sociable, optimistic, talkative, group-dependent, a bit thick-skinned, trusting, and adaptable. The introvert is shy, not very fond of people *en masse*, individualistic, and a bit rigid and suspicious. It is easy to see that 'extraverted' could be confounded with 'well-adjusted', and, indeed, in America, and perhaps in the British public school system, teachers have held up the extravert as an ideal (until recently, when creativity has been found decidedly more associated with introversion).

Among objective test correlations a pattern was known for some years which appeared to be exvia–invia, but only in the last five years have studies shown that the first-order objective test pattern and the second-order questionnaire pattern are the same thing, just as occurred with the corresponding anxiety patterns. The best nine test designs in objective tests for contributing to the exvia-*vs*-invia dimension are listed in Table 15.

It will be noted that the unstructured drawings test was used in U.I. 17 and is illustrated in Diagram 8, page 108. It is not impossible for the same test performance to be loaded by two different factors, for behaviour is almost always determined by several source traits. However, in this case, as in some others, although it is the same test and the same behaviour, a different aspect of the behaviour is scored in the two cases. In this the things seen in the unstructured drawings are not scored for the number of threatening objects but for the total fluency, i.e. the sheer number of objects reported. This tendency of the extravert to report freely, as acceptable, a lot of responses which the introvert is unwilling to own is one of several clues suggesting that

TABLE 15

U.I.32. The Exvia-vs-invia
(or Extraversion-vs-introversion) source trait in objective tests

Objective test	Factor loading
More objects seen in unstructured drawing	+32
Higher ratio of fluency on own personal characteristics	+32
More confident assumption regarding performance level in untried performances	+18
Higher fluency on people's behaviour	+32
Preference for strange, dramatic rather than familiar themes	+20
Higher ratio of favourable to unfavourable self reference in events	+13
Higher ratio of final to initial performance (in children)	+20
Lower accuracy in Gestalt completion	−19

whereas U.I. 17, Inhibition is a general inhibition and caution, Invia (introversion) is a *social* inhibition connected more with the self concept. This distinction is important because Hans Eysenck and some learning theorists have attempted to explain the difference of introvert and extravert simply in terms of an almost neurological quality of inhibition, whereas our distinction of general inhibition and social inhibition gives more role to early childhood experiences with *people* in producing a strictly social inhibition.

This can be seen again in the second test affected by this source trait, where S is simply asked to write down (*a*) good and (*b*) bad characteristics of, (1) himself, and (2) his two best friends. First we find that the exviant has a higher score per minute than the inviant on all four areas. He is simply more fluent *altogether* about social behaviour. But he is *exceptionally* fluent on himself. In this case there is no reason to ascribe the result to egotism in the ordinary sense, and the context of other tests suggests it is more likely due to the introvert's social shyness in regard to saying anything about himself.

The test which records confidence about expected level of personal performance in untried activities is self-explanatory, and the only *caveat* is that so representative a sample of behaviours must be taken as will lessen the chance of anyone *actually* being right in his expectation of being good at all of them! Pictures and illustrative beginnings of stories are used in the test of preference for the strange and dramatic over the familiar and ordinary. Results of the test of the ratio of initial to final performance, on some task such as cancellation or checking synonyms, could be explained either on the grounds that the exviant is a relatively casual starter, who 'warms up', or that the inviant person is more readily fatigued. The former seems far more likely.

In the reaction time experiment a buzzer warning is given in one series of experiments regularly every two seconds before the flash of the light to which the subject reacts. In another series, with which these scores are contrasted, the buzzer comes sometimes one, sometimes two, three, four, etc., seconds before, in other words, quite irregularly. The fact that the exviant takes longer (relatively) with the regular warning could mean either that he fails to 'screw up his tension' to that degree necessary for rapid response, which is possible to the inviant on getting the regular warning. Alternatively it could mean that the inviant is not able to maintain a general alertness over any interval, that is, without the aid of the exactly timed warning signal.

In the 'favourable to unfavourable self-reference' test items of the following kind are presented:

'Do you think that the recent discovery of gold in Pakistan will affect you personally? Yes/No. If you answered "Yes", will it affect you favourably or unfavourably? F. U.' There is no exviant–inviant difference on the first score – the likelihood of being affected – but the exviants are more disposed optimistically (or unsuspectingly) to believe that a random array of remote events will affect them favourably. The last test in the exvia–invia battery, the Gestalt Completion Test, has already been described (p. 107);

the higher exviant score here indicates a certain slap-dash readiness to accept a quick and questionable solution.

A theory of exvia–invia (extraversion–introversion) entertained by some researchers, as mentioned, is that it represents a degree of general inhibition. Against this theory is the evidence here that general inhibition, U.I. 17, is quite a different factor, independent of the present factor in Table 15, which, incidentally, has long been indexed as U.I. 32, simply as an experimental–statistical entity. Our hypothesis about U.I. 32 is that it is a purely *social inhibition* (in the inviant direction). The objective tests, like the questionnaire, indicate the exviant to be a socially uninhibited, fluent, optimistic, person-interested, not self-critical individual. The low social inhibition springs partly from inherited temperamental 'thick-skinnedness', i.e. low susceptibility to threat (for Threctia, $H(-)$, is the most inherited of the component factors), and partly from environmental sources consisting of a more fortunate, less punishing experience with people, presumably in early life especially. These are doubtless bound up in a spiral, in that being easily wounded, temperamentally, can lead to hostile and withdrawing behaviour which in turn increases unfavourable treatment by the social environment. ('Laugh and the world laughs with you. Weep and you weep alone.')

Again, as with Anxiety, one of the first findings as a by-product from standardized measurements is that there are marked cultural differences. Frank Warburton, of the University of Manchester, showed that British university students and schoolchildren are decidedly more inviant, on an average, than their American counterparts. Some initial results by the present writer and Professor Tsujioka point to Americans being very significantly more exviant than the Japanese, and much of this difference persists even for second and third generation Japanese-Americans in Hawaii. These differences are probably partly a matter of explicit cultural ideals. One would guess that the so-called 'Progressive Education' of this generation, in reducing social inhibitions, has tended to an exviant shift, motivated partly by the questionable fear that the inviant schoolchild may be in danger of schizophrenic breakdown or, at least, of maladjustment.

THE PRACTICAL USES AND PROBLEMS OF
OBJECTIVE PERSONALITY TESTING

Effective use of psychological tests requires evidence of good validity and reliability, as we have seen. The proof that tests are concept-valid (sometimes called 'construct' valid) is that factor analysis can demonstrate the existence of a functionally unitary source trait, and that experiment shows the given test battery to correlate with it. The objective tests are in this respect as good as the questionnaires, though instead of a uniform, 'homogeneous' type of test constituted by the series of questionnaire items, the source trait battery consists of an organic whole of very varied parts.

The result is that the O.-A. Battery, as it is called, which has been constructed to measure either twelve or (in the longer form) twenty independent dimensions of personality, takes much longer to give. Indeed the 16 P.F. or Guilford's questionnaire, and others of this kind, typically take only half an hour to an hour, whereas the O.-A. battery, in the child form, takes up to three hours and, in the adult form, up to four hours. It is not surprising, therefore, that educational, industrial, and even clinical psychologists have clung rather conservatively to questionnaires and that the feed-back of theoretically interesting findings which we can confidently expect from objective measurements is not available for discussion at this juncture. One can say 'confidently' because although the O.-A. batteries have only just begun to be applied the *percentage* of effective predictions and analyses from them is decidedly higher than from older tests. Indeed, it is pretty certain that they are yielding several dimensions of behaviour that are not caught by questionnaires at all, i.e. there are some dimensions of a man's behaviour which he never sees.

Objective tests of a limited kind, like the popular Rorschach and the Thematic Apperception Test (T.A.T.), have been in use, however, fairly widely. The former was due to a European psychiatrist and consists of a set of symmetrical coloured inkblots which the subject 'interprets'. The latter is due to an American psychiatrist, Henry Murray, and consists of a set of relatively unstructured pictures which the subject interprets. They fall in the class of 'projective' tests. (The meaning of projection will be taken up in Chapter 7.) However, their use illustrates an important scientific difference between what might be called on the one hand the 'gadget-centred' approach in which the investigator throws in his lot with a particular (to him) fascinating gadget, and by countless studies seeks to extract the last ounce of behaviour prediction from it, and, on the other, the structural research approach, in which one first tries to understand the trait structure and then develops measures appropriate for the major source traits.

The objection to the former – over and above a certain scientific inelegance – is that it is *a priori* unlikely that information about the whole of personality can be efficiently obtained from one limited form of behaviour – whether it be handwriting, or perception of ink blots, or the way a person leaves the tea leaves in his cup. A serious attack on the Rorschach, by Thurstone and again by Davis, showed that only two to five independent dimensions of personality can be squeezed from it, compared with over twenty from the O.-A. batteries. The T.A.T. is disabled by a different difficulty: its low reliability and a confusion of several kinds of projection, as described in Chapter 7. Actually, both of the behavioural performances in these separate gadgets are very worthwhile when included, as blot interpretation and perceptual projection into situations, among the four or five hundred objective tests examined to make up the O.-A. batteries. A clinician who has spent years with the Rorschach can give a fair amount of clinical prognosis with that moderate mixture of accuracy with guesswork which we should expect from having to predict from three or four factors when twenty are required to account for most of the behaviour and clinical outcome concerned.

If one asks why more comprehensive structural approaches are slower to get into wider practice by clinicians and others vitally concerned with personality measurement one discovers some interesting social aspects of science which are little recognized, though they operate also in medical and many other fields of scientific application. First, there is that ego-involvement of most individuals in skills which they have and others do not. This led the weavers of Wigan to smash the new weaving machines, certain unions to oppose efficient automation, and, we are told by military historians, the proposal, as late as the battle of Waterloo, to retain bows and arrows. Many university instructors decline to depart from what they were themselves taught, and it is not unusual to hear a clinical instructor say that since he himself was never taught, say, factor analysis, he cannot aspire to teaching his students the structural concepts and measures based thereon. This tends to give a one-generation lag between research and practice.

Secondly, the man in the street, and the less fully trained but most numerous type of professional, is generally happier with a concrete validity than a conceptual validity, in the senses described above. In this sense he accepts intelligence tests because they predict school performance, though, as we shall see, if an intelligence test predicts school performance too well it ceases to be an intelligence test and becomes a measure of school performance, which is something different. Conceptual validity is a more subtle thing, requiring more subtle methods of demonstration. With personality factors it is even somewhat more difficult than with intelligence tests to point to some single concrete criterion which is nearly *it*. From what single act can one reliably infer ego strength, or surgency, or anxiety? Concrete behaviour, in view of the complexity of human nature, is almost always jointly the product of several traits.

Thirdly, these newer developments towards an objective, quantitative, and rational science of personality have been slowed down by the economic, organizational, and training difficulties necessary for a complex team. Few individual professors have the time or resources for such work. The outcome, historically, has been that most of the advances have come from only two centres in the world, London University, where Sir Cyril Burt and Hans Eysenck and his psychiatrist and psychologist associates at the Maudsley Hospital made an early start, and the Universities of Illinois and Chicago, where some further factor analytic methods were developed and electronic computers were first harnessed to them. From the first 50–100 objective personality measures which London and Illinois jointly covered in the researches of the thirties and forties, the varied range of ingenious. psychologically insightful experimental measurements has been raised at Illinois to about 500 with the help of Frank Warburton of the University of Manchester (who recently gave a B.B.C. account of this work).

The impetus which a truly objective experimental study of personality can give to many applied fields has, however, recently been seized upon far more widely. 'Feedback' has begun from such work as that of Howard at the Chicago Institute of Juvenile Research, Macquarie and White at Toronto University Hospital, the Crichton Royal Hospital in Britain, Sydney University, Boston, Kentucky, Adcock's work in New Zealand, Digman's in Hawaii, Knapp's in the U.S. Navy, Alton State and other hospitals in Illinois, and university departments too numerous to mention. Tatro's recent work at Alton State Hospital has shown that psychologists stand at the threshold of a decade of discoveries of a new type, based on objective possibilities of measuring personality development and therapeutic change. It needs no seer to realize that this is likely to change completely our conceptions and practices in psychotherapy, and to build up a body of scientific laws possessing a certainty and potency of a different order from what we have hitherto known. A glimpse of the first harvests of this third phase of personality study can be given in the last chapters below, but as a brief illustration we may take White and Macquarie's measurement of normals and neurotics on eighteen objective test personality factors. The neurotics were found very significantly different on no fewer than six dimensions, with meanings which throw new light on neurosis. However, the immediate gain is a certainty of diagnosis hitherto unattained. For by combining these six scores in a total, an index is obtained which almost completely separates the neurotics from the normals. No previous measurement devices have been able to match the 'criterion' (the joint judgement of a group of psychiatrists) so closely.

However, in a theoretical sense, we have as yet dealt with only the simplest and crudest aspects of the structural psychologist's personality 'model', and the next chapter needs to tackle somewhat more complex developments.

*

READING

Cattell, R. B., and Warburton, F. W., *Objective Personality and Motivation Tests: A Theoretical Introduction and Practical Compendium*. University of Illinois Press. To be published shortly.

Eysenck, H. J., *The Structure of Human Personality*, second edition. Methuen, 1960.

CHAPTER SIX

Finer Issues in Personality Measurement: States, Instruments, Roles

THE MAIN PROBLEMS IN IMPROVING TRAIT MEASUREMENT

The bold attack which the experimentalists have made on personality measurement, aided by the structuring power of the factor analytic method, produced remarkable advances in the short space of a generation.

Among other things it has yielded a crop of clear-cut, determinate dimensions, measurable by questionnaires, and additionally, by objective laboratory tests ingeniously bringing out the subject's essential personality. The meaning of these functional unities has, in certain cases, already become reasonably clear, for example, in anxiety, exvia, super-ego strength, general inhibition, and regression. Consequently, these measurable entities are becoming the experimental pillars of theory in place of the vague and poorly defined concepts of the clinic on the one hand, or the classical experimenter's armchair notions, represented impotently by single variables, on the other. Finally, they have recently justified themselves to the applied psychologist by a better 'pay-off' in terms of efficiently predicting practical criteria than ever was attained with the older, arbitrary and limited personality tests.

Nevertheless, there are also dangerous pitfalls and unsolved obscurities, as well as successes, on this pioneer frontier. Characteristically, each step forward in science creates new problems and the need for new corrections and modifying conceptions. One of these has been the need to consider 'instrument factors' which, like motes blotting the eye's clear vision, appear in the form of unexpected measurement biases, and susceptibilities to 'test response sets' in various kinds of testing. In short, a test score, even of a well-factored, purely-measured source trait, is not always all that it appears to be.

A second problem to be faced is the invalidation of test results by temporary states of the subject. Every teacher knows the parent who is quick to assert that Johnny was not feeling too well at the time he took such and such an intelligence test or scholarship exam, and in some cases this may really have resulted in a quite unfair evaluation. The possibility that some passing mood of elation or depression, of anxiety or fatigue, has confounded a test result is even greater in the personality and motivation realm than in the scholastic achievement field. Indeed, we must recognize that every personality measurement is taken at a time when the individual is deviant, by *some* small mood state, from his true average position.

Thirdly, we must consider the intrusion of that concept, on which sociologists and anthropologists have lavished so much study, which we call 'role'. A great deal of our behaviour is consciously carried out in one role or another, and perhaps much of the rest is confused by unconscious roles. A role, as was pointed out in Chapter 3, affects powerfully the expression of personality and could blind us and our measuring instruments to the real person. Yet we recognize that, for example, the business executive who has just closed a meeting with authoritative and uncompromising directives when arrested five minutes later for speeding may appear conciliatory and placating to the policeman. The priest who has been laughing and talking volubly with his peers becomes reserved and judicial as he listens to the confessions of a parishioner. How shall we disentangle, in behavioural measurement, that which is personality and that which is role?

This chapter is therefore a point at which we pause and look around and take account of a miscellany of developments affecting the meaning of objective personality measurement techniques.

THE INTRUSION OF INSTRUMENT FACTORS

The long experimental pursuit of tests for the main personality factors has resulted in over 500 very diverse designs, not counting those which have fallen by the wayside.*

One thinks of the classification of these tests mainly in terms of the personality factors which they measure. But, both for the sake of producing that academic tidying which we call 'a taxonomy of tests' and to get a better grasp of the instrument factor effects we have now to consider, it is also important to look at them from other and indeed more superficial points of view.

The instrument factor effect is a tendency for the measurement of trait X through a particular medium, A, not to agree perfectly with its measurement through another medium, B. For example, there are distortions which occur in the questionnaire type of test, such as seeing one's acts through rosy glasses, which do not occur in objective tests, and there are effects in objective tests, for instance, a like or dislike of the examiner giving the individual testing, which do not occur in questionnaires. The instrument factor also shows the nature of its intrusion positively in that correlations arise between behaviours which do not belong to the same trait, just because they are measured through the same kind of device, e.g. a questionnaire, a physiological instrument, a perceptual device, which in fact yield a single factor for the set of measures mediated by the one instrument.

So far, personality 'tests' have been classified only in terms of three main groups of observational 'media' – behaviour ratings or life record data *in situ*; questionnaires or self-evaluative 'opinionnaires'; and objective tests. However, experiment shows that we need finer classifications, because instrument factors are generally found to be more specific and narrow than these. Campbell and Fiske have attempted to handle the problem by a 'multi-method–multi-trait' scheme, in which methods or media classifications on the one hand, and trait classifications on the

* A complete Compendium of objective personality and motivation tests including both those effective in O.-A. batteries and those not as yet locating any known factor is being published by the University of Illinois Press (Cattell and Warburton, 1964), listed in the bibliography of Chapter 5.

other, are used as a kind of latitude and longitude to 'place' any test. The only objection to this – and it is a serious one – is that our subjective ideas of what are 'method' categories of measurement may be quite erroneous. One cannot tell where an instrument factor begins and ends simply by looking at the tests. For example, although a questionnaire is a single instrument or medium to the test constructor it may in fact be (and almost certainly is) subject to two or three quite distinct instrument factor effects corresponding to divisions among types of items which our intuition cannot see and which only an experiment can reveal. Obviously what we want is a 'multi-trait–multi-instrument' classification, which can be made only after research has revealed and demarcated the boundaries of instruments.

As illustration of some of these 'instrument of measurement' factors we may consider, in behaviour ratings, the effect of liking or disliking the person rated. This is called the 'halo' effect, and theoretically it works by causing a person rated high on some desirable traits by this particular judge to be rated high on all desirables. The tendency to 'give a dog a bad name and hang him' has long been known, but the proof of this is difficult, because unless liking or disliking is entirely accidental and circumstantial, *it will depend on the actual traits* which the person has, and not so much create as express them. Furthermore, there *may* be some real tendency for 'bad' traits to go together. Although conceivably a person who steals more than most need not lie more than most, yet surely it is more likely that there *is* a correlation here, due to the strength of the super-ego source trait affecting both. In practice, instead of throwing out all such connexions as due to 'halo', it is much safer to try to reduce any false connexion by such good rating techniques as rating all people on one trait at a time instead of one person on all traits at one time. That is, instead of asking the rater for, say, a 1–10 score for Robert on each of forty traits, we ask him to put, say, thirty people in rank order of sociability, defined as readiness to speak to strangers. Another day, when he has forgotten this order, we move to a new trait, and so on. By this device, and keeping ratings concentrated on actual behaviours instead of sloppy trait terms meaning different things to different people, the halo effect can be largely overcome, as Johnson of Michigan has shown.

Another influence which appears to produce an instrument factor distortion in ratings is the particular role of the rater relative to the ratee. It is not only that (*a*) the role of, say, teacher, parent, sergeant brings special emotional ties to the person rated, but also, (*b*) the person himself behaves differently in the presence of raters in different roles. Parents are sometimes astonished to hear how their children behave in school. Frequently the child is himself so aware of his double personality between home and school that he cannot bear to have his parent meet his teacher; (*c*) actually different hours of the day and different segments of the individual's world may be seen by the different raters. An employer sees the employee over seven or eight hours of work conditions. His family sees him in an eight-hour period that overlaps not at all with the other.

It is not surprising, therefore, that factor analysis shows several distinct 'instrument' factors in ratings over and above those actually reflecting traits. Any estimate of the traits of, say, surgency-*vs*-desurgency, or super-ego strength, will be so contaminated by these intruding instrument factor scores that they will correlate rather poorly when made by, say, employers on the one hand, and friends on the other. And both ratings together will correlate less than a naïve psychologist might expect with scores of these conceptually identical traits on a questionnaire. One must recognize that the so-to-speak Newtonian phase of psychology has given way to an Einsteinian Relativity in which we are more cautious about assuming that our measures are absolutes. Every psychological measurement made in the rating and the questionnaire media contains both the movement of the observer and of the observed. The effect of the perception of the observer must be scientifically allowed for, and, as Digman and others have shown, with sufficient nicety of calculation, something which we may call the real traits of the person can be extricated from its contamination with instrument factors – provided the latter are understood.

As to which medium of observation is best there would seem little doubt that objective tests, as in the O.-A. batteries, are better than questionnaires or ratings. Between questionnaires and ratings there is again little doubt that *having regard to the way in which ratings are done in nine out of ten cases*, the questionnaire is better. It is, therefore, all the more alarming that so many psychologists in applied fields persist in calling the rating medium '*the* criterion', against which a questionnaire or other test is 'validated'. For the recent evidence suggests that the instrument factors in ratings as commonly carried out in schools, business, civil service, or military situations are actually more distorting than those in the questionnaire.

Under ideal conditions, notably with (*a*) at least ten raters for each person, (*b*) ranking on one trait at a time, (*c*) definition of the trait in exact behavioural terms, (*d*) visibility of the ratee over most of the day, it is possible, however, to obtain ratings of quite high reliability. Among the best in the experience of the present writer, reaching reliabilities of 0·9, were those made in tank companies, during the war, where men had seen one another in all kinds of circumstances. Reliabilities of 0·9 have also been reached in groups of women in sororities who, if they had not quite seen such a gamut of behaviour as the soldiers, may perhaps have made up for it by the time and conversation given to studying one another's conduct. Distinguishing, as in Chapter 5, between reliability and validity, we would naturally recognize that a reliability of 0·9 does not imply an equal validity – it may merely mean that a woman's reputation is known more accurately than the woman. It can, however, be shown that these techniques of combining ratings give high validity in some fields where validity can be evaluated. For example, good rating techniques applied to estimating the temperatures of rooms yield, with twenty raters, as Thorndike showed, an accuracy as good as the average room thermometer. A lot of individual judges behave like a lot of test items, the specific errors tending to cancel and the common 'sense' tending to add up. This is perhaps one justification for democracy.

The instrument factors in the questionnaire medium of assessment are more subtle. For example, instrument factors might arise from 'faking good' (sometimes described as a 'social desirability response set'), already discussed, but also from defective self-knowledge, from repression, and from defective knowledge of others (since one's ideas of what is normal inside others are always implicit in assigning an above or below average score to oneself). Regarding the last, one should ask how a man can possibly rate himself reliably on, say, 'tendency to have disturbing dreams' if he has no idea how disturbing the dreams of other people are? What R. L. Stevenson said of the Admiral (in the *Story of a Lie*), 'Between his self-knowledge, which was considerable, and his vanity, which was immense, he had created a strange hybrid animal, and called it by his own name', probably indicates the chief factors in questionnaire distortion. However, social desirability is not one factor but a whole set of distorting factors, depending on roles, as discussed below. In the last few years these observations are becoming so well understood that the worst dangers of distortion in the questionnaire are close to being beaten.

PRINCIPLES FOR INSTRUMENTAL CLASSIFICATION OF PERSONALITY TESTS

These brief glances at the media of rating and self-rating (*Q*-data) will suffice to illustrate the role of the *instrument factor*, in personality testing, definable as 'a single and therefore separable contaminating influence entering into the raw scores estimated for true personality factors, extending across, and characteristic of, a certain medium of observation or mode of measurement'.

Now one of the advantages incorporated in the Objective-Analytic Battery, for the major personality factors, is that the sub-tests for any one factor are extremely diverse (see Tables 12–15) and, as far as the present evidence goes, the danger of contamination by instrument factors is proportionately unimportant.

But what is true about freedom from instrument factor contamination in the main line of research here described, directed to well-marked personality factors and directed by test construction at once boldly and subtly directed in the O.-A. batteries, is not by any means true of certain other objective test approaches. Although the Rorschach test, which deals solely in coloured ink blots, and the T.A.T. or the Rosenzweig 'Picture Frustration' test, which asks for interpretation of social pictures, have already been described, they need to be looked at again from the standpoint of instrument factors.

If our purpose is to describe all kinds of personality tests actually in use by psychologists today, then this section must glance over them, though from the standpoint of the main developments of personality theory we may not necessarily expect them to be in use tomorrow. The various developments which have not put structural personality research and statistical theory first, and test construction as something to be guided by it, have in common only a lack of system and a tendency to have sidled into the area from some adjoining frontier, rather than having imaginatively grappled with its main problems. For example, users of intelligence tests – especially individually administered tests – have noticed that glimpses of personality can be obtained as by-products of the intelligence testing itself. A hesitation unduly prolonged here, an emotionality of expression there, can be made into a standard, scorable clue on some aspect of personality, and, lo, 'personality is being measured'.

It is not surprising that behaviour in almost any situation can be made into a personality test. One could observe the way a person smokes a cigarette, or responds to an interruption, or doodles on a piece of paper. Solomon got good results with offering to chop a baby in two, and Sherlock Holmes by addressing his client as 'Your Majesty' (*A Scandal in Bohemia*). Unfortunately for our evaluation of the interview, men like Solomon and Sherlock Holmes are rare. If one is to compare candidates in an interview situation at all (its reliability is down in the 0·3–4 region) it is best to have a standardized situation, and this can be partly achieved by standard questions and by having something for the interviewee to work upon, to bring out behavioural traits. For as the equation, $R = f(S.P)$, reminds us, our progress will be small if both P *and* S are unknown.

From this standpoint, of standardizing an interview, the development of personality measures out of intelligence tests and other existing procedures is not unreasonable. At the same time, it is conceptually poor stuff compared to the modern structural attack on the problem. It is possible to use a chisel to turn screws, or a sharp screwdriver to chisel a piece of wood, but a craftsman will do neither with enthusiasm.

Classical 'brass instrument' experimenters have similarly observed, as by-products of their work on, for example, perception, or learning, that certain behaviours tie up with apparent individual differences of personality. Very seldom indeed, however, have these been followed up in terms of general personality dimensions and theory. Witkin's perceptual work on individual differences in 'capacity to abstract a percept from its field' becomes understandable in personality terms if seen as a special

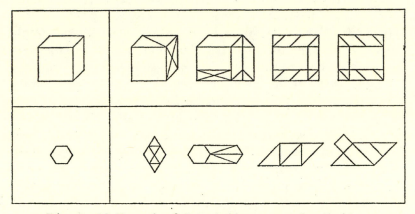

Diagram 15. Example of Gottschaldt: perceptual analysis test

expression of the U.I. 19 or Independence pattern, but not just as a perceptual 'field independence'. In one of his tests the whole room is tilted and the subject, from his rotated chair, is asked to say when a stick is truly (gravitationally) vertical. Correlations as good as or better than this with the general personality factor (indexed as U.I. 19) of Independence can be obtained by the simple pencil and paper tests of Dr Gottschaldt, as shown in Diagram 15.

Because perception has long been an academic category of study within classical psychology its utility for personality measurement has tended to be studied in isolation from that totality of behaviour by which personality factors are better recognized. Personality will naturally express itself in perception, but that expression will again suffer from local, instrument factor effects, and fool us if we confine our study to perception. The special operation in perception known as 'projection' deserves special study, in the following section, but general perceptual effects, such as capacity to abstract, speed of perception, susceptibility to visual illusions, etc., are already involved in the O.-A. battery and their personality meaning is better observed in the context of non-perceptual behaviour too.

Yet another area of special types of objective test is that concerned with 'style', which was pursued far in Germany in the 1940s. We all recognized that the style of a man's behaviour sometimes carried over from one area of behaviour to another. If he is quick and spirited in talking he may, for instance, be quick and spirited with a paint brush. But it is a far cry from this to saying that a single 'life style' pervades every man's life, or to 'reasoning by analogy' from his handwriting that if his strokes are bold he will be socially bold, or if his letters are irregular that his moral behaviour will be irregular. Allport of Harvard, and Vernon at the University of London were first to make more stringent statistical tests of these claims thirty years ago. Neither their work, nor the enormous amount of experiment based on concepts such as 'motor style', 'cognitive style', 'expressive movement', etc., since has yielded a fraction of the returns obtained from general objective tests. 'Life style' and the belief that the whole personality can be inferred from a scrap of handwriting or the lilt of a voice continues to fascinate many, just as does extra-sensory perception or hypnotism. Enormous volumes of records exist, gathered by the most sensitive graphological and voice analysis apparatus; but 'stylists' have been more intuitive and aesthetic than mathematical, and very sophisticated mathematics indeed is needed to capture style. In the present writer's opinion, when these stylistic features are properly analysed and correlated, it will be found that one or two of the main temperament factors, not the whole personality, can be predicted from them.

Yet another of the more restricted approaches to personality measurement is through physical, neurological, physiological, and anatomical observations. The view of Kretschmer in Germany and Sheldon in America that the affectothyme temperament is associated with round, plump body build has been mentioned, as well as Stockard's finding of a more rapid conditioning – perhaps through high anxiety – in narrowly as contrasted with solidly built dogs. An appreciable fraction of psychiatric opinion now holds that schizophrenia is not a psychological disorder but a physiological disorder. Scheier's work on anxiety revealed surprisingly high correlations between physique – small body size and weak muscular performance – and anxiety. Relations have been found between personality factors and blood types, notably with I and J factors (see Chapter 3), as well as with metabolic rate.

That relations to personality should be found in each of these traditional areas of psychological work – physiological psychology, intelligence testing, style or aesthetic preference, perception, the expression of personality in social and political attitudes (as in premsia) – should surprise no psychologist with a broad understanding of personality. But that they are the most profitable place to pursue good personality tests is more questionable. A view of personality structure gained through a more inspired construction of general objective tests has paid off better than these movements, which never really leave the assumptions of the specialized area and are likely to be heavily mixed with instrument factors. The difference in philosophy here reminds one historically of that between the Mediterranean navigators who never let the land out of sight and those who, like da Gama and Columbus, gave up the familiar landmarks and set out on a new ocean.

From the standpoint of *classifying* personality tests in a taxonomic scheme, the categories of perceptual, physiological, stylistic, aesthetic choice, temperamental–cognitive, miniature situational, etc., may have temporary use. But the functional classification and labelling of objective personality tests, in ways to throw light on their construction and mutual relations, is something psychologists have still to achieve.

A step towards a truly operational and comprehensive classification has been made by Warburton (op. cit.) where tests are viewed in terms of the form of the instruction, the nature of the test situation, the mode of the response, and the principles of scoring. For example, some instructions permit a wide variety of responses, others a very restricted channel. Some situations demand perceptual skills, others solution of a problem, others a rapid output, and others an aesthetic choice response, and so on. As to scoring and response, the principal alternatives in responses are here, as in ability tests, (*a*) open-ended, or inventive, in which the subject writes down what he likes, and (*b*) closed or selective (multiple choice) answers, in which he underlines one of several given responses. The latter are, of course, much easier to score objectively and are used whenever possible.

Nothing more can be said in a book of this size about comprehensive taxonomies, and test varieties, but a somewhat more detailed inspection than above will be made in the next section of two or three special classes of major importance in the O.-A. batteries, namely, of the so called 'projective' designs, the exploration of aesthetic choice in music and art; and the exploitation of cognitive style, wit, and humour.

PERSONALITY IN RELATION TO MUSICAL, ARTISTIC TASTES

'Tell me what a man likes and hates and I shall know what sort of a person he is,' is a proverbial remark. Many psychologists have had an almost mystical belief that a person's choices in art, in particular, constitute a sensitive personality indicator, especially of his temperament. One feels that if the subject chooses luscious and meaty Rubens pictures on the one hand or pale and spiritual El Grecos on the other, there is something diagnostic about this. And we are apt, doubtless too glibly, to generalize that a person choosing a weird and stormy Vlaminck landscape, compared, say, to one who likes the peaceful domesticity of a Constable farm scene, has wilder emotions.

Unfortunately, most of the 'inspired' psychiatric theories in this field have received little serious attention from hard-headed psychometrists because obvious scientific checks have not been applied to the results. In one art-and-personality test known to the writer the clinician asserted that the choice of pictures 'a', 'b', 'c', and 'd' denoted a depressive individual, while choice of 'e', 'f', 'g', and 'h' diagnosed a schizophrenic. However, when these tests were administered to a good range of people it turned out that those who chose picture 'a' with high frequency did *not* tend to chose 'b', nor did those who chose 'e' show any systematic tendency to choose 'f'! If these sets were intended to be used as 'scales of depressiveness' or schizophrenia they should at least 'go together' in their parts, in a correlation cluster, or, better, a factor.

By correlation methods it is possible to lay the foundations for the use of art in personality research. Some one hundred paintings, sculptures, and architectural photographs have been so used, independently, by the present writer and by Eysenck. A 'like' or 'dislike' or 'indifferent' judgement is made on each picture by each of some two hundred people and the pictures are correlated with one another to see how many dimensions of taste enter into choice among them. Roughly a dozen such dimensions are found. Their psychological meaning still requires research, but it is at least evident that they do not correspond merely to technical schools of art or historical groups. One psychological relationship already reasonably confirmed is that the more surgent individuals – cheerful, uninhibited, talkative – prefer paintings with clear, 'loud' colours and simple, bold draftsmanship, such as occurs in many post-impressionists and much abstract art, whereas the desurgents prefer the gloom, the suggestive chiaroscuro, and the subtlety of some of the old masters such as Van Dyck. In this case the 'reasoning by analogy' all too frequently indulged in happens to fit the facts. Indeed, as we shall see under humour it is also true that individuals high on surgency prefer jokes which are uninhibited and perhaps unsubtle, compared to the desurgents.

Much experiment has been lavished on the idea that there is something very diagnostic in preference respectively for colour and form. But it is typical of the theory-wrecking complexities in this field that the 'meaning' of such preference turns out to depend much on the particular setting and the actual instrumental procedures. For example, in liking pictures, paired for artistic quality, but showing coloured and uncoloured alternatives, the chief personality factor involved turns out to be the 'regression' factor (U.I. 23, page 111). Persons of low regression and high capacity to mobilize prefer colour to form. Showing more attention to colour in making associations in the Rorschach test seems to have roughly similar psychological meaning. On the other hand giving greater attention to colour than form in *sorting* and in spontaneous attention perception seems largely a function of the 'independence' source trait (U.I. 19 and some U.I. 26) discussed below. Why these differences should exist remains a riddle,

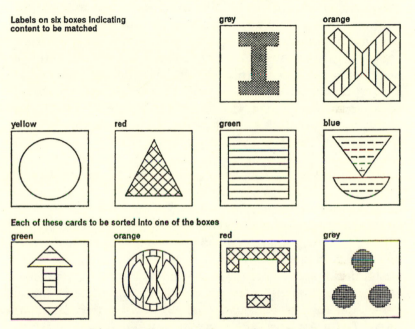

Diagram 16. A colour-form ratio sorting test

though there are plenty of unconfirmed theories. Meanwhile it is used as a test in the O.-A. battery, as shown in Diagram 16, and also in the form of a movie film in a design by Thurstone which makes patterns and colours move in opposite directions.

One of the most extensive theories relating art to temperament is that of Kretschmer, who tried to show that the round-bodied cyclothyme and the lean, narrow sizothyme go in for distinct forms of expression in poetry, art, and architecture. The more 'romantic', full-bodied emotionality of rococo architecture, the opera, and the colourful schools of art he ascribed to the cyclo-thyme (affectothyme) area of Europe – Southern Germany, Austria, and Northern Italy. The more classical, restrained, and either coldly formal or obscurely mystical art he ascribed to the leptosomatic (lean-bodied) predominance areas, like Britain, Northern Germany, and Spain. Gothic architecture belongs to these sizothyme temperament areas. He also applied this to in-dividuals, the lean, sizothyme Schiller producing formal, classical literature, whereas the affectothyme Goethe was a romantic. Statistical analysis shows a slightly significant tendency in the directions indicated.

Recently this pursuit of temperament measurement through taste has gone into the musical field. Incidentally, there has always been a fairly impressive body of opinion, but not among professional psychiatrists, that music must have special powers in psychotherapy if we only knew how to enlist it. Literature is replete, from Homer to Shakespeare and beyond, with allusions to near-madness being cured and emotional devils cast out by just the right music. To Saunders of Princeton, the present writer, and the Music Research Foundation of America, dedicated to music therapy, it seemed that a first exploration of the depth to which music penetrates the soul might be made by determining whether different kinds of mental illnesses show significantly different preferences for music. In view of what had happened in the art field it seemed desirable to begin by first finding statistic-ally what music preferences 'go together'. The I.P.A.T. Music Preference Test of Personality now embodies the results of several factor analyses, in a single long-playing record in which 100 musical excerpts, each heard long enough (about a third of a minute) to strike a mood, are heard. It is found that eleven dimensions account for most of the variation in taste, and, as in pictures, they do *not* correspond simply to technical 'schools' or periods but to some more fundamental temperament differ-ences in toleration of rhythms, speeds, and liking for kinds of emotional stimulation.

The remarkable fact appears that when these 'preference factors' are measured for a group of normals and a group of mental hospital patients, the latter stand at statistically quite different levels from the former. Furthermore, one can distinguish among the mental hospital patients between those suffering from schizophrenia and those who are paranoid or manic. The meaning of the factors as found among normals is consistent with these differences. For example, the set of musical experiences in Factor 8 on the record were found to appeal to normals who are more withdrawn and unsociable. A little later it was found that the score of schizophrenics on this factor tends to be far above that of normals.

At present no one has pursued this research far enough to know how these preferences are determined by the individual's emotional make-up. Possibly there is even some quality in the physical nervous system itself which makes certain kinds of music less pleasant to some people, and this quality may be temperamentally associated with resistance to certain kinds of mental disorder.

PERSONALITY IN RELATION TO PROJECTION AND HUMOUR

It is a natural step from getting people's preferences for art to getting them to tell their phantasies and interpretations as they listen to music and look at pictures. Under the altogether too loose term 'projective' tests, however, research has bogged down in ambiguous conclusions regarding the real worth of such principles.

Projection was originally defined by psychoanalysts as a defence mechanism in which one imputes to others an emotion of one's own which one cannot tolerate ('I don't hate him; he hates me'). It is an 'ego defence mechanism' to support the ego in conflict. A number of other defence mechanisms have been carefully described, notably by Anna Freud, such as phantasy, rationalization, reaction formation ('leaning over backwards', as when a naturally cruel person is for ever praising tolerance and showing exquisite sensitivity to oppression), all directed to enabling a somewhat maladjusted person to live with himself more easily. No proof was given, however, before correlational

researches of Dr Wenig, as to the functional reality and independence of these dynamisms. He showed that rationalization,
autism (believing what it is comfortable to believe), phantasy,
are indeed distinct mechanisms, such that a given person is likely
consistently to use one more than another. He also showed that
there are *two* kinds of projection – *true* projection of unconscious
or barely conscious anti-social motives as described by the
analysts, and *naïve* projection (as the present writer had hypothesized) in which a person (like an inexperienced child) interprets
the behaviour of others in terms of his own personal and limited
motivation system, just as anyone interprets new worlds in terms
of that with which he is familiar.

As Wenig's pictures showed, any person interpreting a picture
'misperceives' it, to some extent. That is, he departs by a given
amount from the central norm (which we may take as the zero
point for scoring) as a result of all these different mechanisms
acting together. If he is angry, but won't admit it, he may, by
true projection, check the answer under the picture: 'The man
seems to be angry.' Or, if he himself finds the environment
puzzling, he may by naïve projection check the interpretation:
'The man is obviously puzzled.' It is not surprising that poor
validities are found for personality characteristics inferred from
tests like the Thematic Apperception Test, if the psychologist's
inference is that the deviations in what the patient describes are a
simple measure of his own deviations. It is true that literature,
and the insight of the ages, are replete with observations on
'projection' in some general sense. Proverbs (26:28) tells us 'A
lying tongue hateth those that are afflicted by it' and Thomas à
Kempis generalized 'What a man is inwardly that will he see
outwardly.' But modern research can show more analytical
capacities, and we recognize that any 'misperception' is the outcome of an aggregate of defences, in which true projection and
naïve projection may act differently. For example, people in
depressed moods can be shown to rate others as more hostile than
usual. This is essentially naïve projection: 'people are unhappy
when they are unloved' and true projection 'I would like
company therefore others are wanting my company' is quite
neutralized in this perception.

1. As a life guard, he is in charge of the beach and is enjoying being 'master of all he surveys'.
2. The swimmers feel secure in having such a confident person in charge.
3. He cannot keep his attention on the swimmers because he finds it hard to take his eyes off the shapely girls.
4. He feels insecure on the high tower and is wondering how firm it is.

This illustrates the weakness of projective tests in their confounding of different defences. For example, a child, by naïve projection from personal experience might choose (4). True projection, by a male, of an unaccepted sex drive, might lead to response (3). High dominance might lead to response (1), by true projection, but by the alternative defence of rationalization, it might lead to (2). The choice of (2) might alternatively arise from a strong need for security. This ambiguity in determining a choice of response requires projection or (better) misperception tests to be accompanied by other tests leading to proper *motivation component* scores in order to give valid results.

Diagram 17. Subject's choice of interpretation

To get a 'projective' or, better, *misperceptive test* (concentrating simply on the process measured) into dependable *conspective* scoring it is necessary to add alternatives as in the following instance from Wenig's work in the writer's laboratory.

A variety of interpretations for aggressive, sexual, fear, and other response items is here offered under the picture. In this case it will be evident that any aggressive interpretation in an unaggressive person is (*a*) opposed by the action of true projection, (*b*) favoured by naïve projection (because he does not realize that most people would not be aggressive here), (*c*) opposed by reaction formation, and (*d*) so on, in a complex overlay of conflicting contributions to misperception.

It is not surprising that, used naïvely, projective devices have given poor validities, as far as general personality traits are concerned. Used with safeguards in the form of over-determined unambiguous response alternatives, however, misperception tests have proved quite effective among the 500 objective devices experimented upon for the O.-A. batteries, and, with further modifications, among objective *motivation* measurement devices as described in Chapter 7.

An area of objective test development which has proved equally intriguing and equally in need of cautious conclusions is that concerned with wit and humour. Freud, in 1904, suggested the theory that our enjoyment of wit springs from the unexpected release of tendencies bottled up in the unconscious. This would obviously explain the great success of sexual and aggressive jokes. The purely intellectual play which strikes us as the essence of the joke he wrote off as a mere 'fuse' or, to be more exact, a small bribe of pleasure to the censor, to permit the essential forbidden expression from the release of which the real pleasure arises. In every country wit and humour are not entirely free, but like all games, follow certain conventional patterns and restrictions.

Pursuit of this idea, by Luborsky at the Menninger Clinic, and other colleagues of the present writer, showed it to be fruitful, but, in the end, in a somewhat different sense from the Freudian one. In the first place, psychiatrists proved quite unable to sort jokes according to the drives or personality traits supposed to be involved in them. If a clinical psychologist put together four jokes alleged to be giving scope to, say, sadism, then it would rarely turn out that a person who enjoyed one would enjoy the others! So again resort had to be had to correlational techniques and it was then found that about a dozen distinct 'bunches' of jokes, each internally consistent in the sense that when people liked one they liked the others, could be found.

The Humour Test of Personality, now published by I.P.A.T. (which has given permission for the following excerpts) yields scores on some eleven factors of personality, plus an intelligence factor (for intelligence can be relatively painlessly measured by reaction to jokes). Scores have been shown to predict personality traits as measured by other devices, e.g. questionnaires, reasonably well. For example, the following two pairs of jokes (Table 16) help distinguish on the extraversion–introversion axis (the exvia–invia source trait). The choice of (a) for the first and (b) for the second characterizes a more exviant person. In this case it eventually proved easy to generalize about the common character of all jokes on this axis. The extravert jokes tend to be hearty, socially uninhibited, and of sexual content; while the inviants prefer jokes which are more dry, cautious, and somewhat acid.

Nowadays it is not unusual for psychologists to complain that the criteria which they are offered, against which to validate their

TABLE 16

Which joke seems funnier to you?

A. 'Aren't you getting tired of this bachelor life, Bill?' asked his friend, Jack. 'Certainly not,' replied Bill. 'What was good enough for my father is good enough for me!'

B. Kind neighbour (to little boy eating an apple): 'Look out for the worms, Sonny.'
Little boy: 'When I eat an apple, the worms have to look out for themselves.'

Joke A is appreciated more by extraverts; joke B by introverts – as a rule.

A. 'I'm looking forward,' she said, 'to my twenty-fifth birthday.'
'Aren't you,' suggested her escort, 'facing the wrong direction?'

B. 'For goodness' sake, use both hands!' exclaimed the girl in the car.
'I can't,' said her escort. 'I've got to steer with one.'

Joke B is the extravert choice; joke A the introvert.

tests, are demonstrably less reliable than the tests themselves. Psychologists have been asked to develop tests of military effectiveness in officers, with nothing better than parade ground ratings against which to evaluate them. A study with a rare degree of realism in the criterion was made in the Korean War, by Dr Meeland and others, where combat effectiveness under war conditions was compared with scores on a wide array of personality measures, mostly pre-factorial (1950).

The Humour Test, already a factored, dimensionalized test, was one of the very few which gave significant predictions. The men who, by knowledge of them on patrols, etc., were voted by observers to be good men to have around, staunch in danger and active in attack, had characteristically different scores from the average on certain humour factor scores, notably on those which distinguish neurotics from normals – but in the opposite direction here. Humour offers considerable promise as a test, because it is difficult to fake and undoubtedly gets at deeper emotional adjustments. Incidentally, as mentioned, the present I.P.A.T. Humour Test also has a hidden intelligence test in it, which correlates well with ordinary intelligence tests – and is certainly more amusing to take!

These brief glances at personality dimension measurement through special classes of instrumentality perhaps suffice to show that art, music, and humour are effective, if somewhat specialized adjuncts to objective testing. They have proved useful with some of the main personality dimensions, such as exvia–invia, intelligence, and anxiety, which retain their unitary pattern form even in these fields of expression. Their measurement may be missed somewhat with a special instrument factor, but they are a valuable addition to the psychologist's measurement resources.

THE DIMENSIONS OF MOODS AND STATES

This chapter promised to look at moods and states as part of a more sophisticated treatment of the measurement problem. But moods and states are more than a mere nuisance to the personality researcher: they are fascinating problems in themselves.

A rationale for their measurement is necessary to move towards laws about them – if laws hold for such capricious entities!

On looking at moods and states the psychologist found just the same bewildering situation as with traits – a vast array of popular terms and no idea of how many real dimensions of independent change exist in human consciousness. In principle it should be possible, however, to apply the same correlational methods here as with traits, and arrive at statements of how many and what kind of dimensions will account for the observed changes and whether they tend to be cyclical or not, etc.

Over the last twenty years research has found two effective ways to get precise accounts of the structure of human moods. They have been called *P-technique* and *Differential R-technique*, and their purpose is to make correlational analysis of *change* as previously, in traits, one made correlational analysis of static structure.

Although we have not bothered with the technical term *R-technique* before, it is the standard designation for the ordinary process of correlating behaviour measures across some hundreds of people and factoring them. In *differential R-technique* the measures which are correlated are not static, but represent increments or changes between measures on occasion 1 and occasion 2. For example, if the psychologist is interested in the effect of a tranquillizing drug on people under stress he may measure 200 people on forty measures of various aspects of anxiety and stress response, psychological and physiological. After half of them have been given the drug he will measure everyone again. The change score on each of the forty measures is obtained by subtracting the first from the second. These forty 'increments' (some will actually be decrements) are then correlated to see what goes with what, and factored to see how many independent influences are needed to account for the changes. As shown below, one obtains not a single dimension of change but a reduction on the anxiety factor, and on the stress factor, but perhaps no simple effect on the regression factor. At least three dimensions are found to be necessary even in the briefest experiments to account for the directions of flow of mood, but if we simplify by speaking of three it is easy to see that the change in any one person would be represented by a line (usually curving) in space plotted according to the shifts on those three axes. A particular mood is represented by a point in this space which combines scores on, for example, anxiety, elation, and regression.

A second way of catching time on the wing is P-technique, so called because it is really a correlational analysis of the single person. Here we would measure the person on the same forty measures – of mood rating, speed of reaction, irritability, blood pressure, breathing rate, etc. – every day for perhaps a hundred days. Correlation over the time series will show which things tend to rise and fall together, and reveal connexions, for example, between psychological and physiological events. Whether we apply stimuli – stresses, tranquillizers, work and rest periods – or just leave 'an awful week' to produce its own differences from 'a delightful week-end' is of no moment. Our interest is in the organism's natural dimensions of 'bounce' under the impact of events. And the number and nature of these functionally unitary response patterns can be located by P-technique and incremental R-technique. A rather more detailed account of P-technique is given below when we study dynamic states – states of desire – but here our concern is mood in the more common sense.

So far these methods have revealed some nine independent dimensions of state change, several of which do fit popular introspections. For example, there is a general fatigue factor which climbs with hour of day, an anxiety factor, an elation-depression factor, and so on. Any *actual* concrete mood state is, of course, a complex combination of levels on these primary state dimensions. The analysis, however, has the advantage that from a weighted composite of any state (or change in state) from actual scores on behaviours a relatively pure estimate can be made of the person's level on any one mood component, in a defined co-ordinate system. This brings the study of ataractic drugs (drugs with psychological effects, such as anti-depressants) to a new level of precision, for one can assign a vector indicating the precise magnitude and mood direction of the change produced in the average person by one milligram of each special kind of chemical.

What then are the behavioural measures used? For each state dimension, as for each trait, one must use a battery of half a dozen tests of demonstrated validity, instead of depending on any single item. The I.P.A.T. Seven Factor State Battery includes the following tests, taken here just for three important states.

Elation-vs-*Depression* (to be precise, Cortertia-*vs*-Pathemia, or
P.U.I. 22)

Verbal fluency	(High)
Reversible perspective	(Fast)
Tempo of arm–shoulder circling	(Fast)
Electrical skin resistance	(Low)
Reaction time	(Short)

In short, people in depressed moods are found to be slower in reaction time, lacking in spontaneous fluency and showing a slow rate of reversal when they press a button in time with the changes in perspective seen in drawings like that shown in Diagram 18.

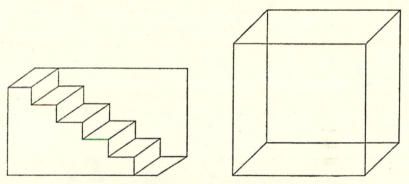

Diagram 18. Examples of alternating perspective tests

Anxiety

Susceptibility to annoyance	(High)
Lack of confidence with untried skills	(High)
Emotionality of comment	(High)
Greater output and lowered alkalinity of saliva	
Greater pulse increase to cold pressor test	
Raised cholinesterase in blood serum	

It will be noticed that some variables here are the same as for anxiety as a trait. For example, both high annoyability and high emotionality of comment define anxiety in a person temporarily anxious and also in what distinguishes a 'permanently' neurotically anxious person from another person.

Excitement-vs-Torpor

Memorizing meaningless material	(Better)
Ratio of non-emotional to emotional recall	(Higher)
Handwriting pressure	(Higher)
Electrical skin resistance	(Lower)
Ataxic sway suggestibility	(Lower)
Size of galvanic skin responses	(Lower)

Three comments may be instructive on the above. First, it will be noted that some dimensions confounded in discussions by traditional experimentalists are found to be distinct, namely, anxiety and excitement – and, one should add, stress response. On the dimension of anxiety, high anxiety is the opposite of low anxiety, but excitement is the opposite of torpor, boredom, or sleepiness, and stress the opposite of ease. In fact, the excitement factor gives better definition than has hitherto been achieved to the notion of 'activation level' which animal experimenters have been tracing to particular neurological action levels in the brain. The distinction of the effort stress dimension from anxiety is also a scientific gain, for lack of which people with real psychosomatic complaints, e.g. stomach ulcers, have been confused with neurotics.

Secondly, one should note that a single variable is rarely an adequate measure of a state and may at times be almost equally an expression of two distinct states. For example, electrical skin resistance falls both in elation and in excitement, and, indeed, also has some contribution from anxiety.

Thirdly, one may note that most states represent a change which affects a set of manifestations scattered across both the psychological and the physiological realm. Some valuable indications of the channels by which mental states affect the body – as in religious miracles – can be experimentally studied now that these state patterns are measurable and better understood. Incidentally, an important difference between fear and anxiety shows up in the above findings, in that whereas fear dries up the mouth, anxiety increases the flow of saliva (as it does that of gastric juice).

The measurement of states is in its infancy, and has hitherto proved baffling because multivariate methods were not employed first to recognize the number and nature of the states. The problem still remains that in certain cases similar test measures seem to be indicated for states and traits. In Chapter 5, page 114, we mentioned this problem for anxiety, where it is particularly acute. A general solution lies in the direction of putting more weight on physiological variables in state batteries, since traits rarely show much physiological correlation. But with increasing research on the seven-state battery we may also be able to discover behavioural measures which, for example, respond to anxiety as a state much more than to anxiety as a characterological trait.

The formal upshot of advance in this new area is that in the specification equation we must always add state factor scores along with trait factor scores. That is to say, when we aim to measure a trait we must either average scores taken over a sufficient sample of different occasions to cancel out mood effects, or we must find ways of measuring the mood factor as such, along the lines just described, and of allowing for it in any trait measurement. The first conclusion is important, for example, in using intelligence tests for scholarship selection. It suggests that instead of one test in an examination week we should average, say, six intelligence measurements spread over as many weeks. Alternatively, when we know something about the kind of mood state likely to be engendered by a particular testing situation, we can measure it separately and discount for its effects on the trait performances.

PERSONALITY, ROLE, AND THE VALIDITY AND RELIABILITY OF PREDICTION

As pointed out earlier, a second main 'disturber' of simple prediction from trait scores is the effect of roles. When a role is obvious, and accompanied by, say, a uniform and ceremonies of office, we have no difficulty in recognizing it. But there are thousands of more subtle roles, from 'the power behind the throne' to 'the household martyr'. The methods for objectively locating the existence and nature of such roles are statistically complex, yet they must be mastered if psychological measurement

graphic plot of
similarity of profile

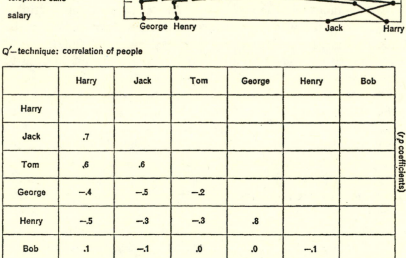

distance walked per day

number of people met

hours of office work

number of senior personnel
to whom the individual has
to report each day

messages carried

telephone calls

salary

Q'—technique: correlation of people

	Harry	Jack	Tom	George	Henry	Bob
Harry						
Jack	.7					
Tom	.6	.6				
George	−.4	−.5	−.2			
Henry	−.5	−.3	−.3	.8		
Bob	.1	−.1	.0	.0	−.1	

(*r_p* coefficients)

Finding role types by Q'—technique
Type 1: *Postmen* Harry, Jack and Tom   Type 2: *Office Managers* George and Henry

Diagram 19

is to mean anything. For roles tremendously modify personality responses. Recently, the head of a certain republic finished lunch, brought his little daughter to shrieks of laughter playing bears and went to his office to sign a firing squad execution for a former fellow student.

Roles may cause sharp changes of behaviour from those of the natural personality, and generate those conflicts with other roles which the novelist never tires of depicting. But how do we locate a role? Postmen, in their occupational role, differ from other men in walking systematically the streets of a whole district, in carrying a bag with letters, and in calling on a large number of people. If we correlated each of 200 people with one another, with respect to a lot of scores, including distance walked, number of people called upon, etc., those who were postmen would form a 'correlation cluster'. A correlation cluster has been discussed earlier (page 58), but it was then a correlation of trait parts in R-technique, whereas here we are correlating people instead of traits, in what is called Q -technique. (See Diagram 19.)

Actually, we should use a pattern similarity coefficient r_p instead of a correlation coefficient to find the similarity of people on their score profiles. This Q'-technique is the basic method for finding 'types' if we are dealing with ordinary personality traits, but when we begin with social role behaviours it is the method for finding roles, like that of a postman, a father, a company executive, a close friend, etc.

Being able to act in a role implies that the individual possesses certain response tendencies, which come into action when the cue stimuli 'call forth' this role behaviour. Consequently, these 'capacities to respond properly for role X' should show up in correlation as a factor just like any personality factor, and we may append it to the *specification equation* on page 79, just like any other predictive factor, thus:

$$R_{ij} = b_{jA}A_i + b_{jB}B_i \ldots + b_{jS}S_j + b_{jL}L_i$$

where R_{ij} is the size of response of person i in situation j; A, B, etc., are his ordinary personality factor scores, and L_i is his role score.

However, L, the role factor, is in some ways different from the class of personality factors. For one thing it affects behaviour in only a relatively limited number of places, whereas a personality factor is much broader. For another, it dictates behaviour which falls in a narrow range of variability: most people, regardless of personality, reply 'Good morning' when so addressed, and a bus driver, no matter what his whims, takes the bus over the standard route. When a role fact loads behaviour it loads it strongly, and otherwise not at all.

Subjectively the possession of a role factor is felt as a 'mental set' which modifies all ordinary responses. The very same stimulus is *perceived* in a different way when one is in the role and when one is out of it, as illustrated by the example of the policeman in and out of uniform witnessing a traffic light violation. Technically, we handle this change of perception the same way in a role as in a mood – both of which can intrude on the ordinary personality – by this special factor, *L*, which can be called a *modulator* factor. A modulator factor comes into action only when the usual, ordinary 'focal stimulus' comes into the orbit of a set of role cues which we may call the 'ambient' or surrounding stimulus. For example, the child's response to the focal stimulus of another putting his tongue out at him is one thing in the playground and another when the ambient stimulus of the classroom atmosphere provides those cues which put him in the role of a pupil. Focal and ambient stimuli now make a new 'global situation' to which he reacts differently, because the *b* value or loading on the role factor which he has acquired is now large.

At this point we step into the region of more complex formulae than can be dealt with in an introduction, but in terms of some practical implications for personality testing the role concepts mean: (1) That in measuring any personality trait the samples of behaviour in our battery should be well chosen across a lot of different roles which people commonly occupy. If, for example, one is measuring the surgency factor in a mixed population (as is usual) of salesmen, diplomats, bus drivers, and teachers it would not do to take all our measures of individual differences in talkativeness (words per hour; which loads surgency) from the 'on the job' role situation. For it is the business of salesmen and teachers to talk a lot, and of bus drivers and diplomats to say little. (2) That in measuring the strength of a person's immersion in a role we should, reciprocally, sample comprehensively across a lot of different trait behaviours. Thus in the end role factors and personality factors must both be measured if we are to get maximum understanding and prediction.

In this chapter our task has been to take a more sophisticated look at the initial simplified picture of personality factor measurement presented earlier. In summary we see that some of the failures and misunderstandings about the technical possibilities of personality measurement arise from: (1) Ignoring certain 'perturbations' in the measurements themselves, due to instrument factors, and the using of single tests instead of batteries properly sampling the demonstrated area of expression; (2) Setting up *ad hoc* 'scales' for this and that arbitrarily designated 'trait', instead of first finding by basic research the structures and states to be measured. Only when we have structured factor measures is it possible (*a*) to allow appropriately for change of the structure with age, environmental influence, physiological condition, etc., as we do, for example, in using the intelligence growth curve to assign an I.Q., and (*b*) to integrate the different traits in a response by the total personality; (3) Failing to allow for the intermittent influences of the mood state and role 'Modulators' we have just discussed.

Chapter 4 has described how psychologists are accustomed to evaluating the quality of tests by the touchstones of (1) *validity* and (2) *consistency*. A glance back at these psychometric test standards, in the light of the more complex considerations of this chapter, should suffice to round off our view of the canons of ordinary psychological testing. The *consistency* of a test, has been defined as the *extent to which it agrees with itself* and has three quite different aspects:

(1) *Reliability:* the extent to which it gives people the same score on occasion A and on occasion B.

(2) *Homogeneity:* the extent to which its different parts measure the same thing.

(3) *Transferability:* the extent to which it goes on measuring the same thing when used on slightly different groups, e.g. in culture or age.

A common mistake in evaluating tests is to assume uniformly that the higher the consistency coefficients the better the test. As far as *transferability* is concerned it is true that a test which is most 'hardy' to changes of climate is generally more desirable.

Even here, however, the property of meeting a wider range of ages and cultures may be purchased at the cost of losing higher validity with that type of group for which it is primarily intended. This question of how far the same traits can be measured across cultures is taken up again in Chapter 9, page 258.

But high homogeneity may not be desirable at all and this has been brought out farther in our discussion of personality trait and role trait, where it has been pointed out that the personality measures must sample from a wide range of different (non-homogeneous) role situations. Usually, in a well-functioning machine or living organism, we judge its efficiency by how well it functions as a whole. We do not expect the parts all to be exactly the same, and, indeed, such homogeneity is a mark of a lower organism. Similarly, any complex and ingenious test, e.g. a factor measure in the O.-A. battery, may need to be put together like a watch, with all its parts properly balanced for some final results. If it is chopped up the scores on its parts need not necessarily correlate highly with one another.

In general, a test for a highly specific thing, e.g. accuracy of addition of small numbers, reaction time to light, or attitude to Senator Jones *should* have high homogeneity. The score on the even numbered items should correlate well with that on the odd (and similarly with any other dichotomy). But with batteries aimed at broad personality factors, whether by objective tests or questionnaires, a high homogeneity coefficient should make us suspicious that it is confounding some narrow trait with a broad trait. Sometimes the test constructor says that parts *A* and *B* are meant to be equivalent measures for the same thing. This happens when several *forms* are made, to give longer or shorter testing periods, or to permit people tested on any one form to be immediately retested without any memory effects. In this case the quite special homogeneity coefficient – which is called an *equivalence* coefficient and is obtained by correlating the two forms – should be as high as is practicable. But otherwise a merely high homogeneity coefficient may imply either desirable or undesirable features.

The necessity is now evident for considering these psychometric properties of tests in a wider context of calculation. Measuring personality is not a simple task, like applying a ruler to a box, which anyone can do given the psychological tests. Nor do ordinary validity and reliability indices always mean what they seem to mean. The psychologist has to recognize that the individual is a living and changing being. If his predictions are to be adequate he must allow for aberrations from instrument factors in his instruments, from moods in his subject, and from the social role contexts in which personality expresses itself.

*

READING

Sells, S. B., *Stimulus Determinants of Behaviour*. Ronald Press, New York, 1963.

Bass, B. M., and Berg, I. A., *Objective Approaches to Personality Assessment*. Van Nostrand, New York, 1959.

CHAPTER SEVEN

The Main Features of Our Dynamic Structure

THE IMPORTANCE OF MOTIVE ANALYSIS
AND DYNAMIC LAWS – OLD AND NEW

Looking back over all that has been said above, about accounting for individual differences in behaviour in terms of ability and general personality source traits, the thoughtful reader may raise the point that although the measurement of these traits accounts for individual differences in behaviour, both in terms of intelligible concepts and in terms of experimental accuracy, yet something is missing. This is an understanding in terms of his inner experience. He is accustomed in his own experience and in popular discussions of psychology to talk about a class of traits which he calls motives, and which, so far, have clearly not entered very directly into our calculations.

Many traits we use in prediction are not registered immediately in the person's consciousness. Some most important differences in behaviour can be predicted from the fact that Mr Smith scores highly on an intelligence test and Mr Jones does not, but neither is aware of this operation of his intelligence level in the behavioural outcome. On the other hand, both are intensely aware of the determination of their actions by their desires and conflicts. This is one reason why the average man finds personality theory from the clinical phase of discussions so much easier to follow. Yet it is a very one-sided account of behaviour. Freud, for example, had practically nothing to say about individual differences in ability and their structure, or about the nature of human temperament differences, and this tradition has persisted in the theory and practice of the average clinical psychologist, who until recently has tried to explain most behaviour in terms of motivation structure and conflict.

Nevertheless, from time to time a healthy angle of realism intrudes into even the psychoanalytic predictions, and someone points out that of two characters, A and B, suffering just the same motivational conflict, A would become neurotic whereas B would not. Or again, it is recognized that an anxious condition in a child is the result of the relation of his intelligence to family, cultural, or school demands. In such insights the limiting conditions in terms of temperament, ability, etc., are recognized as decisive. A balanced view must recognize that the traits we have studied so far have a great deal to say about how well the normal person adjusts to occupation and school, in the family and elsewhere, and that they are important even for the clinical case, though clinicians have been slow to realize this. On the other hand, the experimental psychologist has no intention whatever of saying that motives are unimportant, and indeed the analysis of motives has here been left to last, not with the least implication that it is of lowest importance, but indeed, because it is the most complex and needs the general framework of other traits to define it before it can be understood. For an objective, quantitative science of motivation and human dynamics has also arisen, which is no less successful than that of general personality traits, ability, and temperament, in giving positive understanding and prediction, though it may present some more subtle concepts and elusive mathematical formulae.

Psychologists have been accustomed to define three *modalities* of traits, namely, *cognitive* or *ability* traits, *temperament* or stylistic traits, and *dynamic* traits. In common-sense terms, the ability trait has to do with how well a person handles difficulties, the temperament trait has to do with the general style and tempo with which he carries out whatever he does, and the dynamic trait is concerned with why and how he is moved to do what he does. These traits deal with the sets of incentives to which he has learned to respond. Everyone recognizes these three modalities and for the scholar there exist, in the recommended reading (page 76), more philosophical analyses and more precise operational distinctions made in terms of the way the scores are analysed.

One reason why we are able to predict so much behaviour by measures of ability or temperament traits alone, without taking into account the motivation strength, is that in many civilized performances we are able to deal with situations where the motivation is guaranteed by role and rule to be reasonably uniform. For example, we get correlations of 0·5 between intelligence test measures made on children leaving school this year and their college achievement next year. This much correlation is presumably due to the fact that the school is a relatively standard situation in which motivation and time for study are relatively uniform, so that ability remains the chief discriminator. If we ask about the effect of effort on the intelligence test performance *itself*, we find that moderate differences in motivation in doing an intelligence test have only slight effects upon the score. Indeed, if a person is too strongly motivated in a *complex* situation, like an intelligence test, he may actually do less well than if he is only mildly motivated.

Despite this comparative steadiness of motivation in the school situation, Sweney, Sealy, and the present writer have nevertheless shown in a number of recent studies that a considerably improved prediction of school achievement can be made if motivation measures are added to the intelligence test. Motivation differences may not influence much the immediate score on a pure intelligence test, as just pointed out, but they *do* influence very much the extent to which the person invests his intelligence in school achievements in the day-to-day activities throughout the school year. These positive findings raise the question, to be discussed later, whether selection for scholarships and fellowships should give as much role to motivation tests as to intelligence tests. Actually it is possible to be objective about their relative contributions. The principle of 'additions of variance' used in Chapter 2 in discovering the relative roles of heredity and environment can be applied. When such an analytic evaluation is made, it is found that in determining school achievement individual differences of personality and motivation are of *about the same* degree of importance as individual differences in intelligence.

Probably quantitative evaluations would show about the same balance – a rough equality – in their effects on occupational success. On the other hand, in the field of clinical phenomena, where 'success' means adjustment to life, or, at least, the avoidance of neurosis, rather than performance in some specific area, then there is no question that dynamic, motivational traits become paramount, and abilities of much less importance – though still not negligibly important.

Until psychology supplies the concepts we shall now meet in the science of motivation, the personality structure as so far described remains like an engine with no description of its fuel. The word 'dynamic', of course, conveys this very meaning by its derivation from the Greek term for 'power'. But although dynamic psychology is so important, and so interesting that whole libraries have been written about it in the clinical phase of personality study, an unprejudiced look at these writings forces one to admit that this branch of science during the last fifty years has been as near to chaos as an area of science can well come. Adler, Freud, and Jung disagreed on most things on which it was possible to differ, nor were they the only contestants. Furthermore, clinical differences of viewpoint have been no less fundamental in the last than the first decade of this half century. The confidence of these clashes is partly traceable to the fact that all men are authorities on motive. For all of us – doctor, novelist, or plain man in the street – are acutely aware of our own desires, wishes, and conflicts, and this inside view of the machine encourages each to feel that he knows not only how it works but why it works. Actually, since each person can see only his own dynamics in this way – and if Freud is right, only the conscious fraction at that – his generalizations are 'naïve projections' when he ascribes to others, and even to quite different animal species, modes of reacting that are quite peculiar to himself. Yet to be a part of a process oneself is not necessarily to understand it.

Seen from a little distance, the clinical contribution to understanding human motivation is very little different, in method and concepts, from that which novelists and dramatists, priests and lawyers have developed for hundreds of years. It has perhaps been a little more explicit – certainly more elaborate in its jargon – but no more subtle or delicate than the dissection made by a Shakespeare or Dostoyevsky. Neither offers statistical proof or experimental demonstration. Doubtless the sum total of wisdom about human motivation, from dramatist, priest, lawyer, and medical clinician is very impressive, but the methods used had reached the end of their tether. They frayed into many threads of unsupported personal opinion. The time had come, early in this century, for a science of motivation based on more objective methods.

Some scientists, perhaps appalled by the complexities patently existing in human motivation, have sought the beginnings of understanding in what seems the simpler world of animal experiment. Mazes, and conditioning cages – the Skinner box – hunger and electric shocks have been brought to bear on white rats, pigeons, fish, and sundry other creatures.

One thing at once becomes evident: the resultant terms and concepts mix with the clinical theories no better than oil with water! Actually, although the animal experimentalist's methods are scientifically worthy, the generalizations remain at a relatively obvious level. It cannot be said that any great break-through has yet occurred, except in the placing of these simple generalizations upon an indisputably replicable basis of experiment. It is not pessimistic but descriptively realistic to say that the measurement of motivation and the shaping of dynamic laws remain one of the least satisfactory areas of psychology.

Perhaps most psychologists would agree that out of the chaos of twenty years ago there have emerged some four or five ideas on which a certain amount of common agreement exists. More might be claimed but one might be mistaking some fashions in jargon and a certain weary truce on insoluble issues for scientific agreement. Any rebel could at any moment radically question any one of these 'basic notions' we might list and get no answers equivalent to those which a physical scientist can give to an eccentric who questions the notion that the earth is round or that the speed of light is a constant.

The notions on which, nevertheless, an uneasy consensus exists, include: (*a*) The idea that man inherits certain basic drives, akin to those in higher mammals, which provide the original mainsprings of his actions. (*b*) The notion that certain collections of habits and attitudes become learned through the influence of school and society in such a coordinated way that we can recognize a number of unitary integrated structures. These, which might be called attitude aggregates or sentiments (patriotism, religious beliefs, attachments to the family, etc.), are possessed in some degree by everyone and are characteristic of a given culture. (c) The notion that the learning of attitudes just mentioned takes place through either of two processes, namely, (1) classical conditioning by contiguity, and (2) reward learning, or reinforcement, in which a satisfying outcome stamps in the behaviour which produced it. (d) The notion that a substantial segment of our motivation is unconscious. Most would accept that it is unconscious partly because of the defence of repression, whereby there is amnesia (forgetting) for certain connexions which are painful and embarrassing to contemplate. (e) The notion that there emerges by learning an ego, or self-sentiment, which gains control over the simply reactive impulses from the basic drives, and tries to integrate them in legitimate and socially acceptable expressions. (f) The notion that conflict occurs between different dynamic structures, notably between the ego and the collected drives which the psychoanalysts have called the id, but also between the ego and a sentiment structure called the super-ego, which directs moral behaviour with a categorical imperative. (g) The notion that most clinical, neurotic behaviour arises from imbalances among the powers exercised through these structures, and from the resultant conflicts. Attempts to solve these conflicts result in irrational defences, such as repression, projection, and other dynamisms to be discussed, which issue in the unfortunate neurotic symptoms.

THE NEED FOR NEW METHODS FOR DETERMINING DYNAMIC STRUCTURE

If we begin with the first of these concepts – that of drives – we find, unfortunately, a wide range of opinion among psychologists regarding their number and the extent to which they are innate! Some would argue that a considerable amount of behaviour is specified innately in such fields as sexual behaviour and courtship, aggression, parental protective behaviour, etc., whereas others argue that practically everything but the impulse is culturally determined. There is an amazing amount of disagreement as to the *number* of drives which exist. Freud argued at first for two, namely, libido and the ego forces (or sex on the one hand and aggression and security-seeking on the other). Many animal psychologists argue for three or four, namely hunger, thirst, mating, and parental protective behaviour, and derive all the others from these as 'acquired patterns' under a notion of 'secondary drives'. McDougall, who was as sharp an observer of human nature in a sociological and clinical sense as any, argued for some fourteen to sixteen drives, and Murray, Drever, and others have argued for still other or more numerous patterns of innate response with long names like counteractance, affiliation, and inviolacy. Most psychologists would at least agree with McDougall that the things we are defining have three aspects to them, namely, (*a*) a tendency spontaneously to attend to certain objects and situations as being far more important than others, e.g. for the young male a pretty girl is initially more interesting than a book on Latin grammar: (*b*) a characteristic emotion, which is quite specific to the drive and its action, e.g. fear, anger, sexual feeling, etc.; (*c*) an impulse to a course of action which has a particular goal at its end, e.g. pursuing a fleeing animal and eating it, picking up and hugging and protecting a small child crying in distress.

Now, until the nature and number of these drives can be settled in an objective, experimental, way, we are unlikely to get anywhere with the rest of the superstructure of analysis and theory. Indeed, we are unlikely to get anywhere with the rest of psychology, for it is the dynamic traits which make a man 'go', and the abilities and temperament traits are only qualities in the way the drives to action express themselves. The attempt to settle this taxonomic problem by clinical observation has conspicuously failed, for the various writers have had no real method whereby they could validate their views, and their views in consequence have been just about as varied and inconsistent as they could possibly be. Despite better methodology the attempt to answer it by experiment on animals, as we have seen, has also failed, for the simple reason that we have no logical right to claim that what we find in a rat *must* hold for a different species, namely, the human being, in his obviously complex culture. The related attempt to handle this problem in man *physiologically*, by saying that we will recognize those drives as constitutional for which we can point to a physical basis, as in hunger, sex, etc., also fails through sheer illogical presumption. To say that hunger is a primary drive and curiosity is a secondary drive does not make sense, since our failure to find a physiological, neurological basis for a state of intense curiosity *so far* does not mean that later researchers may not find it with more subtle physiological methods. Furthermore, the attempts to show that the so-called secondary drives are, in fact, 'learned', in the service of the primary drives, has completely failed. Any drive is useful to any other drive at one stage or another of life, or in various situations, and one would have to admit assistance in all directions in this respect.

The real issue which has been overlooked here is, in the last resource, a methodological one. The older method of scientific research, which we described in Chapter 1 as the classical, bivariate experimental method, in which one manipulates what is called an independent variable, A, and observes what happens to a dependent variable, B, is actually very inapt for the problem here being investigated. We are concerned to show the existence or non-existence of a *whole pattern*. That is to say, we are concerned with a multivariate problem or the simultaneous observation and measurement of many variables in behaviour and an attempt to show how they are functionally connected.

In studying, for example, hunger, the animal psychologist has assumed that a single variable, namely, the number of hours by which he deprives the animal of food, is a measure of the strength of the hunger drive. It can be shown that this is only one of many possible measures giving indication of the strength of a hunger drive. The nature of the pattern by which hunger is expressed, and recognition of the best weighted set of scores by which its strength can be assessed, can only be perceived through simultaneous measurement and correlation of many variables, such as the amount of restlessness in the cage, blood sugar level, frequency of anticipatory masticatory movements, and so on. In human beings, due to our greater intellectual capacity to perceive relationships, and the associated complexity of our culture, the expressions of a particular drive can be even more diverse and subtle.

The problem can, therefore, be solved only by the use of those multivariate experimental methods which we stressed in the first chapter. In fact, we should measure many manifestations of human behaviour and find by correlation and by factor analysis which kinds of behaviour go together. When we say 'go together' we mean in many different kinds of situation. For example, if we hypothesize that there is a fear drive, its signs will not only change together from occasion to occasion in the same person, but if we hypothesize that it is also inherited as a whole, then it is likely to be inherited in different strengths by different people. Consequently we should expect that all manifestations of this drive would simultaneously tend to be higher in one person than in another. The person who is more afraid of thunder might also be expected to be a little more afraid of crossing the street, or of burglars. It is not argued that there is *exactly a one-to-one correlation* in the intensity of these things, of course. The factor analytic method never assumes a one-to-one correlation. It simply assumes a *tendency* for a functional unity to show itself simultaneously more strongly in most manifestations – a tendency which will be reduced from a perfect correlation by error and interfering circumstances to a degree which we should be able to calculate. Accordingly, if we were to take a great number of manifestations of what are usually called dynamic traits, interests, and emotional reactions, over the whole gamut of human interests, and intercorrelate them for, say, a good sample of about 300 people, and then factor-analyse them, we ought to get evidence of the number of drives and also obtain patterns which will show the nature of these drives. Possibly, some of the patterns we pick up will turn out not to be drives, but those culturally produced patterns which, above, we have called 'sentiments', or attitude aggregates. But this secondary sorting can be done after the initial structuring has taken place.

The pursuit of this analysis of human dynamics, instead of the armchair or consulting-room approach on the one hand, and the animal cage approach on the other, has involved far more complex organization of research of everyday life observation and measurement than was formerly achieved. It has brought in more complex mathematical ideas, and required a still more imaginative exploitation of the possibilities of the electronic computer. But in the last ten years this approach has yielded quite definite results, which have been well confirmed from study to study, and it is these results with which the reader should first acquaint himself in the following section.

HOW DO WE MEASURE THE STRENGTH OF A MOTIVE OR INTEREST?

The scope and reliability of any statistical or correlational study are as good as, and no better than, those of the individual measurements with which it begins. If we are to analyse and classify motives, in such a way as to lead to a comprehensive taxonomy of drives and sentiments, we must begin, as indicated above, by measuring a sufficient sample of normal and abnormal members of our culture with a good variety of interest and attitude measures. These 'variables', as the experimental psychologist commonly calls them, should be very catholic in their choice, and cover most fields of human endeavour, interest, and emotional attachment. For example, we should have measures of a man's interest in his home and members of his family, in his recreational fields, in his occupational advance and his relation to people with whom he works, his religion, his politics, and last, but not least, in himself as a person.

These elements we shall call *attitude-interests*, for each can be measured as a *strength of interest* in following out *a particular course of action* which is defined when we define an attitude. An *attitude* is thus classical *stimulus–response unit*, defined more exactly below. But these single attitudes are the individual bricks in the house of the total dynamic structure. From these final measurable manifestations we must arrive, by experimental measures and statistical processes, at a picture of the total structure.

Until about ten years ago the measurement of interest was mainly done by opinionnaires or questionnaires of various kinds. The person would be given, for example, a list of activities (or occupations) and asked to check those in which he is strongly interested, those in which he is moderately interested, and those in which he is uninterested. Or, he might be given a set of beliefs, (which essentially get at the same things as attitudes or interests) and asked to check those which are characteristic of his personality. Although such self-evaluation methods may work tolerably well when we are speaking of *general* personality traits, as in the questionnaire factors described in the earlier part of this book, where a person may reasonably state whether he is or is not easily upset by having to stand up in a group to speak, etc., the approach becomes more doubtful and unreliable when one gets to interests which can be vague and deep. If we assume, as most psychologists will, the truth of the clinically based hypothesis stated in the last section, namely, that many interests and motives aré actually unconscious, then obviously it is from the beginning a bankrupt procedure to ask a person to state consciously what the strengths of his various interests are. He may even sin from sheer ignorance, as when you ask a five-year-old how many ice-cream cones he is interested in eating and he replies ten, though subsequent experiment shows that his interest lags after two and changes to revulsion at three.

Fortunately clinical psychology, learning theory, and many chance observations in psychological experiment indicate to us a number of motivational strength manifestations more rich and varied than this approach through the all too obvious recording of people's self-estimates of their interest. For example, there are a whole lot of what psychoanalysis calls 'defence mechanisms', the experimental evidence for which we examined in Chapter 6 in talking of 'projective' tests. Clinical observation suggests that the strength of, at least, unapproved motives should be well indicated by the strength of the accompanying attempts to repress them, to rationalize, to delude oneself by autistic thinking, to project on to others the same motives. Then again, there are learning experiments which show that the sheer memory for certain subjects, or the tendency for them to appear spontaneously through reminiscence, etc., are functions of the strength of the interest involved. Indeed, the sheer rapidity with which one learns new material is obviously tied up with the strength of motive relative to that material.

Looking still farther afield for manifestations of motivation, the young psychologists in this new attack on psychodynamics –

Baggaley in Philadelphia, Radcliffe in Australia, Horn in Denver, Sweney in Texas, Sealy in England – turned next to the physiological signs. They explored the psychogalvanic reflex described on page 106, the change in heart-beat when a topic is mentioned, as well as changes in blood pressure, when an interest is insulted. Psychologists may well suspect also (from the pretty girl on the advertisement) that spontaneous visual attention (eye movement) is a sign of interest, and the same may be said of the fluency of a person on a certain topic, i.e. the rapidity with which ideas rise into his mind upon it. People perceive things more rapidly when they are interested in them, and may indeed sometimes misperceive irrelevant things as what they wish to see, for this very reason. This latter tendency was put into a test by arranging a check list which encouraged the subjects to conjure out of an unstructured drawing the very thing they wished to see. Additional measures have been suggested in the rate of 'warming-up' in a new task, the ability to endure unpleasant or painful stimuli for the sake of attending to something, the level of muscle tension created by perceiving something, and so on.

Over eighty different principles of this kind – each an independent kind of cue to interest and motive – have, in fact, been tried out. Before one can properly evaluate their meaning and validity, however, it becomes necessary to define more precisely the 'criterion' which we are aiming to measure by these devices. We have referred to it above as the basic motivational unity – the 'brick' in the dynamic structure – which we have called the 'attitude'. An attitude, by its dictionary definition, should obviously indicate a readiness to act in a certain direction if circumstances should permit. This readiness to act is created by the pressure of a certain situation. For example, a person might have the attitude, 'I want so much to go to the movies', which might be created by the situation of being on his own in a strange town and, therefore, feeling lonely. When he has money in his pocket and the time is appropriate, this attitude will express itself in actually going to the movies – i.e. we can eventually always refer an attitude to some definable, observable behaviour. An attitude may, therefore, be defined as *an interest in a course of action, in a given situation*.

This brings the attitude into the general paradigm of stimulus–response behaviour, as stated above, and, indeed we may represent its parts in the following generalization:

In these circumstances,	*I*	*want so much*	*to do this*	*with that.*
stimulus situation	organism	interest of a certain intensity	specific goal and course of action	object concerned

There are, of course, transient attitudes, new attitudes, etc., which change rapidly with the situation, and on which the trigger release from inhibition never happens to occur so that they never get into behaviour. But for simplicity of discussion here, we shall assume that we are dealing with stabilized attitudes in an individual which repeatedly express themselves in appropriate action in a measurably stable life situation. That being the case, we recognize that certain provocations in any person's environment cause him at intervals to show the kind of response to the situation defined by the attitude. The frequency and intensity of this response will vary positively with the strength with which the situation stimulates it and inversely with the frequency with which the environment gratifies it. The reader familiar with the sociological–psychological researches on 'attitudes' at the polling booth, and political attitudes, should recognize that the definition of attitude here in the stimulus–response system is quite different from that to which he has been accustomed in polling, where one speaks of an attitude as being only *for or against* an object. Here, on the other hand, the attitude is a course of action, in which an object may be involved, but which is *not* primarily simply for or against the object. It does not make much sense to ask whether a young man viewing a girl on the other side of a bus is for or against her, or whether he is for or against a sunset or a beefsteak. The fact is that attitudes are far more varied than for and against, and this unfortunately rather entrenched sociological–psychological 'attitude study' is a mere travesty of the true dynamic complexity of attitudes. One can feel curious about, reverent towards, interested in overcoming, and so on in the typical real attitude. The formulation of for or against is like a black and white photograph, making a pale imitation of the full colour of the real scene. It abstracts from the total emotional richness some one particular dimension, which may not always be the most important, or one which even makes good sense. Accordingly, let it be understood from this point on that when we talk about an attitude, we mean a course of action in relation to a situation, which course of action is typically allowed intermittently to express itself, by appropriate lifting of the inhibition. Our problem is to measure the intensity of interest in following that course of action. The new motivation measurement principles and devices set out to measure it more validly than by verbal opinionnaires.

OBJECTIVE DEVICES: THE INTEGRATED AND UNINTEGRATED COMPONENTS

If an unsophisticated student were asked to find out how good a measure can be obtained from using a certain principle, he might look around for some 'criterion' of intensity of interest and try to compare the given measure against it, in the case of some given attitude. For example, he might take the amount of money the person is willing to spend to satisfy this attitude, or the amount of time he spends in the course of activity indicated by the attitude. However, our experience with intelligence and general personality traits above has made us rightly suspicious that any *single* concrete criterion could really be able to stand for a *general* concept – in this case, interest strength. For example, the amount of money the person is prepared to spend may depend a good deal also on what he has in the bank, and the amount of time he gives might be much affected by how many hours he has to devote to earning a living. The student in this field might perhaps next suggest that we abandon any single criterion and that we measure the same attitude by *all* of some fifty different devices and then add up the total score upon the lot. By correlating each separate device with this grand total we might find *which* of the single measurements comes closest to the consensus of all of them. This is an improvement, but still it begs an important question. 'What if the thing we are measuring, called motivation strength, is not some single entity – as this "pool of the lot" suggests – but several distinct things?' Moreover, even if it were a single entity, it is possible that our pool of variables is an unbalanced selection accidentally stressing some one kind of measurement approach much more than others, and by this method of validation, perpetuating its own imbalance.

Accordingly, what was done in the actual history of research here was to correlate the methods together, and then by factor analysis to discover what are *the number and nature of independent influences here*. This, of course, was done using the eighty devices upon several distinct attitudes, to make sure the experiment is not obtaining an answer which is true only of one kind of attitude. The experimenters were rewarded to find that the results were, in fact, virtually identical despite different attitude contents or subject matter. It appears now that there are, in fact, some *seven* or eight factors among motivation measurements, and these have been called *motivational components* and identified by the Greek letters from alpha to zeta. The names for them are at the moment interpretations at an exploratory level and need to be intensively examined by further research.

The first of these factors, the alpha factor, has been called the id component in interests, because like the psychoanalytic concept of the id, it involves most of those manifestations which express an untutored 'I wish' or 'I want'. The factor loads such manifestations as autism, i.e. believing what fits one's wish, rationalization – inventing glib reasons to justify what one wants to believe, a quick decision time when deciding what one wants, a high fluency on the cues which stimulate the given course of action, and also a straight statement of preferences in the opinionnaire statement, 'I want to do this'. It is a component of interest and desire which brooks no objection from the outside world.

The second, or beta, factor has manifestations which clearly indicate a matured interest which has been brought into contact with reality. It marks an interest which has learnt its position, so to speak, in the scheme of things. It loads most highly *information* on the topic. That is to say, if a person expresses his interest in a topic, he proves to have a well-furnished mind on the means to attain his end in this area, which shows that the attitude is part of the integrated ego. He also learns a foreign language more rapidly when it has to do with this interest. He can quote readily the kinds of rewards that will follow from such a course of action. He gives a large galvanic skin reflex response if the interest is threatened or insulted, which is a sign of readiness for effective action on behalf of an interest. And he is able in the 'competitive inhibition' situation to bring the perception of things involved in this interest out of their entanglement with other interests. The 'competitive inhibition' test can be illustrated most readily in the auditory realm. A record is played in which a conversation on the topic of interest is over-laid by a good deal of noise and by conversations on other topics. The person is scored on the degree to which he is able to pick out the theme of interest.

For ease of description the above paragraph has outlined the behaviour of a person high on the beta factor, as if he were a 'type'. But these components are in all of us. As far as the evidence goes, every interest of every person has some of each component, but some interests are sustained more by one component than another, and some people have *all* their interests more sustained by a kind of component than do other people. The beta component, which has been called the ego component, shows that the interest has been thought about, put in its proper relation in the person's scheme of things, connexion with the real skills and information necessary to sustain it, and so on. The gamma component, in turn, has the 'I ought to be interested' quality of the super-ego.

One of the most interesting of the motivational components is epsilon, which loads three major manifestations: (1) the psychogalvanic reflex response, (2) a poorness of memory for the given material, and, especially, (3) a poorness of reminiscence. (The psychologist's distinction between memory and reminiscence is that the former is concerned with the amount immediately recalled and the latter with spontaneous afterthought and consolidation – or the converse – which go on after conscious recall is ended.) Investigators had noted many years ago, in experimenting with word associations, that when a word given to a mental patient is known to hit on one of his complexes, he will react to it with a big psychogalvanic jerk, but, half an hour afterwards, will show relatively poor memory for that word, and still poorer spontaneous reminiscence. Consequently, the symptom constituted by a combination of large galvanic reflex (which is generally and normally related to *stronger* memory for a word) with distinctly poorer memory and a black-out reminiscence has long been considered an indicator of a 'complex', in the psychoanalytic sense. Indeed, this and other signs lead us to consider the delta factor specifically as that contribution to an interest which comes from an unconscious motivation from earlier fixations and conflict experiences. It is a capricious interest which both approaches and runs away from its object, as a man may keep prodding with his tongue a suspectedly painful tooth.

The delta component is almost entirely a physiological reactivity in the expression of interest, for it expresses itself most in psychogalvanic skin 'shiver', drop of the blood pressure, etc., though also in greater quickness of decision. Perhaps this is the component which caused Wordsworth's heart to dance with the daffodils or called forth the lines 'My heart leaps up when I behold a rainbow in the sky'. Both alpha and delta components evidently operate partly below the level of consciousness, but they are not inaccessible, whereas epsilon ('complex') interest is something repressed and rendered definitely unconscious as a result of conflict. Indeed, clinical psychologists should get a lot of use from measures set up to determine the epsilon component in an interest, because we would expect it to be particularly prominent wherever a piece of behaviour is of a neurotic nature and springs from repressed roots.

This brief overview of measurement research is perhaps as much as we need to illustrate the wide variety of devices which mark the seven motivational components. Psychologists are beginning to realize that the re-analysis of motivation made in the motivation components system renders obsolete the distinction between 'misperception' or 'projective tests' on the one hand and the great variety of other objective motivation measures. The *real* distinctions, in the seven or so components, are among dynamic *sources* of interest strength, and as far as these are concerned each involves some misperception (projection) devices and some other kinds of device. The form of the test presentation is relatively simple and unimportant.

Both this consideration, and the demonstration of Wenig, referred to above, that projective tests are actually not clear tests of the psychoanalytic projection principle, makes the label an out-of-date one. Even with the more correct operational definition as the *misperception* sub-species of *objective motivation devices,* the tests are not to be recommended as comparable in validity to a properly balanced set of objective tests, grouped under components. For the discussion on instrument factors above makes it highly probable that to measure motive strength solely through 'projective' tests is to contaminate with a large instrument factor error avoided in a set of objective motivation component measures.

The student alert to research implications may have noted too that this discovery of seven distinct motivational components plays havoc also with the traditional method among sociologists of assigning a *single* score to an attitude or sentiment. Obviously any one attitude should really be given seven distinct scores, and our predictions about what the person with this attitude will do will presumably depend upon these score 'qualities' being kept distinct. This is a pretty awkward situation for the applied psychologist, since it seems to complicate tremendously his job of measuring attitudes. For example, if some political prediction requires a poll on the attitude to social question X, then it would seem that we have to describe seven distinct kinds of interest in attitude X and its strength, and that each of these may have different consequences for prediction. This may be one reason why public opinion polling so frequently goes wrong, since current interviewing and survey work apparently depend largely on the alpha component (which contains the opinionnaire or preference sub-test) and neglect the others. Indeed, they depend completely on the device of verbal self-evaluation of interest.

However, since in so many fields of psychological measurement, for example, ability testing, we have found that a number of primary factors may themselves, in turn, be factor analytically grouped to yield some single broader structure the hope arose that the same simplification could be made here. Such a broader structure, if found, normally does not give all the detailed information of the single factors, but it brings about an economy of testing time and may be the best thing to use in measurement. In the present case, the factoring of the seven motivational components does not yield a single broad second-order factor. It yields two such factors (plus some debris), which have been called, respectively, the *integrated* and the *unintegrated* components in interest. The integrated component is determined by the motivational components from the ego (beta) and from the super-ego

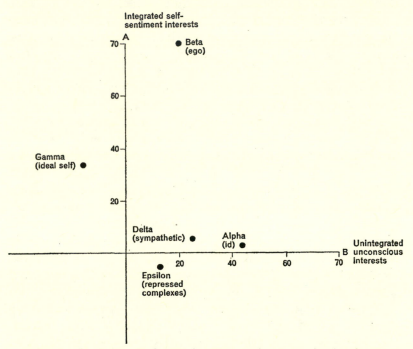

Diagram 20. Relation of second-order to primary motivation factors

(gamma), whereas the unintegrated, or unconscious component is contributed by the physiological measures, (delta), the id component, the hidden complex component, and so on, as shown in Diagram 20. Although U and I (the representative symbols we shall use for these two major factors) are better called Integrated and Unintegrated than Conscious and Unconscious, since some of the contributors to the Unintegrated are partly conscious, clinical psychologists have been apt to call them by the more familiar terms Unconscious and Conscious. Unconscious is not much

amiss, but essentially the U-interest manifestations are unintegrated in the sense that they have an 'I wish' or an 'I want'
quality, but several are, either dimly or even relatively fully,
conscious. Certainly they are associated with day-dream activity.
Furthermore, the I or integrated components may not in psychoanalytic terms be wholly conscious, for it covers the ego and
super-ego, which give social consistency to behaviour, yet the
super-ego is not viewed in clinical theory as mainly conscious.

In the subsequent work which we shall now describe on structuring attitudes according to their content it will be understood
that commonly the battery of several sub-tests used to measure
each different attitude has been a balanced measure of these two
components U and I, which have frequently been added to give
a single score. Like the sociologist, we need to operate at times
with a single total score. However, it is hard to find real rationale
for adding these with equal weight to give a single score – other
than, perhaps, a convention that conscious and unconscious components are equally important! In many cases, it may prove
more interesting to look at the content structure in terms of one of
them only.

The important point to grasp in getting a view over this rather
complex section is that research has now arrived at more valid
ways of measuring the strength of interest and motivation than
through questionnaires and self-evaluations, which have been
used so long, for example, in the Strong and Kuder and many
lesser interest tests. Also the new techniques should eventually
supersede so-called projective devices, as in the Thematic Apperception Test, the Picture Frustration, the Szondi, and countless others. The reliability of these has always been extremely
poor, and different psychologists reach quite different conclusions
from the same responses upon them. As we have seen, true projection, and several other improved misperception measurements,
turn out to have appreciable validity against the motivation component factors, but to avoid instrument factors it is important to
have them balanced by half a dozen different types of device, not
all of which are perceptual, or defence mechanisms. Over the last
fifteen years the new methods of measurement in the objective
domain have been very widely explored by a dozen enterprising

investigators and have yielded batteries – notably the Motivation Analysis Test, called the M.A.T. – which have precisely determinable validities in terms of these motivation components. It is reassuring to the 'practical' man, moreover, that they give quite good predictions against such measures as the amount of time or the amount of money a person spends on an interest activity. The exciting thing to the psychologist, however, is that these measures fit into a quite systematic theoretical framework, with a known mathematical model, which permits all kinds of calculations and insights not possible through simple projective or self-evaluative devices.

HOW CAN DYNAMIC STRUCTURES BE DISCOVERED AND DEMONSTRATED?

At this point our attention moves on from asking how one measures the *strength* of a motive to asking how one determines what its ultimate goal may be. This is what we mean when we ask 'What are his motives?' In psychological terms we are no longer concentrating on measuring the strength of a motive, in terms of component scores, for this has substantially been solved, but we are seeking the methods of revealing dynamic structure.

In everyday life we think we have many ways of deciding what people's dynamic goals may be, and what the main dynamic structures are which make them tick. In fact, the average human being has become very good at this, in an intuitive sense, because survival has often depended upon being sophisticated about the motives of others. Nevertheless, it would defy most people's powers of explanation to describe explicitly the signs by which they judge motives, or what practical arrangements they could best make to carry out 'an experiment' to investigate someone's intentions.

As regards simple strength of motive, popular observation has hit on signs of the same kind as some of those which have been systematically experimentally explored in arriving at the motivational components above. For example, consider our muscle tension 'device'. If Mary gives a start and drops a dish when her mother is talking about Johnny Brown, Mother may become a little suspicious that Johnny Brown means more to her daughter than she hitherto supposed. Or consider the memory signs we have used. If a person knows by heart the telephone numbers of X and Y, but never remembers those of A, B, and C, a similar inference may be made. Not only do we use intuitively quite a number of the principles that have entered into motivational component testing, but we also use what was described above as 'an experiment'. For example, since most people do most things for mixed motives, and since some motives are more respectable than others, a considerable class of social skills has become habitual in most people, either in the interests of self-protection or of tact, in dwelling a little more on the desirable motives than on others which may be neutral or for some reason undesirable. If one is uncertain whether Archibald is pursuing Susan for love or money, then someone may 'experiment' by mentioning that Susan is disinherited. From Archibald's reaction to this news, the observer makes certain inferences.

This complexity of motives has been represented in a model by a device called the dynamic lattice, as shown in Diagram 21 below. The idea shown here is that each attitude 'subsidiates' to another attitude, which, in turn, 'subsidiates' to another, and so on. That is to say, we do A in order to do B in order to gain the satisfaction of C, and so on. For example, a person may study accountancy in order that he may keep his job in a big business in order that he may earn money in order that he may marry and have a family, and so on. The dynamic lattice is thus a 'flow chart' of nearer and more remote dynamic goals. It brings out the important point that attitudes are not just subsidiated in a long chain but that they converge on nodes and redistribute therefrom. What we just refer to as mixed motives means that a single immediate sub-goal often subsidiates to *several* more remote goals.

It will be noted that the various attitudes in the dynamic lattice subsidiate in the last resort to basic 'instinctive' goals, written over to the right of Diagram 21 as ergic goals. It seems that we are so constructed that our final satisfactions have to be instinctive ones, or *ergic* ones. The term *erg*, from the Greek *ergon* for work or energy, is used in the dynamic calculus for a structure which has hitherto been called, at once too vaguely and elaborately, an instinct or drive which is the energy source behind behaviour. As we shall see in a moment, an erg (hard g) can be precisely factor-analytically located and defined, whereas instinct, need, drive, etc., have become all things to all men and can no longer be used with scientific precision. An erg, an ergic (pronounced as in allergic) tension, an ergically determined atti-

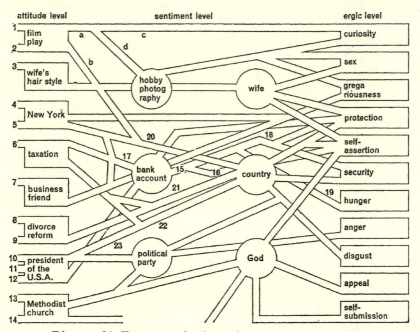

Diagram 21. Fragment of a dynamic lattice, showing attitude subsidiation, sentiment structure, and ergic goals

tude, etc., can, on the other hand, be demonstrated by analysis and measured by objective tests.

From what both animal and clinical study have shown we can contingently best adopt the hypothesis that any series of attitude-interests – of courses of action from sub-goal to sub-goal – must finally end in an ergic goal, as indicated by the need for food, for drink, for security, and so on. The sexual goal and many others are also ergic goals, in that they are pursued, for example, even by primitive peoples who do not know that the begetting of children is connected with sexual intercourse. (And by civilized folk they are evidently pursued far beyond any rational ends of maintaining the population!) An ergic goal is thus a goal in itself, as to the desirability of which there is no arguing, and beyond which no further goal exists *in the make up of the organism.*

How do we determine these subsidiations, and the nature of the primary ergic factor goals to which they lead? The simple way is to ask someone, 'What are you studying accountancy for?' And if he replies, 'To hold my job,' you may say, 'Why do you want to hold that job!' and so on. But in any such string of questions – if your subject is patient and also ready to answer on private matters frankly – you will nevertheless eventually come to a point beyond which he can give you no answer. You come to some such question as, 'Why do you want to eat?' At this point you come to the biological categorical imperative of an ergic goal. Such a 'depth interview' or psychoanalytic 'free association' might permit you to draw a dynamic lattice for the given person, at a rough level of accuracy, showing which particular attitudes subsidiate to which ultimate goals.

Unravelling the lattice by such methods as free association – talking aimlessly – and hypnotism is a standard task in clinical psychology. The greater part of psychoanalytic diagnosis, for example, is concerned with finding out the subsidiations of attitudes – but particularly of the neurotic attitudes we call symptoms – in order to get at the roots of neurotic troubles. The difficulty has long proved to be that often the person does not himself know what the connexions are. In the diagram above, we could and should substitute at many places more short dotted lines for the continuous lines to present connexions that run underground. Free association and the depth interview succeed only to a limited degree, and with much exasperation and guesswork, in exposing these connexions. Fortunately it has recently been shown that the same experimental and statistical methods as have enabled us to disentangle personality structure in temperamental and ability fields will also work effectively here in psychodynamics. Conservative psychologists doubted that the experimental and statistical methods of relating the 'bricks' to find the 'house structure' would work in the more subtle and everchanging world of human motivation as well as they had done in the comparatively straightforward field of abilities. But the pioneer psychologists who tried these methods were surprised to find that the evidence comes out even more clearly than in the traditional ability structure field. Let us see how a typical experiment proceeds.

One begins by measuring the strength of, say, some forty attitudes, chosen to be diverse in the area of life in which they are important. The measurement is done by the objective batteries discussed above. These strength measures are over, say, 200–300 typical persons in our culture. A glance at the correlation matrix shows that various attitudes come together in sub-groups, which means that the members of such a sub-group have a tendency to vary together in strength. Among these we can assume, therefore, that there must be some functional connexion. Indeed, if we go through a complete factor–analytic procedure, we are in fact obtaining objective evidence on the connecting lines in the dynamic (Diagram 21) lattice itself. Thus, for example, all the attitudes which normally subsidiate to the goal of security, i.e. the habitual response patterns which have been built up to serve the erg of fear and escape, will tend to be simultaneously stronger in a person whose need for security is greater than in another who is bolder. This experimental measurement connexion will produce correlations in any group of people, and enable us to see what the associations are.

Alternatively, of course, we can measure the forty or so attitudes in just one person – in what the last chapter defined as P-technique – remeasuring them every day for perhaps 100 days. On some days we would expect a person's ergs, or drives, to stand at higher levels than on others. For example, on one day the individual may feel lonely and his gregarious need is higher, and on another day he may feel more fearful, and his need for security is greater, and on yet another day his sexual drive may be greater and he will be more amorous, and so on. The result of this should be that all the attitudes and courses of action which have drawn their strength and energy from one of these drives should tend to vary together from day to day. It was a woman psychologist, Patricia Cross, who first performed the laborious but crucial P-technique experiment of correlating behaviours and symptoms within the same person over a period of roughly 100 days as mentioned above, and came out with the evidence vital to dynamic calculus theory that the same drive structures in fact appear as in the inter-individual method.

From the standpoint of fifty years of speculation about human and mammalian drives and their roles the striking results of either of these approaches is that they finish by demonstrating a clear-cut set of ergic structures such as have long been conjectured by clinicians and social theorists. They are much the same also as animal observers ('ethologists' as they are now more accurately named), such as Lorenz, McDougall, and Tinbergen have inferred from watching the natural behaviour of the higher mammals. The latter resemble us so much in their general physiology, nervous system, and even anatomical structure, as Darwin first clearly brought out, that it would be extraordinary if we did not also share with them whatever constitutional impulses, emotions, and spontaneous attention capacities exist in the main ergs.

By these newer methods it has thus become possible to show that some at least of the earlier conjectures are correct in supposing

TABLE 17

Fear erg attitudes

I want my country to get more protection against the terror of the atom bomb	0·5
I want to see any formidable militaristic power that actively threatens us attacked and destroyed	0·5
I want to see the danger of death by accident and disease reduced	0·4
I want to see those responsible for inflation punished	0·4
I want never to be an insane patient in a mental hospital	0·4
I want to see a reduction of income tax for those in my bracket	0·3
I want to take out more insurance against illness	0·3
I want to become proficient in my career	0·3
I want my country to have power and influence in the world	0·5
I like to take part in political arguments	0·3

(*a*) separate ergic sources of reactivity or energy, (*b*) particular natures and goals for these ergs. Speculations had ranged from two or three 'instincts' (Freud) to sixteen (McDougall) to twenty-eight (Murray). The experimental verdict so far is that there are some ten main dynamic structures, of the general nature of ergs, in human beings. They include sex, fear, gregariousness, self-assertion, parental pity and protectiveness, pugnacity, etc. The evidence for any one of these resides in a particular pattern of 'loadings' on a set of attitudes. Thus, Tables 17 and 18 show the loadings or sets of attitudes on the fear drive and the sex erg,

TABLE 18

Sex erg attitudes

I want to fall in love with a beautiful woman	0·5
I want to satisfy my sexual needs	0·5
I like sexual attractiveness in a woman	0·5
I like to see a good movie now and then	0·4
I like a novel with love interest and a ravishing heroine	0·4
I like to enjoy smoking and drinking	0·4
I want to see more good restaurants serving attractive food	0·3
I want to listen to music	0·3
I want to travel and explore the world	0·3

respectively. It should be remembered that each of the attitudes stated in terms of a verbal phrase here has actually been measured by some sixty separate measures on six different motivation component devices. The latter, as discussed in Section 4 above, include the psychogalvanic response to words having to do with that attitude, the extent to which beliefs and perceptions are autistically misperceived, the memory for words having to do with that attitude, the amount of information the person has on courses of action helping the attitude, by the rate at which he can learn new material that has to do with that particular goal, and so on through the objective tests which ultimately lead to the integrated and unintegrated component scores. When the results of such an experiment come through the computing machine, it is found, regardless of the theorist's wishes from older *a priori* lists, that the attitudes neatly segregate themselves into those which would be expected on the hypothesis of the above nine or so ergic structures. That is to say, all the attitudes having a single, emotional goal, despite quite diverse social-cultural situations, come together in a single erg.

THE NATURE OF THE MAIN SENTIMENT STRUCTURES,
INCLUDING THE SELF

As researchers extended their coverage of many human interests and attitudes they were surprised to see factor patterns coming out of the experiments which could not be identified with the nine or so drive patterns just mentioned, and which did not look at all like constitutionally given interests. For example, the patterns did not resemble anything which our biological relatives, the primates and the higher mammals, possess. They turned out to form a class of patterns the content of each of which, in general, centres upon some one social institution, such as the family, one's job, one's church, one's chief recreational hobby interest, one's nation, and so on.

These new dynamic structures, visible as common reactive patterns on which most people have some degree of endowment, have been called *sentiments,* since the common use of the word 'sentiment' has always had this connotation. It is presumed that if one person, for example, goes to church much more than another person, then he will acquire not just one attitude, but *a whole set of attitudes* (attitudes functional in church membership) in some stronger degree than the person who does not go to church much. That is to say, a learning experience goes on which *simultaneously* raises the strength of all these attitudes and thus

TABLE 19

Sentiment to religion

I want to feel that I am in touch with God, or some principle in the universe that gives meaning and help in my struggles	0·6
I want to see the standards of organized religion maintained or increased throughout our lives	0·6
I want to have my parents' advice and to heed their wishes in planning my affairs	0·4
I want my parents never to be lacking the necessities of comfortable living	0·3
I do not want to see birth control available to all	0·2
I want more protection against the atom bomb	0·2
I want my country to be the most powerful and influential	0·2
I want to help the distressed, wherever they are	0·2
I do not want to spend more time playing cards	0·2

produces a structural unity among them, which is something quite different from the structural unity of the innate ergic patterns of interest.

Examples of such patterns are shown in Tables 19 and 20. The first is clearly a confirmation of the religious sentiment about which we have just been speculating, while the second, derived from an experiment with objective motivation measures on Air Force men, clearly refers to a 'sentiment to one's profession', in this case that of an officer pilot. The first way in which one notices that a sentiment structure is different from an erg is that the

TABLE 20

Sentiment to career
(Air Force)

I want to make my career in the Air Force	0·70
I like the excitement and adventure of combat flying	0·63
I want to get technical education such as the Air Force provides	0·58
I enjoy commanding men and taking the responsibilities of a military leader	0·44
I do not want to take more time to enjoy rest and to sleep later in the mornings	−0·41
I like being up in an aeroplane	0·41
I want to satisfy my sense of duty to my country by enlisting in its most important defence arm in threatening times	0·39
I want to become first-rate at my Air Force job	0·36
I do not want to spend more time at home puttering around	−0·36

emotional (ergic goal) qualities which enter it are very diverse, whereas in an erg they are all of one quality, e.g. gregariousness, sex. From inspecting 'content' (see Tables 18, 19, and 20) we notice that in an erg there is one drive goal quality and many different social learning fields. But in a sentiment there is diversity of emotional roots and satisfactions along with a single sociological object or institution. The sentiment brings together attitudes, in fact, with several *different* ergic roots, but only *one* source of learning – the repeated experiences of rewarded behaviour simultaneously affecting a wide set of attitudes. In Table 20 it is the attitudes which make a good officer in the Air Force organization. The existence of such unitary pattern makes it possible to set up a battery of objective tests from the scores on which one can speak with some confidence of the strength of a given individual's total interest in his occupation, or the strength of the sentiment and loyalty which he has developed to home, wife, abstract values, or any other environmental experience.

So far we have distinguished the erg and the sentiment on a purely experimental basis, pointing out that one can recognize a natural tendency of dynamic factors to fall into two descriptive classes. It has also been pointed out that the origins of the cor-relations among attitudes could be due in the one case to a com-mon biological source of energy – as when all hunger manifesta-tions vary together – and in the other to a common experience of learning – as when the degrees of adoption of all church attitudes vary together. But what does this mean in dynamic terms? Animal psychologists have referred to something fairly close to these human research findings in a jargon of 'primary' and 'secondary' drives; but this misses the main point: that they are totally dif-ferent in origin. The sentiment, it is true, may be said to have 'borrowed' its energy from the ergs, but its form and origin is entirely due to the impress of the cultural learning pattern. Fur-thermore, its drive quality is not the uniform drive energy of an erg, but is a confluence, borrowed from several ergs. The senti-ment, it is true, is an existing source of interest and energy, but it is only a 'holding company' for the energy basically coming from ergs. Like an erg, it is called a dynamic structure, because it is a predictable source of interest, attention, work, and learning; but unlike an erg it may, in the course of experience, disintegrate again and decay to nothing. This is uncommon – the statistical evidence shows that after twenty our interest systems remain pretty stable. But under psychoanalysis, or political brainwash-ing, or a transplantation to another culture, sentiments are cap-able of great change.

One of the largest and most psychologically significant of the sentiment patterns which have so far appeared is that shown in Table 21. Consideration of the attitudes involved shows that it must be regarded as the 'sentiment to the self'. Since the early literary analyses of the self concept carried out with such superb skill by William James and McDougall, psychologists have been well aware that each individual develops a set of attitudes centred upon himself, just as he does for any other important sentiment object in his environment. Developmentally we recognize that at two or three years of age he often begins to refer to himself in the third person, 'Joe is a good boy'. He is becoming capable of conceiving himself as an object, with real characteristics like any other entity he thinks about. Furthermore, he soon shows signs that he can regulate his behaviour by an increasingly accurate self-conception, in regard to physical powers, mental capacities, and so forth. He becomes motivated to preserve an acceptable self-concept in his own eyes and in what he believes to be the opinion of others. This self-concept comes, by virtue of the dynamic resources vested in it in the self-sentiment habit

TABLE 21

The self-sentiment

I like to have good control over all my mental processes – my memory, impulses and general behaviour	0·4
I want never to do anything that would damage my sense of self-respect	0·4
I want to be first-rate in my job	0·3
I want to take part in citizenship activities in the community in which I live	0·3
I want to maintain a reputation for honest and high principles among my fellows	0·3
I like commanding men and taking the responsibilities of a leader	0·3
I want to satisfy my sense of duty to my country	0·3
I want never to be an insane patient in a mental hospital	0·3
I do not want to spend more time in sleep	0·3
I want to give my wife the good things she should have	0·3
I want to spend more time reading	0·3

structure, to control the impulses of ergs and to integrate the lesser sentiments, within a consistent working system. A measure of the strength of the self-sentiment thus might be expected to help predict the degree of socially acceptable behaviour which the person can manage and the consistency of his self-organization. This has already been shown by the M.A.T. and S.M.A.T. (School Motivation Analysis Test) batteries to be true, for the measure correlates positively in high-school children with school achievement, when intelligence is constant, and negatively with delinquent tendencies. Parenthetically, one may note that the studies of the 'achievement motive' in various modern societies by McClelland at Harvard are closely connected with this self-sentiment. Its pattern is obviously going to vary from culture to culture, in that for some societies physical courage will be a required trait of a self-respecting person, in others civility, in others achievement. The motivation towards achievement can be shown actually to spring from three distinct dynamic sources: (*a*) the self-sentiment, as here, (*b*) the super-ego, to be discussed, and (*c*) a simple erg of self-assertiveness, akin to that which shows itself in display in male mammals, as mentioned under ergs above.

Before proceeding further let us ask to what foundation of practical measurement in the motivation field these research developments lead. Obviously the shift must take place from opinionnaires and verbally stated preference tests to objective devices of known motivation component validity, and freedom from a single instrument factor. Secondly, psychologists are setting out to measure dynamic traits which have research demonstration as unitary structures.

The Motivational Analysis Test (M.A.T.) and the School Motivational Analysis Test (S.M.A.T.) are among the first tests designed to meet these requirements, and they present themselves as batteries for either group or individual administration. If given in the group form they include only four types of objective sub-test: (1) Autism, (2) Projection, (3) Word Association, and (4) Information. But if circumstances permit individual administration, (5) Reaction Time and (6) Galvanic Skin Response are added. Examples will be given below.

The tests measure the strength of the ten largest known dynamic factors, including five ergic tension levels – for sex, self-assertion, fear, etc. – and five sentiments – to home, to the self, etc. The choice of dynamic structures in M.A.T. is such as to orient it particularly to clinical work, whereas S.M.A.T. is intended for general school psychological work, including prediction of scholarship achievement, analysis of adjustment problems, and vocational guidance. Examples of the items for the various devices are given in Table 22.

Granted that strengths on the principal dynamic structure factors are scored, they can be used either as ergic tension level

TABLE 22

Example of items from M.A.T. (Motivational Analysis Test)

Autism

Self-assertion: What percentage of people feel that a person's status is properly shown by his appearance and that 'clothes make the man or woman'?

80%	50%	20%	0
3	2	1	0

Fear: The money spent by cities to protect their citizens from atomic attack has gone up in ten years by:

20%	50%	100%	200%
0	1	2	3

Utilities

More research money should be spent on:

Self-assertion: (a) Dressing the nation in smarter styles and new fabrics.
Fear: (b) Finding cures for radiation sickness.

More newspaper articles should stress:

Super-ego: (a) Self-control in facing sexual distractions.
Self-sentiment: (b) Gaining happiness by being socially useful.

Information

A stoic is:

    (a) a person who seeks pleasures of a physical nature.
    (b) a basic coin of Ethiopia.
    (c) *a person not affected by passions.*
    (d) a small haystack in a field.   *SELF-ASSERTION* *

Which of the following has the highest reputation as a man of honesty and principle?

    (a) Talleyrand
    (b) Charlie Chaplin
    (c) Theodore Roosevelt
    (d) *Woodrow Wilson*   *SUPER-EGO*

Paired Words

Red ⟨ cross (*SUPER-EGO*) / lips (*SEX*)   Country ⟨ club (*SELF-ASSERTION*) / cottage (*HOME*)

Autism

Self-sentiment: How many people feel it is more important to be honest than popular?

100%	80%	60%	40%	20%
4	3	2	1	0

Self-assertion: How many people would like to be head of the government?

90%	70%	50%	30%	10%
4	3	2	1	0

Information

What people think of you is called your:

        (a) *reputation*

        (b) experience

        (c) disposition

        (d) ambition   *Self-sentiment*

Which official is responsible for the accuracy of the financial report?

        (a) President

        (b) Vice-President

        (c) Secretary

        (d) *Treasurer*   *Self-assertion*

Paired Words

STUDENT ⟨ body (*Self-assertion*) / learn (*Curiosity*)   BOOK ⟨ Bank (*Acquisition*) / Bible (*Religious sentiment*)

Memory

Subject looks at this list for several seconds:		Then subject turns page and tries to pick previous words from this list:	
Bank	(*Acquisition*)	Defend	Most
Rest	(*Sensuality*)	Gloomy	Invitation
Invitation	(*Self-sentiment*)	Rest	Outline
Unselfish	(*Super-ego*)	Conceit	Century
Defend	(*Patriotism*)	Date	Unselfish
		Bank	Church

---

* (The categories presented in capitals are, of course, not printed on the test itself.)

indicators, guide clinical practice or physiological research or social learning studies interested in drive tension levels and the formation of sentiments, or to make predictions for individuals on particular attitudes and interests by the same type of 'specification equation' as has been used for general personality prediction. The familiar specification equation weighting factors by situational indices according to their involvement in the particular behaviour now becomes:

$$I_j = s_{jE_1}E_1 \ldots + s_{jE_k}E_k + s_{jM_1}M_1 \ldots + s_{jM_l}M_l$$

where I_j is the strength of interest in the course of action stimulated by the particular situation designated j. The E's are the ergic tension strengths (k of them), and the M's are the strengths of the sentiments (l of them). (Specific factors are omitted, in order not to obscure the main statement of the equation.)

SITUATIONS AND SATISFACTIONS AFFECTING SCORES
ON DYNAMIC TRAITS

From our common sense experience, in our own behaviour and that of others, we realize that these sentiment-strength and ergic tension measures will obviously not stay constant for one person over time in the way that general personality factors and abilities tend to stay tolerably constant. For example, a person's sense of security or insecurity may be provoked by happenings reported in the newspaper, or by something that happened to his bank account, or fear of illness in a relative or himself, thus changing the whole level of his ergic tension on some basic erg. Not only will the general fearfulness level of the individual thus fluctuate from time to time, and situation to situation, but even the strengths of' sentiments will alter steadily with learning or decay with time and circumstance, as Keats regretted that sentiments to loved objects cannot last 'Or new Love pine at them beyond tomorrow.' As these underlying factors change, so a person's reaction to any particular concrete stimulation of interest will change. For example, it is well known, and can be shown even by measurement, that a person will show more of a startle response to some small stimulus when he is already in a state of fear tension about some major situation than in other circumstances. Shakespeare used this mechanism to show the degree of tension under which Macbeth was living, starting in his guilt at every sound. When he heard some frightful cry, his wife merely 'heard the owl scream and the crickets cry'. Our ergic tension levels are all the time changing with their general stimulation by environment and the amounts of goal satisfaction they currently receive, but in ways not yet understood in detailed formulae. From the above account of the structure of motivation components and dynamic traits the reader eager to master the subject would naturally wish to proceed to the laws and principles describing how these measures change with learning, with physiology, with motivation and conflict, home and life experience. But we have to confess that the road ends not far from here, like a half-constructed highway. One can go farther, but only into the speculative and contradictory jungle of the clinical phase of theorizing. When more of the research surveying teams can push this solid experimental work into clinical, educational, and other applied fields, these instruments will demonstrate the capacity to give us our laws and principles of human dynamics. Meanwhile, except for certain rewarding practical predictions by objective dynamic measures to be described in the 'applied' Chapter 11, what follows is a logical analysis with far more scant experimental basis than the findings reported to this point.

An obviously important area of research is the relation of ergic tension levels to physiological causes. It has long been known that hunger sensations are associated with the onset of stomach churnings, that sexual desire is deficient in eunuchs, and that water-seeking behaviour in animals is a comparatively simple function of their physiological dehydration. Perhaps the whole secret of motivation resides in physiology? Some psychologists have thought so, and yet one has to be suspicious of the tendency of psychologists to escape into 'good concrete physiology' whenever the going gets difficult in the strictly behavioural field. And, as we have seen, it *did* get difficult to make headway in behavioural experiments until the researchers shifted from the cramped bivariate to the more comprehensive multivariate experiment. Interaction between two scientific disciplines is greatly to be encouraged, but only if trade is two-sided. Now that psychologists can go to physiology with clear concepts of drives and sentiments, and reliable measures of them, it should be richly profitable to look for physiological connexions. But not earlier, when psychologists could offer nothing precise with which to connect physiological measurements.

On the physiological side the work has been very largely with animals. Numerous interesting connexions of behaviour with kinds of deprivation have been shown by Young and O'Kelly. Some countercheck to too simple a physiological account of drives has been offered by Harlow of Wisconsin, who shows that Rhesus monkeys will often do more for the sake of curiosity, or mother love, than for the grosser physiological needs. In fact, some interesting comparisons of strengths of drive have been made in choice-box experiments with animals, which put hunger above sex, and maternal protectiveness above hunger.

More recently physiological psychologists have shown by implanting electrodes in the under-brain (hypothalamus and thalamus) of rats and cats that particular desires – to eat, to drink, to fight, to escape – can be powerfully excited by electrical stimulation there. In this way, or by injecting chemicals in the right zone, particular drives can be excited, akin to a mood, so that a cat, for example, will get angry with everything it sees. There is no doubt that the neurological areas of drives are now tolerably well located in animals. But all this helps us only a little way along in understanding the laws of complex motivation in man.

Human behavioural experiments show that ergic tension levels are quite susceptible to physiological deprivation. For example, an individual who has not eaten for a long time can become excruciatingly sensitive to the smell and sight of food. Moreover, his thoughts and imaginings turn constantly to food. Therefore, evidently, we should expect our best measures, such as the fluency test, the misperception test, etc., to be determined partly by a physiological component, at least in *some* drives. In the formula developed below we shall represent gratification level by the symbol G, and, therefore, the absence of gratification, which we now observe to have effects on test results, by $-G$.

Secondly, the tension level in a particular erg will be determined partly by the more remote history of that drive. There are studies which show, for example, with puppies, that those who did not get their full experience of suckling at the breast when they were small, continue to show an interest in manipulating and sucking things with their lips. Freud stressed that the state of the adult sex drive, particularly such aspects as its insatiability, its liability to homosexual turns, its fixation upon particular types of people, etc., were (according to his clinical hunches) frequently strongly affected by things which happened when the individual was only two or three years old. This kind of effect has become quite familiar in recent years through what are called 'imprinting' experiments with animals. Thus, for example, if a duckling is brought up with a hen instead of with a duckling at a certain stage, it will continue throughout its life to seek the company of hens rather than other ducks. There appears to be a developmental stage in most drives in which their whole intensity and direction can be rather powerfully influenced by experience. In our summary below of what effects an ergic tension level, we have symbolized the things we are discussing by letters in formulae and this 'personal history' influence is symbolized by the letter H. Presumably, we must also add a term C for constitutional and hereditary effects, which, as every observer of families recognizes, sometimes cause some individuals to have what is apparently an innately stronger need in respect to a certain drive, e.g. self-assertion, sex, fear, etc.

Naturally, any equation expressing the influences affecting ergic tension must include a term for the strength of the stimulus provocation which is going on in the person's life at the time. There is some debate in progress as to whether some drives, at least, can possibly operate without *any* stimulus at all, since they seem to be so very much inwardly determined. One does not have to be reminded of food in order to know that one is feeling hungry. One of the problems in human adjustment in the sex area is that, in the male at least, sexual drive is more dependent on inner than outer stimuli, so that sometimes quite unsuitable stimuli will be reacted to. It is for this reason that the constant k has been introduced into the following statement of hypothesis, because it means that when the stimulus, S, drops to zero, the total drive still does not vanish.

So far we are moving towards some such formulation as that E, the ergic tension, is a function of the stimulus situation ($S + k$) multiplied by the need strength ($C + H$). However, it has also just been pointed out that the tension on a drive will also be a function of the degree of satisfaction intermittently received. In a country where famine is prevalent, we might expect to find a totally higher level on the hunger drive measures than in a society where food is available readily at short intervals. In this respect, it is of some interest perhaps that the present writer's researches with the factor analytic measurement of motivation cues and devices failed to show any hunger drive at all in British and American populations! It is possible that our schedules never allow us to get so hungry that this drive shows up in sufficient variance strength to be statistically significant.

However, although the majority of people in civilized countries are nowadays more concerned about over-eating than under-eating, even the most paternal government cannot guarantee the reduction of all ergic tensions, and the needs for self-assertiveness, gregariousness, sex, etc., continue to show some variability. It may well be found when analyses of the effect of gratification on ergic tension measures are made that in some drives the effect of gratification operates at two different levels. For example, when a person is hungry certain kinds of behaviour can be shown to be a function of the excessive lowering of available glucose in his blood serum. If one could inject glucose directly into his veins, would this hunger and food-seeking behaviour cease, even though he has not gone through the motions of obtaining food, chewing, and swallowing it? There are some signs that the complete satisfaction must have both its mental, behavioural, and its physical components. Accordingly, in our formulation represented

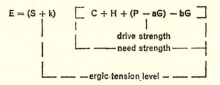

Diagram 22. The components in generating an ergic tension level

in Diagram 22, we write a gratification, G, change operating in respect both to the physiological terms and the total ergic tension, as shown here, with different constants, a and b, for the two domains of action.

This formula seeks to express very briefly three distinct concepts to help clarify measurement research on dynamic laws. They are (*a*) *Drive Strength:* the individual's natural strength of drive at that time in his life, apart from current stimulation or gratification conditions. As Diagram 22 shows, this covers C, H, and P (the normal physiological condition component); (*b*) *Need Strength*, which means the strength of the need at the time, but still only as it is inherent in the person and his current gratification, but apart from stimulation; finally, (*c*) there is the total *ergic tension level*, as actually measured in such batteries as M.A.T. and S.M.A.T., which represents the final outcome due to the combined action of need strength and stimulation level.

Preliminary experiments with the M.A.T. show that ergic tension levels do indeed fluctuate with stimulation and gratification roughly as required by this formulation, and that they also change with such influences as psychotherapy, where Sweney has shown significant reductions on successfully treated cases. Somewhat more surprising is that changes also occur in certain sentiments, as shown in Diagram 27 below, notably in the self-sentiment, though most sentiments, like those to one's career, to a recreation, etc., do remain reasonably constant. What makes them fluctuate as much as they do is not yet clear. Although a man may have sustained sentiments to his home or to his job, there are days when he is not as interested in his job as on others, and possibly, in some men, days when he is so fed up with his home that he will welcome a few days away! Presumably these fluctuations hinge on the punishments and rewards of the main drives that support the sentiment, and through which it has come into existence. For it is obvious that since the ergs are really the main original sources of mental energy, as McDougall so cogently argued in his book on social psychology and personality, all our other interests must in some way drive from them by subsidiation and be ultimately dependent upon them.

Thus, if a person builds up a substantial set of interest habits in his career, he does so because the activities of this career subsidiate to a variety of ergic satisfactions, just as we have shown in the dynamic lattice above. For example, they may contribute to his self-assertive satisfaction, in so far as he holds an important role in the business, to his gregarious erg, in so far as he likes the company of the people around the office, and so on. There is one school of thought, of which Allport in America is representative, which argues that when a habit has been in existence long enough, it gets an intrinsic power of its own, independently of the ergic goals to which it is subsidiated. On the other hand, Freud and the psychoanalysts have always stressed that when a course of behaviour no longer contributes to some final ergic goal, it becomes defunct and disappears. Of course, even the latter view does not deny that with increasing age there occurs some rigidity of habit systems – which makes the falling away of a particular kind of behaviour, when it fails to contribute to the final ergic goal, less quick and less evident, though no less inevitable. For the evidence for most instances of alleged functional autonomy, i.e. the ability to obtain satisfaction through something which no longer feeds a basic goal, has always been exaggerated. It has overlooked subtle indirect satisfactions which continue to feed the sentiment. As conceived in the dynamic calculus of human interests the sentiment structure is a sort of intermediate 'holding company', expressing ergic energy through certain facilitating habits, but liable to become obsolete if energy is ever directed elsewhere. These more subtle issues of motivation change and conflict will be pursued in the next chapter.

*

READING

Lindzey, G., *Assessment of Human Motives*. Rhinehart, New York, 1958.
Young, P. T., *Motivation and Emotion*. Wiley, 1961.

CHAPTER EIGHT

The Clinical Measurement of Conflict and Maladjustment

WHAT DO CLINICAL PSYCHOLOGISTS NEED TO MEASURE?

Viewed in terms of the amount of medical help and hospital space which have to be set aside for it, mental illness is socially the most serious form of illness in our times. Psychiatrists recognize broadly two kinds of mental illness: psychosis or insanity on the one hand, and neurosis or nervous disorder on the other. The magnitude of the first of these problems may be grasped from the fact that in most civilized countries about one person in twelve spends some time in a mental hospital. The frequency of neurosis is much harder to assess, and estimates as to the number of people who would benefit from treatment for neurotic conditions range from about one in fifty to one in five.

In the last resort, the decision as to whether it is worth while to give treatment becomes an economic issue. Doubtless one person in five could be made happier by having some advice and help from a psychiatrist or clinical psychologist, but it is economically quite impracticable to have the percentage of doctors in the population which would be required to do this. Treatment for private patients by a qualified psychiatrist costs at the present time roughly £5 or $20 an hour, and a reasonably thorough psychoanalytic treatment may run to 200 hours. These estimates of the extent and the cost of dealing with mental illness, incidentally, leave out of the total the cost of hospitals for the mental defective, who constitute about 1 per cent of our population.

Obviously the only hope of meeting the needs of society reside in drastic improvements in the efficiency of diagnosis and of methods of treatment. If we face the question of the effectiveness of therapy without illusions we have to admit that on a national basis the situation is not so different from that pertaining to cancer. Almost everyone knows some afflicted individual, and the urge to do something, even though we do not know exactly what to do, is very great. This has led to a lot of expenditure directly in clinical treatment which might have been much better directed to basic research, a position which the wiser members of our community are now beginning to take.

What we really need is more progress in the scientific analysis of personality, considering the normal and the abnormal as part of a single problem. The funds available for particular research areas run ten to one in favour of medical psychological research compared to basic, direct scientific study of personality as a natural phenomenon. Yet to compare again with the case of cancer, we know that some of the most valuable leads have arisen from basic research in fields which had nothing to do with cancer primarily, such as genetics, the study of viruses, and biochemistry.

Research in clinical psychology broadly divides into research on therapy and on diagnosis. Better understanding of diagnosis would, of course, enlighten therapy too. In the first place, we have only the vaguest ideas at present about the *frequency* and incidence of various lesser forms of mental disorder, as indicated in the above-mentioned variation of estimates as to the frequency of neurotic conditions from one in fifty to one in five. Surveys are just beginning to be made across most civilized countries to discover, in town and country, what the state of the average citizen may be. This has been made possible only by new measurement instruments. But measurement is even more important in evaluating the effectiveness of particular kinds of therapy or treatment. Until we know what we are treating, the direction and planning of treatment is obviously wild and vague. And until we can demonstrate how much patients have benefited from this kind of treatment compared with that kind, we have no objective way of deciding whether any treatment is an improvement on its historical predecessor. If the matter were so simple that we had only to deal with people who are sick and people who are well, this emphasis on diagnosis would not arise. But the fact is that neurotics who have been treated for a very long time are sometimes slightly better, sometimes obviously much better, and sometimes in such a condition that we doubt whether the treatment did them any good at all. Progress in the measurement of the mentally ill is, therefore, very closely dependent indeed upon progress in mental measurement generally, and on new diagnostic techniques in clinical psychology in particular.

Historically there has been a tendency for clinical psychology to develop its test devices in isolation, as instanced in the Rorschach, the M.M.P.I., etc., from the basic research on measurement in the normal individual. Indeed, initially there was not only a separation of applied psychology from its parent science, but also an isolated development of quite local systems for clinic, school, and industry. Such separate 'cook books' existed also in chemistry and other studies in their infancy. Most people who have followed the Hollywood expedition into the realm of the psychiatrist and of pathology, in a number of dramatic films over the last decade, have become familiar with the coloured ink blots which constitute the Rorschach test, as shown to patients to get their free associations, and have heard here of the T.A.T., or Thematic Apperception Test. The schools, however, followed a practice which knew nothing of these but only of the Binet, while industrial personnel work has often concocted such local and secret devices as to present a charlatan's paradise.

Fortunately the last decade has seen a relatively rapid knitting of different practices around more professional psychometric evaluations. One difficulty in bringing general personality and motivation measurement into fruitful interaction with clinical psychology has been that clinical theory itself, as we have seen, has been biased by the oddity of its sample. There were actually, before about 1950, far more people studying abnormal than normal personality psychology, and there was a marked disinclination to recognize that the abnormal might be better understood if one took the trouble to study 'control' cases of normals. Indeed, whereas control groups are a matter of course to the scientist, practically no psychoanalyst has reported analysis of normal people together with his explanation of the abnormal.

Part of the difficulty in focusing the needs here arises from the use of the word 'disease' in regard to mental abnormality. In the

realm of physical medicine, a disease process is commonly something very different indeed from a normal process. In a whole lot
of cases it may mean an infectious disease, engendered by a germ
which is simply not attacking most healthy people. In that case
something quite different is happening in the diseased person from
what is happening in the normal person who is not infected. In
the realm of mental disorder, on the other hand, there seem to
be far more instances where the abnormal process is just an
extreme form of something which is visible in the normal individual, and in which the illness may be said to be functional in the
sense of an imbalance between things which go on in a more
balanced way in the normal.

Although it is true that certain forms of psychosis, especially
those caused by some physical disturbance of the brain, are
pretty close to physical illnesses, yet the neuroses, and what are
called the character disorders, on the other hand, pass without
any sharp break into what we call normal behaviour. There is an
old story about two Quakers in conversation in which one says,
'George, all the world is a bit queer except thee and me, and
sometimes I am not so sure about thee.' Practically all the neuroses
and an appreciable fraction of other mental illnesses are in this
category. The clinical psychologist, therefore, really needs to
concern himself more than he has before with measuring essentially normal processes, using norms and scales which will allow
him to recognize when the process has moved to an abnormal
range. Also, he needs a 'model' in which he can put these measurements together so that he may understand the imbalances
which occur in a functional disorder in terms of universal psychological laws.

THE HIDDEN PATTERN OF NEUROTICISM

There are various ways of defining neuroticism. A psychoanalyst
may prefer to define it in his theoretical terms as a particular
kind of conflict, with generation of anxiety, between the ego, id,
and super-ego. He regards it as a kind of knot or tangle in those
same motivational channels which we were studying in the last
chapter. However, he has generally not thought of looking into

personality factors of a different kind than dynamic ones, and the substance of our Chapters 3, 4, and 5 would seem to him a bit irrelevant. However, we notice that other practitioners, less wedded to the rather elaborate yet also elegant psychoanalytic theories, are content to describe neurosis almost as if it were simply a high level of anxiety. Finally, in a very pragmatic sense, there is only one definition of neurosis – that it is the pattern of behaviour shown by those individuals who come to a clinic for aid because they feel themselves to be in emotional difficulties (and who do not have that kind of disorder which a psychiatrist recognizes as psychosis). Thus if we accept neurotics as a socially set-aside group, marked operationally by coming to a clinic for help, then our theoretical understanding of neurosis must begin by finding what measurements differentiate this group from the average group which constitutes our population.

With this aim, a great number of tests have been given by psychologists to neurotics and normals, and either some tendency to differ or some substantial degree of difference has been found on some of them. For example, on the Rorschach there is a tendency to make associations to ink blots of a certain kind more frequently than others. Eysenck, for example, has shown that – quite apart from fewer colour responses and such things – neurotics actually make *uncommon* responses, just in terms of the average frequency characteristic of the general population. Also, the kinds of associations in the forms of stories that are given to the pictures of the T.A.T. differ. Differences exist also in some ways of responding to intelligence tests, and even on the frequency of adjectives and nouns in interview conversation. Most of these measures, however, are not very reliable, and even though they give some differences, it is not easily possible to make much sense out of them in terms of personality structure.

Accordingly, the more recent systematic approach has been to take personality factors which are already recognized as basic dimensions in the normal personality, and to compare normals and neurotics for their average score on these. Some of the earliest work in this field was done by Eysenck and his collaborators at the Maudsley Hospital in London, who showed pretty clearly that the factor which the Illinois team called, among normals,

U.I. 23 or Regression (page 109), distinguishes neurotics from normals but does not distinguish psychotics from normals. On the basis of this they have rightly argued that neuroticism is not just a lower degree of the same mental illness which appears in psychoticism, but is quite different in kind. This conclusion may have to be revised a little, in that there are indications that on some personality factors, neurotics and psychotics deviate from the general population in the same way, but there is no doubt that in the *total profile* of dimensions the neurotic is quite a different person from the psychotic. Naturally, as in most illnesses, there is unfortunately no guarantee that because one has one disease one cannot have another, and this alone may be responsible for occasional measurement overlap.

Before we scrutinize these findings in the objective test measurements, however, let us look at them in the perhaps more easily interpretable questionnaire measurement factors. Until recently clinicians have regarded the questionnaire as perhaps too simple for their purposes, but Eber, Scheier, Tatro, Swenson, and others have shown striking results from the 16 P.F. and the H.S.P.Q., measuring the same personality factors as in normals, and Hathaway, Meehl, and others have shown that a surface trait questionnaire, the M.M.P.I., dealing with abnormal syndromes, can also be valuable to the clinician in assessing abnormality more objectively.

Karson, Pierson, Scheier, and others who began systematically to collect personality factor scores (by the 16 P.F. for adults and the High School Personality Questionnaire for child guidance cases) were prepared to find some cultural differences in this diagnosis, but the surprising and convincing finding is that the type of profile found among neurotics in the south of America, in the north of America, in Canada, in Australia, and in Britain is essentially the same. The central tendency in this profile is shown in Diagram 23 below. It can be shown that there is a statistically significant difference from normals on no fewer than six of these factors, some of which we have already recognized in Chapters 4 and 5 to be measures of anxiety, and others which are not merely forms of anxiety.

Now the personality profile in these primary personality factors is not just a *descriptive* account of the pathological behaviour as in the M.M.P.I., *surface traits* but an analysis in terms of the underlying personality structures i.e., *source traits*. It tells how this person is adjusting, in terms of the personality processes which are common to all men. Indeed, a number of interesting further calculations and interpretations can be made in terms of the dimension values obtained. In the first place, since we recog-

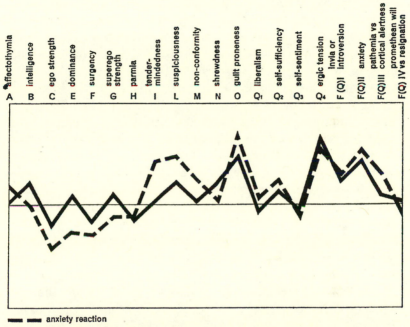

anxiety reaction

conversion reaction or conversion hysteria

Diagram 23. 16 P.F. profile of neurotics

nize that the neurotic is in a bath of anxiety, which may be partly a temporary state and hides more permanent personality flaws, we can 'partial out' (as the statistician says) the score on the general (second-order) anxiety factor (Chapter 5) by subtracting it from O, $Q4$, etc., and see what we have left. What one has left is some still very marked differences on five factors, namely a tendency to be low on C, ego strength, to be high on M, the factor called Autia, to be high on I factor, called Premsia, and to be low on Dominance (E) and on Surgency (F).

The personality dimension which has been labelled *M*, or Autia, expresses itself in high subjectivity and disregard of the external world. Autious people are wrapped up in their own thoughts, inclined to disregard practical, social necessities, disinclined to alter their ideas in response to brute facts, and so on. It is easy to understand that this might get a person into unrealistic positions on emotional issues which would sow the seeds for a neurotic breakdown later. Our understanding of *I* factor, which is perhaps the most important factor besides anxiety in neuroticism, extends so far to the notion that it represents an over-indulgent early upbringing. Individuals high in *I* factor are, as Chapter 4 points out, sensitive emotionally, capricious, and somewhat 'spoilt'. Again, it is not surprising that this kind of general orientation would result in a difficulty in handling needs which cannot be satisfied. The more realistic *low I* individual is likely quickly to reconcile himself to certain deprivations, where the *high I* individual may show the typical neurotic hesitation in which he is unwilling either to give up an impulse or to accept the consequences of retaining it.

The low *C*, ego strength, score of the neurotic actually fits very well the general psychoanalytic clinical theory. It means that the individual is easily swamped by his own emotionality, is subject to moods and a jaundiced attitude to life, and cannot adjust his behaviour to the realities of a situation. Further work by Scheier, Tatro, Eber, Costello, and others shows, furthermore, that low *C* score is the central feature of *all* kinds of psychopathology. It turns up in all varieties of neurotics, in alcoholics, homosexuals, exhibitionists, psychopaths, drug addicts, and most psychotics.

The low scores on *E*, dominance, are not so universally found in pathology, e.g. psychopaths are high *E*, and occur most markedly in neurotics, probably being a consequence of the primary disorder, as loss of self-confidence is a consequence of many illnesses and misfortunes. The desurgency (low *F*) of neurotics is most marked in depressive neurotics but is also characteristic of the great majority of mentally ill people (manics excepted). Surgency declines with age and mental disorder increases with age, and we may be facing some problem of energy-economics here, the desurgent person lacking the resources to readjust to major difficulties. Both submissiveness (low E) and desurgency (low F) tend to be responses, also, to major frustrations, which may explain their universality in the mentally ill.

For the practical purpose of quick diagnosis in general practice, or for assessing the *degree* of neuroticism, in individuals included in social surveys, etc., it has been possible to take the key items from the above personality scales and put them into a brief forty item *Neuroticism Scale Questionnaire* (N.S.Q.). The kind of items used in this scale, though not actual items from the published scale, are shown in Table 23.

TABLE 23

Some items from a parallel form of the N.S.Q. (*Neuroticism Scale Questionnaire*)

1. I like going out and meeting new people.
   | Yes | Sometimes | No |
2. I tend to get upset when I have to travel.
   | Generally | Sometimes | Never |
3. If someone interrupts me when I'm doing anything, I find it hard not to get confused.
   | Yes | Sometimes | No |
4. I like a bit of strenuous physical exercise every day.
   | Yes | Uncertain | No |

These questions are in some cases 'disguised', as in (1) and (4), but in others 'face valid', as in (2) and (3). Neurotics more frequently answer (1) No, (2) Yes, (3) Yes, (4) No. (Note the design of balancing yes and no answers.)

The items sampled here also have 'face validity' (and could therefore be faked), but such are chosen for the readers' benefit in understanding the actual nature of neurotic behaviour. But others – and they are the best items – are obscure to the average person, despite good correlation with the total neuroticism score which the N.S.Q. sets out to measure. There is, of course, some correlation (about $+0.5$) between the neuroticism and the anxiety scales, because high anxiety is a part of neuroticism. But not all neurotics are really high on anxiety and certainly not all people high on anxiety are neurotics. It is of interest to the theory that some cultures are likely to generate neuroticism more than others and that quite significant differences have been found between countries on the N.S.Q.

PERSONALITY STRUCTURES IN THE VARIETIES OF NEUROTICS AND DELINQUENTS

Although it is useful to have a single brief 'special purpose' test like the N.S.Q. to indicate degree of neuroticism – especially in the general practioner's office where he wants to get an objective indication of whether a physically ill person is also mildly neurotic or so severely neurotic as to need referral to a psychiatrist, yet this is a mere beginning.

The important thing, as far as an intelligent therapeutic approach to cure is concerned, is knowing the total personality structure of the patient. Because the *average* personality profile of the neurotic on sixteen distinct personality factors is as shown in Diagram 23, it does not, of course, follow that every person coming to a clinic with neurotic complaints will have just such a profile. In the first place there are differences among the syndrome groups which psychiatrists have long separated out, notably the anxiety reaction types, affected principally by a vague, pervasive anxiety; the conversion hysterics, who complain mainly of physical symptoms, and the obsession-compulsives who have irrational compulsions to various acts. To show at the same time how we may go in and out of representation alternatively by the primary factors or by the second-order factors derivable from the 16 P.F., the differences found among these groups are shown in Diagram 24 in a four-factor second-order profile.

The story of how the clinical psychologist would react to each feature of the individual 16 P.F. profile is too long for an introductory account. Some neurotic individuals will have such a low C score that almost any trivial environmental conflict would have precipitated the neurosis. Another is perhaps neurotic despite tolerably high C and an extravert endowment in the constitutional H factor. In one an excessive anxiety may spring from a general ergic frustration, as shown by a high Q_4 score on ergic tensions, whereas in another it may be associated with a strong guilt reaction, as shown by a high *O* score, and so on.

Consideration of the individuality of the profile brings us to recognize the narrowing gap which the modern psychologist sees between the person suffering from mental disorder, and the delinquent. This is shown at the practical level by the Child Guidance Clinic being about equally concerned with neurotic and delinquent children and, at the theoretical level, by psychiatrists defining a class of neurotics as 'acting-out neurotics' or 'behaviour disorders'. At the adult level the law continues to treat as punishable any anti-social behaviour not committed by

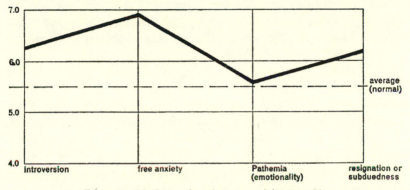

Diagram 24. Second-order neuroticism profile

someone actually insane. Some reformers, rather high on *I* factor, think it unfortunate that a neurotic criminal should be punished rather than treated. But society has other people to think of besides the delinquent. A man beaten over the head with a piece of lead pipe is likely to have only a mild interest in whether his wanton assailant was a simple or a neurotic criminal. Much harm has been done to public acceptance of careful scientific work in psychology by extravagant claims and illogical, sentimental arguments from the intuitive clinical phase of psychology. The fact is that no demonstration has been given that punishing the criminal fails to exercise a deterrent effect on a large number of potential criminals. And since psychiatric experience is that certain types of psychopath scarcely respond at all to therapy, the logical conclusion is that they should be locked up with the therapist until they do – probably for the rest of their lives. Every effort should be bent to supporting research which will make the treatment of delinquency scientifically effective, but the present state of our knowledge justifies little interference with the law.

A generation ago it was customary to say that neurotics and delinquents deviate on opposite sides from the normal, in that neurotics suffer from excessive super-ego guilt and delinquents from insufficient. Questioning the clinical tradition and the Freudian position, Mowrer, in America, has argued that *both* suffer from super-ego defect. Still working from the consulting room type of evidence, he has concluded that the guilt of the neurotic is due to the fact that he has actually offended against moral standards, and failed to keep his impulses under control, relative to the healthy person.

The situation as revealed by personality factor measurement is more complex. First delinquents show lower than average C factor score, just like neurotics and psychotics. They are unduly emotional, and unable to control their impulses and moods. Sir Cyril Burt, in his classic, *The Young Delinquent*, studying objectively the whole gamut of causes of delinquency in London children, noted this central fact many years ago, and was inclined to consider the general emotionality of the low-C individual as constitutional. He viewed it, like low intelligence, as a constitutional handicap exposing the individual more sharply to the effects of unfavourable environment. Our more recent data (Chapter 2) shows that a constitutional component exists in C, but leaves a lot of room for environmental improvement.

As to super-ego strength, G factor, the results show it clearly to be sub-normal in the delinquent and psychopath, but also somewhat defective – and certainly not above average – in the neurotic. The neurotic is experiencing guilt, O factor, not because he has unusually high standards, but because his phantasies and impulses more frequently offend than in the better controlled non-neurotic.

Much of the clinical-intuitive belief that the neurotic is over-exacting with himself may be a confused perception of the fact, supported by measurement, that he *is* over-inhibited socially. In other words, neurotics are more frequently made out of introverts and delinquents more frequently out of extraverts. The tendency of delinquents to be more extravert is borne out both by the questionnaire data in Diagram 25, and by the objective measures on the factors in Table 24. The data in Diagram 25 is due to Dr George Pierson, from his organization of state agencies research on delinquents in Washington State, and it uses the High School

H.S.P.Q. factors

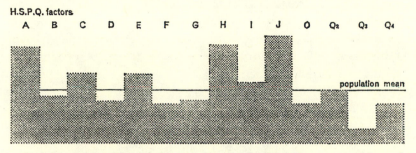

Results are combined influence from I.P.A.T. delinquent sample and papers of Pierson and Kelly, *Journal of Psychology*, 1963.
Prediction of parole success of delinquents
(Courtesy of G. Pierson, *Journal of Social Psychology*, 1963)
Weights assigned to personality factors in predicting likelihood of judges' agreement on case being successful on parole:

A	B	C	D	E	F	G	H	I	J	O	Q₂	Q₃	Q₄
·03	·09	− ·46	·31	·03	− ·14	·60	− ·17	·24	·17	·22	− ·29	·05	·19

This shows that if a lad is delinquent despite high ego strength, C, and self-sufficiency, Q_2, the probability of change is poor. Excitability, D, emotional sensitivity, I, guilt proneness, O, and a good super-ego, G, apparently associate with a delinquent (possibly caught in a more situational or impulsive delinquency) having prospects of good parole behaviour.

Diagram 25. Personality Profile and prognoses of delinquents
Average profile of over a thousand teen-age delinquents
(For descriptions of these traits, see Chapter 12)

Personality Questionnaire (H.S.P.Q.) which, however, deals with the same primary factors as with adults.

Although one calls delinquents 'extravert' in the short-hand of the grosser second-order factor system, it is interesting to notice that this extraversion has a special quality in that the primaries show dominance, *E*, to be more involved than is usual in the second-order picture, and F less involved. However, at the second-order level – and this is supported also by the careful rating studies on delinquents by Quay and Peterson – the delinquent is low in C and associated adjustment measures, low in super-ego strength, and high in extraversion.

To the psychologist, understanding the meaning and genesis of these factors, some causes and treatments for delinquency become more clearly evident. However, in treatment, in the last resort, each case must be guided by the individuality of the primary personality profile, and these profiles, in maladjusted individuals, will range from about the neurotic to around the delinquent pattern.

MEASUREMENTS ON THE MALADJUSTED – NEUROTICS, DELINQUENTS, AND PSYCHOTICS – BY OBJECTIVE ANALYTIC FACTOR BATTERIES

Although modern questionnaires, measuring a dozen to twenty independent factors, as in the Guilford–Zimmerman and the 16 P.F. Questionnaires, demonstrably cover far more of the personality than earlier questionnaires, yet we have seen reason to doubt that they capture all aspects of personality. For example, the six second-order factors in the 16 P.F. may correspond to six factors in the Objective-Analytic battery (the O.-A.), but this still leaves a dozen or so untouched, as if some forms of personality will only come out in behaviour, not in what we *see* in our behaviour.

Both for this reason, and because some risk of error from faking lurks in questionnaire data gathered in uncontrolled circumstances, the differences of neurotics, psychotics (insane persons), and delinquents have also been studied by objective batteries. A comparison of neurotics and normals is shown in Table 24. The dimensions on which differences exist at a high level of significance (besides the general anxiety factor (Chapter 5), U.I. 24 on which neurotics are decidedly higher) are the factor of emotional frustration, U.I. 22(–), on which neurotics are naturally higher, the regression factor, U.I. 23, of which some description has been given (Chapter 5), and the extraversion–introversion factor,

U.I. 32. The latter shows the expected tendency for neurotics to be more introverted, and there are significant differences on two or three other factors we will not pause here to describe. The kinds of test which appear in these factors may be seen back in Chapter 4 and in the larger book by Warburton and the present writer (end of Chapter 5).

TABLE 24

Summary of data relating first-order objective-test factors to clinically judged neuroticism-vs-normalcy

Factor title (positive pole)	U.I. No.	30 Normals 24 Neurotics Toronto	32 Normals 25 Neurotics Illinois
Cortertia	U.I. 22	+2·62	+8·33
Responsive will	U.I. 29	+5·62	+7·95
Ego strength	U.I. 16	+4·47	+8·73
High mobilization *vs* regression	U.I. 23	+3·60	+5·73
Independence	U.I. 19	+3·87	+1·04
Exuberance	U.I. 21	+4·53	+3·68
Anxiety	U.I. 24	−2·01	−1·34
Invia or introversion	U.I. 32	−2·10	−3·94

Unless the sign is positive, neurotics are higher than normals. The figures in columns three and four are the *differences* between neurotics and normals expressed as a multiple of what is called a standard score difference. (Normals are subtracted from the neurotics' average.) When this difference is more than twice as great as the standard score, it is statistically significant.

What is important in this new trend in diagnosis, however, is, first, that the degree of separation achieved by these measures between neurotics and normals is very impressive (see also Diagram 46 p. 330). Second, we observe that the nature of the factors indicates that neuroticism is something more than a tangle in the motivation system alone, such as is studied more intensively in Section 5 below. It is true that neurotics do show a high degree of conflict and of anxiety, etc., but they also differ on other factors, e.g., extraversion–introversion, and on certain temperament dimensions, some of which have quite a marked degree of inheritance.

From the evidence on twins, also, by Eysenck and Prell, one

is forced to conclude that there is a certain type of constitution which is more likely to become neurotic than another. These temperament predispositions include that inviant tendency to avoid people, the U.I. 17 tendency to be relatively easily inhibited by failure, the U.I. 21 (—) lack of fertility in trial and error solutions to a problem, the U.I. 23 tendency to subjectivity and rigidity, and perhaps a general tendency to become emotional in disturbing situations. In Diagram 46, the scores of a set of normal and a set of neurotic individuals are shown upon a weighted composite of the six or seven personality factors which most distinguish neurotics from normals. It will be seen that an almost complete separation of the two groups is obtained in terms of this score. Indeed, the separation is probably as good as would be obtained from the consensus of a number of psychiatrists who had studied the patients for weeks, yet the test only took a couple of hours to administer. Of course, one needs much more than a mere diagnostic separation, in the long run. One needs also to know which of the personality factors is fateful for the particular case, and why it operates the way it does. This is something which still lies ahead in the field of research.

The first explorations of what personality factors 'go wrong' in delinquents was made by Dr Knapp in the case of Navy men thrown 'in the brig' for relatively serious or persistent offences. A somewhat different type of delinquent – the Chicago street gang type – was studied by Drs Cartwright and Howard, and their sociologist team mates, trying to get at the totality of influences – psychological, biological, sociological, and economic – of which all crime is a function. A third application of the general O.-A. battery was made on hardened criminals at Joliet by Damarin and Warburton. All of these studies are too recent for a simple popular digest to be made; but it is quite evident that criminals differ from the average non-criminal significantly on certain personality factors and certain constellations among personality factors.

The dimensions on which delinquents are conspicuously different are U.I. 20, Comention (tendency to go with the gang); U.I. 24, Anxiety and maladjustment; U.I. 26, a kind of vanity and self-centredness; low U.I. 28, i.e. low super-ego strength;

U.I. 29, called over-responsiveness; and U.I. 30, aloof independence. At first the U.I. 20 association is a bit surprising, since Comention was so named ('thinking together') because its behaviour seemed to indicate a kind of group solidarity. In fact it was called colloquially in the laboratory the 'Cat and Dog' factor, in that high comention has that dog-like characteristic of ready emotional response to the immediate group and loyalty to it. Possibly more 'immediate groups' are against the abstract moral values of society than we realize!

It may be of interest to look at the behaviours which come together in a factor not previously set out, namely, U.I. 26, as in Table 25. That this factor should be higher in delinquents is

TABLE 25

U.I. 26. Narcistic self-vs-low egotism

Objective test	Factor loading
Higher proportion of fluency on self	+47
Lower motor rigidity	−27
More preference for form over colour in sorting	−24
Better immediate memory for attitudes checked	+31
Higher ratio of final to initial performance: C.M.S.	+41
Higher proportion of threatening objects perceived in unstructured drawings	+23
Higher ratio of final to initial performance: backward writing and reading	+27
Higher achievement (grade point average)	+29

perhaps not so surprising when one looks at its self-centredness or 'prima donna' autonomy. The individual high on these experimental measures tends to be highly fluent about his own interests, but also fluent in general (to a slightly lesser extent). He accelerates under approval and takes disapproval badly. He shows great persistence in reaching his goals, and achieves good marks at school relative to his intelligence. Finally, he shows an unusually explicit self-concept, a lively emotionality of comment, a good control of immediate behaviour, and, by inference, a certain argumentativeness. The origins of the U.I. 26 pattern are at present uninvestigated, and because it contributes to delinquency we should not assume it is a wholly undesirable trait. One can see certain positive social performances, e.g. in art and literature, to which it might contribute, but it is also fairly evident that such 'vanity' might favour individual delinquency.

The other five or so source traits distinguishing delinquents are equally interesting, but U.I. 26 has been chosen as entirely new in discussion here. They all make sense psychologically, in terms of what is yet known, but far more research is needed to trace their natural history as source traits. All we can say definitely at this juncture is that except for Anxiety (U.I. 24) which is shared with neurotics, and I.U. 28 and 29, which operate towards the *opposite* extreme from that in neurotics, the factors are different from those which distinguish neurotics from normals. Consequently, and in view of the magnitudes of the differences, it should be possible to make up a weighted score on the O.–A. personality traits which would substantially separate those deviants we call delinquents and neurotics from the general population and from each other.

Finally, let us turn to the third great group of maladjusted – the insane, or the 'psychotic' as the modern psychiatrist calls them. It has already been pointed out that the researchers at the Maudsley Hospital in London have cogently argued that the deviation of psychoticism differs in kind from the deviation in neuroticism, and results agreeing with this have been independently obtained, though not yet fully published, in the United States in the Illinois laboratories and by Brengelman and Frank in New Jersey. The possibility must also be considered that whereas neuroticism is always a matter of 'more or less', with a fairly wide range over which it is practicable to measure the severity of neurosis, yet psychoticism may be more of an all-or-nothing matter in that the individual is either in contact with reality or not.

What we see at the common-sense level is that the neurotic shows some difficulties in his social life, some failures to measure up to the needs of his family, and some inefficiencies in his occupation, but he is generally able to 'look after himself' to a reasonable degree. Moreover, he is generally aware of his problems, perhaps too painfully aware of them. On the other hand, the psychotic is generally completely unable to look after himself, and perhaps unsafe to be left with others, and he very often shows a pretty complete lack of insight into the fact that he is in such a state and has problems.

Since there are several distinct varieties of psychoticism, such as manic and depressive disorders, schizophrenia, senile psychoses, paranoia, confusional disorders from infectious conditions, it may seem unreasonable to expect any single personality dimension or characteristic to distinguish psychotics. If a psychiatrist is asked to say why he calls them all psychotics, despite these varied behavioural expressions, he is likely to seek some such generalization as that all of them are out of touch with reality, or that all of them show emotional reactions which are in some way inappropriate to their situations. For example, the schizophrenic shows no apparent emotion in situations where normal people would react, or he reacts violently at trifling things which seem meaningless to others, while a manic or a depressive is clearly showing an emotional mood which is monstrously out of proportion to the causes for joy or sadness in his immediate environment. One can, of course, find individuals on the border-line in manic and depressive conditions, such as in what is called hypomanic behaviour, in which the excitement strikes us as inappropriate but not so severe as to require restraint; but by and large there is little difficulty in recognizing that a manic or a depressive has passed a normal boundary.

Perhaps the chief exception to the tendency to an all-or-nothing diagnosis of psychotic conditions lies in paranoia, in which individuals have systematic delusions without hallucinations and often without much emotional oddity. In fact, some paranoids have delusional systems differing so subtly from the normal that it takes one a very long while to realize that one is not talking with a perfectly normal individual. Furthermore, normal individuals can have paranoid states when they get excessively tired, or have been subjected to prolonged emotional harassment. In many cases it would require a very nice judgement to decide when a system of ideas is delusional or true and whole cultures might be and have been judged to be delusional by people from other cultures who happen not to share the given beliefs. Thus in this case the notion of a sane or not sane category certainly fails, and we have the same kind of situation as in neuroticism where a difference in degree needs to be measured.

Although psychoticism is relatively sharply visible it does, of course, show gradations, and researchers in this field in the last ten years have sought for tests which will operate as if they are measuring degrees of abnormality. With their measures they are prepared to let the verdict of experience show whether the distribution is continuous or broken. At the questionnaire level the best-known device in this respect is the Minnesota Multiphasic Inventory, which is specifically directed at the particular syndromes in mental disorder. Again, though we cannot repeat items from the actual M.M.P.I. test, Table 26 will show the type of item which is employed.

TABLE 26

Questions used to score on psychopathological syndrome scales in tests like the M.M.P.I. (Minnesota Multiphasic Personality Inventory)

1. I have a feeling that something dreadful is going to happen, I do not know what.   True   False
2. Terrible ideas get into my mind and I cannot get rid of them.
                                                   True   False
3. My digestion seems all wrong most of the time.
                                                   True   False
4. People seem to treat me badly without any real cause.
                                                   True   False

Psychologists, by diligent statistical sifting of responses, have also learnt that certain responses to the ten Rorschach ink blots distinguish psychotics to some extent from normals. For example, associations which indicate attention mainly to the *colour* of the ink blots are said to indicate a warm, outgoing, impulsive personality. Various abnormalities of personality are inferred also from the total 'response productivity' (what we should call 'fluency' in the O.-A. battery), as well as from whole and part responses, and from the proportion of associations describing movement relative to those which do not. However, as Vernon and Cronbach, respectively in Britain and America, have shown, the reliabilities are low and the validity of prediction is much poorer than clinicians have become accustomed to believe. Predictions from personality factors in questionnaires and objective test batteries could almost certainly be shown today to be far better than from the Rorschach. Anastasi, whose surveys of tests have been fairly and shrewdly made, points out that part of the trouble with 'projective' tests is a lack of sophistication in scoring. For example, the separate categories are not scored ipsatively (see above on motivation measures), while such things are not recognized as that responses indicative of disturbance in the adult may be quite normal in the child (and *vice versa*). The real cause of failure in most 'special gadget' tests, relative to the broad approach through source trait tests based on research on personality structure, is that their blind empiricism of interpretation permits no link-up with structural calculations while the narrowness of behaviour sampled in the test makes effective total personality predictions unlikely.

On the Sixteen Personality Factor Questionnaire, some extensive clinical insights have recently been gained. Tatro and Komlos, in a large Illinois state hospital, have shown that paranoids deviate significantly in the direction of harria, $I(-)$, inflated self-sentiment, Q_3, and subnormal ergic tension, $Q_4(-)$. Individuals low on intelligence, $B(-)$, conservative in temperament, Q_1, and high on super ego, G, are more frequently found in the affective psychoses; while schizophrenics are significantly different from normals in showing ego weakness, $C(-)$, high self sentiment, Q_3, low drive tension, $Q_4(-)$, and introvert scores on $E(-)$, low dominance, and $F(-)$, desurgency. These source trait findings make good sense dynamically, but whether a weighted composite of these scores will fully separate psychotics remains to be seen. Low C factor (poor ego strength) seems common to practically all pathology of personality; but it may be that the questionnaire is not capable of getting at the whole psychotic difference. Meanwhile it is evident that it helps a great deal and assists also in revealing the former dimensions of a personality, upon which some abnormal process has settled down.

In terms of objective tests, the work of the Maudsley group and of the Illinois group has so far produced tests of only modest validity and usefulness, though a break-through may occur here at any time through incoming results from mental hospitals. Eysenck has used such tests as Gestalt completion, alternating perspective, size of writing and copying, computational skill, and sense of time required in what is called a mirror drawing task. It is perhaps a little surprising that sheer computational skill should enter in, but one must remember that the tests which are given are very simple figures, and one is testing not so much the speed and skill, such as a practised accountant might have with figures, but rather the sheer capacity to reason logically about numbers. At any rate, the psychotic, even when made roughly equivalent in intelligence to the normal group, makes far more errors and gives a poorer performance in simple addition and subtraction.

This factor which Eysenck found powerfully to distinguish psychotics from normals has been known as U.I.25 in the Universal Index series, and in its 'positive' (non-psychotic) direction has been found to contribute to various kinds of efficiency and adjustment, e.g. freedom from delinquency. It may help to look at a few experimental measurements individually. The difference between the psychotics and the normals in the Gestalt completion test is in the direction of the non-normals making faster and less accurate estimates. A specimen of this test was shown in Diagram 7 above. Another test already illustrated in Diagram 18 above is that of alternating perspective. The psychotics in general show a great instability of perspective here and change over more rapidly. From the discussion in Chapter 6 it will be evident that this is a multiply-determined test response, since it can be used to contribute at any rate to two factors.

Another test in this battery is that which has to do with the size of reproduction of a drawing or of handwriting. Eysenck's results show that the handwriting size tends to get large in psychotics, and our studies show that if a person is asked to draw on a sheet of paper some simple figure flashed on a screen, the psychotic will tend to draw it out of proportion in relation to the paper. (Generally too large, as with handwriting, but also excessively small.) Some uses similar to this have been made in a single test – the Bender Gestalt – not used as part of a general source trait battery. Specimens of drawing by such abnormals are shown in Diagram 26.

Intensive studies are in progress, in Illinois, London, and Boston, which may substantially increase available valid objective tests. The results of Tatro, at Alton State Hospital, already show that the diagnostic power of the O.-A. type of measurement of personality factors is going to yield as powerful a diagnostic aid with psychotics as White, Scheier, Swenson, and others found with neurotics. Very large and significant differences from nor-

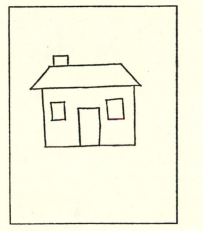

normal   psychotic

Diagram 26. Psychotic and normal copy of drawing

mals have been found in the direction of weaker ego strength, U.I.16(−), high restraint, U.I.21(−), regression, U.I.23(−), low realism, U.I.25(−), and especially in a curious behaviour pattern, U.I.30(−), which expresses a tendency to dissociate in frustrating situations. In contrast to the theoretical position of Eysenck, this leads us to the theory that psychotics deviate on some source traits − e.g. ego weakness, U.I.16, and regression, U.I.23 − in the same direction as psychotics, though *the total pattern of psychological inadequacy is quite distinct*. Indeed, the O.-A. type of test battery yields us a set of source trait scores having a very different diagnostic pattern from that for either of the other two large deviant groups − neurotics and delinquents. In view of the legal and social problems connected with trying to decide when mental disorder is serious enough to require hospitalization, some reliable diagnostic aids extra to the legal and psychiatric judgement would have very universal value. At the same time, as in all factor analytic experiment, the nature of the mental aberration involved in the separate factors (for we can no longer speak of *one* psychoticism factor) could greatly clarify understanding and efforts at individual therapy.

THE CONTRIBUTION OF DYNAMIC MEASUREMENT TO CLINICAL CONCEPTS

So far the aim of this chapter has been to show that there is more to clinical diagnosis, i.e. the understanding of neurotic, criminal, and psychotic deviants generally, than the older picture of an entanglement and conflict in the individual's dynamics. It must now be evident that neurotics, for example, differ from normals, on the average, also on a variety of temperament traits and general personality factors, some of which could be causes and some consequences of the conflict, anxiety and dynamic frustration. Any skilful prevention or treatment of mental illness will not only use these personality factor evaluations as a profile for diagnosis but also as a statement of the original constitutional resources, and of the present conditions in the patient, to be taken into account in solving the problem. In Chapter 10, on Personality Learning, the way in which some of these traits can contribute either to neurosis or to recovery will be systematically discussed. Here we have to note only that these general personality trait differences have been shown indubitably to exist.

Nevertheless, this does not mean that the dynamic conflicts beloved of the earlier clinical theorist do not exist. They exist to be studied by more quantitative methods, and when we integrate this knowledge with the quantitative study of general personality traits just covered, psychotherapy will indeed begin to acquire effective diagnostic ideas and powerful control of therapy. Chapter 7 has described what concepts basic research has developed in regard to the dynamics of the normal individual. What application could these experimental measures of ergic tensions, of sentiments, super-ego and self-sentiment strength have to understanding the dynamic problem in clinical psychology?

General evidence supports the clinician's position that the typical patient is suffering from frustrations of sexual and other ergs, which, *in extremis,* he has sought to handle by repressions

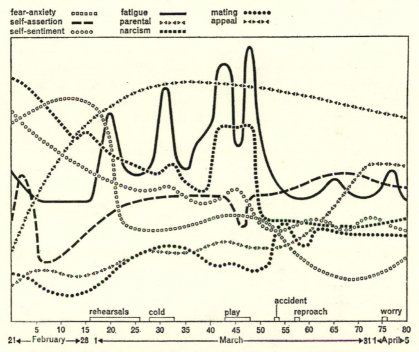

Diagram 27. Ergic tension (and sentiment) response to stimulus (*S*), internal state (*P*), and goal satisfaction (*G*).

and other ego defence mechanisms. Early childhood experiences, depositing regressive tendencies, cause the ego strength to be inadequate to face the joint assault from the demands of the undischarged ergs (the id) on the one hand and guilt imposed by the super-ego on the other. The therapeutic task is to find where the ergic tensions are high, what particular forces are in conflict, and how an acceptable expression can be found for what is now expressing itself in symptoms.

Are the ergic tensions described in the last chapter the same as those which concern the clinician? Diagram 27 shows the daily changes in ergic tension levels from a case measured by objective motivation component devices (the M.A.T.). These were recorded every day over the dates shown at the bottom and a diary was kept by the patient at the same time. He was a student, having some conflict with his family about studying drama instead of science, and he was also anxious to be accepted to act in a college play. Without space to analyse an individual case history here we may yet note that (*a*) each ergic tension level behaves in its own characteristic way, as would be expected from the basic research showing this number and kind of ergs to exist in man; (*b*) the changes of the tension levels with stimulation and gratification are such as might be expected from the formula at the end of the last chapter.

For example, when he is accepted as an actor his anxiety level falls. The 'showing off' on the stage stimulates the narcistic drive level, which remains at a high level through the week of the play. The protective 'succorant' (Murray) drive is stimulated by a severe automobile accident to his father, at the point shown, where he went to see his father in hospital. One ergic need not too clearly evidenced in other studies is the sleep-seeking or rest need. Here it mounts spasmodically to startling proportions in the measurements as his diary complains of late rehearsals and early risings making him dead tired. Finally, we note that when his professor told him that he might fail his exams through too much time on the play, the fear erg measures shot up.

Objective dynamic measurements, however, supply not only the means of ergic tension measures but also, as the formula on page 232 shows, the basis for a 'quantitative psychoanalysis'. Any attitude or symptom can now have 'loadings' calculated for it which express the extent to which its satisfaction involves each erg and sentiment. To restrict an example simply to two ergs, it is possible that the attitude 'I want to marry Jane' will be found on factor analysis to have a $+ 0.5$ projection on the gregarious erg and $+0.4$ on the sex erg, whereas the attitude 'I want to marry Sally' would have $+0.3$ projection on gregariousness and $+0.6$ on the sex erg (see Diagram 28A). In ordinary language we should say that the quality of satisfaction which the vacillating bachelor anticipates from each of these prospective wives is different – in one case there is more intellectual congeniality which gives more satisfaction to gregariousness and in the other more appeal from feminine beauty. One of the first advantages of the dynamic calculus is that it enables us to represent these differences in a way to make calculations possible about preferences and choices. As Diagram 28 shows, the strength and emotional quality of any dynamic attitude can now be represented by what mathematicians call a vector, such that its length is equal to the *strength* of motivation and its direction to the *emotional ergic quality*.

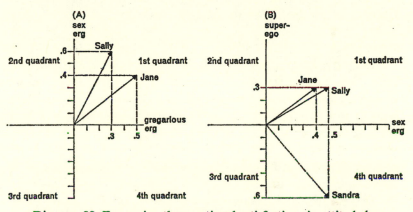

Diagram 28. Expressing the emotional satisfactions in attitude by vector representation

Since symptoms are, by the above general definition of attitudes, just one kind of attitude, the method offers us, experimentally and conceptually, what might be called a quantitative psychoanalysis. Furthermore, since mathematical rules exist for adding vectors, we can perform all sorts of interesting calculations about, for example, what one attitude would be an acceptable substitute for two or three others in a learning process.

Of course, the projections are actually on more than two ergic coordinates – research at present suggests nine are important. So other drawings are possible and necessary. For example, Diagram 28b shows that the interest in marrying Sally and Jane is equally acceptable to the super-ego, and, on three factors, the vector formulae would run

$$I_{Jane} = 0.4E_{sex} + 0.5E_{greg.} + 0.3M_{super-ego}$$ (*M* being for a sentiment)

$$I_{Sally} = 0.6E_{sex} + 0.3E_{greg.} + 0.3M_{super-ego}$$

For a person whose sex and gregarious ergs and super-ego strength were equally strong the two attitudes above would exactly balance in strength and present an insoluble choice. But if gregarious needs were stronger a decision would be made in favour of Jane.

Now, it sometimes happens that a loading works out to be negative, as in the following case of Sandra.

$$I_{Sandra} = 0.5E_{sex} + 0.2E_{greg.} - 0.6M_{super-ego}$$

This negative loading means that the super-ego strength throws its weight against Sandra. She is evidently the sort of girl with whom a respectable man is ashamed to be seen. Since she is attractive a conflict situation develops here. He can go on seeing her only at the cost of minor conflict and 'the expense of spirit in a waste of shame'.

A course of action thus fraught with conflict is represented as in the dotted line vector in Diagram 28. It was found quite early in dynamic calculus research that most attitudes have values which cause them to fall in what we have learnt to call in algebra the 'first quadrant', relatively few in the second and fourth, and none in the third (when all axes are considered). The reason for this is soon evident in what has sometimes been called the 'pleasure principle', or more accurately that no action is undertaken which does not bring tension reduction. For the third quadrant means negative satisfaction on all ergs.

Diagram 28, and the associated specification equations, thus provide us with a calculus for handling dynamic conflict, either in terms of (*a*) two courses of action between which a person is trying to decide, or (*b*) the extent of persistent inner conflict in a course of action which he had decided upon as the best possible compromise in an imperfect world.

Incidentally, it will follow that in a happily well-controlled person, whose impulses are in the main subordinated to more remote socially desirable goals, the terms in the dynamic specification equation for the self-sentiment and the super-ego must be capable of outweighing any cabal of ergs. The self-sentiment, as Table 21 shows, is a system of attitudes whose satisfaction is the preservation of the physical, social, and moral status of the self. That such attitudes can be learnt and sustained is due to the fact that they are rewarded by all the satisfactions which are alone possible through an intact and socially respected self. To the extent that humans are better able than animals to think about tomorrow, and to the degree that parents and teachers reward with approval behaviour issuing from an integrated and socialized self-concept, the strength of the self-sentiment will reach values permitting such control of ergs. The possibilities of measurement here open up new areas of study in personality development, as we shall see in Chapter 10.

THE CLINICAL USE OF DYNAMIC MEASUREMENTS

The integration that is now becoming possible between the personality factor measurement approach to neuroticism and delinquency on the one hand, and the dynamic approach which ascribes everything to a tangled conflict on the other, should begin to be evident. When the psychometrist says that neurotics differ significantly on a number of general personality factors from normals he is calling attention to defined personality resources ignored by the psychoanalyst, but he is also recognizing that some of these general personality factors, e.g. ego strength or the self-sentiment, can be changed in the right direction by the analyst's untangling of a conflict. In other words, some of these general dimensions, as we shall see in a moment, are functions of the accumulated conflicts in many local areas.

But when it comes to these zones of conflict themselves the personality structure theorist also wishes to use improved methods from the dynamic calculus in the understanding and unravelling of the dynamic problem. One persistent source of misunderstanding here arises from the belief that since conflicts are absolutely idiosyncratic to the individual the measurement of general traits cannot be applicable. First, as Chapters 3 and 4 have brought out, the individuality of the individual can be expressed as a unique combination of traits common to everyone. Secondly, as we now inspect P-technique (page 154) more closely it will be evident that it copes with the absolute idiosyncrasy which characterizes the field of interests.

Let there be no doubt that interests, more than abilities and temperament traits, need more resort to truly unique traits for their description. The conflict which Mr X has deals with his *own* father; his present interests in medieval music will fit no common sentiment; and his personal history can be told only in accidents peculiar to his life course. However, if the practitioner is prepared to use free association and familiar clinical exploratory methods to *reconnoitre* the apparent important issues, he can then get more dependable and quantitative information about the dynamic constellation of fixations and conflicts by P-technique. As the reader will recall, this involves testing the person on perhaps fifty attitudes, marking the familiar ergic factor and sentiments, as well as the symptoms and fixations important in the particular case. By repeating these measures on the given individual for about a hundred days one gets correlatable time series which show how things change together over time, with the onslaughts of daily events. From factoring these one gets the ergs and sentiments, and the attitude vectors described in the last section, *except that these now show the investments of drives, etc. by that particular person in his particular interest*, not the values for people in general.

The method has received little practical application as yet, except in research and special cases, because it demands more time than either patient or doctor is normally willing to give, but also because few psychiatrists indeed have the mathematical capacity to handle it. However, the advent of the electronic computer, with its technician attached to psychological research centres, has banished half the problem. The technician could now return in an hour with a print-out, saying 'This is the dynamic structure and source of symptoms of Patient X'. Whether the second half of the problem can be solved – a reduction of the testing time –

no one can say at present, but science has a way of surprising us by performing the impossible, and it may be that some rapid succession of measurements will some day become practical.

Such P-technique results offer not only a means of objectively focusing the roots and magnitudes of conflict, but also of calculating the magnitude of a given conflict, for a whole dynamic system or a whole person. In principle this can be done by comparing the total magnitude of the negative loadings with the positive loadings. For example, if the loadings of attitude I_j are

$$I_j = s_1 E_1 - s_2 E_2 + s_3 E_3 + s_4 E_4 - s_5 E_5$$

then the conflict in the attitude, C_j, could be written:

$$C_j = \frac{s_2 + s_5}{s_1 + s_3 + s_4}$$

Such a conflict index, C, can be worked out for a whole erg or sentiment to answer the question 'How much conflict does X have in his religious sentiments (or his sentiment to home or to self)?' If the psychologist is careful to sample the total realm of interests of the typical member of our culture he could, further, compare one person with another as to his total degree of conflict, adding all the negative s's across all attitudes in the numerator and all positive ones in the denominator.

This interesting experiment, crucial for the theory, was carried out by J. R. Williams, a clinical and school psychologist in Illinois, comparing a number of mental hospital patients with normals. As the theory required, the patients showed significantly higher conflict indices (C's) than the normals. Furthermore, the C indices were higher in those rated by the psychiatrists as having more conflict, and, also, as theory requires, the 16 P.F. measure of ego strength showed the higher conflict cases to have lower ego strength. It therefore seems that the dynamic calculus, using P-technique, could be used diagnostically to find (*a*) the severity of conflict in an individual, (*b*) the ergic tension regions with which it is most concerned, and (*c*) the roles of particular structures, such as ergs, super-ego, and self-sentiment in producing and sustaining a given symptom. Nevertheless, for the practical reasons cited above, this remains a dream of the future so far as the average patient is concerned, though research can lever itself to new heights of precision by these techniques.

A quite different approach to measuring conflict has been one which seizes on the possibilities inherent in the age-old signs of conflict. Clinicians and others have long recognized that a person in a state of conflict will show more than the average amount of hesitation, will go to others for support, will drag in things that are not really connected with the conflict, will show undue sensitiveness to praise and blame on the decision in question, will have phantasies about what he is reluctantly turning down, will become accident-prone when the issues are provoked, and will show odd memory effects, some things staying in consciousness obstinately and others vanishing, around the area of conflict.

Just as with any other psychological idea, researchers needed first to examine, by correlation, what concepts would be suggested by the way in which these signs of conflict cohere. It turned out that, much as in the general motivation field, some seven or eight distinct directions of expression exist. Among these are (*a*) a tendency of the individual in conflict to avoid stimuli which 'prod' the conflict (psychoanalysts have glimpsed this as 'restriction of the ego', but have never measured it); (*b*) a tendency to suppress one side of the conflicting impulses, which is accompanied by heightened tension (even muscular tension) and increased general impulsiveness and motor overactivity; (*c*) a tendency to phantasy about possible happy solutions. Others are more complex but Sweney's work shows clearly that these conflict dimensions can now be experimentally measured.

The existence of (*b*) may account for some findings that persons who pursue athletics and out-of-door activities show reduced neuroticism. For, at least in minor conflicts, these findings suggest that increased motor activity may aid in maintaining adjustments. A leading statistician lecturing for the tobacco companies on possible flaws in the evidence on smoking and cancer argued that many borderline neurotics just manage to keep their tensions under control by this habit. Planned physical exercise has at least equal claim and happier effects. Actually, however, our whole knowledge of how people handle and disperse minor conflicts is rudimentary, all attention having previously been centred on the grand neurotic conflicts seen in the clinic. The work of Sweney and others offers objective batteries for measuring the severities of conflicts, major or minor, and thus opens up possibilities of social research on such problems.

*

READING

Pennington, L., and Berg, I. A., *An Introduction to Clinical Psychology*, Third Edition. Ronald Press, New York, 1960.
Hall, C. A., and Lindzey, G., *Theories of Personality*. Wiley, New York, 1957; Chapman & Hall, 1957.

CHAPTER NINE

Analysis of the Concept of Integration of Personality

BEHAVIOURISM, REFLEXOLOGY, AND THE HIGHER DEVELOPMENT OF THE BEHAVIOURAL EQUATION

Scientific progress is a rhythm of analysis and synthesis. So far the main chapters have sought to show how the experimental psychologist, with behavioural observations and measurements, with mathematics and the computer, can take the total behaviour apart into meaningful and useful abstractions, such as traits of general personality, ability, or motivation. It is sometimes alleged that the psychologist does not know how to put Humpty-Dumpty together again. The last chapter's discussion on conflict and the self-sentiment shows, however, that we are approaching the ideas necessary to deal with the total functioning of the organism. If we are not merely to talk about 'integration' and 'adjustment' in rhapsodizing generalities, but to proceed to show a scientific capacity to predict and test, some return to mathematical ideas is essential in this integrating chapter.

If the reader will glance back at the first page of Chapter 2 he will recall the basic stimulus response equation with which behaviourism began and which is reproduced again here. For when psychologists *grew* shy of introspection, rightly recognizing that an observation by this method could never be scientifically checked by a second observer, they pinned their behaviouristic faith on what is often called the stimulus–response paradigm. They proposed that we define the stimulus with which the organism is presented and measure its response thereto, and then seek to find laws connecting the two. Thus the essential symbolic representation was:

$$R = f(S)$$

where R is a measured response and S a measured stimulus and f is some mathematical function which would contain the scientific laws we are seeking.

Unfortunately, the branch of behaviourism which began with Pavlov in Russia, and which has been particularly popular in America since the boost given it by the simple-minded Watson, left the organism and *its nature* out of this equation. Most professional psychologists (except for a few idiosyncratic philosophical psychologists) are behaviourists nowadays. But the form of behaviourism on which learning theory, in particular, has sought to nourish itself is really only one form or model within behaviourism, though it is sometimes mistaken for the whole. For clarity this particular sub-model should be distinguished as *reflexology*. It is entranced by the penny-in-the-slot model in which everything is reduced to the impact of a stimulus and the triggering of some motor behaviour called a response.

The behaviourist position as it developed in personality theory, however, casts doubt on the adequacy of so simplified a model to investigate the complexity of human behaviour and has introduced some different notions. In the first place it writes instead of the above equation the *general behavioural equation*:

$$R = f(O.S)$$

where O is the organism or person. It thus states that the laws describing the response must have terms both for the organism and the stimulus, and implies that it is poor strategy to try to find merely stimulus–response laws. For example, it would be useless to try to find relations between the daily work done and the weight of food eaten unless one recognized the species of animal or the occupation of the individual concerned.

Personality theory, in fact, has always considered both response and learning laws in a very different context from the 'conditioning' of the reflexological 'learning theorist'. Learning theory, it is true, has recently come around to putting O in the equation, and is even inclined to claim that it thought of the idea. But personality theory has meanwhile expanded O into a whole series of terms, each representing a dimension on which any given personality can be represented. These terms are the facts we have described. And as our first introduction of 'the specification equation' on page 79 shows, we can now re-introduce the person into the general behavioural equation as a whole pattern of dimensions.

Let us now go over the specification equation with a little more concrete illustration and attention to implications. This requires asking just how the pattern of dimensions for an individual is to be set out in measurements, *before* the individual's pattern is put in any behavioural equation.

THE DIMENSIONAL REPRESENTATION OF A PERSON

It has been agreed that out of the infinite number of 'behaviours' which different people or professional psychologists might care to list, and to which a variety of terms could be given, most meaningful prediction can be obtained if we restrict ourselves to those which have been shown by correlational investigations to constitute unitary traits. They alone have claim to being functional unities in action and in development. For example, the ego strength source trait, factor *C* (page 73) is in some dynamic sense a functional unity, controlling impulses, exploring acceptable modes of expression, etc. It is also a unity in growth, for a curve of change with age can be plotted for it (see below) which is characteristic, and different from that for any other personality source trait.

To get an individual's score on any of those source traits which we have so far learnt to measure we add up his performance scores on a set of varied items (in the questionnaire) or sub-tests (in the O.-A. battery) which have been carefully chosen for their variety and their experimentally demonstrated good 'loadings' on the factor. For example, in the *C* factor answers (0, 1, or 2) on some 26 questionnaire items in the 16 P.F. contribute to the factor measurement. In the Binet or Wechsler intelligence tests the individual's source trait (intelligence) score may be contributed to by a synonyms sub-test, a number of series item, an analogies and a classification sub-test, etc., as Eysenck has explained in a companion volume to this book. Just the same is done here for personality source traits. For instance, in the neurotic regression factor, U.I. 23, as the previous chapter shows, one would add up scores on the rigidity test, sway suggestibility, error/speed ratio, etc., sub-tests to a *single* source trait score.

There are certain psychometric niceties about this addition.

We need not bother about them here, except to indicate that each sub-test should ideally be put in comparable 'standard score' form and that the sub-test with better correlations with the factor could be given more weight. While talking of scoring tests we might point out that the psychologist expresses most of his measures in standard scores because his raw scores, unlike these of the physical scientist, are not very meaningful as they stand. The metre, the gramme, and the degree of centigrade are all related, but every one of 900 tests has its own score units.

For example, the range of scores on the rigidity test happens to fall, in terms of the ratio of letters done per minute under the two conditions, from about 0·5 to 7·5. The sway suggestibility test may yield a score in centimetres, from say 10 to 300. If these diverse ranges and units have somehow to be added together with equal weight to each, then we must begin by converting each to a standard score. A standard score simply asks what the distribution of raw unit scores for the given test is in our population and then expresses the total range as a standard number of units. Typically a standard score ranges from −2·5 to +2·5 with the population mean at 0. Nearly 70 per cent of the population on such a scale fall between +1·0 and −1·0.

The I.Q. is really another form of 'comparable' score and so also is the 'percentile score'. The percentile score of a person simply says what his rank order would be in a typical 100 people (with one at the bottom). Thus a percentile score of 81 on ego strength would mean that 80·9 per cent of the population fall below that person on this source trait. A very useful form of standard score is the *sten* (an abbreviation for 'standard ten'). In this scale the ordinary standard score ranging from −2·5 to +2·5 is for convenience freed of decimals, and shifted on its base, so that it ranges from 1 to 10, and the central, average value for the population is 5·5. It is this sten scale which we shall use for our profiles here since it fits our mental habits gained through the decimal system.

Granted that the individual has been scored on the one to two dozen source traits (*A*, *B*, *C*, etc., or U.I. 16, 17, 18, etc.) which cover so much of personality behaviour (because ultimately based on the 'personality sphere' of our daily behaviour) then

athletes, olympic champions   41 cases*

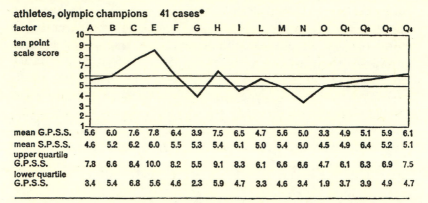

factor	A	B	C	E	F	G	H	I	L	M	N	O	Q₁	Q₂	Q₃	Q₄
mean G.P.S.S.	5.6	6.0	7.6	7.8	6.4	3.9	7.5	6.5	4.7	5.6	5.0	3.3	4.9	5.1	5.9	6.1
mean S.P.S.S.	4.6	5.2	6.2	6.0	5.5	5.3	5.4	6.1	5.0	5.4	5.0	4.5	4.9	6.4	5.2	5.1
upper quartile G.P.S.S.	7.8	6.6	8.4	10.0	8.2	5.5	9.1	8.3	6.1	6.6	6.6	4.7	6.1	6.3	6.9	7.5
lower quartile G.P.S.S.	3.4	5.4	6.8	5.6	4.6	2.3	5.9	4.7	3.3	4.6	3.4	1.9	3.7	3.9	4.9	4.7

This profile is devised from measures on the leading American and British champions at the 1952 Olympic Games, as carried out under the guidance of Professor T. K. Cureton and reported by Heusner, W. V., in *Personality Traits of Champion and Former Champion Athletes*, M. A. Thesis. University of Illinois Library, Urbana, Illinois, 1952.

Diagram 29. 16 P.F. profile of athletes

the personality profile of eminent researchers

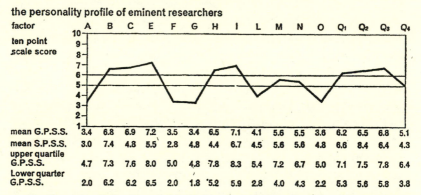

factor	A	B	C	E	F	G	H	I	L	M	N	O	Q₁	Q₂	Q₃	Q₄
mean G.P.S.S.	3.4	6.8	6.9	7.2	3.5	3.4	6.5	7.1	4.1	5.6	5.5	3.6	6.2	6.5	6.8	5.1
mean S.P.S.S.	3.0	7.4	4.8	5.5	2.8	4.8	4.4	6.7	4.5	5.6	5.6	4.8	6.6	8.4	6.4	4.3
upper quartile G.P.S.S.	4.7	7.3	7.6	8.0	5.0	4.8	7.8	8.3	5.4	7.2	6.7	5.0	7.1	7.5	7.8	6.4
Lower quarter G.P.S.S.	2.0	6.2	6.2	6.5	2.0	1.8	5.2	5.9	2.8	4.0	4.3	2.2	5.3	5.6	5.8	3.8

Credit to Dr John Drevdahl, University of Miami, and to the Institute of Personality and Ability Testing, the *Handbook for the 16 Personality Factor Questionnaire.*

Diagram 30. 16 P.F. profile of researchers

we can represent his individuality in one of two familiar ways. A favourite device is a profile, as illustrated in Diagrams 29 and 30. Here, of course, each column represents a source trait and the height corresponds to the sten score thereon. The first illustration is the average profile of forty-one Olympic athletes, but for discussion it might be considered as a single typical athlete. We note that he is high on ego strength, C, on dominance, E, and also on parmia, H, which is a kind of autonomic toughness. In other respects, except for a low guilt proneness, O, it is a fairly average profile. The dominance stands him in good stead in heightening competitive motivation and the ego strength in tolerating the tense waiting hours before a race. Indeed, one may conclude that there are probably mute, inglorious athletes actually faster than those who win Olympic laurels, but whose lack of these worry-resistant personality traits rules them out from performing dependably in such exciting public situations.

The second illustration is that of a group of leading physicists and other scientific researchers. One notices that they are decidedly 'introvert' – sizothyme ($A(-)$) and desurgent ($F(-)$) – and also sensitive ($I+$), while being nevertheless above average in ego strength and dominance. This is a combination to produce those inner tensions of 'warring heredities' which Kretschmer believed were important for creative genius. Apart from some similarity in high E and low G – frequently found in people who are 'a law to themselves' – the Olympic athlete and the leading researcher profiles are considerably different, as one might expect.

A second way to represent the individual's unique combination of source trait scores is, of course, as a point fixed by as many coordinates as there are factors. For example, the athlete and the researcher above can be represented as far as the first three factors, A, B, and C, are concerned by the three side 'views' or projections of a cube shown in Diagram 31.

What we have in Diagram 31 could be represented by an actual cube, in which the athlete, the researcher, and as many other people as we like, could be represented each by a point. (A similar axis system was used above for representing an attitude as a vector.) Since ultimately far more than three dimensions are needed, as we have seen, to represent the richness of facets of the human personality, our coordinate system must expand beyond both the simple two-coordinate graph, and the cube, to a set of axes in 'hyperspace', as the mathematician would call it. This representation is not as handy as a chain profile, as in Diagrams 29 and 30, to show us at a glance the nature of the individual, though it has some special utilities for calculations which we shall not pursue here.

An important measurement ('psychometric') question often raised about the description of individuals by factor is 'How can you give proper regard for the absolute uniqueness of the individual when you are using *common traits*, i.e. traits measured in the same way for everyone, to describe him?' Along this line Allport has suggested that we should also use *unique traits* to

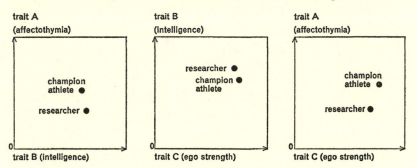

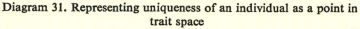

Diagram 31. Representing uniqueness of an individual as a point in trait space

describe individuals and in the last chapter's account of the extreme individuality of interest and motivation systems we saw that unique traits may assume real importance. As an ordinary example of common trait usage one might say that one person has an I.Q. of 110 and another of 120, and in so doing we are using a common trait describing intelligence in exactly the same way for both of them, but giving one more of the dimension than the other. A sensitive observer might here say that the quality of the intelligence he sees in one is more imaginative than in the other, and assert that we are missing something when we measure both on the same common trait.

This problem became still more apparent in the last chapter's examination of dynamic traits. It is proverbial that two men equally strong in the sex drive may express it in ways so different, e.g. in the ethical standards and social effects involved, that to say the drive is equally strong seems beside the point. Or again, a dynamic trait of self-assertion and dominance may express itself in one person in school, in another about the home, and so on.

Nevertheless, so long as we are dealing with the prediction of *individual differences* in behaviour we logically have to deal with common traits on a common numerical scale. As indicated above, in scoring a common trait we give weights according to what correlation, on a typical representative set of people, yields as 'loadings' on particular expressions. The weights given to sub-tests in a battery express the *average* use of that outlet by members of our society.

The logical difficulties of the initially attractive idea of a unique trait are rarely met by its sponsors. To use unique traits means that separate trait concepts and scales (many such, in fact) have to be set up for each individual. How should we compare people in physical size, e.g. the sizes of noses, and ears, if we let each person have his own peculiar ruler? The truth is that the idea of a truly unique trait has meaning and negotiability only when we are out to compare the *states* of one individual on different occasions, as we did by P-technique in Chapter 6.

This conclusion does not mean that we turn a blind eye to the problem of uniqueness as exemplified in different qualities of intelligence. The fact is that such unique qualities can in the end always be represented by special combinations of common traits. We have no difficulty in representing the endless physical idiosyncrasies of man by means of combinations of measures on three dimensions in space. Because each nose is unique, and a snub-nose is only with difficulty compared as to length with an aquiline one, we do not despair of describing physical appearance by common concepts, and the same should be true when we are faced with mental idiosyncrasies.

For example, we have said above that anxiety is a second-order factor principally involving five first-order personality factors, ego weakness ($C-$), guilt proneness (O), paranoid tendency (L), low self sentiment (Q_3-), and high drive tension (Q_4). Although two individuals may stand at the same level on the common second-order general anxiety measure, this total may be made up in different degrees from different primary factors. Incidentally, this is one reason for not trying to handle individual differences in terms of too few and too gross second-order factors instead of the full keyboard of primaries.

In the end, therefore, provided enough common factors or source traits are taken into account, the uniqueness of the individual *can* be fully represented, mathematically and quantitatively by the uniqueness possessed by a point fixed on many coordinates. A star needs only three dimensions for the mathematician to fix its position in space, but the personality of the human being can have its uniqueness defined only by a point in hyperspace.

THE UNIQUE PERSONALITY MEETS A UNIQUE SITUATION

With this sketch of the simple 'model', as the scientist would call it, with which we express individuality in terms of different numerical scores on a set of traits – regardless for the moment of what the trait list may be – let us return to the problem of expressing the interaction of stimulus and organism in the behavioural equation.

Chapter 4 introduced what we in general called the behavioural specification equation (henceforth the behavioural equation). If we take any response or performance P_j, which everyone makes in situation j, a factor analysis, or a correlation of P_j with source trait measurements, will give us the weights or 'behavioural situation indices' by which to weight each person's scores on his factors in order to get the best estimate of his magnitude of response.

This is an artificial, simplified illustration, for if, as in Chapter 11 below, we were to set out to make the best estimate of how well a boy or girl might do in high school, many more source traits – in abilities, personality, and interest – would need to be taken into account. Using H.S.P.Q. trait measures for an example, the behavioural indices would be approximately:

Grade (in standard score)
$$= -0{\cdot}4A, +0{\cdot}5B, +0{\cdot}3C, -0{\cdot}2E, + \text{ etc. (see page 79)}.$$

One can see also that these weights, loadings, or tangents are psychologically meaningful. The loading of $0{\cdot}5$ on B means that for every two stens he is above average on the intelligence score, a person is likely to be one sten above average on school attainment. On the other hand, the negative loading, $-0{\cdot}4$ on A (equation (4) above), means that sizothymes do better than cyclothymes (other things being equal) in school performance. This is not surprising, for the aloof, withdrawn, precise sizothyme has a 'bookish' temperament, and although he may not get on too well with people, his interests in ideas and words favour good academic performance.

For example, if only intelligence and ego strength were considered, we might have John with a standard score of $+1 \cdot 0$ on intelligence and $-0 \cdot 5$ on ego strength, and Harry with scores of $+0 \cdot 5$ and $+2 \cdot 0$ on these. Let us next suppose that performance in football, P_f, has been shown by correlation to have the behavioural equation

$$P_f = 0 \cdot 1 T_I + 0 \cdot 6 T_E$$

(where T_I is the trait of general intelligence and T_E that of ego strength). Performance in poetry appreciation (rated, say, by teachers) has different indices, thus:

$$P_p = 0 \cdot 7 T_I - 0 \cdot 1 T_E$$

P_f for John and Harry will then be estimated as follows:

$$P_{f(J)} = (0 \cdot 1 \times 1 \cdot 0) + (0 \cdot 6 \times -0 \cdot 5) = -0 \cdot 20$$
$$P_{f(H)} = (0 \cdot 1 \times 0 \cdot 5) + (0 \cdot 6 \times 2 \cdot 0) \quad = 1 \cdot 25$$

Thus John is slightly below average and Harry much above. P_p, or poetry appreciation on the other hand becomes:

$$P_{p(J)} = (0 \cdot 7 \times 1 \cdot 0) - (0 \cdot 1 \times -0 \cdot 5) = 0 \cdot 75$$
$$P_{p(H)} = (0 \cdot 7 \times 0 \cdot 5) - (0 \cdot 1 \times 2 \cdot 0) \quad = 0 \cdot 15$$

whence both are predicted to turn out above average, but now the leadership is with John.

In the above specification of achievement, the loading of $+0 \cdot 3$ on C or ego strength shows that good control and absence of neurotic emotionality favour learning as they do most kinds of effective use of whatever intelligence one has. Some speculation has been stirred by the finding, now in several studies, that higher dominance, E, is slightly ($-0 \cdot 2$) inversely related to school examination achievement. It may be that the more docile, low E individual simply serves up what he has been given, and is thus a good examination-passer. Other hypotheses are that the high E pupil is less liked by teachers, or that independent, critical thought is time-consuming and gives him an examination disadvantage relative to the parrot-learner. It is noteworthy that in original creative work (see the researcher profile above) the higher E person tends to be above average. Somewhere along the way, therefore, our schools 'change gear', favouring the docile examinee in the high school and the early undergraduate years but recognizing the sturdy, independent thinker (if there are by then any left!) in post-graduate research or business life.

However, our job here is not to debate educational philosophy, but only to illustrate how the specification equation values are experimentally obtained and used in a field familiar to most people.

It will help, finally, to look at the behavioural equation in its most general form, with the symbols T_{li} to T_{ki} to represent the scores of individual i on the personality, etc., traits T_l to T_k. (The 'specific factor' peculiar to this one response R_j in situation j has been omitted because the equation

$$R_j = s_{j1}T_{1i} + s_{j2}T_{2i} \ldots + s_{jk}T_{ki}$$

is complex-looking enough without that, though to anyone who has gone through school algebra it is actually a very simple linear equation.) The s's are the *situational indices* (obtained as loadings) which, as we have seen, are merely statements of *how much each given trait is involved in the given response*. Each s has a j under it to show it appropriate and peculiar to the response to the situation j. And it has the number of the trait it is attached to to show it is peculiar and appropriate to that given trait also.

Now the point to be made here is that the values

$$s_{j1}, s_{j2}, \ldots \text{up to } s_{jk}$$

are as characteristic of the situation as the values

$$T_{1i}, T_{2i}, \ldots \text{up to } T_{ki}$$

are characteristic of the person. We have no trouble in understanding that these k scores are the *profile* of the person. They uniquely define his personality. Similarly the s numbers can be put into a profile which uniquely defines the situation. For example, the values above for the school situation say, in brief symbols, that classroom performance is an intelligence-demanding, introvert-favouring, emotional-stability-testing, docility-rewarding situation.

This 'profile of the situation' does not describe it *physically*. Indeed, it would be quite possible for two situations which are very different in social or physical description to be very similar in the situational index profiles, which describe *psychological similarity*. For example, if a neurotic reacts with overwhelming anxiety on one occasion to a thunderstorm and on another to seeing a black cat, the dread and avoidance responses to both of these situations are likely to be highly loaded on the anxiety factor, etc., and to have the same *meaning* psychologically although physically different.

There has never been any difficulty for the psychologist in describing and measuring situations physically. But until the above factor analytic developments took place there was no way of quantifying and expressing the *psychological meaning of a situation*. The profile of situational index scores not only allows us to express the unique quality of each situation, but also to ask how much one situation resembles another. Thereby we can proceed to an objective classification of situations according to their psychological rather than their physical resemblances. For example, here is an objective, experimental way whereby one can classify jobs according to their psychological demands (in so far as we use ability trait indices) and satisfactions (in so far as we use dynamic trait indices).

If now we return to our original behaviourist's basic formulation:

$$R = f(O.S)$$

we see that the advance of objective personality analysis has permitted a multi-dimensional description of the individual to be brought into interaction with a multi-dimensional description of the situation (in a way we first encountered in Chapter 6). For the organism, O, we now enter the profile of the organism, namely, a set of T values. For the S we substitute the values for the profile of the situation, bringing them together according to the rule of the specification equation.

(Organism's properties)

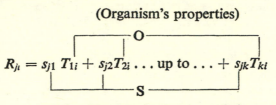

$$R_{ji} = s_{j1}\,T_{1i} + s_{j2}T_{2i} \ldots \text{up to} \ldots + s_{jk}T_{ki}$$

(Stimulus situation's properties)

This is how we begin to put Humpty-Dumpty together again, and in doing so we have enriched our concepts of person and situation and also increased our accuracy of prediction. Indeed, in theory, if we knew every factor involved in the person, and the s's for every class of situation, we could make accurate predictions rather than rough estimates.

HOW TRAITS INTERACT

The last section has shown how modern quantitative psychology can represent the unique individual personality and the equally unique situation, and combine them in a 'specification equation' to predict the response which the person is likely to make. Normally we choose a situation where a certain kind of response is being made by everyone but where its magnitude varies. In many life situations the actual quality or kind of response also varies. However, we can handle this with our formula, as we did in the motivation field, by finding for one individual which course of action would be more strongly impelled, and taking this as the response.

From the standpoint of developing any truly scientific analysis of personality, questions of the above kind have to be asked. A scientific theory must finally be expressed in a 'model', and a model forces us to ask exactly what our assumptions are about mathematical formulae, causal connexions, and so on. In Newton's 'machinery' for the solar system, his model made certain clear assumptions. He simplified by considering the masses of planets as concentrated at points, and he applied the formula which said masses attract by their products and inversely as the square of their distances. This model fitted so well that there was no need to change it until the extremely small divergences from the model of separate mass and velocity values were investigated at the challenge of Einstein's alternative model.

In the present model of the structure of personality the effects of the various traits are supposed to combine additively. The effect on behaviour of T_1, namely, $s_l T_1$, is added to $s_2 T_2$, and so on through the specification equation. Other models are obviously possible. We could try the idea that the behaviour-contribution varies as the *square* of the trait quantity, or that it is a consequence of the product instead of the sum of traits. Certainly it is easily *possible* to conceive situations psychologically where a product makes good sense. For example, if we take a group of people living together, say in a student dormitory or an officer's mess, and get a measure of sociometric popularity, i.e. essentially by how many people each person is liked or disliked, it is found that this popularity score is systematically related to personality factors. A specification equation can be written for popularity. It loads A positively, C positively, G positively, and I negatively. In rough terms for these factors, a warm, dependable person of strong super-ego and no airs of sensitivity tends to be liked, and persons who have some of the major components in neuroticism are disliked. (This may be *one* reason why the unfortunate neurotic is ready to pay so much just to have someone – a medical man or psychiatrist is best of course – listen to him!)

However, when the figures are examined more closely, a curious relation emerges in regard to surgency, or F. If the person has the type of profile which is liked he will be liked still more if he is surgent. But, similarly, if he has the type considered objectionable, then, if he is talkative, sociable, and irrepressible, i.e. surgent, he is disliked more than if he were desurgent. Thus the surgency factor acts as a sort of catalyst, or, simply, a magnifying glass for the effects of the other qualities. This is understandable, for the surgent individual reveals his personality more rapidly, as it were on a wider stage, than does the desurgent. Surgency in a person makes us react more strongly to either the good or the bad in him, for the uninhibited temperament thrusts his quality more powerfully upon us.

If this analysis is correct then the usual additive specification equation breaks down. The simple model then no longer fits the psychological nature of the real life interaction. One possible adjustment would be to have the score in surgency *multiply* the other factor scores. Another would be to add surgency in but give weights suitable to a *curvilinear* relation of the response

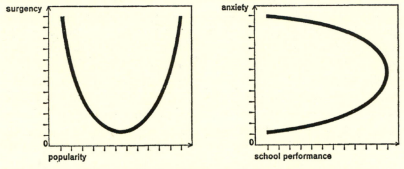

Diagram 32. Curvilinear prediction relations

(evoking popularity in this case) to the factor. Certainly, it is possible to think of instances where a curvilinear relation, as in Diagram 32, seems a better model. For example, there is some evidence that school performance may be so related to anxiety level.

The appropriate procedure in science is to choose the simplest model that seems workable and stick to it unless and until it fails in some respect. The additive and linear model evidently suffices for a great deal of human behaviour, and it can be modified at points like the above where some particular trait behaves in an unusual manner.

If we continue with the theory that one trait 'helps' another in an additive way in producing any performance, a number of interesting 'riders' and dilemmas follow. For example, it follows that two different people can achieve the same result by a different combination of trait combinations. They achieve the same score but with a different 'quality' in their styles. For simplicity let us suppose that success in fencing depends on only two factors, an intelligence trait, *I*, determining good tactics, and a manual dexterity trait, *D*, determining good execution of tactics. Let the weights (situational indices) found for these, by factor analysis of many people in many matches, be $+0.3$ and $+0.7$ respectively, so that performance P_f can be analysed:

$$P_f = 0.3I + 0.7D$$

If we substitute for *I* and *D* the profile of Mr Smith who is intelligent but clumsy, with a standard score of $+2.5$ on *I* and -1.0 on dexterity, we get a performance of $+0.05$, roughly average. If next we take Mr Brown, a not very intelligent man, with an *I* score of -1.0, but a dexterity somewhat above average, $+0.5$, it will be found that he goes to a drawn match with Mr Smith, for his performance is also $+0.05$. However, in the one case the performance is achieved by able tactics despite poor control of the foil, while in the other we watch a quite different style, characterized by deftness and dexterity. This principle applies across the whole range of personality expressions, and explains what we notice in terms of different styles of behaviour despite equal success. In the dynamic trait realm it also explains why two people perceive the same object or situation with different meaning – emotional meaning – despite the relations being in terms of the same common traits.

Another conception introduced in rough form earlier which can now be more clearly handled is the idea that one trait is more powerful than another. For example, we said cyclothymia–sizothymia was labelled *A* in the factor trait series because it was the largest factor and that this agreed with the psychiatrists having first recognized such a dimension in clinical experience. What, in fact, is the basis of calculation for placing source traits as *A*, *B*, *C*, etc. (or U.I. 1, 2, 3, etc., in objective tests) in declining order of size or importance? To give meaning to this we must start with what is called a 'stratified sample' of the 'personality sphere' of everyday life behaviour performances. On such a set one source trait, *A*, may have large loadings – say, 0·5 or more – on many performances whereas another, say, the *N* trait, may have only a few high loadings and otherwise have loadings mainly about zero. Provided our sample of performance is really representative this permits us to say that A, cyclothymia-*vs*-sizothymia, is a really important trait, because it affects so much of behaviour and to such an extent, whereas N, the 'shrewdness' factor, operates only in restricted fields and is not so important in describing the personality as a whole. By this criterion the three most important traits are *A*, the cyclo-sizo temperament differentiator, *B*, general intelligence, and *C*, ego strength or emotional control, and it is noteworthy that, in their popular terminology, these are constantly in use in describing personality.

THE USE AND MISUSE OF TYPES

The contrasting habits of describing personalities by *types* and by *traits* was mentioned at the outset of our discussion, with the

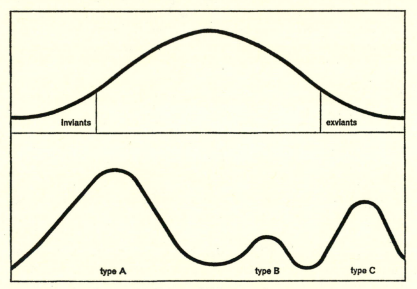

Diagram 33. True and false use of type concept

comment that they are really supplementary rather than inconsistent methods. In accordance with the theme of this chapter, which is to bring all concepts into a logical, conceptual integration, freed of fallacies with which the popular treatment of personality is plagued, we ought to return to some tricky aspects of this relationship.

So long as people are distributed on traits in an essentially normal scatter, in the well-known bell-shaped fashion shown in Diagram 33, there is really no point in using type concepts. Merely, as a convenient manner of speaking, one can refer to the persons at the end of such distributions, as shown by the shaded portions, as surgent or desurgent, exviant or inviant 'types'. But this says no more than the trait scores say. Indeed, it leaves the middle group vague and unnamed. It also forces us to be arbitrary about the point at which we cut off those we designate as types.

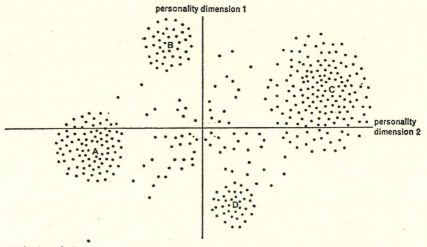

Diagram 34. Species types

Unlike the situation in the first 'distribution curve' in Diagram 33, there are somewhat less common instances where people are found with especial frequency at some level of score, as at the 'modes' *A*, *B*, and *C* in Diagram 33, and it may then be useful to speak of belonging to these types. Even then it is not so useful, when people need dozens of different traits to describe them, to talk about their appearance just on one trait and so the notion of type acquires its full usefulness only when people simultaneously cluster on several characteristics at once, as shown by the swarms of points in Diagram 34. If we imagine this carried into hyper-space, as discussed above, in the scheme to represent people on *all* traits, as point positions in space, then there *could* be swarms of points in this space. When such swarms of similar people are separated by empty spaces, like galaxies in astronomical space, it gives real advantages, which we shall now discuss, to use the term 'type' and to use 'types' in calculations.

The usage of type stated in quantitative terms here is really no different from what we recognize in qualitative terms when we deal with species of plants, or, say, breeds of dogs. Each differs from the other not only on some one measurement, but on *a whole pattern*. Indeed, sometimes the single measures may overlap but the patterns or ratios among them do not. For example, in a mixed kennel of fifty whippet dogs and fifty bulldogs there may be overlap of the breeds in body length, or even in some cases in leg length, but the ratios or total patterns of leg, body, and muzzle lengths and widths are such that we never for a moment confuse one with the other.

When we think of types in their essential nature as galaxies in a uniform space it is at first rather surprising that this space is not uniformly full of living representatives of all mathematically possible combinations of measurements. If the traits are or can be continuous, why are their combinations not also represented at every possible point? It is a mystery which we take too much for granted, in plant and animal and personality. For biologically, and culturally, as far as human societies are concerned, gaps confront us on all sides. There are no spiders or beetles with the human type of eye or hand. There are no cultures combining the industrial revolution with cannibalism. The Greeks noted these holes in biological space and filled a few in with creatures like the centaur, and later the Teutonic dragon, with reptile head and bird wings, filled another empty quadrant.

The reason for these unfulfilled possibilities is fairly evident. Certain combinations, though mathematically and logically possible, either do not work out functionally or simply have not been tried. Is the same true of human personality? As far as the major personality traits are concerned we know that people tend to be normally distributed on them, according to any ordinary scaling of scores, and all mathematically possible combinations are also apparently biologically and culturally possible. Admittedly, some combinations may be less pleasant than others for their possessors. The high *E* trait (dominance) which combined with high intelligence (*B*) might make a pioneer in science (awkward to live with, perhaps, but very useful to society), when combined with low intelligence – so that the dominance cannot easily express itself – might make a criminal. Obviously, some biological selection is bound in the long run to make awkward combinations less frequent, and we do see some correlations of traits which suggest this. For example, the primaries *A*, *H*, *F*, *L*, and Q_2 tend to get correlated in the second-order exvia–invia factor (page 123 above), but it is still possible for a person to be very high on *A*, and therefore very fond of human society and parties, while being very low on *F*, and therefore so dull, inhibited, and passive that few people invite him to a party.

But selection, by social learning or biological survival, cannot go far to eliminate awkward combinations in a freely inter-marrying society. If certain traits are useful at certain levels in one sort of combination, they will persist in cropping up at those levels in other combinations which are less fortunate. For ex-ample, the elements for good musical or artistic talent sometimes appear in individuals of low intelligence, who cannot express that talent or make a living by it. Thus quite distinct 'species types' (as they may be called for accuracy) are not demonstrable in broad primary traits. But distinct types *can* be found (*a*) in certain inherited patterns, (*b*) at the opposite extreme in the most highly acquired patterns, such as patterns of occupational skills, and political or religious attitudes, and (*c*) when disease syndromes produce particular patterns. As an instance of the last, the schizophrenic, for example, shows a set of traits which mark him off as, so to speak, a separate species of mind. He is withdrawn from and ignores his environment, his laughter and annoyance occur without any obvious relation to events, though mostly he seems without emotion. He hears imaginary voices and sees hallucinatory images. To say that someone is a schizophrenic is, therefore, at once to convey to another psychologist what would take a long time to describe in single traits.

The inherited 'types' are very few, and, of course, because they come from medical observation, mainly pathological. A quite distinctive type of mental defective has long been technically called a Mongolian imbecile because he has physical features resembling someone of Mongolian race and a pattern of mental defect (not associated with the Mongolian race) which is quite specific among forms of low intelligence. It means a verbal ability characteristically not so low as the other abilities, a cheerful, friendly disposition, and other pattern features. To take another kind of pattern which, though hereditary, comes on in middle age, we may mention Huntington's chorea, where a mental degeneration is associated with palsy, in a pattern which a psychiatrist readily recognizes.

The hatreds with which some people accompany recognition of racial differences (in which practice Hitler's Nazis have unfortunately been by no means unique) should not blind us to the fact that it is not, *a priori*, unreasonable to expect that a pattern of physical differences might be accompanied by a pattern of temperamental differences. One might not expect any significant intelligence differences – at least among races coping equally with their cultural environments today. (Though as between present and past races, such as Neanderthal man, there is every sign of significant intelligence and cranial capacity differences.) On the other hand, one might expect differences of temperament associated with long selection to fit a particular climate or a particular culture. As seen in Chapter 2, Kretschmer and Sheldon have both shown some association of cyclothyme temperament with broad body build and sizothyme temperament with slim build. But in terms of total physical type no such equivalent mental patterns have yet been established,* though the finer measurement methods available today may, with pattern analysis computer programmes, yet reveal them.

* A curiosity pointed out in this connexion by the present writer, and since confirmed at the University of Chicago, is a difference between light-eyed and light-haired people on the one hand and dark on the other in terms of a three-element pattern covering (in the direction of dark-eyedness) higher motor-rigidity (on the test on page 110), stronger emotionality, and more interest in such subjects as history and religion, compared to mathematics, crafts, and science. The contrast in interests may be interpreted as a difference between 'dry' topics, lacking immediate emotional content, and those with emotional values immediately woven into them. Doubtless a number of other such physically tied patterns will crop up as systematic measurement investigation proceeds.

Although instances of discrete 'species' pattern types in behaviour are thus not easily instanced at the temperament level they stare us in the face when we turn to environmentally produced occupationally acquired skills, and the beliefs and attitude systems of political and religious groups. These need no illustration. The predictive power of a type category is evident, however, when we think of how much it means to us if when being introduced to a person we are told that he is, say, a surgeon, a republican, or a member of the Presbyterian church. From the purely statistical point of view the assignment to a type brings two advantages in prediction. First, personality variations *within* a type can usually be more reliably and closely related to a criterion than across a conglomerate population of types. For example, I.Q. may predict salary within a group of surgeons, all with similar training and opportunity, more reliably than in the general population. Or, if I am told that a certain person uses bad language in public, my prediction of other traits will be more accurate if I am told whether that person is a man or a woman, instead of leaving the group unspecified. The mathematically inclined reader will recognize that the point made here has to do with using non-linear instead of linear relations in the equation on page 253. Secondly, when several traits come together in a particular way they may produce effects which philosophers have called 'emergents', which theoretically cannot be predicted simply from the traits. For example, it is said that no one knowing only the properties of the metal sodium and the gas chlorine could predict the 'saltiness' of the product formed when they combine. It would take us into too abstruse mathematics to ask how the specification equation needs modifying for type effects, but at least the psychologist gains something by locating these type clusters, when they exist, and recognizing that new features are brought in.

One area in which type patterns are particularly important is in the relation of people with people. For example, quite apart from explicit group affiliations, people of the same age group tend to associate together, from infancy to late maturity. Another type difference, which there is little danger of overlooking, is that provided by the species types of the two sexes! Since the days when Havelock Ellis wrote his classical *Men and Women*, inadvertently mixing in some superstitions with his scientific data, a good deal of new and quantitative psychological data has accumulated, notably through such patient researchers as Lewis Terman, who compared abilities, personality traits, attitudes, and interests. Incidentally, he made a psychological masculinity–femininity scale which worked reasonably well, despite showing young men as more masculine than old men – due to the trend of both sexes towards feminine sensitivity with age in cultural societies.

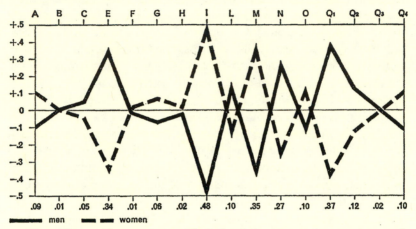

Note: The profiles are symmetrical about the average because men and women jointly *make* the average.

Diagram 35. Difference of 'Type' of men and women on personality factors

Somewhat to the surprise of many whose ideal is a bigger and better sex difference, the correlational studies of behaviour show a very similar trait structure. As far as the major source traits are concerned the important observation is apparently that men and women are primarily human personalities and secondarily of a particular sex!

On these personality factors, however, they certainly tend to stand at different levels. The principal factors on which statistically significant differences exist, as found for men and women, and confirmed for boys and girls, are shown in Diagram 35. The five most significant differences show women to be less dominant (*E*), more premsic (*I*) (emotionally sensitive and over-protected), autious (M), i.e. given to letting inner wishes determine belief, autistically; more child-like in expressing attitudes, and more conservative (Q_1). Also, they are more cyclothymic (A), and less self-sufficient (Q_2).

There is no inconsistency at any point of these test results with life behaviour statistics or even literary evidence. The higher dominance of men and higher emotionality and conservatism of women are proverbial. The first and last agree with the far higher crime-rate of men. One of the new slants which the testing brings out, however, is that the higher emotionality of women is only to a small degree that moody emotionality due to lower ego strength and mainly a function of the higher emotional sensitivity measured by the premsia factor, I. This protected emotional sensitivity is nevertheless higher in neurotics, which fits again the statistics of more frequent neurosis in women. Again, the finding that the male average is decidedly lower on A, i.e. that men are more sizothyme, agrees with the clinical finding that men are more than twice as prone as women to schizophrenia whereas women are significantly more prone to the 'affective' psychoses of manic behaviour and depression.

Age, sex, and occupation are among the outstanding, but not the only instances of the whole pattern of adaptation simultaneously changing in a way which justifies our switching to predictions which use type concepts rather than trait concepts alone. Another striking instance, often confounded with racial type differences, yet distinct from them, is presented by the type patterns due to particular cultures. As measurement has been brought to bear on national cultures it has revealed the differences to be very substantial, whether considered in terms of such statistics as percentage of marriages ending in divorce, number of musical compositions per 100,000, number of murders per 100,000, and so on, or in terms of psychological tests.

Diagram 14 (page 122) shows some of the substantial differences found on measured anxiety level, and we have also referred to the Manchester–Chicago results showing Britons to be decidedly more introvert than Americans, especially on the sizothyme (cool, aloof) component. This work, on a truly adequate measurement basis, is only just beginning, but it looks as if what the sociologists wanted to consider as imaginary national 'stereotypes', or even slurs, may have a substantial core of truth, though doubtless caricatured in different directions according to the observer's side of the fence. If we consider, for example, the charming politeness of the average Japanese, or the emotional reserve of the average Englishman, it is clear that to interpret an absolute score level on a particular trait in a particular individual the psychological type to which he belongs must also be taken into consideration.

With these examples we recognize that our 'model', to get good predictions, must measure and recognize types as well as traits. In a type the trait parts stand at the levels they do because there is functional fitness in such a combination. The giraffe's neck is long because, with long legs, he still has to get his mouth down to the pool. The low dominance (E factor) score in women might similarly be due to a certain incompatibility between high emotional sensitivity (I factor) and the results of rough-shod dominance behaviour. At any rate, what the statistical analysis of type clusters teaches us is that not all the possible combinations of more or less continuously distributed traits are 'occupied'. Persons are, in some respects, clumped together in 'galaxies' in the hyper-space of trait dimensions. Some of these, such as culture pattern types, may be restricted more or less through accident: other combinations have just not been tried. But in others a necessary functional connexion with the environment has brought the parts of the psychological type pattern together and multiplied cases at that position.

ADJUSTMENT, ADAPTATION, AND INTEGRATION OF PERSONALITY AND ENVIRONMENT

The purpose of this chapter has been to give a glimpse of the final model, in which quantitative and analytic research on personality culminates, before applying it in remaining chapters to some practical problems. A trait, it will be evident, is not something existing in a person: it is a concept and a measurement derived from his relations to his environment, though it hinges on him.

From another aspect, behavioural traits are the necessary negotiations or compromises between the physiological demands of the organism on the one hand, and the physical and social demands of the environment on the other. The organism is a tremendously ingenious arrangement of protoplasm, set to seek only to maintain life in itself and to propagate itself. All the motivation which builds up elaborate trait habits must spring from these physiological needs, and these traits will reflect, in form, the conditions of the physical and social environment. If the reader asks what has happened to the soul one reply would be that the modern psychologist is as afraid of mentioning the word in public as a Victorian curate might have been of mentioning sexual intercourse. Each is showing respect for something a little outside his area of specialization, yet in neither case can it be ignored. At the present moment the path from protoplasm to the soul is too far for the psycho-physiologist to span. But as we reach the rather cloudy heights of such concepts as 'adjustment' and 'integration', and try to put them into measurement form, we realize that we are approaching the neighbourhood of what has intuitively been called the soul, and that some day greatness of soul may be contemplated as something more than a metaphor. Whoever scales these scientific heights will be using concepts and mathematical models which will make very elementary those background statistics which we have refrained from introducing here except in simplified form.

A definition can be given to adjustment in terms of the conflict index of Chapter 8 (page 235). For if by adjustment we mean the extent to which the individual is gaining satisfactory expression for his given nature, i.e. his degree of realization and happiness, then this will be the inverse of his ergic loss in conflict. Thus we may write Adjustment, A, in a calculable figure:

$$A = \frac{1}{C}$$

where C is the conflict index, i.e. the sum of negative s's over positive s's from a P-technique analysis of his dynamic structure. If the theories about measuring U, unintegrated, and I, integrated motivation components by different batteries (and manifestations) are right we should also expect a fairly close relation of A to the difference, $I–U$, over a representative set of interest areas. Furthermore, since conflict and anxiety develop together from an insoluble clash with environment, we should expect that these A (adjustment) measures would show a substantial inverse relation to general anxiety factor measures, and this also is borne out by the first studies, in the last two or three years.

Two other concepts of the total personality which are much discussed are adaptation and integration. It seems best to restrict the former to its biological and social meaning, namely, to the extent to which the individual's behaviour aids him in surviving, and, indeed, succeeding. Obviously, adjustment and adaptation can be at appreciably different levels in the same person. An unsuccessful criminal is maladapted, but he may be giving every possible expression to his ergs, without inner conflict. A miserable miser may be maladjusted but excellently adapted, in terms of survival.

Integration is a more baffling concept. Essentially, we mean by a well-integrated man one whose various purposes cohere in a single harmonious life goal. He does not, for example, try to be a gourmand and an athlete at the same time, or to let his left hand undo the work of his right in any field. The concept is hard to get into measurement form because what 'interferes' depends so much on individual *values*. By values we mean the social, artistic, moral, and other standards which the individual would like others and himself to follow. Most value attitudes are found embedded in the self-sentiment and the super-ego structures. The calculation of the degree of integration present in the individual's values is a social calculation, as well as an individual one, for it requires us to find out how well society would do with various combinations of values; and this is something for the future.

This consideration reminds us, however, that personality has a long social frontage. 'No man liveth to himself, and no man dieth to himself.' He plays roles – if 'play' can be used for such serious matters – in a family, a social status group, a school, a job, a country, a religious sect, and so on. The *sentiment* structures which contain these roles are a very important part of his trait structure.

Thus, in summary, as far as we can at present quantify behavioural performances, our most effective model is one which uses a behavioural equation covering the following terms:

$$P_j = s_{ja}A \ldots + s_{jtY}T \ldots + s_{je}E \ldots + s_{jm}M \ldots + s_{jr}R \ldots + s_{js}S$$

where *A* represents ability source traits – how *well* the performance is done;

    T represents temperament traits: the style of behaviour;

    E represents ergic drives, the first class of dynamic trait;

    M represents sentiments, the second class of dynamic trait;

    R represents a role trait, the third class of dynamic trait;

    S represents temporary moods and other modulating *states*.

Our prediction will be best if we recognize the type to which the individual belongs, and measure the traits and the situational indices appropriately for that type.

The fact that we need to know the *s*'s means that prediction requires an understanding as much of the social and general environment as of the person. For this reason the team-work with sociologists, which psychologists like Cartwright, Cook, Newcombe, and Scott have been vigorously pursuing, is an indispensable part of the scientific analysis of personality. In terms of mathematics and models the position we reach here might be called an *intersection* theory of personality, for it makes the individual the main intersection point of physiological and sociological concepts. But he is the most important point in all of it, as the hub is the most important part of the wheel, for on what happens in his integration, action, at the focus of the human will, the fate of the rest depends.

*

READING

Wepman, J. M., and Heine, R. W., *Concepts of Personality*. Aldine, Chicago, 1963.

Hare, P., Borgatta, E. F., and Bales, R. F., *Small Groups: Studies in Social Interaction*. Knopf, New York, 1955.

CHAPTER TEN

The Development of Personality

THE ROLE OF CLASSICAL CONDITIONING
IN PERSONALITY LEARNING

A reminder of the necessity of proper perspective on the interaction of learning and hereditary maturation, in determining the
individual personality, has been given in Chapter 2. That approach was meant to give some realistic conception of the limits
set by each, but the *process* by which motivation and learning
interact in personality formation remains to be considered.

Three forms of learning have been briefly described in Chapter
2:

(1) Classical conditioning, where a new stimulus gets attached to an old response by occurring a moment before the
old stimulus;

(2) goal path reward learning, where a new way to an existing
goal is learned because it is more rewarded;

(3) integration learning, also under reward, but where a
readjustment is made among goals, some being denied or given
restricted effect, in the interest of the organism's *total* satisfaction.

The relative roles of these in personality formation is still unknown. Only one thing is certain: the textbooks have given excessive attention to classical conditioning and insufficient thought
to how integration learning occurs. Indeed, as far as personality
learning is concerned the learning theorists have insisted on the
penny-in-the-slot reflexological model much as the nostrum salesman is ready to claim it will cure all, before he even hears what the
disease is. Few have looked at measured personality changes, to
see what they first have to explain. How, for example, would the
increase on the ego strength factor, C, shown to occur in therapy,

be accounted for by a large number of conditionings of specific behaviours? When a reduction occurs on the anxiety factor, U.I. 24, are we to suppose it is because each of the specific anxiety responses, to thunder, snakes, lost income, etc., has been separately reduced by de-conditioning (extinction) of the particular fear? This is possible – a factor measure is an average of responses in many situations – but in Chapters 7 and 8 we have favoured additionally or alternatively the view that a drive or trait may change *as a whole*. This is the meaning of the *H* – History of the drive – term in the equation on page 202, which says that experiences, especially early experiences, may do something to a general personality trait *as a whole*.

Experimental and statistical evidence in support of this comes from the work of Spitz and others, showing that children brought up in inferior orphanages, with defective personal affectional ties, show defective capacity in later life to make warm human contacts compared with those brought up with affection from a mother or mother substitute. Harlow's work with rhesus monkeys shows similarly that the early experience of love relationships in infancy affects whole trait patterns later on. Possibly, as Eric Erickson's insistence on the first stage of infant development as establishing 'trust' implies, we should also find that individuals brought up in less predictable, more confusing, and frightening environments tend to show more paranoid behaviour in later life, as Benedict recognized in whole cultures, such as the North West Coast Indians.

In short, we cannot suppose that classical conditioning can explain all of personality learning, and the simple laws which many years of experiment have established about conditioning in cognitive situations and for specific muscular responses have shown no great efficacy in explaining personality learning. Laws have been established about the optimum interval for conditioning, about the effect of excitement level at the time of conditioning, the effect of frequency of repetition of the conditioning experience, and so on. One finding of some interest with regard to personality is that of Humphreys and others: when the conditioned and unconditioned stimuli are only intermittently associated the learning endures longer. If you have been used to the light sometimes coming on and sometimes not when you press the switch you will go on trying this longer, when it finally goes out of order, than if it had worked regularly right up to the moment it went wrong. Many of our personality responses are thus learnt on a 'probability basis': we are vaguely aware that they work much of the time.

The role of classical conditioning is probably greatest in our unconscious learning and it certainly plays a part in some powerful, irrational emotional attachments and phobias. Elsewhere we have described Watson's experiment with attaching a fear response to a white rabbit in a small child by making a frightening crash immediately after the rabbit's appearance. Thereafter the child cringed when the rabbit appeared. What is called 'behaviour therapy' today applies the successful extinction procedure which Watson applied to this child, namely, repeated exposures to the rabbit (or its equivalent) at short intervals in a reassuring, pleasant environment, i.e. without the 'crash'. One of the incompletely explained findings in this field is the extraordinary persistence of an emotional response conditioning to a single powerful emotional experience. The suggestion is that the very strength of the response causes some dissociation from fresh cognitive experience, and that relearning can occur only with emotion reaching the original level.

THE ROLE OF GOAL PATH, REWARD, AND PUNISHMENT LEARNING

By goal-path learning we mean learning new behaviour to reach an old goal, as presented either in an erg or a sentiment. By a piece of unnecessary mental acrobatics one can call this 'operant conditioning', but the important thing about it is that it requires reward, whereas conditioning does not. The simplest physical illustration is a rat running a maze to get food. If he is punished by an electric shock for entering certain alleys, he gradually drops them. If he is unrewarded, by getting no food down blind alleys, he learns to drop out those energy-consuming detours and follow the paths which lead most directly to food reward.

Much of our personality learning occurs by this 'law of effect', as it is called. A boy has a sentiment towards athletic prowess, for example, and discovers that good exercise and diet may contribute to this goal; or a business man has a sentiment towards his career as a salesman and discovers that knowing a certain foreign language would help him. In this way the boy may acquire much knowledge and good habits on diet and the businessman a subsidiary sentiment of interest in languages. Indeed, most of our learning in the building up of dynamic structures is of this kind, and it can be represented in the dynamic lattice (Diagram 21, page 186), which maps these connexions, as a 'growing back' of new paths from the ergic goal end of the lattice, as shown in Diagram 36.

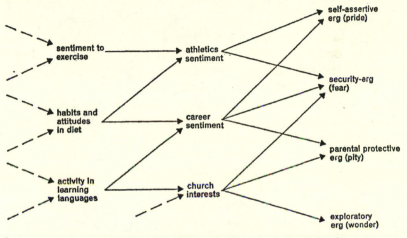

Diagram 36. Goal path learning in the dynamic lattice

This lattice helps to remind us that sentiments must ultimately subsidiate to ergic goals, and that the growth of structure, in a complex culture, is always towards the left. The dotted lines show the gradual crystallization, out of random behaviour and experience, of new habits and attitudes. They are no longer rewarded *directly* by ergic satisfactions but by contributing to an existing sentiment which in turn draws its motive power from ergic satisfactions. Ignoring this theoretical model many experimenters have sought to implant new attitudes or to change attitudes by movies and exhortatory propaganda, and have seemingly been surprised at their failure. A new attitude is not implanted by frontal attack but by showing how it will subsidiate to some existing sentiment (as wise old Ben Franklin realized, in his autobiographical report).

Another characteristic of human emotional learning which the dynamic lattice brings out is what may be called *confluence learning* – the acquisition of behaviours and attitudes which simultaneously subsidiate to two or more different goals. Thus in Diagram 36 the salesman's learning of a foreign language might simultaneously be found useful in aiding some foreign charity supported by his church, and thus also give satisfaction to his religious sentiment. And the boy's interest in diet, in connexion with athletic prowess (we have built the boy and the man into the same lattice in Diagram 36) may prove useful to him in staying in good condition for his career also.

So far nothing has been said about *how* these learnings occur, but only *why* and *where*, through the law of effect. Some learning, even in personality, is entirely rational, as when a man takes stock of his needs and decides to learn these skills, adopt the attitudes of that group, or practise self-control. Some of it is a more or less conscious imitation of admired figures – especially of parents, etc., in childhood, and of historical or living eminent men and women in adolescence. But much of it is almost certainly as unconscious as that which occurs to the rat or pigeon in the Skinner box. Therein we behave randomly and are rewarded fairly consistently only for certain behaviour – for no obvious reason. We do not know just what the family, the peer group, the church, the career organization are rewarding, by approval and disapproval, company and loneliness, sexual encouragement and frustration. Nor do they. The conscious statements in a family of what is approved behaviour may not coincide with what is actually, unconsciously rewarded – a fact which Sir Cyril Burt first brought out clearly in his finding of inconsistent discipline in the families of delinquents. But the law of effect remains our soundest principle for understanding much personality development – provided we recognize that unlike the maze animal, responding mainly to hunger and thirst, the human responds to ergic tension reduction on all those ergs which dynamic structure research has revealed – assertiveness, exploration, gregariousness, protectiveness, etc. – and these, moreover, require subtle perception in tracing their action.

In the notion of confluence learning we have encountered already the idea that learning needs sometimes to be considered in relation to the totality of the organism's drive satisfactions, not merely in terms of the goal path satisfaction to a single ergic goal. The formula for conflict (page 232) has also reminded us that a course of action may sometimes be settled upon which is punishing as far as one drive is concerned but sufficiently rewarding on two or three others to be adopted. About the rate of exchange among different drives – or whether they can be easily measured in the same 'quality' – we are uncertain, though the discussion on relative magnitudes of traits (page 265) provides an avenue of research.

In an animal or young child the behavioural outcome of a conflict seems to be decided by the relative strength of ergs at the time. This obviously does not lead to *maximal satisfaction of the organism over any given time period*, because what the child does then may prevent his satisfaction in some other way later. For example, by taking a jam tart from the cupboard now he may find his mother denies him any supper. Inhibition comes from foresight or from interference of some other drive, but these are not so different since the fear drive – fear of loss of satisfactions – may operate at the time to effect the restraint, i.e. much foresight is fearsight.

That which the child builds up, as a restraining mechanism, and which few animals can acquire, lies in the form of two structures which we have already experimentally recognized – the self-sentiment and the super-ego. The latter is a comparatively straightforward set of categorical imperatives, based on guilt motivation, to do this and not do that, and we must leave its description to the experimental literature (Readings, page 286) and to the psychoanalysts. The former is a more complex and intriguing affair, the main attitudes found in it being set out on page 194. How the growing child builds up attitudes around his self-concept has already been described. But what function does this serve?

In the first place, the preservation of the self as a physically healthy and intact going concern is obviously a prerequisite for the satisfaction of any sentiment or erg which the individual possesses! So also is the preservation of the social and ethical self as something which the community respects. The amount of other satisfaction, ergic and sentiment, which depends on this may not be immediately appreciated. But among primitive peoples a broken taboo which puts the individual outside the tribe has been

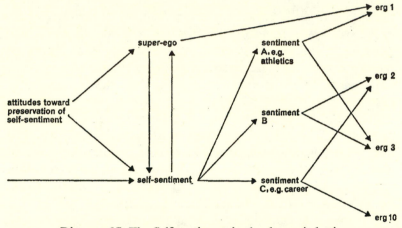

Diagram 37. The Self-sentiment in the dynamic lattice

known to cause comparatively sudden death; Roman and Greek citizens of antiquity have fallen on their sword blades rather than go into exile; and excommunication has brought emperors to supplication. Dynamically, the sentiment towards maintaining the self correct by certain standards of conduct, satisfactory to community and super-ego, is therefore a *necessary instrumentality* to the satisfaction of most other of our life interests.

The conclusion to which this leads is that the self-sentiment must appear in the dynamic lattice at the position indicated in Diagram 37, far to the left and therefore among the latest of sentiments to reach a ripe development. It contributes to all sentiment and ergic satisfactions, and this accounts also for its dynamic strength in controlling, as the 'master sentiment', all other structures. In our account of the behavioural equation (page 80) we pointed out that in any sample of reasonably controlled persons it must have such a weight as will enable it to outweigh any single erg or set of ergs, thus:

$$P_j = s_{e1}E_1 \ldots \div s_{en}E_n + s_{m1}M_1$$

where s_{m1}, for the self-sentiment M_1, must be greater than s_{e1} and s_{en} for the ergs, $E_1 \ldots E_n$, which might be involved in any situation. A still inadequately mapped part of the lattice is that relating the self-sentiment to the super-ego, where a two-way action may exist: satisfying the super-ego is instrumental in maintaining the self-sentiment, but also maintaining a sound self-sentiment is incidentally necessary to satisfying the super-ego. The correlations of measures of these two with each other, and with such performances as school reports and freedom from delinquency, argue for a relation approximately as shown.

Integration learning is the essential producer of both general sentiments and the self-sentiment, but shows its nature most clearly in the latter. We may safely assume that trial-and-error learning plays a large role again. It has been said of the adolescent, who is particularly beset by the problems of self-sentiment learning, that we should be patient with his posturings and inconsistencies because he is trying on many faces to see which best fits his resources and dynamic needs. It may not always be trial-and-error learning in the sense of something blind and unconscious – the individual may be well aware what ideal or compromise he is trying, but the answer can come only from experiment. Until he tries a dental college, for example, he may not know whether he has the abilities and fortitude for dentistry.

The satisfactions and dissatisfactions of particular drives in various situations are something which a psychologist, with the aid of the dynamic calculus – and a good computer – may some day be able approximately to work out for a given individual. Meanwhile he has to experiment for himself, by changing a job, by marrying or not marrying, to see if the sum total of satisfactions to all drives shows a gain or loss in the transaction.

Let us next see how integration learning proceeds in terms of the readjustments it occasions in the individual.

THE DYNAMIC CROSSROADS, OR CHIASMS, IN ADJUSTMENT PATH ANALYSIS

In connexion with the dynamic calculus, and particularly its use in studying integration and adjustment, the clinician's experience of human conflicts has been schematized into a potentially quantifiable system called *adjustment process analysis*. This considers all the possible alternatives in trial-and-error 'emotional learning', providing a scheme of successive 'dynamic crossroads' whereby any individual's particular learning position can be codified.

One naturally begins in the Adjustment Path Analysis Chart (Diagram 38) with an individual stimulated with respect to a certain drive and asks what happens from there. If he immediately finds satisfaction the story ends – until the drive is active again. No learning needs to occur. But at this choice point or crossroads (or chiasm, if you prefer science in Greek), several other roads are possible. The person may fail to find satisfaction and, like a thirsty traveller in the desert, continue in deprivation, or he may perceive what he needs but encounter a frustrating obstacle between him and it. These are indicated as paths A_1, A_3 and A_2 at the first chiasm, A, in Diagram 38.

If he continues to fail to circumvent the barrier three things can happen at the barrier chiasm, B. He can get very angry and succeed in smashing it, B_1, or he may attack it in vain (and receive retaliation, since many barriers are live ones), B_2, or he may stay deprived and daydream, B_3. Standing next at chiasm C, the now unfortunate individual can give way to despair and appeal, at C_1, to decide to give up that ergic satisfaction (or that path to it) at C_2, or persist with non-adjustive (because hopeless) pugnacity cycles at C_3.

The D chiasm, which follows from the renunciation decision at C_2, is a very critical one for emotional learning. It leaves the individual with the necessity of handling an unexpressed drive, and on the way he does this depends his mental health and his character growth. The alternatives are first D_1, deflexion to some other path, or (if we are considering all practical paths blocked) *sublimation*, i.e. change of the goal itself, as when sex needs are expressed in art or religion. Secondly, D_2, the person may get no solution and stay in a turmoil of inner conflict and anxiety, or, thirdly, by path D_3, he may be able to summon up the ego strength,

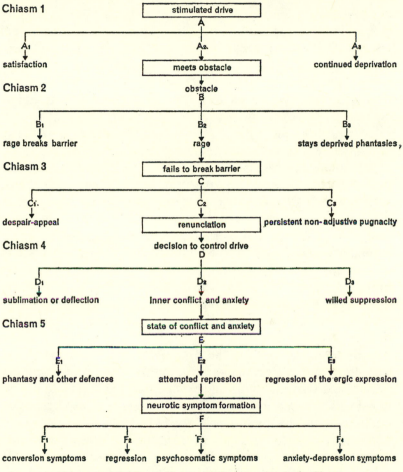

Diagram 38. The Adjustment Process Analysis Chart

if his past development has been fortunate, calmly and consciously to suppress the behaviour pending some more appropriate situation.

In most individuals the conflict and anxiety at E will tend to induce defence reactions and, especially, an attempt at repression.

Other responses are shown in Diagram 38. At F we are definitely in a neurotic path and the alternatives are mainly those governing the form of symptoms. It should be noted that though we have followed in the A.P.A. Chart the paths which lead on to the cul-de-sac at F, the numerous side paths are actually more frequently followed in healthy learning. Thus at B, the individual learns that there are occasions to 'summon up the blood' and break a barrier, as Christ whipped the money-lenders out of the temple. There are also times, as at C, where a prayer for assistance from others may yield a solution. D_1, the path of sublimation and deflexion, is particularly valuable. Through deflexion, new sentiment structures are built up, and confluence solutions, as in Diagrams 36 and 37.

Psychoanalytic theory contains the idea that the more the individual has succeeded, in the past, by these confluence, etc., solutions in finding realistic expression for his needs, the stronger his ego structure will be and the less he will need in future to resort to ego defences like repression. This remains to be experimentally checked. But certainly the capacity, by a calm act of suppression, to hold an ergic expression in limbo while one looks around for appropriate realistic outlets is superior to rigid repression as part of an emotional learning process. For it allows plasticity, trial and error, and the building up of new sentiments instead of complexes.

A defect of considering the dynamic aspect of personality in isolation is that it gives the impression that virtually anything can be attained by suitably arranging the learning. Watson, the reflexologist, was led on, by a similar impression that in principle anything could be conditioned, to make the statement that he could convert a mental defective into a doctor or lawyer by conditioning the right responses. Recognition of integration learning avoids this error and reminds us that other dimensions of personality put limits to the manner of learning. The intelligence level, for example, puts a limit to learning by reward. For when the individual can no longer discriminate whether his response is right or wrong in terms of leading to success, 'success' cannot reward him.

More importantly, there is some limit in one of our personality factors – perhaps U.I. 21, Exuberance – to the restraint a person can learn. If the reward or punishment follows the action by more than a few seconds an animal like the worm does not learn, and this period is only moderately longer for a rat, a dog, and so to an ape. In *every* species tested by animal learning experimenters, learning is *poorer* with increased demand on future reference. If the punishment is too many steps away for the given organism or individual he will go on repeating the wrong behaviour and being punished. Incidentally, we know that the frontal lobes of the brain are particularly concerned with this future reference, and if they are defective, or damaged, the individual shows reduced capacity for integration learning.

In this connexion there is obviously a problem for parent and teacher in not trying to demand of a younger child greater restraint than he can muster. There is a time for removing powerful temptations rather than attempting to teach: we do not put the bottle to the baby's mouth and punish him for drinking before the clock strikes the hour. There is an argument for using personality tests whenever there is doubt about the level of ego-strength development, e.g. in an older delinquent, for when the individual *can* learn it is equally a mistake not to teach him self-control and autonomy. But the notion that a stronger temptation can always be overcome by a stronger reward or punishment is fallacious beyond a certain point on the curve – and our law courts are recognizing this.

The effect of increased motivation, to the point of stress, was shown by Lazarus, Eriksen, and others to increase speed but also errors. Other work (Jones) shows also a tendency under marked frustration and stress for learning to be slower, and for responses to be more 'stereotyped'. That is to say, the individual reduces the variety of his trial-and-error responses and may even go on 'stupidly' making an inappropriate response time after time.

THE INTERACTION IN DEVELOPMENT OF
MATURATION AND LEARNING

When some curves of personality change with age are discussed in Diagrams 40–41 below, one must keep in mind that development can be maturation, learning, or an interaction of the two. An important principle here, in regard to the maturational limits in learning, is brought out by Hilgard, in regard to his own experiments and those of others on children's acquisition of walking, language habits, reading, etc. It is that learning by a certain age can generally be accomplished more rapidly when maturation has proceeded further. This is conspicuous in learning to walk, where long early training gives negligible advantage over short practice at a later period.

On the other hand, the work of Hess and others on imprinting, already mentioned, shows that with animals there is usually an optimum time for learning, and that unless practice occurs when the 'instinctive' mechanisms are about ripe, later learning may fail to have the required effect. Donald Hebb, Lashley, and others experimenting at the Orange Park ape colony, showed that if young apes are blindfolded and deprived of vision during the period immediately after birth, when their vision is normally maturing, later learning experience will never fully develop their visual powers. Incidentally, since the basic 'fluid intelligence' reaches maturity in man between fourteen and sixteen, it is probably a loss not to have really bright children at the university at sixteen, to expose them to ideas with which they can cope at a time when their receptivity is keenest.

No adequate experiment yet exists on human drive maturation and its relation to learning. Is it possible, for example, that cultural sublimation of the sex drive is achieved most readily in adolescence, and that absence of excessive sexual stimulation then favours such sublimation? At least there is a belief in higher civilizations that postponement of marriage well beyond the physical maturation level, and some segregation of the sexes, produces cultural vigour which is not attained merely by opportunities for longer study.

In considering changes which express hereditary, neurological, and hormonal developments it is easy to forget that maturation implies downward as well as upward changes. Since it is part of human heredity to be set to die, as if we were experimental models to be scrapped, decline and death must also be considered as maturation, not learning. In the case of intelligence, very adequate experiment has now established a typical curve of decline of intelligence as well as a natural rise (Diagram 39). The I.Q. remains constant only over the period of growth. That this ratio stays pretty constant (especially if we divide by the age from conception instead of the age from birth) during the growth period, despite environmental ups and downs, argues for this being a maturational process, but the chief argument arises from the high degree of hereditary determination as described in Chapter 2.

Insufficient research has been done on the life curves of other personality source traits to justify firm conclusions about maturation and learning, but we can glean some tentative conclusions from circumstantial evidence.

For example, the source trait *H*, parmia versus threctia, shows a slight but steady rise through the whole life period over which it has been tested, as shown in Diagram 39. That is to say, people become a little less shy, less sensitive to social inhibition as they grow older. In the childhood period this is a matter of common observation, since we see a movement from the four-year-old, hiding behind his mother's skirts when visitors appear, to the relatively brash twelve-year-old. Some fluctuation between shyness and boldness occurs during adolescence and then a steady diminution.

One form of behaviour loaded by the source trait *H* is 'talkativeness' (Table 9, page 95). Records of small group behaviour, for example, show that high *H*-scoring individuals tend to ramble on more and cause some criticism from more laconic colleagues. A tendency this way seen in older people supports the questionnaire score evidence of Diagram 39. Rupert Brooke draws a picture of Menelaus and Helen returned from Troy and ageing, till Menelaus 'waxed garrulous, and sacked a hundred Troys 'twixt noon and supper'.

It is interesting to contrast with this the typical age curve of *F* factor, surgency-*vs*-desurgency, for this also loads talkativeness, but obviously of a very different quality. The curve for surgency runs high in adolescence and drops steadily thereafter. Incidentally, it will be realized that the units vertically in Diagram 39 are not raw scores, which, not being comparable, would not allow us to say that one trait climbs or falls more steeply than another.

They are standard scores taken at twenty years of age (which is why the curves intersect at 20), i.e. we express the change *between* and over years in terms of the individual difference range *within* a typical year.

That the qualities of surgency – enthusiasm, impulsiveness, high spirits, loquacity – decline with age is common observation and the subject of many a poet's lament. The typical human being becomes more sober, judicious, careful, less inclined to go out to parties, and so on, with age – the very qualities of desurgency.

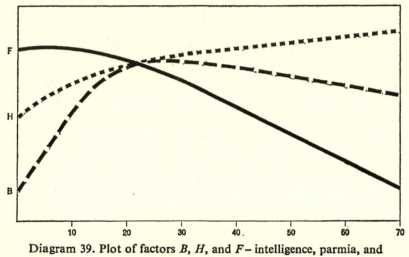

Diagram 39. Plot of factors *B*, *H*, and *F* – intelligence, parmia, and surgency – early life course

What is the cause of such change? One can speculate that it might be either reduced energy or increased inhibition or both. Actually, we have contrasted *H* and *F* because nature–nurture analyses show *H* to be a substantially genetic temperament trait and *F* to be very largely environmentally determined. In fact, desurgency has been theorized to be a function of the amount of failure and punishment which the individual's activities have encountered. If each of these traits were *wholly* determined by its predominant determiner we should have to explain the rising curve of parmia as an entirely maturational change – some neurological or hormonal change in that parasympathetic–sympathetic balance which the name parmia indicates – in favour of the person getting less susceptible to threat (threctic) and more thick-skinned with age.

Conversely, we should have to explain the increase in desurgency as due to accumulated experience of the failure of human enterprises – that 'the race is not to the swift nor the battle to the strong neither yet bread to the wise, but time and chance happeneth to them all' – and possibly to a misanthropy based on the continued spectacle of human foolishness. However, on common-sense grounds one might equally explain the decreasing shyness of *H* as due to more extensive knowledge of people, and the increasing soberness of *F* as due to declining energy. Until further research, the maturational, physiological explanation of the *H* trend and the reward–punishment ratio view of the *F* trend must be accepted as more probable (older people in well-cushioned societies remain pretty surgent!). Incidentally, since both *H* and *F* are prominent in the broad, second-order extraversion–introversion factor, yet behave in opposite ways here, we again see the approximateness which is involved in dealing with these cruder second-order concepts rather than the first order, as represented in the sixteen factors of the 16 P.F. test and others.

Although the objective test factors of Chapter 5 have only been accurately measured as yet over a few years of age range, equally definite and characteristically diverse trends appear, as shown for three representative instances in Diagram 40.

The rise in U.I. 17 shows the same general increase in caution and capacity to inhibit which we have seen in the desurgency curve. Life, for the young, is an increasing acquaintance with situations in which one can get into danger, and a corresponding acquisition of inhibitions. That U.I. 21, Exuberance, shows a sharp decline suggests a possible connexion with rate of metabolism. Indeed, the high constitutional determination of Exuberance, and the experimental check which shows that it does indeed have some relation to metabolism, strongly suggest a physiological basis and that we are dealing with a maturation curve. The decline in U.I. 28, which is a form of rigid, authority-dependent behaviour, might, on the other hand, be due to the learning of independence as the child moves out more from the family. As explained earlier (page 121), one pattern, U.I. 24 or anxiety, has been traced across most of the age range and it shows a high level in adolescence, followed by a drop to a fairly steady level at about thirty-five and then a rise about sixty to sixty-five. The rise in adolescence fits the general rise of conflict then, but the reasons for the rise about sixty-five may be either physiological or cultural. If it has to do with retirement and loss of status it may not show

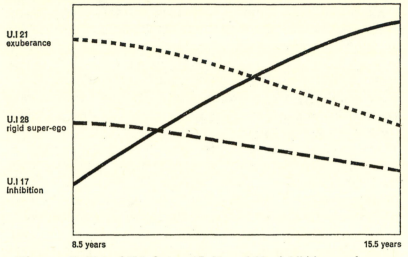

U.I 21
exuberance

U.I 28
rigid super-ego

U.I 17
inhibition

8.5 years   15.5 years

Diagram 40. Plot of U.I. factors 17, 21, and 28 – inhibition, exuberance, and rigid super-ego – early life course

up in all cultures, but if with illness and death, it might be more universal. A public health programme, in its mental health aspects, needs to know more about these trends.

THE CALCULATION OF PERSONALITY LEARNING

From the above curves for a few major factors, to producing something like a scientific equivalent for Shakespeare's seven ages of man, from 'the infant, muling and puking in his nurse's arms' to 'last scene of all . . .' is a substantial undertaking. But one can see already the advantages of exploring those changes in terms of well-defined source traits instead of arbitrary special tests. As the measurement of pure source traits is pushed farther down the age range – and it is now at the four to six year level –

the researcher on development is able to formulate his conclusions with increasing accuracy and continuity. Alas, 'child development' has been, from a scientific point of view, one of the weakest areas of psychology, because the practical lore of the nursery school and the reading needs of the average mother have dominated it. But it is far too important an approach to understanding personality to be left at a 'popular' level of technique.

Now that personality measurement is becoming tolerably practicable, that kind of research on development can begin which relates personality to the attitudes of parents in the home, to the social status group and neighbourhood influences, and to the accidents of early life. That quite significant relations can be found when measurements of, for example, parental attitudes and home atmospheres are employed, is shown by the extensive studies of Baldwin, Becker, Sealy, and others in America and Britain.

Initially, we need not ask which of the above three learning laws – conditioning, the law of effect, or integration learning – are at work. We can simply relate personality changes to experiences in an empirical way. However, in so doing we must go beyond what the learning theorist does with his animal in a cage, and recognize that any experience produces learning in more than one dimension. Indeed, it is necessary to recognize the definition that personality learning is a *multi-dimensional change in response to a multi-dimensional situation.*

Now we *have* the capacity to record a multi-dimensional change, because of our source trait batteries ready for various ages. The multi-dimensional situation we can conceive either in terms of the situational indices (page 248) for each particular situation, or, perhaps more profitably, by considering the person's whole life as a situation. And what is more vitally important about the person's whole life than the ups and downs of expression, frustration, and compromise which his dynamic needs have suffered in the Adjustment Path Analysis?

If the following of a certain path at the crossroads typically produces certain effects on several personality factors, then we can write a strip, or vector, as the mathematician will call it, describing those multiple changes. For example, the path B_1

(Diagram 38, page 275) of successfully breaking a barrier might affect some six personality factors in the following way:

Path Personality Coefficients

A	B	C	E	O	Q_4
O	0	$+0.2$	$+0.1$	-0.3	-0.3

That is to say, this overcoming of a barrier to something he felt he ought to do – say persuading his father to let him go on with studies – has reduced general drive tension, Q_4, by the standard score — 0.3, reduced guilt, O, equally, raised dominance slightly, and given increased ego strength, by $+ 0.2$, because of the increased experience in coping with life situations. Presumably, as in most learning, the repetition of a certain path of behaviour will in some way multiply the effects from a single experience. Thus if we know the multi-dimensional learning effects of a particular path and the number of experiences the individual has had of it, we can theoretically calculate his expected personality learning.

Conversely, if we know the personality change between two measured occasions and the frequency of experience of a particular path we can calculate what may be called the path-personality vector of coefficients, as above. However, the whole life experience of the individual will not be relative to one path but to all the paths in the Adjustment Path Analysis Chart (page 275). He will have his own particular frequencies on these, which can also be written as a strip of figures or a 'vector'. It will, in fact, constitute the most succinct possible statement of his adjustment life history – of the emotional frustrations he has met and how he has handled them. By what is called 'matrix multiplication', which a computer can perform, we could put this path frequency information – this description of the multi-dimensional life situation – in with the path-personality association figures and obtain the multi-dimensional personality change expected from these experiences.

This conception of Adjustment Process Analysis is at present only theoretical, but it offers an all-inclusive way of studying personality development experimentally, without any immediate assumptions about particular learning models. In time it could throw light on these learning mechanisms as they actually operate in personality change. There remains, however, one complication about the path-personality indices which the reader may raise. If we find, empirically, that people who follow with greater frequency the path of repression, E_2, are more anxious than the average, we still do not know whether this is because more anxious people more often choose that route at the chiasm E, or whether the greater anxiety is the result of experience of that route. By simple retrospective analysis, such as would be simplest to make, this could not be decided. But the answer is given when

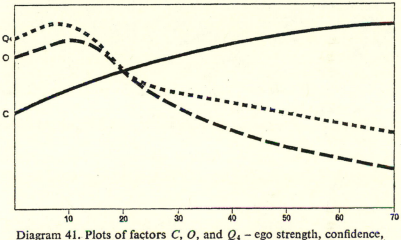

Diagram 41. Plots of factors C, O, and Q_4 – ego strength, confidence, and ergic tension – over life course

we can test a large number of people, wait for something to happen to them, and retest them.

No research of this kind has yet been engineered, partly because adjustment path analysis, as a study of typical life situations in our culture, has not by any means reached the level of personality source trait measurement – and both are needed. However, one can glimpse the ultimate practicality of such study of the *individual* personality development from data already available on the *average* personality development. For example, Diagram 41 shows the plots recently obtained by Sealy for life change on C, ego strength, O, guilt, and Q_4, undischarged ergic tension level.

A certain coordination in these curves suggests some common influence. The difficult period of adolescence, in which the individual is struggling for economic, social, and sexual recognition, shows itself doubtless by many experiences of the path of frustration and, indeed, of the later paths of internalizing conflict and undergoing repression. This seems to be accompanied by a rise in guilt experiences, O, a decided rise in ergic tension, Q_4, as drive remains undischarged, and a reduction in ego formation, C. As these problems gradually get solved we see a simultaneous reduction of guilt and excessive drive tension and a strengthening of the ego structure which continues through years of ripening experience.

*

READING

Mowrer, O. H., *Learning Theory and Behavior.* Wiley, New York, 1960; Chapman & Hall, 1960.

Guilford, J. P., *Personality.* McGraw-Hill, New York, 1959.

CHAPTER ELEVEN

Personality Testing and the School Child

SOCIETY'S REACTION TO PSYCHOLOGICAL TESTING

The dedicated scientist, labouring for the increase of human knowledge, is sometimes completely dismayed at the use made of it. Unfortunately the obviously dramatic nuclear bang has taken attention from possible misuses outside physics which may be just as serious. Among these, for example, are the use of psychology for mass persuasion, and others too complex for brief reference. The potentiality of 'persuasion' is undoubtedly there, for example, as mentioned under motivation. It is possible to plant electrodes in the brain of a dog and, by pressing buttons, make him do almost anything. His 'will', as he presumably experiences it, is the whim of the experimenter. Because the electrical connexions in our TV sets are not actually in our brains there is no reason for being less alarmed at what a perverted science might do for 'persuasion' on political, social, and commercial matters. Parenthetically, a fairly common delusion among schizophrenics is that someone is controlling their thoughts by electrical apparatus. Yet this nightmare hallucination could become the day-by-day experience of mankind unless the highest ethical standards are maintained in applied science.

Our purpose in this chapter is to look in a practical way and from several angles at the applications which can follow from the theoretical findings of the last ten chapters. So far, the main fields of application of personality psychology have been in the clinic and mental hospital, the school, and industrial and military personnel selection. However, some newer fields are opening up, such as the adjustment of advertising appeal to the particular personality type which is likely to use a certain product; the provision of advice before marriage on marital compatibility; and the application of 'group dynamics' laws concerning the way in which certain constellations of personalities will work out in teams. Perhaps some day we shall even be able to implement Bernard Shaw's suggestion, implicit in Plato's *Republic*, that political leaders should be selected, or voted to office, in the brighter light of published personality and ability test results.

Some further comment on the above introductory recognition of moral problems in applied science is called for because there are currently signs that the public has become confused over some issues in applied psychology. No problem exists in the clinical applications that is not already covered by the medical Hippocratic oath. The only moral indignation likely to be encountered by the practising clinician is from the researcher who can rightly claim that so many are lagging behind the treatment efficiency of the newer methods which research holds out. The current issues occur in education and industrial selection, where books like Hoffman's *Tyranny of Testing* and Gross's *Brain Watchers*, have confused the imperfections of prediction, which psychology shares with medicine and meteorology, with a supposed 'prying into people's minds' and infringement of the individual's liberty.

Individual liberty, even from a benign but fussy bureaucracy, is vital. But psychological examination infringes on it no more than does a medical examination. The real objections of some people to mental testing are emotional, and the rabble rousers only supply rationalizations for them. There is no one more confident that intelligence tests are theoretically all wrong than an 'intellectual' who has just 'failed' a practical item. And naturally, perhaps, there is no one more fluent on the psychological, moral, and educational wrongness of a scholarship examination than an unhappy housewife whose son has just failed to gain a place. Social snobbery, and perhaps a deeper narcissistic revolt against evaluation as a fundamental reality of life, make such frustrations more intolerable than they need be. When children are raised to espouse and develop a mature competitive philosophy (in the Adlerian sense of deriving no pathological inferiority sense from fair interaction) in which they can accept that others can always be found who will be superior to themselves in one way or another, there is less need to seek a scapegoat in the test. Let it be recognized that the greatest genius still fails miserably in some field or another. Dalton, the great chemist, surprised a child by not being able to pass a test of colour vision: Cavendish was quite unable to make small talk and was a social failure; Newton never won the love of a woman he wanted to marry. A substantial part of 'personality learning' consists in focusing correctly on our own limitations, and we should be grateful to any test which helps us objectively to 'know ourselves'. But let us not forget that all human estimation of humans is fallible.

As one would expect from its roots in deeper weaknesses of human nature, the objection to testing, even by the gods, is very old. In Fitzgerald's *Rubá'iyát of Omar Khayyám* a day of judgement is dismissed by the wishful thinkers in the tavern:

'They talk of some strict testing of us.'

'Pish! He's a good fellow and 'twill all be well.'

Yet the individual is actually being evaluated all the time, by his fellow men and his physical environment. As far as the testing and evaluation by his fellow men is concerned his real choice is only between having it done somewhat more accurately and justly on the one hand, or less accurately and with more prejudice on the other. If the mother, whose son has been directed to a secondary modern instead of a secondary grammar school on the basis of an intelligence test, believes injustice has been done, she may be inclined to claim that an interview evaluation or some other alternative would be preferable. Psychologists, however, have investigated the relative predictive reliability and validity of the interview and it shows up very poorly indeed compared with psychological tests. It is, moreover, liable to every prejudice of the examiner, set off, for example, by the child's physical appearance, dress, or accent. Most of the alternatives to the exacting 'eleven plus' examination in Britain suggested in Parliament and the popular Press are in fact quite sorry substitutes. The research psychologist himself might suggest, on the other hand, that this particular evaluation would be more just if based on at least half a dozen tests, spread over a couple of years. It could also be made more fair by the use of culture-fair intelligence tests (see page 301 below) instead of traditional tests now in use, and more accurately selective of those who will do better later by introducing also personality tests which will be discussed below. For the rest, some attention to a philosophy of life is important. If society fails to give as much honour to the man who paints a house superbly as it does to, say, the mediocre editor of a newspaper, this is the fault of the values of that society, not the fault of the tests which evaluate these kinds of abilities.

HOW SHOULD THE PSYCHOLOGIST BE ORGANIZED IN THE SCHOOL?

Applications of personality and motivation measurement to children, with which this chapter is concerned, arise largely in the school. They have to do with examinations, methods of teaching, and promotion in the school proper, but also with the child guidance clinic's handling of emotional maladjustment and delinquency, and with counselling of the choice of an occupation. If we are serious about the school's goal of developing personality and character, over and above the mere imparting of skills and information, then personality and motivation measurement can bring new help also to the specifying of goals and the testing of claims to character education. If a famous educator is right in saying that teachers take seriously only the teaching which can be measured in examinations, then these new possibilities of measurement could be the forgotten slipper which brings this Cinderella of education – character education – back to proper recognition.

If the psychologist's work in the school turns out to be creative it will be accidental, for he is the teacher's technical aid, not a definer of the philosophy and aims of education. Scientific psychologists have deplored as much as anyone the disastrous products of, for example, the 'progressive education' aims which their less scientific but more vociferous colleagues palmed off upon education as an alleged education 'rider' on Freud's alleged theorem about the evil effects of suppression and repression. Here Rousseau rode again, on a scientific horse of purely spectral quality, and doubtless other fads are yet to come, dressed in the scientific jargon of the day.

In other instances minor incursions into the realm of defining goals have been more justified. For example, the teaching of skills practically never used again, as in Latin and Greek, on the grounds that they disciplined the mind in other fields, was exploded by psychological experiments showing remarkably little transfer of training. Again, when the nineteenth-century followers of Seguin and the twentieth-century followers of the reflexologist J. B. Watson aimed to impart to all mental defectives the high scholarship required in the professions – and merely ruined the defectives' disposition and health – mature psychologists had to point out that this aim was scientifically absurd.

However, apart from almost accidental connexions of aims, the role of the school psychologist may be briefly defined by saying that he applies learning theory to the curriculum; psychometrics to the improvement of examinations; and personality theory to the treatment of maladjustment and the problems of personality and character education. In regard to these purposes there exists at the moment, however, a gap between the qualifications of the psychologist and the complexities of his task. If we are to understand some current problems in organizing the psychologist optimally into the school, occasioned by this gap, it will help also to look at history.

A history of the association of psychologists with the school will show that though psychology may have done much for education, education has probably done more for psychology. It was through the constant support of education that psychologists produced the Binet test, developed useful theories of abilities, and developed concepts of validity and reliability around the objective, multiple-choice achievement test. Educational support joined with the social sciences to sharpen the 'itemetric' psychometry of most attitude and verbal interest scales. On the other hand, a very special problem arose in regard to any equivalent mutual stimulation of education and psychology in the personality and emotional learning areas of psychology. When education authorities began to set up child guidance clinics – roughly in the twenties – to handle nervousness, delinquency, and defects of personality development, they hesitated between calling in the psychologist and the psychiatrist. Actually, at that time psychology had very little but pretentious and untried theories to offer, and it was not surprising that practical leaders in the community turned sometimes to that trusted friend the doctor, and placed child guidance clinics more frequently in the hands of medical psychiatrists than psychologists. Actually, in terms of being properly equipped with a body of knowledge about the *normal* child personality, it would be hard to say whether psychology or psychiatry was wider of the mark.

As Chapter 1 documents, clinical practice became the first area to supply psychology with the more useful – or, at least, plausible – personality theories. But they came from the psychiatrist, and the tendency was for the school psychologist to become a sort of eunochoid practitioner in the house of the medical psychologist. He dealt with intelligence tests and school achievement, but left emotional problems strictly alone. In more conservative countries this acceptance of the psychologist's limited role continued even after psychology had begun to build its experimental personality and learning theories. So long as this persisted the assessment of the child's problems was split in two parts: the examination of the cognitive characteristics of his personality by the psychologist and of the emotional aspects of his personality by the psychiatrist. Of course, they spent hours in conferences to put him together again, but the result did not always have the insight which results from one person seeing and knowing the whole. (Committees are useful, but the camel, we are told, is the result of an attempt to design a horse – by a committee.) This 'division of labour', which has been largely abandoned in America, Scandinavia, and some Commonwealth countries, is obviously as prolific of unnecessary problems as a national frontier running through the middle of a densely populated city. For cognitive and emotional life obviously interact intimately in one person and every process. Since some degrees of specialization are inevitable, because our minds are small, a better division would really be that of having a medical man handle the physiological problems and a psychologist the psychological problems in a single team, as Freud essentially argued in his book calling for the lay analyst.*

* Even if life were much longer it is questionable whether it would be economically possible to produce many practitioners qualified both with an M.D. and a Ph.D. A better practical solution is for a fully psychologically trained and a fully medically trained person to work together.

As often happens, the social machinery for handling an acute human need got crystallized before science really had the means of meeting the need, and this crystallization got in the way of the more enlightened scientific developments. Thus surgeons for centuries operated from barber shops, because their lore was not part of the ancient dignity of medical philosophy. Similarly, the scientific study of personality by psychologists made substantial headway after the social role of the psychologist had in some places become confined to ability testing. Now the more refined, instrumental concepts in personality examination often involve statistical and learning theory concepts which are not part of the psychiatrist's equipment. Of course, it does not matter whether we call the specialist in human personality a psychotherapist or a psychiatrist, but it does matter that his training should cover most of what is now taught in the doctorate in psychology.

Through some interesting interactions of culture and science which space prevents our following here it turned out that the combination of plasticity in the American culture, and the generous support of psychological research there, resulted in America taking the lead in creating a new specialist and a new profession – the psychologist trained as a psychotherapist. There, and to a lesser extent in places ranging from Paris to Jakarta, psychologists have appeared as state-qualified clinicians, in mental hospitals, as school counsellors and psychological specialists, in many educational systems, and in industrial personnel work. In schools and child guidance clinics they deal with the backward, with designing scholarship tests, with vocational guidance, as well as with individual emotional and adjustment problems. The universities in America followed suit with counselling centres, staffed with psychologists who advised students not only on their abilities and study habits, but also on emotional problems, passing on to psychiatrists only the uncommon pathological cases requiring custodial care.

Counselling centres and counsellors, which, in a typical large university, may deal in some way with as many as a thousand cases a year, have been helped in their work by the advancing *armamentarium* of personality and ability tests, and have recently tried motivation tests too. They have particularly been helped by neuroticism scales, here described in Chapter 8, for screening purposes by a brief, widely applicable test to locate those who may need more intensive diagnosis or treatment. In one university known to the writer, where about 200 students out of 20,000 had spontaneously come to the counselling centre in one year with emotional problems, the use of a ten-minute screening device yielded another 300 with scores showing equally severe maladjustment, and who, when interviewed, confessed to such serious behaviour as suicide attempts and were plainly in need of treatment, but who had not been able to find their way to the available services.

Since as much has been said about the tests, as such, as space permits, in Chapters 4, 5, 6, and 8, our concern here is only to explain strategic choice and organization of tests in schools and universities. At the present time the tests in use cover not only the newer structured tests, like intelligence tests, the factored questionnaires (the 16 P. F., Guilford–Zimmerman, the High School Personality Questionnaire, the Thurstone inventory, etc.) and such interest measures as the Kuder and the School Motivation Analysis Test, but also special-purpose tests like the Strong Occupation Interest Blank and the Holtzman adaptation of the Rorschach to group administration.

Four or five developments obviously indicated on scientific grounds are in practice only in their infancy. First, the testing and the keeping of records in any large system, be it school or industry, needs to be organized simultaneously for ability-achievement predictions and for individual, therapeutic and training treatment. Hitherto these have tended to grow up in a false separation, due to different pools of tests being used for each. But now that structural measurement has brought out that the same traits are really relevant to both, they need, as described in more detail below, to be organized in a single record system available for both uses. Secondly, there needs to be more exploration of the more difficult but more valuable *Objective*-Analytic batteries worked upon by Eysenck, Hundleby, Damarin, Pawlik (in Vienna), Tsujioka (in Japan), and others. These can be given either in an individual clinical test situation, or as a group test in a classroom, and a dozen to twenty independent personality dimensions can be covered. Thirdly, only a few pioneer counselling and educational psychologists have yet realized the substantial extent of the gain in prediction of scholastic and other achievement from adding personality and motivation measures to the ordinary intelligence and scholastic tests. Fourthly, the time has come to overhaul our intelligence testing, in favour of culture-fair tests, as described in the next section. These are major issues of progress, but there are also lesser improvements, such as using machine scoring and spreading the routine testing over more occasions.

In connexion with practical 'test installations' a big issue has been whether group or individual testing is better. The latter is far more costly of time, and the widespread assumption that all the psychological advantages in reliability and validity reside with the individual test is false. A child who works well on his own may actually be embarrassed and awkward in an individual interview situation. Moreover, more than a little of the examiner's own personality may also enter into the child's score in an individual situation. One cannot so reliably compare the scores of twelve children each individually tested by a different examiner as one can those of the same children all tested in a group. In a recent case where parents had their child tested privately, yielding an I.Q. of 127 – above the grammar school scholarship selection average of 125 – they not unnaturally demanded that the child be given a scholarship. The education authorities whose group test results had *not* assigned a scholarship to this child stood their ground, saying that they did not believe 'in giving advantages to those who could afford private consultation'. Their action perhaps strikes one as a disingenuous appeal to the envious *hoi polloi*, but the decision could have been defended better on the technical ground of poorer comparability of test results in the individual situation.

In tests either of intelligence or personality, properly designed for group administration, the only advantage of giving them one at a time is that one can prevent sheer and absolute misunderstanding of the instructions, or complete non-cooperation. However, there are means in most tests of reliably spotting complete failure to understand, or an attempt at sabotage, in the group test situation. It is far more economical to use the group situation and examine only these cases of 'misfire' afresh in an individual test. Sometimes the cost of individual testing is used as an argument for doing no testing at all. Better the average result of group testings on two or three occasions – even if it were true that group testing is less reliable – than no analytical information about the child at all.

A considerable boon to the practical side of test administration has been machine scoring, which in its simpler form has been in use for decades. Recently it has advanced by (a) becoming applicable to multi-dimensional personality tests, sensing patterns, and printing out the several factor scores, as in the National Computer Systems scoring of the 16 P.F.; (b) using light-sensitive cells to respond to the pencil marks on paper, instead of depending on brush contact, involving special pencils or holes punched in cards; and (c) yielding simultaneously the primary factor raw scores and the weighted combinations of these which give second-order scores, neuroticism diagnoses, or various specification equation predictions of criteria. What would, with a few hundreds of subjects tested, need some weeks of scoring by ordinary methods, or still more hundreds of expert man-hours by interview methods of evaluating personality, can be done in a few hours on the 16 P.F. by computer systems, yielding all derived scores for each person at the same time.

A related but very recent development is the improved accuracy and economy in the actual administration of tests which has been made possible by automation. Seated comfortably in a booth, with no interrupting noises, and headphones conveying instruction in a pleasant voice from the psychologist, several subjects can be tested simultaneously. Dr Herbert Eber, in vocational rehabilitation work, has found it possible to handle far more guidance cases in this way, and with demonstrably improved reliability. There are few psychologists, indeed, working with a stop-watch in an individual testing situation who do not, in distraction, accumulate timing errors. The use of recordings, in automatic test administration, does a better job of standardizing voice tone, time, and several other aspects otherwise not controlled to the degree desirable in a good 'psychological experiment'.

THE NATURE OF INTELLIGENCE IN
RELATION TO PERSONALITY

Discussion of school psychology presents the most natural place in this book to raise some debated questions about the interaction of personality and intelligence. Everyone has views about the relative importance of the latter and the layman often has decided views about their mode of interaction in test situations and life situations. Actually, some amateur views on intelligence, though based on little but fiction, turn out to be no stranger than the remarkable facts which research unearths.

Let us glance at the history and status of intelligence testing. A phase of construction of intelligence tests on an 'intuitive' or at best 'verbal–theoretical' basis began with the great success of Binet and Simon in 1905 in putting together an intelligence test which diagnosed mental defect more reliably than had ever been done before. Many imitators appeared, and what began with an inspired construction by two men of genius inevitably ended in a wild proliferation of 'intelligence tests' for all kinds of school and industrial use. Lacking any solid scientific basis, such testing practice was soon in theoretical bankruptcy, expressed in the cynical conclusion that 'intelligence is what intelligence tests measure'.

Fortunately the monumental work of Spearman in England, and, later, of Thurstone in America, had meanwhile established that there exists a general factor of intelligence, akin to those general factors discussed above in the personality domain. This factor runs across a diversity of what Thurstone calls primary abilities, such as verbal ability, spatial problem solving, numerical ability, and even good memory. That is to say, there is a tendency for people who are better at finding exact synonyms, or solving arithmetical problems, also to be better at recognizing analogies, memorizing new material, and working out spatial puzzles.

Theoretically and practically the important fact is that this general ability source trait is 'determinate'. That is to say, its unique composition can be fixed, in terms of contributory measures, by the factor analytic rotations and a score assigned on this factor to any given individual. Thereby it is possible to ascertain the *concept validity* (p. 85) of any proposed intelligence test by finding its correlation with this general factor score. Any arbitrariness and subjectivity of opinion among different test authors can thus be taken out of intelligence test design. This is the practical gain, but the theoretical gain lies in the possibility that we can interpret the nature of general intelligence from this defined, located set of expressions. When one looks over various areas of intellectual ability 'loaded' by the factor, the first conclusion is that it is a factor very general in its effects and remarkably ubiquitous in its behavioural influence. It extends from such simple perceptual processes as judging one's distance from a door, or judging the difference in pitch of two notes, to understanding a book by Einstein or judging the style of classical Greek prose. However, the former loadings are quite small and it reaches its purest expression whenever *complex relationships* have to be perceived, which explains why such performances as completing analogies, as in Table 27, or understanding classifications, as in

TABLE 27
Analogy items

(a) Foot is to leg as hand is to: ———— (open ended)
(b) Stitch is to shirt as nail is to: ————
hammer, table, needle, jacket (selective)
Brighter people on the intelligence test as a whole give: (a) arm, (b) table.

Table 28, are among the sub-tests correlating most highly with the

TABLE 28
Classification items

| (a) Pool | river | house | ocean | stream | (selective) |
| (b) Eat | run | swim | crawl | walk | (selective) |

Brighter people on the intelligence test as a whole give: (a) house, (b) eat.

general intelligence factor. 'Series' tests are also very familiar in intelligence tests and these very obviously involve 'eduction of relations', since one tries the relation perceived between the first and second term upon the second and third and then, if it fits, employs it to get the missing last term.

Incidentally, most intelligence tests are *selective*, not *inventive*. That is, the subject is presented with a multiple choice situation, evaluating several *given* alternatives, one of which is correct, instead of facing an open-ended test. In the latter, as shown at (*a*) in Table 27, the subject invents his own answer, and this provides scoring problems. The test no longer has full *conspective* (page 103) reliability. But is some value in intelligence testing lost if the person only selects the right answer from given alternatives? Correlations with the general factor show that selective answer tests are just as 'saturated' (loaded) with intelligence as inventive answers. The latter involve more use of memory and fluency factors, but these are not intelligence. Consequently, the selective design is now more universally used.

To the layman it may appear a little puzzling that an intelligence test is validated against this rather abstract thing – a source trait or factor concept – since he may feel that he wants to be sure that it is predicting something of assumed practical value. He perhaps has definite personal ideas of what intelligence is and would like to substitute some *concrete* validation, against a particular performance. Not uncommonly, it must be confessed, the layman's suggestion turns out to be something in which he has done well – a businessman may say ability to make money is the real test! Even if he prefers some impersonal concept like the 'capacity to learn', 'adaptability to new situations', or 'success in life' the concretization of such verbal definitions is not easy to find! One university president has written a book in which he has actually said that he can accept a definition of intelligence only as 'that which brings success in life'. This obviously merely 'passes the buck', for success is defined peculiarly by every man, according to his philosophy. Compared with these shifting sands the operational unity which is presented by Spearman's general factor (*B* in our factor size series) is a rock, and indeed it behaves as is required by the central tendency in most definitions of intelligence. It correlates with all kinds of problem-solving ability, with ability to think abstractly, with success in learning more complex matters in the school curriculum, and, less uniformly, with salary level and complexity of occupation. On this apparently theoretically firm basis the test construction of the present generation of psychologists (Burt, Vernon, Parry, Warburton, and others in England; Cattell, Guilford, Wechsler, Thurstone, and the Educational Test Service psychologists in America; and Meili, Arnold, the Australian Foundation for Educational Research elsewhere) has been built. The I.Q. derives its meaning as a pure measure from this source, and the calculations for predicting school achievement from intelligence tests are based on this conception.

But now, around the middle of the century, just when everything seemed neatly packaged, a doubt appears. It seems to be the nature of science that a theory is born to die, and is often killed by new research appearing just when it has become most widely accepted. Fortunately, perhaps, the revolutionary overturning of a theory commonly leaves many practical procedures only moderately or slightly changed. Artillery officers – but not astronomers – can take Einstein or leave him, for they still find Newtonian mechanics entirely adequate. But a new theory *may* add some quite new procedures and possibilities, as in the present case. Twenty years ago the present writer and his colleagues, and Hebb in Canada, began to have a suspicion that Spearman's general factor is really two things, not one, and papers were read to that effect before a sceptical psychological convention. Actually the frequently repeated intensive correlational analyses made in the field of abilities alone would, for technical reasons, be capable of revealing this. But when intelligence is examined *among* personality measures, as has been done increasingly in later years, the situation is different. Perhaps what happens can most quickly be indicated by reminding the reader that the exact form of a figure is best perceived when it is seen against a ground of a different colour. When personality or motivation measures are introduced among ability measures they provide such a ground. And this step, together with more sensitive statistical tests of the number of factors, enabled us to see in the computer output, alongside Spearman's general factor pattern, a spectral second factor of much the same shape. The findings which apparently confirm this are too recent to be more than tentatively stated. Pending further research, not all psychologists will accept it, but at least the theory is an interesting one and may have far-reaching results.

SOME PRACTICAL IMPLICATIONS OF THE THEORY OF
FLUID AND CRYSTALLIZED GENERAL ABILITY

The new theory claims that there are actually *two* general ability factors which, from their properties, have been called *fluid* and *crystallized* general ability. In intelligence test practice the quickest way of designating these two is by pointing to the culture-fair and the traditional (verbal and numerical) tests, respectively. Culture-fair tests were implicit in the work of Spearman's students, Fortes, Line, and Cattell, in the late twenties, demonstrating his argument that it does not matter what subject matter is used among the elements between which one asks the subject to perceive relations. Provided the relations are complex enough one can, for instance, generate an analogies test among shades of colour. The systematical application of this to producing tests which would be comparatively free of cultural influences did not begin, however, for nearly another decade, when the present writer, with his students Sarason and Feingold, and Raven in Britain, developed tests which have since been called the I.P.A.T. Culture-Fair Intelligence Scales and the Progressive Matrices. (The Culture-Fair tests include Matrices as one of four sub-tests.)

The present writer first sought to generate sufficiently complex relations among 'fundaments' which are common to people all over the earth and which would not, of course, be presented in verbal symbols, but as pictures. (Intelligence tests given pictorially are, of course, far from culture-free.) It seemed that parts of the human body, sun, moon, and stars were about the only things common to cultures. But, additionally, any shapes on paper, or in plastic, that do not represent objects peculiar to a culture, or have names, proved effective. Diagrams 42 and 43 show respectively a series and a matrices test made up out of such material. Such 'perceptual' tests were shown by Feingold, Sarason, and other researchers with the present writer, as well as by Raven, (*a*) to correlate very well with general intelligence estimates and the general factor – much better than 'performance tests' with form boards, etc., and (*b*) to show no cultural effects. For example, Feingold compared immigrants to the U.S. on these and traditional tests (i) on entering, and (ii) a year or more after acclimatizing.

The traditional tests were woefully misleading but the culture-fair stood firm. The C.F. tests have since been shown to be effective in China, Africa, India, and across most culture varieties.

What is called the *fluid* general ability factor (because it is free of particular investments) shows itself particularly in the culture-fair tests but also by other characteristics. First, it separates as a distinct but correlated factor from crystallized ability. Secondly, as an ability to perceive relationships in any material, new or old,

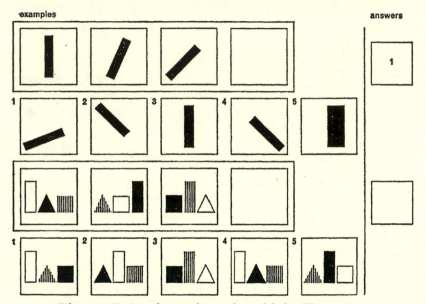

Diagram 42. A series test in a culture-fair intelligence test

it reaches its maximum level at about fourteen or fifteen years, as the brain finishes its growth. But crystallized ability may go on being deposited with further investments in training, education, and experience beyond this age and in college populations the test performance curve does not 'flatten out' till twenty-one or so. Age or brain injury may bring a general reduction of the fluid ability level, but the crystallized ability retains the 'shape' which fluid ability and experience have given to it – just as the coral rock formation retains the form reached by the once living coral organism, so that only quite special areas, such as verbal facility, may be damaged.

This metaphor of a coral growth brings us to the crux of the meaning of 'two general abilities' and requires that we take stock of our understanding of the statistical pattern which we have all along been calling a 'factor'. Fluid ability appears as a general

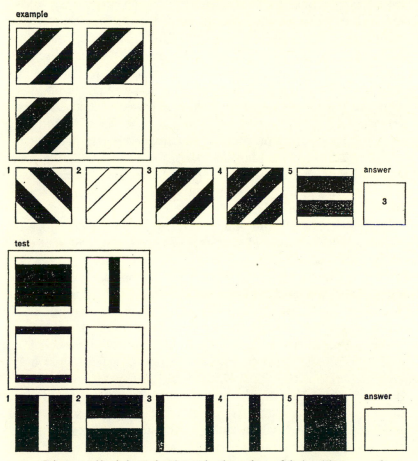

Diagram 43. A 'matrices' test in the culture-fair intelligence scale

factor because it is some sort of active mental capacity or energy, which is thrown now into this problem and now into that. The different performances correlate, i.e. a person high in one tends to be high in all, because people differ in their endowment in it, and it is the same force now exerted here and now there. But the correlation found among the parts of the crystallized general ability, e.g. between judgement in English, in mathematics, in history, etc., is of a different origin. It springs largely from the uniformity of our school curriculum, whereby a person who has been twice as long at school as another will simultaneously know *more* of all these things. If this is the case, one may ask: 'What then is the difference between crystallized intelligence and what we simply call general school achievement?' General school achievement includes much that is known merely by rote, i.e. by good memory and school interest, and which required no great fluid intelligence for its acquisition. What we call crystallized intelligence is the collection of *skilled judgements* a person has acquired by applying his fluid intelligence to his school opportunities. It is a sort of 'holding company' for what fluid intelligence and school experience have jointly produced, and as such it has a life of its own in that its skills tend to generate more skills like them.

The difference of fluid and crystallized ability is brought out most clearly if we consider persons raised in two different cultures, say in Britain and France. It would be unfair to make any precise inference about an English seventeen-year-old's intelligence from his decisions on the correctness of synonyms in French or the shrewdness of his comment on the domestic policies of Louis Quinze. Within any culture the differences are not so great, but social status, locality, and opportunity differences still make the correlation between fluid and crystallized ability only about $+0.6$, not the $+1.0$ which would justify deriving an estimate of a child's natural, fluid intelligence by the traditional intelligence test (crystallized ability) rather than by the fluid intelligence factor (as in a culture-fair intelligence test). Again, this can be sharply brought home by the fact that one simply cannot compare, say, American and Chinese children on an intelligence test by an American or Chinese intelligence test. Yet, when the I.P.A.T. Culture-Fair test is used, the Chinese in Taiwan and the Americans in Illinois have been demonstrated to possess almost exactly the same average score and scatter. Naturally, the mere fact that the identical test gives the same score in these two circumstances does not alone prove that the test is getting at native ability. A good culture-fair test should *sometimes* decline to show differences between people in different cultures because the cultures may alone distinguish them, but at other times it should even show differences when both groups are within one culture. Such tests, in fact, show lower scores from the north island of Japan than from the south (a fact which Japanese understand), and lower scores in southern Italy than the north (a fact which Italians understand). The finding that Chinese in China score the same as Americans fits other indications of Chinese intelligence, such as the equal performance of their descendants in America in traditional intelligence tests in English. (The prize for Gaelic poetry has recently been given to a Chinese girl brought up in Ireland.) Whether the lower scores found on these tests by anthropologists working in the Congo is to be explained by temporary conditions is something for science to investigate.

Within one country the discrepancy between individual intelligence levels as measured respectively by traditional 'crystallized' intelligence factor measures and culture-fair measures of the fluid ability factor is not great *during the growth period*. But after school there is increasing divergence. One person may begin investing his fluid ability in entirely new fields – say mining engineering – while another becomes a school-teacher and another concentrates on the verbal skills of a journalist. Because skilled habits in any field get dusty with disuse, the traditional intelligence test, like the Terman–Binet, the Wechsler, W.A.I.S., etc., will deal rather unfairly with the cowboy, the farmer, or mining engineer, compared with the teacher or journalist, if they are re-tested at, say, forty years of age. This has been noted in the selection problems of Mensa, a society in England and America, entry to which depends democratically upon the individual, no matter what his background, scoring above a stipulated high I.Q. level on an adult intelligence test. The selections made by traditional tests (the Cattell Scale III, for superior adults) and culture-fair tests have only a moderate degree of consensus. In Diagram 44 the two coordinates represent scores on the two types of test, the angle between them being adjusted to give the correlation of about 0·7, which is approximately correct for such tests among *general adults*. (Among students, having the same educational background, the agreement would be much higher than 0·7.) It will be seen that the same cut-off points – the top 5 per cent and the top 10 per cent on the two tests garners a different crop, and that the number in common to the two crops gets lower as the selection point is made higher. In one survey made by the writer the highest score on the I.P.A.T. Culture-Fair was made by a young sailor – a very intelligent man who, through an adventurous and easy-going temperament, had become a deck-hand –

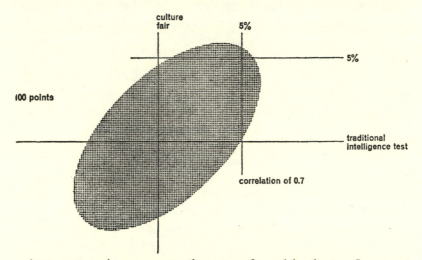

1 per cent are in common to the groups formed by the top 5 per cent by culture-fair and traditional intelligence tests.

Diagram 44. Differences expected in selection of bright people on culture-fair and traditional intelligence tests

and the highest score in the Cattell Scale III traditional test by a classics student at Oxford. Each was pretty high on the other test too, but if we accept fluid ability as 'native intelligence' the sailor was the brighter man. The difference in membership of such a society, according to whether it adopted the fluid or a crystallized intelligence factor as its definition of intelligence, illustrates the general importance of the choice of test in the social application of intelligence tests.

However, the greater discrepancy between fluid and crystallized scores among adults arises not only from the fact that crystallized ability is no longer being 'pushed along', just ahead of, and by the growing fluid ability in the common learning environment of the school. For a gap between them develops also from the fact that fluid ability can *sink down* below its late adolescent level. To take an extreme case, a brain injury to the parietal area of Broca may cause some *general* loss of fluid, adaptive ability, but in the crystallized ability measurements it will affect only one of the circle of skills commonly measured in such an intelligence test, in that it will cause specifically some verbal aphasia, i.e. a loss of skilled use of words. Thus if the traditional test used happens to measure the individual on crystallized abilities *not* affected by the locality of injury a wrong impression of his general mental capacity is obtained.

In adult life particularly, when a prediction is required of how intelligently a person will operate in some entirely new field, e.g. in wartime induction testing, assigning new job areas, a fluid ability measure by a culture-fair test is the wiser measure to use. But even at the school age where the two measures are usually in closer agreement, injustices can be done by a test which looks backward to past opportunities rather than forward to potential performance in a new type of school. The work of Dr Douglas and his colleagues at the London School of Economics brings this out clearly by showing that on traditional intelligence tests the average I.Q. of children from lower social status homes drops relative to that of more environmentally favoured children when retested over the age range from eight to eleven plus. For if the alleged intelligence test is actually contaminated with school achievement and home cultural background, the obtained apparent I.Q. will deviate from its proper constancy in the one case in an upward and in the other in a downward direction.

In the coming decade, with increasing interest of the general public in effective and fair application of mental tests, we are likely to see considerable debate on the proper roles respectively of traditional and culture-fair tests. Against the advantages of the latter, two arguments are likely to appear. First, they do not have 'face validity'. That is to say it is hard to see from looking at them why they test intelligence. For example, a frequent comment is 'This test involves no word skills whatever. How can it possibly predict capacity to succeed in English?' The professional psychologist, but not the general public, has long given up face validity (or 'faith validity' as the specialist calls it), recognizing that the first reaction of the general public to the automobile was 'How can it possibly go without a horse?' In one group in which varied students were subsequently subjected to intensive English training the culture-fair actually predicted English achievement better than an ordinary verbal intelligence test.

A second criticism is that *within the same year* and among students *all in the same kind of school*, the culture-fair does not correlate with ('predict') achievement quite so highly as the traditional test. This is not only admitted, but treasured by the exponent of the newer tests. The reason that the traditional test gives a better immediate 'prediction' is that it already contains an appreciable admixture of the school achievement it is supposed to predict. If all we want to do is predict, in March, children's school achievement in, say, July, we can do better than any intelligence test by predicting from their school achievement scores in March. The very object of an intelligence test, however, is to be *analytical*. As we study any individual child we are interested in the *discrepancy* between his native intelligence and his school achievement, and the more clearly and reliably this is brought out the better the test. The claim of the culture-fair tests is that it will make a more fair selection for future performance when the passage of some years has given a chance for the present accidental inequalities of achievement opportunity to be ironed out.

Beyond two such apparently real criticisms it has been said by shrewd observers that since the professional interest of educators and sociologists is specifically in culture they are not likely to be enthusiastic about a measurement which aims to ignore it. Indeed, it is less than a generation since the majority of sociologists taught their students that there are no innate differences in intelligence, and that 'native intelligence' must be a figment of the imagination. The researcher's position, stated in Chapter 2, is that it is possible to infer the relative contribution of genetic and environment variation to the observed population variance in any trait. What fresh light then does this newer analysis of intelligence into two general factors throw on the old and vexed question of how far intelligence is inborn? With tests in use before the advent of culture-fair scales an 80/20 per cent ratio in favour of heredity has commonly been found, but recent results suggest that the hereditary determination is higher than this for fluid ability and possibly lower for crystallized ability. However, one must insist that the constitutional determination is still well short of 100 per cent for fluid ability, i.e. it is not properly labelled the individual's innate ability level. For its level is affected by accidents of gestation and birth, and thereafter by physiological environment, head injuries, etc., if not by the school environment of the individual. Thus this issue, like many others, is likely to become more understandable as research clarifies the new theory of two general ability factors, fluid and crystallized.

PERSONALITY AND SCHOOL ACHIEVEMENT

It is a commonplace among experienced observers in almost any field of endeavour that personality and ability together decide the outcome, their relative importance varying according to the form of achievement involved. It should be understood that we include here, under personality, also motivation and values.

Consequently the educational psychologist has hitherto taken a peculiar position, for in fact he has devoted his efforts to predicting achievement from abilities alone. For example, when schools in Britain select pupils for the eleven plus scholarship selection, or for entry to the university, they do so by an academic attainment examination and by an intelligence test. And when a psychologist in a child guidance clinic looks for the causes of backwardness in a child referred for very poor school performance his examination begins – and all too frequently ends – with an intelligence test. Until a few years ago this limitation was necessitated by the absence of valid tests of personality and motivation. But if the factors examined in Chapters 3–7 indeed cover much of the personality and motivation area, then the practising psychologist should not be denying the new resources held out to him, but should revise his ideas and rise to the challenge of new powers – and, of course, new problems!

The first information on the extent to which personality and motivation measures affect and predict school performance has come from studies on normal children by Pierson, Sweney, and Sealy in America, Connor and Radcliffe in Australia, and Butcher and Warburton in Britain. There have also been special studies on personality influence in backward children by Wright, O'Halloran, and others. Immediately it has become apparent that personality factors do indeed contribute just about as much as abilities themselves to school achievement. Many a schoolteacher would have been ready to bet on this conclusion without the evidence of tests, but the test experiment brought objective confirmation of the magnitude of these influences and also on the directions in which temperament and dynamic traits act.

When the High School Personality Questionnaire, which measures fourteen distinct factors, and requires no more than an hour's testing time, has been given to groups of some 300 boys and girls, of around twelve years of age, or the 16 P.F. to students of eighteen, the 'specification equation' obtained (see page 79) averages as follows:

$$A_c = +0 \cdot 2A +0 \cdot 5B +0 \cdot 3C -0 \cdot 2D -0 \cdot 2F +0 \cdot 4G +0 \cdot 2H \\ -0 \cdot 2I -0 \cdot 2M +0 \cdot 3Q_2 +0 \cdot 3Q_3 -0 \cdot 1Q_4$$

This formulation states that a child's achievement score in English and arithmetic combined (A_c) is best estimated by weighting his affectothymia temperament score (A) positive, his intelligence score (B) positive, his ego strength (C) score positive, his excitability (D) negative, and so on, by the decimal fractions indicated, and then adding the lot (in standard scores). The reader can remind himself what the factors are by looking them up under the letter symbols in the glossary at the end of this book. Incidentally, different research articles have reported slightly different weights, according to type of school, age of subjects, country, etc., and as discussed below, we should, psychologically, expect such variation. The reader may also be reminded that these weights are approximately the same as the *correlations* of the given personality factors with the 'criterion', the child's score in the basic subjects – English and arithmetic. They show how much the given personality source trait concerned helps or hinders achievement and when we look at their natures the results make good sense.

For example, other things being equal (and this is what we mean when we speak of a weight for a given factor) a child who is more outgoing, adaptable and warmly related to the teacher (all aspects of *A* factor) will learn faster (+0·2). The child who is more emotionally balanced and less easily upset (*C* factor, ego strength) will also learn more easily (+0·3). The individual of greater conscientiousness (*G* factor) will make more progress (+0·4) for the same intelligence, and so on.

Nevertheless, not all these personality connexions discovered by research are so self-evident. For instance, the more dominant child (*E* factor), according to these measurements, learns more slowly than the more submissive. Why should this be? Some perspective is given on this by the finding that at a much later stage, with post-graduate university students and scientific researchers, the reverse is true. The more dominant turn out to be more creative and to achieve more in the field of research. As pointed out in discussing the nature of dominance, the docility and imitativeness which make a good examination-passer are not what make a good independent, critical thinker. Some may regard this finding as obliquely exposing something wrong with our school system. This is not necessarily true: perhaps class teaching is only possible with some degree of docility. But it raises a deeper question, discussed below, concerning whether a scholarship should select for good school or good *post*-school performance.

The weights on various personality factors will also change with the school subject concerned. They are, in fact, somewhat different for performance in English and performance in arithmetic, the subjects which we have averaged above to give a general school performance. In this respect it is surprising to find that introverts (to be exact, sizothymes – *A—* – and desurgents – *F—*) tend to have better vocabularies and grammatical skill than extroverts, who actually do more talking. A simple possible explanation is that introverts read more, and the people they meet in reading have better vocabularies and grammatical styles than the people they would meet in everyday life. But it is also possible that they love words more because they live more in a world of ideas than with concrete things.

The manner and degree in which a personality factor aids the expression of ability in producing achievement also varies with circumstances and age. For example, the big temperament dimension, affectothymia-*vs*-sizothymia, or A factor, actually changes its direction of influence somewhere between twelve years of age and the university student period. In the former, affectothymia correlates positively with classroom achievement, whereas among students all of equal intelligence the sizothymes get better grades. The loading or weight changes from $+0{\cdot}3$ to $-0{\cdot}4$! Presumably we are seeing here a change from social reinforcement of effort in the classroom, well responded to by the sociable affectothyme, to more individual, internal direction at the university level, where the sizothyme enjoys his autonomy. In the university, also, the largest positive loading shifts to Q_3, i.e. the person with a well-integrated self-sentiment gains the advantage.

Whereas it is very rare for any known *ability* to load an achievement performance negatively, personality factors are frequently good for one kind of achievement and bad for another. Among various abilities the worst that can be said of, for example, musical ability is that it is unimportant in contributing to one's drawing ability. It does not *interfere*. (Having a higher spatial thinking ability, as Thurstone showed, actually goes with slightly better than average verbal ability.) The ambivalent action of personality factors, on the other hand, is shown by A and E above, and also by the sharp contrast between the negative loading of surgency, F, in examination success and its substantial positive association (perhaps due to liveliness, talkativeness, and limelighting) with effectiveness in small groups and election to positions of leadership. Again, desurgency – $F(-)$ – as Drevdahl has shown, is characteristic of original thinkers. This opposition between popularity for elections, and original, creative thinking may well explain why democratic leaders so seldom lead! There are, however, countless other instances where personality factor weights flip over from positive to negative with different kinds of achievement. This is the personality analyst's expression of the fact that 'it takes all kinds to make a world', though, to be realistic, the uses for some kinds of personality endowment are hard to discover!

THE EFFECTS OF MOTIVATION AND VALUES
ON ACHIEVEMENT

It is commonly assumed in the exhortation 'try your hardest' that the relation of motivation to achievement is a simple one. It is certainly a powerful one, but not always simple. For example, performance on intelligence tests fails to improve beyond a quite moderate level of effort and may decrease. As Sarason has shown, when people are at a high anxiety level greater effort may actually lead to reduced performance, notably in committing to memory.

Our evidence here is largely on various ergic tension levels and on sentiment structure development in relation to school achievement. To understand the answers it is necessary to introduce one more statistical notion, namely, that the percentage of the variance (variability) in a certain criterion accounted for by some personality (or other) measure which predicts it is the *square* of their correlation, *not* just the coefficient itself. For the present this may need to be taken on faith, but obviously it is a useful notion when we want to account for the fractions out of a total performance which are associated with particular sources.

For example, the correlation typically found between an intelligence test and school achievement is around 0·5 (0·55 in a recent survey in Scotland, but perhaps Scots are a little more careful not to waste any intelligence!). This means that $(0·5)^2 \times 100$, i.e. 25 per cent of the range observed in achievement is associated with the intelligence variability in the particular population. Or, looked at another way, if we could instantly eliminate differences of intelligence – or take a lot of people all chosen to be just at the same intelligence level, the variance in school performance would still be appreciable, namely, 75 per cent of what it now is.

This kind of statistical calculation is very useful in giving us an idea of the relative importance of various causes – and also in showing us how much we still do not know. For the various contributions should add up to 100 per cent and no more. Now we are approaching the question of the relative importance of abilities, personality traits and motivation factors. Many experiments have converged on reliable estimates for the abilities. If we use several primary abilities, as in Thurstone's tests, we may predict a shade more than from intelligence alone, but the figure usually stands at 25–30 per cent.

An estimate for personality factors may be obtained approximately from squaring the correlations in the equation above. (Actually, because of rounding and some correlations among factors the literal value is too high, and the best estimate would be roughly 40 per cent.) The experimental evidence on motivation measures, with M.A.T. (The Motivation Analysis Test) is too recent for any precise conclusion to be drawn until checked, but it looks as if about 20 per cent will be found associated with motivation. Allowing for slight overlaps among the measures from these three *essentially* independent 'modalities' of psychological measurement, a shrewd estimate might be that the three batteries will account for 60–80 per cent of the variance in achievement.

To some unfamiliar with general psychological measurement this may not seem a very high efficiency of total prediction. But actually we should be surprised and suspicious if it were much higher. For this tells us how much we can predict from *qualities within the student*, and, as every student well knows, something depends on relatively accidental circumstances outside himself, e.g. an illness, a good tip on what is likely in the exam, a lost notebook, the conditions for working at home, the attitudes of his parents and his peers, and so on.

As to the particular dynamic factors which seem systematically to associate themselves with achievement the work of Connor, Horn, Pierson, Sealy, Sweney, and others already converges, on their varied student groups, to a decided unanimity of conclusion. This is summarized – necessarily roughly because of the absence of common units – in Diagram 45.

Some of these differences fit other sources of evidence. For example, since the self-sentiment and the super-ego are already known to load achievement when measured on the 16 P.F. questionnaire, it is not surprising that they should do so also when measured by these objective motivation strength measurement devices. Nor is it surprising that the general strength of curiosity should advance learning.

The quite large negative roles found for ergic tension levels on sex, pugnacity, and narcissism, however, are striking and will lead to some new developments in our thinking. A simple type of explanation of the effect of sex tension level might be that the student experiencing higher drive is more distracted from his studies. A more sophisticated and perhaps more likely one is tied up with Freud's generalization that culture is sustained by sublimated sex drive. Possibly the individuals who have achieved more

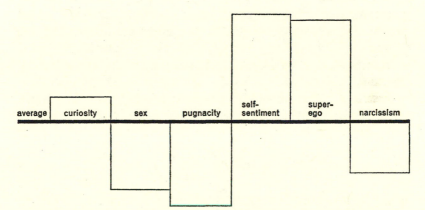

| average | curiosity | sex | pugnacity | self-sentiment | super-ego | narcissism |

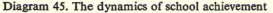

This profile of the high achiever compared with the low achiever shows on what dynamic structures the former tends to excel and to be below average.

Diagram 45. The dynamics of school achievement

of such sublimation, and thus reduced the tension for direct sex expression, do better because of these greater resources for cultural attainment.

On the other hand, the higher pugnacity is probably better explained as a consequence than as a cause of poorer achievement. Pugnacity (which is, incidentally, a demonstrably quite different factor from the self-assertiveness erg – see Chapter 7) is the consequence of a frustration situation. And at the stage of life when schoolwork occupies so large a sector of the life circle, in a competitive school system, what could generate more pugnacity and sadistic tension? Although M.A.T. measurements do not yet exist for pre-schizophrenics, one sometimes sees a high build-up of pugnacity in the late adolescent who repeatedly fails in occupational try-outs and moves towards a schizophrenic intransigence.

Alternative explanations as cause and as effect have also been offered in response to this new finding that narcissism has a quite powerful negative relation to achievement. The narcissistic drive, as far as the dynamic analysis of Chapter 7 shows, is a general sensuality, with a sexual quality, but directed more to the individual himself, much as psychoanalytic clinical observations have always described it. However, the factor pattern shows a somewhat broader quality, with self-indulgence, avoidance of work, selfishness, rejection of moral demands, and much which, in a group, would be the very antithesis of high morale. Some clinical explanations have considered this to be essentially a 'regression', and doubtless certain early massive discouragements might contribute to it. But it seems far more probable that the poor achievement is a consequence of this pervasive self-love.

SOME FINER ISSUES IN MOTIVATION AND ACHIEVEMENT

The two preceding sections have tried to show the results of recent advances in ability, personality, and motivation testing, indicating what each area contributes when the other is held constant. For example, the contributions from dynamic tension levels assume intelligence to be the same when the achievement differences are affected by motivation differences. It has been shown that the three modalities are very roughly equal in their contribution to achievement and that they account for about two thirds to three quarters of the 'explanation' (variance) of individual differences in performance. Although, as Tennyson reminded us, 'science moves but slowly, slowly, creeping on from point to point', and these findings of the present pioneer decade will need to be confirmed in diverse situations, the potential advance of educational practice from what could be done with ability tests alone is almost staggering.

Before trying to focus some conclusions for practice, and some social implications, let us consider a little more the full scientific complexity of these findings. First, how general are they?

Actually, the results of the American investigators above have already received reasonable confirmation by Radcliffe in Australia and by the lively work of Butcher (Edinburgh) and Warburton (Manchester). Much the same personality and motivation factors are active, though there are some slight but interesting differences of emphasis too. Secondly, how do mechanisms vary with different ages of students and different types of educational system? Thirdly, how do the three kinds of trait interact?

As regards the latter, it is reasonably sure that certain abilities and general personality factors determine interests rather than vice versa. For example, how can anyone get very interested in the amino acid structure of D.N.A. or excited about Bessel functions if he does not in the first place have the *B* factor (intelligence) level necessary to *see* the relations? And again, in Chapter 4, we have seen that a whole set of dynamic attitudes and social interests, called by Eysenck the tough-*vs*-tender-minded pattern (see Chapter 12, page 358) is apparently an expression of the general personal source trait of premsia-*vs*-harria (*I* factor). Other instances of the generation of interest and dynamic trait patterns between the pressures of environment on the one hand, and the ability, personality, and physical 'givens' of the individual on the other, exist in recent research.

Regarding the second question above, the predictive weights required for various personality and dynamic factors will obviously change, statistically, with local social characteristics and school selection. The 'importance' of traits will vary.

University students, for example, have already been selected for intelligence, so one would no longer expect differences of intelligence to be so important in predicting the differences in achievement among them. In fact, one would anticipate that personality differences would now climb to the paramount position as the decider of grade performance – and recent results support this. Secondly, one should note that the weights will also vary with the situation in which the learning is carried out. For most students the change from the ordinary school, where a teacher treats them with the solicitude of a good hen for a brood of children, to the university, where they are (more in European than American universities) expected to be their own managers, is one which takes some adjustment. New qualities of personality come into action. We have already seen that the loading on *A* factor, affectothymia–sizothymia, actually seems to reverse its sign. This says that students who respond strongly to the social milieu do well in school, but that the detached and self-sufficient do better at the university.

In particular we can expect a more complex set of laws to develop regarding prediction, especially from motivation measures. In the first place these measures will not be so relatively constant from month to month as will ability and general personality source traits. A drive tension level in particular may change with the general stimulation level of the environment and the degree of intercurrent satisfaction. We need to know more about how big these changes are and how changes of achievement in turn affect them. Again, some curious differences have appeared between the measurement of a dynamic structure in its unintegrated and its integrated motivation components. For example, the self-assertive erg in its integrated manifestations seems to contribute positively to achievement, whereas the scores on its unintegrated component battery are definitely negatively related to achievement. We have much to learn about these differences of meaning among the distinct motivation components, and when these insights are gained our control and prediction should reach new levels.

The relation of personality and motivation scores to performance throw light not only on the individual, but on the school system. Differences can be seen between the personality and motivation structures which command success in one type of school and in another. In the last two or three generations there has been more concentration in the art of the teacher on attaching new ideas to existing interests of the child instead of driving him, like a donkey, with blows from behind. Different personality traits will obviously contribute to success under two such different systems. What is perhaps constructively of more importance is that the emergence of reliable, objective measures of dynamic strength will enable the educator to get reliable information about the strengths of sentiments on which he can hope to build at various ages and with various types of student.

The facts already cited above – that sizothymia is negatively related to performance in grade school and positively in the university; that docility (low E) favours examination-passing but is a defect when research work and creative art are the goals, etc. – may suffice to show, however, how measurement in schools can help to throw light on the teacher and the accepted institutions as well as on the individual.

Finally, research is beginning to throw light on the meaning of these personality and motivation factors in achievement considered in a broader context than the school alone. This will be considered in the next chapter, where it is pointed out that if the selective school is preparation for something *beyond* the school, then we should be selecting for it by the qualities which give success later, rather than those which give success only in its examinations. In these later successes there is reason to believe that the balance of weighting tips over and that dynamic traits, instead of being third in order of their contribution to achievement, as in the school, become paramount.

SOME PRACTICAL PROBLEMS IN SCHOOL PSYCHO-LOGICAL SERVICES

Let us now consider the implication of the above findings for an efficient school psychological service. It has already been pointed out that such a service must be many-sided. It must think of at least four aspects: (1) keeping records of achievement and making predictions and scholarship selections; (2) understanding the emotional and social adjustment of the individual child, at recurrent 'problem' occasions, as in Child Guidance Clinic work; (3) giving vocational guidance at the close of the school period; and (4) understanding what the classroom institutions and teaching methods are demanding of the pupils.

Many school systems in advanced countries supply at least the first three of these. But all too often they do so through different persons and offices, using testing devices which do not interlock and records which are not easily mutually available. In view of the scientific advances which have oriented testing to organic realities in the individual, psychological testing, like medical testing, has become integrated, and the administrative segregation of functions like child guidance treatment of problem children, special school treatment of backward children, scholarship examination, a guidance teacher's handling of vocational guidance, etc., is a wasteful disregard of modern possibilities. A school psychological centre should handle all of these with one or two fully qualified psychologists (or more in a city centre). Records of the total personality and ability would then be preserved from the beginning at the central school psychologist's office. For example, the psychologist handling clinical cases would not be left to find, the first time that a child is referred for help, that no earlier data whatever exists on his former personality and interest development, nor would the examination of scholarship potential be a mechanical procedure divorced from knowledge of the emotional make-up and interest of the particular child.

However, the more effective and far-reaching the psychological care of the child becomes, the more the psychological scientist is going to have to come out of his laboratory backroom and justify and explain his procedures to the public. As pointed out earlier in this chapter there have been minor revolts against his procedures, largely rationalizing an unrealistic, narcissistic wish that one should not be measured against environmental demands, but partly on the misunderstanding that a psychologist commands when in fact he merely advises. However, as present-day examples of how involved these issues may get in popular superstition and political slogans one may instance the burning of personality test papers in Texas and the decision of a socialist London County Council to abolish the scholarship examination's recognition of individual differences in ability, on 'the principle that no London child must be labelled "suitable" or "unsuitable" for any particular form of education' (*Evening Standard*, 1 July 1963). The danger of scientifically uneducated politicians, writers, and journalists propagandizing public opinion in a world where the understanding of man and society has also become an intricate science, with many gifts to bestow, is nowhere better illustrated than in the schools. To show that science can be misunderstood from any political angle, a conservative newspaper of the same city (*Daily Telegraph*, 2 July 1963) said in an editorial on scholarship selection: 'Some of the greatest men of our own time – Sir Winston Churchill is a primary example – showed singularly little ability . . . in boyhood.' These varying types of development are well understood by psychologists. Churchill, Darwin, and others would have been recognized by intelligence tests whereas they were not recognized by ordinary school examinations. Churchill is clearly an example of, among other things, the lawful relation on page 311 above, where high dominance factor, *E*, detracts from school performance but contributes to original performance in later life.

These arguments are against poor, unimaginative, and bureaucratic use of psychological tests, not against more effective use. But it is ironical that the writers think the solution is to go back to no selection at all – the bright and the backward going at the same frustrating lock-step in the same classroom – or to selection by interviews, essays, and teachers' all-too-human personal prejudices. This is done in the city where Sir Cyril Burt, around 1910, pioneered with the most up-to-date psychological testing programme then in existence and published, in 1921, results demonstrating solutions which have become classical in mental testing, and which fully answer the confusions voiced in 1963.

Misunderstandings, by parents or politicians, of what tests aim and do not aim to do, and what degrees of accuracy they can and cannot attain, are, nevertheless, being increasingly eradicated. But wider confidence in testing can come only if certain real technical shortcomings of psychological measurement are faced. For example, as tests are recognized to affect positions, salaries, and practical affairs, there will be increasing efforts to 'beat' them, by coaching, faking, etc. That coaching for intelligence tests can be met by coaching everyone, with effective reduction of test sophistication differences, has been shown by Dr Eysenck in a companion volume to this book, and we need say no more. The issue of faking in personality tests is a more complex question, which needs some essential comments.

Psychologists have recognized and experimented upon the tendency in questionnaires to 'fake good' and give 'socially desirable' responses. When subjects respond as truthfully as possible, in an anonymous situation, and then do the same test again where they are limelighted and the results have bearing on their future, the latter situation turns out to produce an aberration which is not along a single 'social desirability' dimension but along several dimensions, turning upon the 'role' which the subject chooses to play.

There are three ways of handling this 'motivational distortion' influence. First, by hiding in the test certain items aimed to evaluate the degree of 'faking'. Thus the M.M.P.I. has a 'lie scale' and a 'faking scale', etc., and the 16 P.F. has an M.D. (motivational distortion scale). These may assume, as an approximation, a single distortion shift, and correct each personality factor score by its amount. However, in the broader sense psychologists have to recognize two major possibilities in test taking: motivational distortion and sabotage. The latter is rare, but we have to recognize that in every society there are one or two who take perverse pleasure in wrecking. For example, a non-cooperative person might check every alternate answer, or try to answer randomly. By certain probability tests, applied by computer, such departures from any natural structure can almost infallibly be recognized. Nothing can at present be extracted from such a response sheet, but at least it can be set aside as sabotaged. The motivational distortion problem, on the other hand, is comparatively small and looks as if it might be solved in a decade.

Secondly, one may seek items which correlate with the required personality factor but do not obviously look as if they should, i.e. have no face validity. This is a promising line and has been followed in the High School Personality Questionnaire. Lastly, one can shift from questionnaires to objective tests, as described in Chapters 5 and 6. Because of the greater demands on technical psychological skill, and the increase of the testing time demands by a ratio of 4 or 5, this valuable step forward is only being made slowly.

A second major respect in which testing must put its house in order as it comes increasingly into practical life is in demonstrating more regard for what should be the real criterion. For example, in the stress of war conditions military psychologists had to accept the infantry officer schools' grades as the 'criterion' of a good officer, there being no opportunity to record subsequent behaviour in the field. The ability and personality tests used succeeded in so cutting down the rejection rate among those taken into training that millions of man hours and dollars were demonstrably saved. But still the criterion was an artificial one, and it was not until the Korean War that records of actual battle behaviour were meticulously obtained and used as the true criterion against which any test had to stand up in prediction. Less dramatically, but equally realistically, in peace the psychologist has to adjust his selection to the criterion of 'the long run' rather than some immediate performance.

Actually the tendency to depend on the cheap and immediate criterion has nothing to do with psychological testing. The psychologist develops his tests of personality structures and the prediction he gives is usually more limited by the unreliability of the criterion he is given than by his own tests. The criterion for scholarship selection, for example, should not be success in school but success after the school. Shrewd observers in education have long objected that pupils who are skilled examination-passers, and who may also do well in intelligence tests, do not always live up to the promise after school. They may be colourless, or lack enterprise, or fail to show a sturdy interest in hard work. Though success in particular occupations to some extent requires particular traits, there are certain traits which are necessary for successful use of one's abilities in almost any area, and it would not be unreasonable in awarding school scholarships to give weight to those traits important for the occupations served by such schools. Such weight would almost certainly raise personality factor scores to the same order of importance as intelligence tests. The ordinary school examination may actually weight these at present in the wrong direction, as in the above instance of higher score on dominance (E factor) being associated with greater creativity in art and scientific research but lower score in exams, whereas higher docility systematically contributes to good examination-passing.

Yet another social aspect of psychological testing arises from the extreme complexity and many years of necessary research in modern test production. The day of the 'patent medicine' test, made up by the individual by a stroke of alleged inspiration, is gone, as also is the test made up specially for the occasion by the psychologist, like the old-fashioned doctor going into his back room or garage to concoct his own pharmaceuticals. There is indeed considerable parallelism between the great pharmaceutical houses, developing in their research laboratories biochemical and other 'drugs' of a complexity beyond the individual pharmacist's scope, and psychological test publishers who supply the psychologist. The question of whether there should be a single state monopoly or a careful arrangement of adequate competition among several private enterprises is one which is likely to be answered too frequently by a political response. In America there are half a dozen major independent test research centres – the Psychological Corporation founded by McKeen Cattell; the Educational Testing Service, supported in part by universities and colleges; Science Research Associates, founded by Thurstone; I.P.A.T., the Institute for Personality and Ability Testing, and certain general book publishers, e.g. the World Book Company, which maintain test development centres in which standardizations, relations to criteria, and improved scoring facilities are worked out. This variety has permitted an open-mindedness to new possibilities which a single bureaucratic 'authority', unassailable by competition, has usually not shown. At any rate, it is unquestionable that America has gone farthest in technical level of test development, in providing computer and other facilities, and in 'lending' its tests to other cultures.

One substantial advantage of the factored ability of personality tests, such as the Thurstone Primary Abilities Test, the 16 P.F., the G–Z questionnaire, the O.-A. Batterie., etc., is that the criterion relationships, the occupational profiles, the clinical diagnostic weights, etc., which are built up at such cost of human effort, do not have to be thrown away when the test is scrapped or revised. With a 'patent' test, as with a patent medicine, all we know is that a certain amount predicts a certain result, and we have no idea through what functions it works. On the other hand, when we establish that so much general ability (Spearman's 'g', our B) is required for a certain occupation, or that surgency (F), and parmia (H) are respectively positively and negatively correlated with prognosis in a mental disorder, this information preserves its value and meaning when, after perhaps ten years, some slight improvements are made in the method of test measurement of, say, surgency, parmia, or intelligence.

*

READING

Burt, C. L., *The Young Delinquent*. Appleton Century, New York, 1925; fourth edition, University of London Press, 1944.

Cattell, R. B., and Butcher, J., *The Prediction of Achievement and Creativity*. Bobbs Merrill, Indianapolis, U.S.A., 1965.

Klausmeier, H. J., *Learning and Human Abilities*. New York, Harper, 1961; Hamish Hamilton, 1961.

CHAPTER TWELVE

Personality Measurement and the Solution of Some Social Problems

THE USE OF TESTS DIAGNOSTICALLY IN CLINICAL WORK

The previous chapter has looked at social applications in the special realm of the school. Apart from incidental references in the course of describing measurement theory as such, however, we have not systematically looked over the general area of *applied* measurement. In this chapter we propose to do so, and with reference to wider issues, such as community mental health, industrial organization, and socio-political organization.

Although countless writers have familiarized the public with the ways in which our three- or four-hundred-year-old scientific and industrial revolution has transformed the life of the typical individual in our culture, few have attempted the still more imagination-demanding task of recognizing what advances in the *human* sciences could do. Actually the changes which a substantial advance in psychological science could produce might be far more radical and demand a far more searching examination of our social values and goals in life than has ever been thrust upon us by the impersonal *physical* sciences.

Among the more obvious fields of psychological application in which a reliably developed personality, ability, and motivation measurement could play its part are: a happier use of human resources in occupations; more informative advertising in obtaining effective distribution of goods; the selection of political leaders; the control of crime and broader but less dramatic anti-social behaviour; the diagnosis of mental illness and the evaluation of therapeutic gain; advice in marriage and family problems; and the evaluation of social trends.

Taking first the use of mental tests in individual clinical work, we need to hark back to findings in pure research set out in Chapter 8. There it was pointed out that the use of normal personality source trait measures reveals neurotics to have a different profile from normals, both on questionnaires and on objective tests. The same is true of psychotics and of other special groups, e.g. homosexuals, as shown in Diagram 47 below. It was also pointed out that emphasis in diagnosis has shifted from pigeonholing cases in particular 'syndromes' to understanding the adjustment·in terms of quantitative analysis on personality structures and dynamic source traits which constitute the unique constitution of the individual. In scientific concepts psychiatry has tended to move from an 'Aristotelian', 'all-or-nothing' typification into an understanding in terms of *degrees* of traits common to all – the so-called 'Galilean' approach. Thus, instead of merely saying, 'This person is a hebephrenic schizophrenic,' and putting him in the right ward in a mental hospital (with perhaps the associated notion that little more than diagnosis can be attempted, one evaluates his level on each of a number of scales, e.g. anxiety level, degree of contact with reality, ego strength, constitutional degree of schizothyme temperament, and so on.

This advance must not blind us to the theoretical possibility that some mental disorders may also be different *in kind*, in their processes and traits, from anything in the normal range. They may not lie on the extreme of some 'normal' dimension, but may require additional sets of measurements. Certainly some mental disorders, e.g. epilepsy and schizophrenia, give evidence of being more analogous to physical diseases, where a germ or a special disease process has taken over and introduced new processes. Others, however, such as the neuroses and paranoia, give evidence of being only extreme functionings, separated by no sharp break from the so-called normal person. Psychologists have consequently begun to give increasing attention, in clinical diagnostic research, to the dimensional scales derived from that 'structural-approach' by correlation which has been described in the main chapters here.

What this will do to the *armamentarium* of tests available to the clinical psychologist in the present decade is not hard to see – though like every change it will cause some anguish in those who have given much to acquire obsolescent skills. On the one hand, as we have seen, there are a number of special, 'gadget' tests where the behaviour seems more or less intriguing to the inventor and from which he hopes to extract evidence of personality, as, for instance, from handwriting. In earlier chapters we have glanced briefly at these: the ten ink blots offered for interpretation in the Rorschach test; the Szondi with its forty-eight pictures of psychiatric patients to which the subject reacts 'like' or 'dislike'; the T.A.T., in which the projections of the scorer are apt to get mixed with the already mixed defence systems of the responder; the 'Picture Frustration' test which makes the doubtful assumption (page 183) that what a person reads into a picture is his own motivation, and so on.

On the other hand, there is a slower, more disciplined development of experimental knowledge about personality structure, leading to construction of 'structural tests' aimed at the emerging personality structures. This development provides the clinical psychologist with measures, sometimes from a great variety of objective, performance, 'projective', etc., tests as in the Objective-Analytical personality battery; sometimes, from questionnaire items as in the series from the Pre-School Personality Questionnaire to the 16 P.F.; and sometimes from objective devices (autism, word association, projection) in attitude–interest tests like M.A.T. and S.M.A.T., all of which are directed to clear-cut structures and dimensions, such as the cyclothyme temperament, ego strength, sex erg tension, general intelligence, dominance, radicalism, guilt proneness, surgency, regression, and super-ego strength.

Intermediate between these are such tests as the M.M.P.I., the Kuder Interest Test, the Strong Interest Blank. The two last do not use objective measures (and the Strong is not in unitary trait scores), while the M.M.P.I. organizes its answers, as we have seen, not in source traits but surface traits. These latter have the unity of a set of symptoms which 'go together' in a syndrome, but do not necessarily correspond to underlying structures or source traits in the normal personality structure.

The trend of practice over the last twenty years shows the M.M.P.I. gradually supplanting the special gadget type of test, and, as the questionnaire (buffered by motivational distortion devices), becomes accepted more widely, it is likely in its turn to be accompanied in most examinations by the source trait measures in the 16 P.F., H.S.P.Q., and so on. For the combination of source trait measures (causal influences) and surface trait measures (combinations and effects) could be peculiarly effective. The comparatively slow acceptance of the questionnaire in clinical work must be ascribed partly to justifiable fears about its fakeability, but also, as an experienced observer of the last generation of clinicians must confess, to a certain pleasurable sense of artistry which the clinician gained with the 'crystal ball' type of test. Actually the scope for nice calculation and an artistic judgement, along with scientific insights, is greater with the structured type of measurement, but the clinician then works with figures supplied him by a technician or even an automated test apparatus, and for some this is less emotionally satisfying than a sense of face-to-face penetration with the patient. However, the fact remains that the brute empiricism of trying to tie up particular shades of response in a 'limited behaviour' patent gadget test with a scientific understanding of personality has had poor success. Actually, in the Rorschach, for example, Eysenck has shown that an unprescribed measure, namely the sheer oddity (statistically) of the associations given, is a better measure of neuroticism than any of the prescribed measures extracted. Since such a measure derives reliably from more sources in the O.-A. battery, there is little point in setting up a special test to get it.

This brings us to the question of the role of the O.-A. source trait measures in clinical work. If clinicians have doubts about the questionnaire it might seem that the solution is to switch to objective measures. But, as stated, the O.-A. battery is at present complex and time-consuming, and since it is the scientific essence of personality trait assessment to catch the behaviour simultaneously in several areas, it has been difficult to get the battery shortened. Consequently its application is at present mainly in research in clinics and mental hospitals, and there is little to show in the way of routine experience. Nevertheless, this is a rather sad reflection on the up-to-dateness and the perspective of values of many practitioners, for, as the Maudsley and Crichton Royal Hospitals (to name but two) in Britain have shown, the power of diagnosis from such factor scores is a substantial advance on that of older instruments. In Chapter 8 we pointed out that some six distinct source traits in the O.-A. battery significantly (statistically) distinguish neurotics from normals, as shown by the pioneer work in Toronto, Tennessee, and Illinois. The resultant combination of these scores yields a separation of neurotics from normals

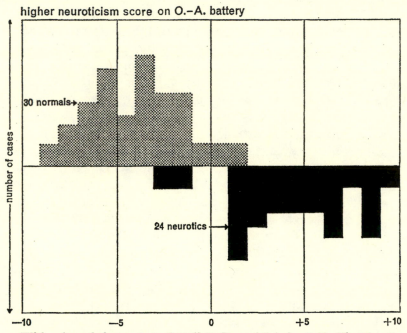

higher neuroticism score on O.–A. battery

30 normals→

number of cases

24 neurotics →

—10   —5   0   +5   +10

With acknowledgements to Cattell, R. B., and Scheier, I. H., *The Meaning and Measurement of Neuroticism and Anxiety*, Ronald Press, 1961 (adapted).

Diagram 46. Frequency histogram of the linear discriminant function for 30 normal and 24 neurotic subjects on objective test personality factors

as shown in Diagram 46, which is practically as reliable as the criterion – the pooled judgement of several psychiatrists who have seen the patient.

However, even with questionnaire means of measuring source traits the diagnostic effectiveness has been high. In the first place. as stated introductorily in Chapter 8, the profiles of different mental hospital groups are characteristic and throw light on the underlying mechanism of the disorder. For example, Diagram 47 shows the profile of a group of homosexuals in prison. (That this is not a *De Profundis* 'prison' profile and is different from other convicts is witnessed by the profile of unconvicted homosexuals being similar.) The homosexual has been a stumbling block to

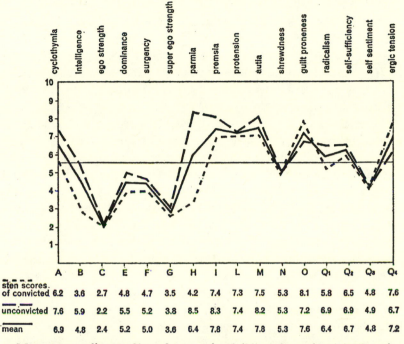

	A	B	C	E	F	G	H	I	L	M	N	O	Q₁	Q₂	Q₃	Q₄
sten scores of convicted	6.2	3.6	2.7	4.8	4.7	3.5	4.2	7.4	7.3	7.5	5.3	8.1	5.8	6.5	4.8	7.6
unconvicted	7.6	5.9	2.2	5.5	5.2	3.8	8.5	8.3	7.4	8.2	5.3	7.2	6.9	6.9	4.9	6.7
mean	6.9	4.8	2.4	5.2	5.0	3.6	6.4	7.8	7.4	7.8	5.3	7.6	6.4	6.7	4.8	7.2

Mean personality profiles of unconvicted (33) and convicted (100) male homosexuals.

Diagram 47. 16 P.F. profile of homosexuals

many clinical theorists – especially in that he fails to respond to treatment – and he has been described as obstinate, uncooperative, etc. The profile places him actually as an anxiety neurotic, perhaps as a result of undischargeable ergic tensions, but also with a peculiar emphasis on extraversion and radicalism. Thus unlike the introverted neurotic he is impelled to 'act out' his difficulty, and to do so without conservative inhibitions. The question of inferences for therapy belongs to the next section.

TESTING AND PSYCHOTHERAPY

Until recently tests were used in diagnosis, but very little in therapy. The older type of test, merely categorizing a patient, in any case gave few leads towards therapy. The more analytical test would be expected, on the other hand, to give much insight as to how the trouble arose and how its sources might be attacked. For example, a high anxiety score, on the second-order questionnaire measure (page 118), may have its emphasis in a low C factor score (ego weakness), in a large temperamental timidity ($H(-)$ factor), or in guilt proneness (O), or in high ergic tension (Q_4), which (at present interpretation) is general undischarged drive.

Additionally, however, the more analytical kind of measurement brings advantages in the course of therapy itself, akin to those in physical medicine which come from plotting charts of clinical thermometer readings, or a series of analyses of blood sugar content. Actually traditional psychiatric practice has not even had the means to prove that the patient gets any better at all, and Eysenck recently raised some fuss and feathers by a forthright declaration that from all data examined he could find no evidence that patients treated by the customary psychoanalytic procedures recovered at any faster rate than an untreated group.

Similar results have been reported elsewhere and some have been found and not reported. Brunswik at the University of California reported a substantial number of failures to reduce neurosis and pointed out that when change occurred it was sometimes in the form of substitution of a 'character disorder' (emotional and anti-social behaviour) for a neurosis. Incidentally, this is what we should expect from the measurements of the neurotic profile shown in Chapter 8. The neurotic has a basic emotional instability as shown by low score on the C factor of ego strength. He holds this in check by higher super-ego control, which at the same time may generate the neurotic symptoms. Consequently, many a psychoanalyst reacts to the super-ego demands as his main enemy and, in practice, he spends much of his time whittling away at the super-ego. Naturally, if he succeeds, he releases the impulsive, insufficiently developed ego and produces a 'behaviour disorder'. A proper measurement comparison with normals would have shown that the super-ego is only a surface problem and that the main contribution to neurosis lies in other factors.

Apart from some shifts of symptoms of this kind, changes of a magnitude to be expected from an effective, theoretically sound therapy are believed by a substantial number of psychologists to be missing from present practice with neurotics and still more with psychotics. One eminent critic of psychoanalysis has said, 'In the acceptance, promulgation, and practice of Freudian psychoanalysis and derivative therapies, we psychologists and psychiatrists have "sold" enormous quantities of a still unvalidated product.'

Incidentally, what is perhaps more serious in the long run is that the faulty conclusions from unchecked assumptions of cure with this small group of abnormal cases have been applied to the lives of healthy members of society, e.g. in 'progressive' education, and all kinds of rationalizations have been used to support that fundamental resistance to moral demands which exists in everyone. In the last thirty years it has sometimes become 'intellectual' to be amoral. As Mowrer, one of the world leaders in psychiatric research, has recently said, 'We are getting ever clearer indications that psychoanalysis is not only far less effective as a therapy than we had originally supposed; there are many competent observers also saying that, to the extent that psychoanalysis has been adopted by the public as a philosophy of life, we are *sick*.' The sociologist, Lapierre, in *The Freudian Ethic*, has documented in this area what has been broadly evident to psychologists for many years.

Parenthetically, the reader should not assume that the criticisms here are directed only upon psychoanalysis. (As regards social theorizing, let us recognize that Freud himself, e.g. in *Civilization and its Discontents*, showed that he appreciated the need for society's inhibitions. It was the journalists, and the lesser psychiatrists misunderstanding the basic theme, who rode a wave of reaction against 'Victorianism'.) Rather the attack here is against the whole fanciful and presumptuous theorizing of pre-metric, pre-experimental theory, based, moreover, almost exclusively on abnormal cases, as in the writings of Adler, Freud, Fromm, Jung, and countless others who have claimed authority to instruct the public, on clinical therapy in particular and psychological laws in general.

The responses in the last decade to doubts about theories from the purely clinical phase of observation have taken two main directions: (1) exploration of biochemical theories and drug or physiological approaches, as in electric shock therapy, thorazine, meprobamate, and the tranquillizers, and (2) what is called *behaviour therapy*, and hinges on conditioning or operating with the current reward system or 'dynamic lattice' of the patient. The former remedies have certainly reduced the problems of mental hospitals, but most psychiatrists consider them palliatives rather than 'cures'. Measurements with the I.P.A.T. anxiety scale, and other approaches to pure anxiety measures, do show quite definitely, however, that tranquillizers such as meprobamate combined with mild therapy lower, and keep lowered, the level of anxiety in neurotics. In regard to behaviour therapy we should note that at the moment clinical schools are splintered in many ways, but the most important division is between (*a*) those who think troubles are tied up with specific personal interests and incidents, as in psychoanalysis (but not only psychoanalysis) and who believe the historical origins of the neurosis must be retraced to effect a readjustment, as in most Jungian, Freudian, and other theories, and (*b*) those who instead follow Pavlov in believing that we can forget the past and that it suffices to bring about a change *now*, sometimes only of the symptom itself. The latter is the essence of 'behavioural therapy' and it aims essentially at reconditioning the faulty responses. This view can perhaps be likened to that of practical surgeons who are less concerned to ask what past stresses produced the stomach ulcer, but believe in operating to remove it.

From the standpoint of our present concern with personality measurement, either can be reconciled with the view that changing a specific behaviour will contribute to general personality source trait change. When a broad personality factor such as ego strength is shown to be deficient, one may well be able to trace this to a succession of ego-weakening incidents and it is possible that reliving them and re-evaluating the emotional habits set up by them (or behaviourally reconditioning the specific expressions) will result in an improved score on this dimension. To recognize that one can measure the height of a whole building as a unitary characteristic does not deny that many distinct small acts of construction have brought it about. But both the psychoanalyst and the behaviour therapist have perhaps overlooked, in their preoccupation with the bricks and girders, that one is out to raise the level of the roof!

It may be true that the patient wishes only to get rid of the annoying or debilitating symptom, and it is possible that behaviour therapy or psychoanalysis can do this. Yet the personality measurements show that in neurosis the whole personality pattern is defective in terms of necessary levels of functioning. They remind us that the historical incidents and tangled personal conflicts are really important only in so far as they produce losses of energy and other 'energy economic' effects in the total personality. On the other hand, at least in the popular conceptions of psychiatry, the 'historical trauma' view of neurosis has prevailed over the 'economics of energy' view, with its measurable general dimensions, because people enjoy reading a dramatized personal story more than a book of economics. Regardless of which side we take on the above issue – cure by unravelling history or by 'surgical' direct conditioning – we conclude that a complete view requires both measurement of the factors and an understanding of what accumulation of experiences has resulted in their being what they are. Moreover, the personality source trait measurement reminds us that the old-fashioned, 'purely personal, historical tangle' psychiatrist has also generally neglected certain constitutional personality factors which set limits to the patient's capacity to behave otherwise, and suggest the kind of adjustment best likely to succeed in terms of his available resources.

In Chapter 8 the P-technique method of measuring an individual day after day on a set of interest measures has shown how even the most unique constellation of historical interest attachments and symptoms can be clarified by methods more quantitative and objective than those of free association. This is the bridge which will eventually relate the particular and historical personal interests and symptoms of the individual to his levels on the basic source traits measured by the common factor batteries. If the clinician objects that the demand on mathematics and computing which P-technique makes is inappropriate to psychology, one can only reply that when one considers how much more complex the living organism is than any man-made machine, it is surely realistic to expect that the mathematics required of psychologists will be more complex than that which every engineer has to learn. If the general laws of psychology are mathematical, the decisions affecting a particular patient are bound to involve calculation, just as they are beginning to do in those biochemical and functional disorders of physical medicine which are more than germ infections or broken bones.

Meanwhile the common factor batteries are destined to be increasingly adopted for (*a*) checking the initial classification as hysteric, anxiety neurotic, sociopath, paranoid schizophrenic, alcoholic, or whatever *category* the profile indicates (see pages 211 and 217); (*b*) understanding, in terms of the quite individual constellation of personality factor strengths and weaknesses, how this given individual is dynamically out of adjustment, and (*c*) checking the degree of real progress being made in therapy by actual tests, in the course of therapy, on such source traits as anxiety, ego strength, surgency, dominance, and the tension level of particular ergs.

PERSONALITY MEASUREMENT IN BROADER MENTAL HEALTH PROGRAMMES

By contrast to these complexities in unravelling the unique trait structure of individuals, the less ambitious aim of measuring 'rough' common traits in large numbers of people as part of social and mental health surveys is theoretically simple though beset with some practical problems. For the sub-tests which would be required to produce sound measures of anxiety, or of neuroticism, or of degree of conflict, it is necessary to search among the sub-test forms shown to be valid in the factor analyses referred to in Chapters 3–6 above. The only novelty here is the demand for a test brief enough to be acceptable to large numbers of busy people; intelligible enough for persons of the lowest educational level to follow; and mechanical enough for relatively untrained assistants to administer.

Health surveys, aiming to put a finger on the pulse of a whole population, are increasingly a feature of well-organized societies. General medicine has obviously been able in the last twenty years to move increasingly towards a prophylactic practice. It anticipates and heads off disease, from typhoid to rabies, and now to cancer and heart disease, before they occur. Action of this kind demands good information regarding the movements of 'the enemy'. It requires surveys and statistical analyses to show just what the frequency of certain diseases may be, and whether they and their known causes are increasing or decreasing. To obtain this information, some invasion of the citizen's 'privacy' is inevitable; but mankind cannot expect to enjoy all the benefits of a modern society without some degree of cooperation with community services. Organized surveys are as necessary to the social body as sets of sensory nerves are to the proper functioning of the physical body.

Whereas data on the frequency of tuberculosis, venereal disease, and typhoid fever are now obtainable for a majority of advanced countries, mental health survey results are comparatively new and rare. Data exists, it is true, for a score of countries on basic admissions to mental hospitals, perhaps classified under a few major headings. But this means comparatively little, if only because the sheer number of admissions often depends on the hospital accommodation available! Even within the more prosperous United States, there appear on paper to be twice as many mental defectives in a certain state X as in state Y, and one's suspicions that X is not really more stupid than Y are aroused only upon noticing that state X has twice as large a mental health allowance as state Y: more hospital beds are available. Moreover, in any country, it seems that somewhat psychotic or mental defective individuals are left to go around unsupervised in small villages whereas the same persons would be placed in mental hospitals in a large city. (The rate of commitment for mental disorder is about twice as high in cities as in the country.) Similarly we are in doubt about changes with historical periods. Emil Ludwig, for example, in *Son of Man*, argues that the Middle East at the time of Christ was rife with mental disorders, with wandering individuals seeing hallucinatory visions and hearing voices, and the epidemics of St Vitus dance in the Middle Ages by contrast suggest a shift only from a schizophrenic to an hysteric culture. Certainly, by our present standards, such acts as the crucifixion of a thousand Spartacists along the Appian way are understandable only as bizarre and horrible lunacy.

Evidently the mental health of a community needs watching for other reasons than anticipating mental hospital accommodation requirements. To begin with smaller issues, however, do we really know whether cities provoke more madness than does rural life, as L. Hausman and B. Russell, among others, have implied? It is at least possible that the gross figures merely reflect differences in available services and efficiency of diagnosis. And as to the latter, in Chapter 8, where we discussed the things which clinicians need to measure, it was pointed out that almost fantastic disparities exist among various estimates of the frequency of neurosis in our population. Some say one person in fifty is really in need of clinical treatment as a neurotic. Others say one in five. Some say one person in fifty might advantageously take tranquillizers on account of a too sensitive anxiety level, but the sales in several countries suggest that one in five must be taking them. Estimates of the frequency of psychotic personalities, dangerous to themselves and to others, similarly vary from one in ten to one in a hundred. Roughly one person in twelve spends some time in a mental hospital or under mental treatment, in countries where records are available, but as to lesser degrees of disorder we are in the dark. An eminent statistician, speaking recently on lung cancer and the incidence of smoking, suggested that so many borderline neurotic persons hold themselves together by this vice that, if smoking were prohibited, the gain in reduction of lung cancer would be offset by a loss through increase of mental patients. His implication that smoking helps mental balance is entirely unwarranted; indeed, much could be quoted to the contrary, but it illustrates at least a statistician's view of the prevalence of lesser mental disorder. As soon as governments set out seriously to take stock of the incidence of this and that tendency to mental disorder, related in various occupations, age, and sex groups, etc., it is almost certain that new and valuable connexions will become apparent, as happened, for example, in the instance of lung cancer quoted here.

Since the admission of an individual to a mental hospital as insane depends on many accidental circumstances, such as the provision of hospital facilities, the patience of his family, etc., and

The numbers by each country indicate the size of sample gathered

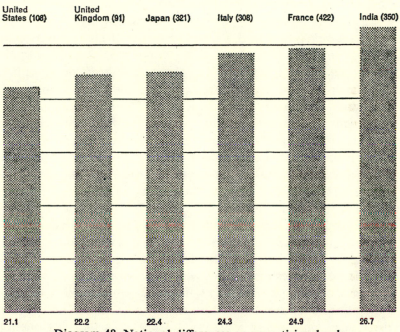

United States (108) United Kingdom (91) Japan (321) Italy (308) France (422) India (350)

21.1   22.2   22.4   24.3   24.9   26.7

Diagram 48. National differences on neuroticism levels

the number of neurotics being treated is a close function of money available for psychiatrists, it is obviously desirable in assessing community mental health to depend less on hospital or clinic figures and more on actual measures made on fair samples of the population. In the last decade the advances in knowing precisely what we are measuring by mental tests have made this decidedly more practicable. For example, brief verbal Neuroticism Scale Questionnaires of about forty items each and taking less than ten minutes for the average person to complete are available for such surveys. Although no truly large scale work has yet been done, one particular version of a neuroticism scale, that by Scheier, has been translated into several different languages and applied to equivalent groups (technical college students) in different countries. The results reveal quite remarkable differences in average mental health level, as shown in Diagram 48. If substantiated by additional, more varied samples, these findings should provoke much thought and theory about the relation of various aspects of culture to neurosis.

The nature of the forty-item short verbal anxiety scale has already been discussed and, as a comparison of Diagrams 14 and 48 will show, there is a tendency for countries higher in neurosis also to be higher in anxiety. In source trait terms neurosis has been demonstrated to be a complex entity, due to the conjunction of several personality characteristics of an individual or of a community. Indeed, the results of surveys would be decidedly more intelligible, and more far-reaching in their reliable implications, if they were routinely made with a battery covering several distinct personality factors, as in the 16 P.F., the Thurstone Inventory or the High School Personality Questionnaire, from which anxiety and neuroticism, etc., can be derived as secondary scores, instead of being directed only to a purely pathological symptom measurement such as anxiety. The evaluation of such a whole set of factors, making community comparisons, would certainly throw more light on the origins of symptoms in different settings and communities. For any intelligent planning of prophylactic mental health programmes will need first to know what features of our culture are responsible for various personality deviations.

Actually, at this pioneer stage, we happen to know more about the distribution of psychological traits in terms of these new source traits through private enterprise, by the advertising industry, and by medical supply houses, than we do from any governmentally instituted surveys. Very complete coast-to-coast surveys have been made by the 16 P.F. In some fields buyers of different products differ significantly in personality. For example, women buyers of a certain rather flamboyant cosmetic turn out to be significantly more extravert than those who buy a more demure one. Similarly, personality relations on the *I* factor (sensitive-*vs*-tough) are very clear in relation to such political issues as compulsory vaccination, corporal punishment in schools, armament expenditure, etc. In both politics and advertising appeals can be adjusted to be most effective for the temperaments concerned. In research by pharmaceutical houses on tranquillizer use it has been shown, by the I.P.A.T. anxiety scale, that private patients seeking such medication from general practitioners are in fact at a high anxiety level, as Diagram 49 shows. This diagram also shows that general internal medicine

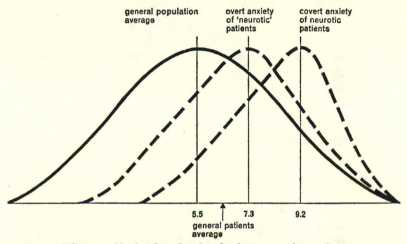

Diagram 49. Anxiety levels of private practice patients

patients are also somewhat above the general anxiety level, and that the patients with mental symptoms are actually higher on covert than overt anxiety. (These are two parts of the I.P.A.T. anxiety scale measuring less conscious and more conscious anxiety; for anxiety can be 'bound' or below the surface.) Thus these patients, far from being hypochondriacs, have more emotional disturbance than they are prepared consciously to admit.

Population personality measures, carried out in the mental health field, could lead, via our knowledge of the dynamics of source traits, to predictions of the effects of various kinds of social legislation upon mental health. Even before that they are useful simply to ascertain the need for clinics and mental hospital accommodation in various areas.

When the psychologist gets interested in the social aspects of personality, the problem arises that in the last resort the task of producing the instruments proves less difficult than that of producing the subjects! The 'man in the street', so glibly summoned up by journalists, is in fact a very difficult species to catch. Almost any group which is accessible – students, military men, hospital inmates – constitutes a selected and misleading sample. The boy in the street is less difficult: schools give an excellent cross-section. But unless steps are deliberately taken to get a 'stratified sample' of normal subjects, on a 'panel', organized perhaps by a state statistician and paid for their trouble, the psychologist and the psychiatrist will continue to lack vital information about the true average man of our time.

Such an organization of a 'professional subject' sample would also permit the use of more satisfactory tests, such as the Objective-Analytic types of battery, which need more time and a trained psychologist, instead of those all-too-short verbal tests which can be given from door to door by a social worker. As the psychologist gets nearer to the average man he often discovers, incidentally, that the style of his tests needs real revision, from the standpoint of educational level, in reading, etc. The public was surprised and incredulous to hear that the enlisted men measured by psychologists in the First World War had an average mental age of twelve years. The construction of ability and educational achievement tests has by now thoroughly adapted itself to realities unknown to people who read books; but adaptation of personality tests to all ranges of education (at present all too many seem written for university students!) has been carried reasonably far only in a minority, such as the above-mentioned brief anxiety and neuroticism scales. However, Dr Eber, working with the Vocational Rehabilitation Services in rural Alabama, has shown that it is possible to produce a 'low literate' version of the 16 P.F. which works with that substantial fraction of the population whose education opportunities have been limited and whose vocabulary is consequently minimal.

In any wide application of mental testing, as in these adult mental health surveys, or in the general school testing considered in the last chapter, it is necessary to consider and allow for the phenomenon technically known as *test sophistication*. By test sophistication we refer to the extent of changes in a test score through one subject being more familiar with the test than another, notably with the selective answer procedure, the timing, and the response habits. For example, in intelligence tests, it is true, as Vernon and Parry have shown, that a person's score is slightly higher in a normally equivalent form of test B if he has already taken test A. The improvement with increasing experience is greatest between the first and second exposure to an intelligence test and is negligible by the time we compare the fifth and sixth exposures. Test sophistication must be distinguished from *actual improvement of the trait*, e.g. intelligence, by environmental advantages. It is a mere adjustment to the testing situation, and occurs equally in culture-fair intelligence tests and traditional, education-contaminated intelligence tests.

Psychologically, one would expect that test sophistication effects would appear also in personality tests. Recent work by Howard in Chicago, making repeated applications of the 16 P.F. questionnaire to the same subjects, shows that some change does in fact occur. However, it is quite small and it is mainly in the direction of increasing reliability and validity of the test. In the questionnaire medium, at least, it is as if the asking of the questions draws the subject's attention to his own behaviour, so that after pondering on it, in, say, half a dozen test repetitions over two or three months, he observes and reports more accurately.

The only widely practicable way of overcoming errors of evaluation due to differing levels of test sophistication is to arrange that all the population gets *some* common test sophistication. (Alternatively, as in some of the present writer's own tests, the user is advised to administer two or more equivalent forms in succession and throw the first form away.) The problem is in part being taken care of through a natural public reaction. For the lively response of certain opportunists to the immense parental concern about children's school intelligence test performance has been to flood the market with booklets of test specimens by the use of which the child may be coached to the best possible test sophistication. The more stuffy professional psychologists shuddered and protested, when wisely they should have welcomed it as a solution to the problem of test sophistication. The policy of the American Psychological Association, in forbidding its 20,000 members to supply tests to unqualified members of the general public, seems to be partly motivated by this questionable desire to avoid test sophistication, but also by other and sounder reasons. It seems likely that in the end the only solution will be to get *all* people test-sophisticated, since in the actual test situation we must spend time bringing them first to the same level of familiarity, to get good results. Such books as the present, and Eysenck's *Know Your Own I.Q.*, provided they do not infringe copyrights, or give whole tests whereby a layman might, with his limited knowledge, draw false and dangerous conclusions about someone's personality or mental health, may perhaps accomplish something in this direction. If educators are really sincere in quoting the philosophers on the importance of self-knowledge, they will be less concerned with bureaucratic protocol in withholding test results from parents and children than in spreading that psychological education whereby test results can be properly understood.

VOCATIONAL GUIDANCE AND SELECTION

Public education and occupational opportunity were chaotic when the savant Pascal made his oft-quoted remark that that which takes most of a man's waking hours – his job – is commonly decided by accident. Schools, business organizations, and government schemes have since concentrated mightily on remedying this situation, but the extent to which any well-intentioned plans succeed hinges, in the last resort, on the technical powers of the psychologist. For example, until a decade ago psychologists could measure nothing but abilities with tolerable reliability and validity, yet every shrewd observer of life realized that personality and motivation differences are probably the greater part of the story of occupational success and satisfaction.

Regardless of whether we deal with vocational guidance, i.e. finding the best-fitting job for a given group of individuals in school, employment agency, or vocation rehabilitation unit, or vocational selection, i.e. picking the best person for a defined, necessary job performance, certain general principles apply.

First, the truly comprehensive view requires that we consider society as well as the individual. In society there is a population with such and such resources of intelligence, training, emotional stability, etc., partly biological, partly the result of existing training. If one directs more good ability into, say, the fine arts, there may be less in medicine, and if the economic system pays race-course touts more than, say, teachers, the level of intelligence characteristic of teachers may be less than it would otherwise be. All fitness for an occupation is relative to supply.

When we face the choice for a man who might do equally well as a lawyer or a painter, we have to consider also how many other people are heading for these occupations and what society needs. A vocational guidance psychologist known to the writer treasures an indignant letter received during the war from a saxophonist who was drafted (for good reasons, in terms of his rapid computing ability) to anti-aircraft artillery. He complained bitterly of the stupidity of the authorities in putting him in artillery when his natural job was making a noise on the saxophone! Statistical psychologists have worked out some nice mathematical theorems which neatly ensure the maximum utilization of abilities in a system of competing sub-groups, each demanding a somewhat different emphasis on abilities for success. But these are beyond an introductory exposition; only the principle can be noted; and except in an ideally cooperative set of people it could not be used!

A second general principle concerns that difference between adjustment in a job (largely in terms of satisfaction) and efficiency at a job which we have noted earlier in talking about the specification equation. It was there noted that the efficiency in a job can be defined by a 'criterion score' or rating. This can then be estimated by our familiar specification equation, weighting each ability and personality factor by what research has shown to be its importance for that criterion. For example, in a study by Dr Joseph King of Industrial Psychology, Inc., New York, several hundred bakery route (door-to-door) salesmen, on equivalent rural types of routes, were measured on intelligence and the 16 P.F. test personality factors. The correlations of these scores with the criterion – amount of product regularly sold – were as follows

$$C = 0.2A + 0.2B + 0.3C + 0.2F + 0.3G + 0.2H - 0.2I - 0.4L \\ - 0.3O - 0.1Q_1 + 0.4Q_3 - 0.2Q_4$$

That is to say, the effective salesman in this type of situation tends to be of cyclothyme temperament (warm), surgent (talkative), and of sufficient ego strength not to suffer if brushed off – and so on. The combination makes sense in terms of most people's experience of salesmen! The figures could be used as they stand for vocational selection, but for vocational guidance statistical adjustments would have to be made for the salesman already having a different range, in some traits, from that of the general population. Essentially, however, by this method, we should get an 'efficiency at the job' estimate through multiplying each candidate's personality source trait scores by these weights, and adding to a single criterion score estimate.

By contrast, the 'adjustment to the job' principle proceeds as follows. One takes a sufficient sample of people who have stuck to that job, and finds their average profile. Such a central profile for each of four different jobs on sixteen personality factors and five ability factors (four primaries and general intelligence) is shown in Diagram 50, and it will be seen that they differ considerably. One could now take the individual profile for a given candidate seeking vocational guidance or selection and set it alongside these (and other occupations similarly analysed) to decide which it best fits. In a small test installation one might depend on assessing the relative goodness of two people, in the fit of their profiles to the model by eye, but the decision can be made more reliable by working out a pattern similarity coefficient (written r_p to distinguish it from r, the correlation coefficient) between the ideal and actual profiles. One thus sees which of a number of jobs or job families the individual best fits. However, this says how well he is 'adjusted' in agreeing with the type of person society has hitherto called to that job, and who has stayed 'successfully' in that job. And there may well be some appreciable discrepancies between the adjustment as thus calculated and the

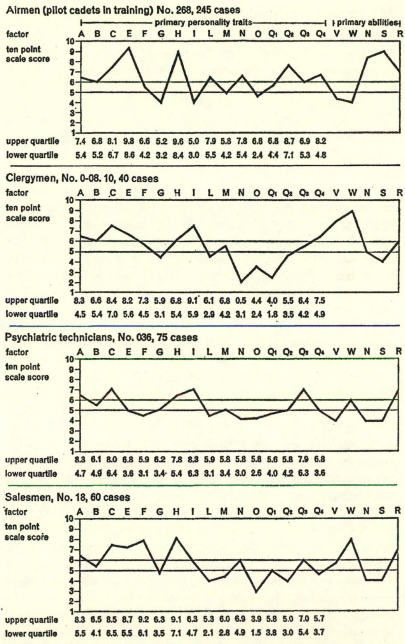

Airmen (pilot cadets in training) No. 268, 245 cases

factor	A	B	C	E	F	G	H	I	L	M	N	O	Q₁	Q₂	Q₃	Q₄	V	W	N	S	R
upper quartile	7.4	6.8	8.1	9.8	6.6	5.2	9.6	5.0	7.9	5.8	7.8	6.8	6.8	8.7	6.9	8.2					
lower quartile	5.4	5.2	6.7	8.6	4.2	3.2	8.4	3.0	5.5	4.2	5.4	2.4	4.4	7.1	5.3	4.8					

Clergymen, No. 0-08. 10, 40 cases

factor	A	B	C	E	F	G	H	I	L	M	N	O	Q₁	Q₂	Q₃	Q₄	V	W	N	S	R
upper quartile	8.3	6.6	8.4	8.2	7.3	5.9	6.8	9.1	6.1	6.8	0.5	4.4	4.0	5.5	6.4	7.5					
lower quartile	4.5	5.4	7.0	5.6	4.5	3.1	5.4	5.9	2.9	4.2	3.1	2.4	1.8	3.5	4.2	4.9					

Psychiatric technicians, No. 036, 75 cases

factor	A	B	C	E	F	G	H	I	L	M	N	O	Q₁	Q₂	Q₃	Q₄	V	W	N	S	R
upper quartile	8.3	6.1	8.0	6.8	5.9	6.2	7.8	8.3	5.9	5.8	5.8	5.8	5.6	5.8	7.9	6.8					
lower quartile	4.7	4.9	6.4	3.6	3.1	3.4	5.4	6.3	3.1	3.4	3.0	2.6	4.0	4.2	6.3	3.6					

Salesmen, No. 18, 60 cases

factor	A	B	C	E	F	G	H	I	L	M	N	O	Q₁	Q₂	Q₃	Q₄	V	W	N	S	R
upper quartile	8.3	6.5	8.5	8.7	9.2	6.3	9.1	6.3	5.3	6.0	6.9	3.9	5.8	5.0	7.0	5.7					
lower quartile	5.5	4.1	6.5	5.5	6.1	3.5	7.1	4.7	2.1	2.8	4.9	1.5	3.8	3.0	5.4	3.7					

Note: The personality scores on the 16 P.F. are from the number of cases indicated. The Primary Abilities values, however, are based only on demonstration cases and are to be considered only as likely illustration.

Diagram 50. Four job profiles on personality factors and primary abilities efficiency decisions as found by the estimation from the equation for goodness of performance. For example, Mr A, who is a business executive, might be more efficient as a janitor than Mr B, but how long would he stay in the job, and is it good for society so to place him?

Even among those who stably stay in a job the two indices will rank people somewhat differently. For example, scientific researchers (Diagram 30) are more premsic ($I +$ factor) than the general population. That is to say, they are more emotionally sensitive, which is probably due to the fact that more educated persons, especially from homes well cushioned economically, are in general more premsic, through being relatively protected from harsh demands of reality. But when correlations with a criterion of productivity and effectiveness, such as patents gained, researches published, etc., are made in a group of researchers it turns out that premsia is negatively weighted. The harric ($I-$) individual, i.e. the tough and realistic scientist, actually does a better job. Incidentally, since I factor tends to be associated with more indulgent upbringing, the finding of higher art and music interests in premsic individuals fits the statistical finding that scientific leaders, relative to leaders in music and arts, come from less privileged homes.

Formerly (and, alas, in many places today) vocational guidance, however sound the assessment of the individual, was based on comparatively amateur impressions by the counsellor of what various jobs would demand. A slight advance is made when ideas are derived from some 'job analysis' in terms of what *acts* the person carries out in the job. But research often shows that a job makes unseen demands, and these confident impressions from job description can be quite wide of the mark. Occupations with apparently very dissimilar activities can demand a very similar personality profile and apparently similar jobs make very different demands. For instance, air pilots, Olympic athletes, and firemen are quite similar; while research professors and teachers are quite dissimilar. This lack of real knowledge about what a job is really like and what it demands has been a source of criticism of job interest tests, of which the Strong Interest Blank and the Kuder are among the best examples, in which the person literally checks off the occupations and activities he thinks would most interest him. It is true that in these test devices the test constructors have not taken these statements entirely at their face value, but have made statistical analyses showing the choices which people in particular occupations make. However, such vocational guidance does not permit scores to be interpreted and understood through intermediate psychological concepts, such as temperament traits and drive strengths, which would enable one to add psychological to statistical prediction.

The advantage of a vocational guidance system based less on crude empiricism and more on test scores which represent known temperament or dynamic structures is that much can be brought to bear in the latter system from our knowledge of the natural history of the traits, and the sociology of the occupation. For example, we know that some source traits, like cyclothymia, intelligence, and threctic ($H-$ factor) are largely constitutionally given, while others, such as premsia (I factor), super-ego strength, surgency, etc., are susceptible to substantial environmental change. To know from the scores which of these traits account for the person fitting the occupational profile or criterion at a given moment is important. Statistically, at the moment of examination, two people might show an equally good fit, but psychologically we would know that one would be doing much better in a year's time. For we know that some factors follow a typical life course, e.g. in the steady decline in surgency after adolescence, and the rise of ego strength. Consequently, knowing the natural history of the source trait measured, and the occupational fact that, say, the demands on ego strength do not come until later, one would present different occupational advice, with the help of tests yielding meaningful source trait scores, from that offered with batteries which merely tie up statistically some inscrutable score on a patent test with some probability of success in a particular occupation.

Vocational guidance when well done is no simple procedure for which a score on an intelligence test and an achievement test will suffice. The number of source trait scores likely to be needed to reach as good a prediction as is virtually possible may easily reach thirty or forty. Both statistically and psychologically the prediction will gain from going to about ten abilities, sixteen personality traits, and a dozen dynamic traits. Incidentally, in almost any adjustment prediction, one does well to spread the available testing time far more evenly over the three modalities than has hitherto been done – when dynamic traits were neglected and concentration was on abilities. It is true that in vocational terms routine testing still does not know nearly enough about the roles of the dynamic factor measures, as in M.A.T., or in a recent test by Sweney called the Vocational Interest Measure. However, one can see from pure research that the objective tests are valid, and from clinical insight one can see that certain occupations would give greater scope to certain drive tensions. There are occupations which an assertive person, or a person of high gregarious need, or a person of inordinate need for security, for example, would clearly prefer. But since measures of these in objective terms (Chapter 7) rather than in the self-evaluating procedures of, say, the Edwards Personal Preference Inventory, are as recent as 1960, few vocation investigations have yet been made.

Incidentally, the above testing principle of spreading one's measurement widely does not apply only to different modalities – ability, personality, motivation. Even in one modality it is better to measure *several* things in spite of the reduced reliability found in short tests for each, than to measure only *one* thing with very high reliability. One great advantage of factored tests of any kind is that one's test measures are guaranteed to be well spread out, each tapping an entirely new aspect of personality, whereas other tests frequently overlap and repeat themselves very wastefully. The time demand, in getting an adequate evaluation of an individual's personality, even with the most judicious use of tests and scoring methods, is likely to be perhaps four hours or more. But, in all conscience, this is precious little to take from a person's time for advising him on a life career. Indeed, both industry and the general public have a serious responsibility for remedying two major abuses in personnel selection, affecting the lives of millions. First, there is this absurd discrepancy between the importance to employees and employers of having the right rather than the wrong man in a job, perhaps for years, and the idea that twenty minutes is enough to give to testing. Three or four hours is needed, even with an uncommonly good choice of factored ability and personality tests, to get reasonable coverage. Secondly, there has been a careless dependence on impressive charlatans, with little qualification in psychological testing and still less understanding of the simplest statistics. The almost invariable defence of these types, as they miss the most obvious statistical advantages of procedure, is that they depend on subject insight and 'clinical' feeling. They exploit the stereotype that there must be some inverse relation between scientific efficiency and crystal ball insight; but in some experiments actually carried out on interview 'insight' these humbugs have done decidedly less well on personal reliability of subjective impression than have objective methodologists.

In large businesses, and organizations such as the civil service, much economy can be brought into the whole testing procedure for promotion and allocation to special jobs by the installation of what has been called *the two-file system*, briefly referred to in connexion with school-testing installations in the last chapter. This aims to increase reliability and to bring 'developmental depth perception' to bear upon any single set of test results. It involves preserving the individual's profile of source trait scores by testing on the same agreed set of centrally important source traits in personality, etc., at regular intervals of perhaps a couple of years. Alongside the resulting file of individuals' scores is kept a file of the adjustment profiles, on the same source traits, for the various occupations, promotions, and specialities in which these individuals might be interested. This occupational data file would naturally cover data accumulated both for adjustment (mean profile) and effectiveness (weights for the specification equation, obtained by keeping records over years) profiles.

The two-file system implies a potential matching of every individual's profile from the first file with every job profile from the second file. It is not difficult to foresee a time when electronic computer methods could be brought to develop this two-file system towards the principle of maximizing the utilization of talents and interests for the good of society as a whole as sketched above. Although the statistical principles of the maximization of use of resources are complex, a glimpse of their working can be given on a comparatively simple instance. It is sometimes pointed out that in terms of I.Q. there are probably ten times as many people at a level capable of profiting by university education (as now defined) as there are among those of good intelligence (I.Q. 120 plus) who at present actually go to universities. However, fitness to succeed in universities, as in any occupation, is determined by a suitably high score on several *other* traits, beyond intelligence. Let us consider only four independent factors, on each of which only the highest 25 per cent are fit for some exacting occupation. The fraction of the population *simultaneously* 'passing' on all four will be $\frac{1}{4} \times \frac{1}{4} \times \frac{1}{4} \times \frac{1}{4}$, or one in 256. Thus it is easy to be deceived into thinking that human resources are not being used if one omits reference to the simultaneous need for several qualities. It is the virtue of the psychometric system we are speaking about that it searches out resources in terms of such combinations.

What is said here in statistical terms about the rarity of the requisite multiple trait combination to do a job is well known to managers and teachers. Of a hundred children who might, say, eventually do valuable scientific research, eighty (in America where one in five goes to a university) will fail to reach university entrance, and ten of the remaining twenty will show a disinclination or disability in mathematics. Of the ten left, five will be women who will marry before graduate school, and go to higher things. Of the remaining five, two may be offered more money in some routine job, and two may have neurotic personality disabilities which prevent their even finishing anything!

In Kipling's poem about the garden and gardeners, he insists that the garden finds work 'for everyone', but he admits that 'some can pot begonias and some can bud a rose, and some are hardly fit to trust with anything that grows'. But the fact is that for any occupation to which multiple cut-off scores are applied, one gets inevitably into the above 'ten little nigger boys' culmination. It has been said, for example, that intelligence requirements for entry to the Guards could be raised if the stature requirements could be lowered, and this, suitably expanded, is the problem in all occupations. The psychometrist has to compromise between finding the perfect niche sought by the person and the perfect person which society wants in that position – and this turns out to be a nice problem in relativity.

MENTAL MEASUREMENT AND SOCIO-POLITICAL LIFE

Literary gentlemen have speculated very freely about the impact of mental measurement upon society. On the one side, philosophers from Plato to Bernard Shaw have sketched utopias in which leaders are selected on explicit test data rather than dubious popular report, and, on the other, Aldous Huxley, Orwell in *1984*, and Young in *The Rise of the Meritocracy* have poked fun at or drawn unpleasant caricatures of the systems demanded by these idealists. What these three reactionaries have overlooked is that the advance of the social sciences, which they regret, is entirely compatible with a democratic framework. Science and democracy owe much to each other. Indeed, the capacity of democracy to survive in competition with other systems will depend on a rich application of the findings of behavioural science, with the individual's consent and insight.

However much the Orwells may implicitly sentimentalize about the good old days, they do not seem to have been very happy either, with the Chamberlains on the one hand or the Mussolinis and Hitlers on the other. It is our present methods, or lack of methods, which throw up such men as leaders. There can surely be little doubt that the present processes even for 'democratic election' of political leaders are extremely inefficient and erroneous. The Press creates an 'image'; the candidate appeals to the prejudices of the less intelligent mass of voters, and is photographed with a benevolent smile patting small children on the head. It is impossible for the intelligent voter to find what he is really like, how emotionally stable he may be or how firm psychologically his attitudes are on vital values. Nor could a psychologist, from the journalistic evidence available, usually hope to fix his I.Q., with any confidence, within an error range from 95 to 145. Shaw's suggestion implying that the intelligence, educational–informational level, and personality and motivational measures of the rival candidates should be put up on a public slate is inherently a good one, and psychology has reached a stage where something of this kind could in fact be done.

Although the abilities of leaders, including most royal lines, give evidence when closely examined of being well above the population average, there are no technical difficulties in constructing intelligence tests, for example, to reach the most rarefied heights. For example, there are intelligence tests where not one person in ten thousand reaches the 'ceiling', and there are emotional stability measures which are virtually unfakeable (though sabotageable). A development of this kind would, of course, imply the secondary development of technical advice to the voter on what these scores mean, just as the modern buyer of a complex electronic product or medicine consults a *Consumer's Guide* or some equivalent for technical evaluation.

Meanwhile the experimental study of politics and group behaviour by such psychologists as Guetzkow, Rummel, Wrigley, Osgood, Stice, Gibb, Fiedler, Triandis, and others has told us a good deal about what *does* happen in the present methods. In the first place, it seems that most groups if left to themselves spontaneously develop a leader. The anarchist is wrong in supposing that anarchy is a preferred state of society. Stice, Gibb, and the present writer set a hundred groups of ten men each in competition (for money and privileges) group with group. The intergroup performance was measured in a large variety of ways, from a simple tug of war, to factory production, to committee arrangements, and so to strategic decisions akin to those in war. Given the alternative of working with or without a leader, it turned out that all groups, after a little experience of the conditions of survival, decided to elect a leader. The leader could be changed after an interval. The primary aim was to study the personality of the leader and its relation to group success, e.g. the methods of leadership, the followers' changing attitudes, etc., but evidence was also gathered on the dimensions of groups. It was soon found that the naturally emerging elected leaders, in a face-to-face situation, turned out to have a personality profile characteristically different from the followers. In long-term leadership, it is conceivable that holding the position might be partly responsible for developing the traits. But in this case the personality must be the cause of the rise to leadership, because the 16 P.F. and the intelligence testing were done *before* the event.

Diagram 51 shows curves for three types of leader, but the differences are minor, and of the significant common trends, we may choose for illustrative comment the following: (1) elected leaders are significantly above average intelligence; (2) they are higher

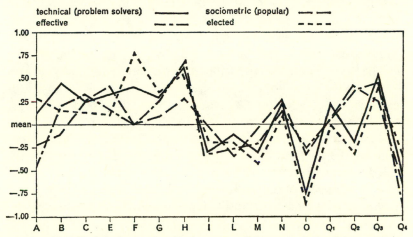

The 16 P.F. has been peculiarly successful, compared with more restricted tests, in selecting successful leaders in face-to-face, direct-contact groups. These generalizations are from a study of 100 groups of 10 men each, in which the performance of each group was measured in many situations. The profiles for leaders are given for three distinct bases of leader selection: (1) effective leaders, as rated by observers watching the group performance; (2) elected leaders, who were popularly elected and retained the position; (3) problem-solving leaders, who may not have been rated as leaders but who had to their credit the greatest number of contributions to solving group problems.

Diagram 51. The personality profiles of leaders: effective, elected, popular, and technical

on ego and super-ego strength (factors *C* and *G*); (3) they are more extravert, particularly on the surgency component (*F*). Regarding the first, there is some evidence that a leader does well to be more intelligent but not too intelligent. If the gap is too large, leadership is lost. Terman's work on the I.Q.s of scientists and of political and military leaders suggests that leading scientists have little chance of making good political leaders for this reason (as well as other reasons implicit in the personality data below). As to the C and G factor findings, the high ego strength and emotional stability are necessary if a leader is not to retire disgusted into private life in face of the irrational pressures and ingratitude he encounters. Similarly, the high super-ego strength is necessary because morality is the life blood of a group – the condition by which groups exist – however detestable some *individuals* may find it! As evidence of this, we note that among some twenty traits which followers rated for desirability in a leader, 'fair-mindedness' and 'standing up for the right' were at the top.

The third group of traits – the extraversion factors of A, F, etc. – are also easy to explain but harder to justify as rational desirables. Affectothymia (A factor) brings, it is true, a warm-heartedness which followers like. Frederick the Great, who responded to his soldiers' apprehensions before battle with 'surely you don't expect to live forever!' would scarcely have been an electioneering success. However, he, and our definitely $A(-)$ Queen Elizabeth I did better for their countries than, say, the warm-hearted Richard I and Charles II. For $A(+)$ brings sentimentality, emotionality, and lack of foresight.

The contribution of surgency ($F+$) to election is obviously that of making the person more 'visible', for the surgent is talkative and enthusiastic and uninhibited (see correlations, page 92). Unfortunately this trait brings in its train several real behavioural disabilities for good leadership. Shrewder and more sober judgements are made by desurgent people – leading researchers and doctors, for example, tend to be desurgent. Moreover, the surgent individuals, like Mussolini, Hitler, and many another, are temperamentally glib and confident in their promises. The public learns (although slowly), for in these small group experiments, on second elections, the highly surgent and also the highly dominant lose some of their initial popularity. Only in those who worship movie idols are these characteristics perennially admired.

This brief glance at personality measurement and leadership suffices to show that psychological tests *can* locate at least the individuals the public (in face-to-face contact) will pick, and that scientific principles apply to leadership dynamics. Such research also strongly suggests that although the present haphazard process manages to select people with some characteristics which a good leader needs, it also accepts others which may be positively dangerous. The pages of history are full of dominant, surgent, and affectothyme psychopaths whose histrionics have crowded out better leaders. The fault lies in the followers, who are not wise enough to discount these traits. It is within the realm of practical possibilities today to improve the process of election by making objective psychological measures available.

In saying 'the fault lies in the followers' we recognize that the voting behaviour of followers depends not only on the personality of the leader, but on their own personality and intelligence. Any community with a large fraction of people below an I.Q. of 85, for example, will stagger like a water-logged ship, for intelligence below roughly 85 can be the prey to every oversimplified slogan. Not much is yet known about the effect on social life of community differences on general personality factors, though it is certain that there *are* significant differences between nations, regions, and social classes on these factors. For example, there is a statistical tendency for individuals of lower social status to be less dominant and less surgent, and also, but less clearly, less emotionally stable (C factor). Differences on anxiety have already been cited (page 114), and one may point to both Warburton's and Butcher's finding on the 16 P.F. of a substantially more extravert score by Americans compared with equivalent British groups. Accumulating test evidence often shows that 'national stereotypes' are not altogether figments of the imagination. There are also differences between urban and rural groups which may have importance for social organization. Butcher, comparing scores on the High School Personality Questionnaire, found rural children less anxious and more parmic ($H+$) than town children, while individuals who live in the centre of town rather than in suburbs have been found more surgent. It has been said that Britain built up its civilization in its country houses, and has regarded cities as an unfortunate necessity, whereas the more surgent Italian wants to live in the chatter at the heart of a city. Certainly differences of temperament have social implications for the success of colonization, for city planners, and for the manufacturers of recreational material.

When William James and others asserted that the differences in intellectual conclusions among philosophers could be traced more to their differences in temperament than to any differences in facts available to them, they stated a principle which has since been experimentally verified. In understanding the 'rational viewpoints' of whole peoples as well as individuals one must frankly recognize that logically reached attitudes are often secondary products of personality. The personality analyses carried out by the present writer and his colleagues in the forties showed two personality factors in particular which influenced view and values, namely, the radicalism–conservatism factor, indexed Q_1, and the tender–tough-minded dimension (later called premsia-harria), indexed as I factor. Thurstone had independently located the attitude pattern Q_1, showing its extensive determination of 'willingness to change' over more than political fields, and Eysenck has independently extended our knowledge of the range of the tender–tough effects of I factor, from art to zoology. Table 29 shows some attitudes affected by these two personality dimensions.

One must keep statistical and psychological perspective in looking at Table 29, for it does not mean that by any means all of variance in these attitudes is due to these single factors. Attitudes are thought of by psychologists as belonging mainly to dynamic modality, i.e. to the realm of interests, drives, etc., and much of the individual difference on the above attitudes would indeed lie in particular developments of dynamic interests. That is to say, we must look for part of the explanation of these attitudes in rationally determined or, at least, socially understandable sentiments and loyalties rooted in personal history. But some more general influence lies beyond these rational sources in sheer temperament. If a small boy and an old lady differ in attitudes about having a window open, each will have a solidly connected irrefutable chain of logical syllogisms, but one will begin with the premise of a high and the other of a low personal basic metabolic rate. Personality – the inborn, or, at the very least, the present and pervasive temperamental sensitivity – acts as a hidden premise in the individual's logic arguments, and leads two reasonable individuals to incompatible conclusions.

TABLE 29

Attitudes expressing the personality factor, Q_1,
radicalism-vs-conservatism

1. The Bible is true in all parts.

    True   False

2. If one's country is threatened, it is often necessary to go to war.

    True   False

3. Our greatest need today is that all people should learn birth control.

    True   False

4. It is the government's duty to provide security and medical services for all.

    True   False

5. It is not desirable to have divorce obtainable simply by mutual consent.

    True   False

The radical (Q_1+) answers to these attitudes are (1) False, (2) False, (3) True, (4) True, (5) False.

Attitudes resulting from the projection of the personality source trait,
premsia, I factor, into socio-political beliefs

1. It is more important that people have artistic surroundings than a raised material standard of living.

    True   False

2. To ensure scientific advance, it is necessary that operations be performed on live animals (vivisection) with proper anaesthesia and other safeguards.

    Yes   No

3. In sexual matters, people should be free to do and teach what seems reasonable to *them*.

    Yes   No

4. Parents should have the right to excuse their children from vaccination for epidemic diseases.

    Yes   No

5. People who are certain to pass on serious hereditary defects should be compulsorily sterilized.   Yes   No

The premsic ($I+$) responses are (1) True, (2) No, (3) Yes, (4) Yes, (5) No.

There is a sense in which the $I+$ individual, with his culturally cushioned background and resulting 'overprotected emotional sensitivity' (premsia), has a general belief that the world is a much more benign and restful place than the harric ($I-$) individual assumes it to be. His Rousseauian beliefs about the natural goodness of man, the lack of necessity for punishment, the objectionableness of government coercion (e.g. on vaccination) follow logically from a childhood protected by a veneer of civilization which has never, in his experience, startled him by breaking through. The harric $(I-)$ individual, on the other hand, though less comfortable to be with, is also more dependable in the sense that he feels less entitled to follow his whims and is more prepared to accept and cope with the reality of an intractable world. (A general personality tendency allied to premsia, but to be differentiated, is the tendency to what is known as autism, discussed in motivation measurement – page 195 – by which one tends to believe what it is pleasant to believe, and to do, regardless of physical consequences or morality, what one wishes to do.)

There are some suggestions that older cultures, particularly those not faced with the responsibilities of leadership, run higher on premsia. Results from India, for example, are far higher than for America. One may suspect that when the Romans 'sighed and went away' from Britain they left a premsic population. Possibly there is a trend in that direction in this century, since the increasing application of science has made life easier and death more remote for everyone. People are inclined to credit this gain to their own political intelligence, and the increase in tender-mindedness to some moral superiority over their ancestors; but social science will probably show the unearned *dolce vita* of the many to be built on the hard-headed reasoning of the scientific few. A sudden build-up of life pressures, for example, through population explosions, could easily shift the level on the I axis, restoring nineteenth-century beliefs in such things as martial ventures and the summary hanging of murderers, and reducing the concern for lost titmice in Bournemouth or the excess of homework in East Ham. There have apparently been swings on this dimension before, and students of historical cycles, like Raymond Wheeler and others, have even tried to associate tough–tender oscillation in history with recorded climatic swings.

Certainly there is some very interesting work ahead in relating both more constitutional personality factors, like A, and more environmentally determined, like I, to social and aesthetic differences and trends. Kretschmer's *Psychology of Men of Genius*, which relates low A to Gothic art, classical purity in literature, etc., and high A to rococo art, opera, and the romantic schools of literature, has already been mentioned and is a bold attempt in this direction. However, of all associations yet found between average population scores and general social outcomes perhaps the most striking is that between morale of the group as a whole and the number of neurotics in it (or the average personal neuroticism score). The ability of small groups to perform tasks on time, to withstand efforts to break them up (as an 'operational' definition of group morale), and even to perform in a tug-of-war (with the rope wired for continuous electric shock) can be shown to relate significantly to personality factors, but to none so much as the neuroticism factors. The mean level of neuroticism (or the percentage of neurotics) is the most powerful known reducer of the morale and the effectiveness of a group. Indeed, on the strength of this one might be tempted to define neuroticism in social rather than in clinical terms. Psychoanalytic literature has been endlessly concerned with the unfortunate things that society is said to do to the neurotic; but the experimental approach reveals some equally important things about what the neurotic does to society!

A WIDER LOOK AT THE SCIENTIFIC ANALYSIS OF PERSONALITY

Although the main applications of personality measurement and analysis are covered by the above topics of school organization, industrial selection, treatment of the neurotic and delinquent, etc., there remain some more delicate and also more pervasive areas of effect, for example, in marriage, religion, and personal realization.

With increasing mobility of population it is becoming less common for a youth to marry the girl next door. Yet if Blaise Pascal thought that choice of career was largely decided by accident, what could he not have said of choice of a spouse? Two principles have been considered by psychologists as governing non-accidental aspects of marriage choice: (1) assortativeness – the tendency of like to choose like, and (2) social compensatoriness – the tendency of both so to choose that together they make an effective team. The latter can but does not always work in opposition to the former. If someone feels that the obvious fact that they must be sexually attracted has been omitted, it is because it *is* obvious that they must have in common a difference of sex!

Assortativeness of mating was noticed long ago in relation to physical characteristics. Correlations of husband and wife range from 0·3 to 0·7 with respect to height and weight, hair and eye colour, and even to such minor traits as ratios of chest depth to width! Willson and the present writer found in 100 married couples a correlation of +0·7 in intelligence. It has since been shown that compatibility is associated also with similarity on measured personality factors. Affectothyme husbands choose affectothyme rather than sizothyme wives: surgent young women prefer surgent young men, and so on. These positive correlations are even more consistent among dynamic traits and interests. Lowell Kelley tested over 400 husbands and wives with the Allport–Vernon Interest Values test, which yields scores on aesthetic, theoretical, economic, social, political, and religious investments of interest and found better agreement of husbands and wives than people at random. Others have concluded that successfully married couples are more alike on these personality and interest traits than are those who get divorced. Whereas the obvious fact that people tend to marry persons of their own race and religion might initially be thought of as an accident due to contiguity, therefore, these results from analysis of measures where contiguity is not involved suggest rather that it is part of a general and deeper tendency for like to seek like.

The compensatory principle can also, though with more difficulty, be revealed by measurement and statistics. A marriage may survive one member being extravagant when it could not survive two. The lack of any substantial positive correlation on the *C* source trait, ego strength, or emotional stability, suggests similarly that an unstable person may unconsciously seek out a more stable one on whom to lean. And since marriage is give and take, this is probably traded for some return compensation on traits good in another direction. The poet Byron considered he had traded good looks and brilliance for money and steadfastness, but his wife in that case grew dissatisfied with the bargain, and there must always be a risk in the working of the compensatory principle. The only source trait known to be reported negatively correlated in researches is the L factor of Protension, which has not been discussed here as a factor. Protension is an acronym from 'projection of inner tension', which is the main basis for paranoid behaviour. The high L factor person distrusts most people, is of a dour disposition, feels superior, and makes friends slowly. It seems that if one person is high the other tends to be low on this trait, presumably because no marriage could last with two protensive people.

For a variety of reasons – of which the delicacy of the state of engagement is one – comparatively little of scientific value has yet been done on personality and marriage. Yet the technical resources are now becoming available, in questionnaires and O.-A. batteries, interest-value measures, the I.P.A.T. Humour test of personality (surely compatibility of humour is important), and the motivation measures, which would permit far greater insight into the nature of the success of a proposed marriage. Cupid and a computer may seem poles apart; but, compared with the wreckage of happiness represented by one divorce in every four marriages they might, on a basis of joint and tentative advice, improve the human lot considerably.

Yet another comparatively untouched and as yet speculative area of psychological application is towards the development of those values in personality which make for a better society. For many peoples in this generation a better society has meant a more prosperous society, and advertisers have done their best to make 'better living' mean a cluttering of life with more material possessions. Yet sooner or later the material sufficiency made possible by physical science will need to be extended to a spiritual richness made possible by psychological science. Ministers of religion and psychologists have tended to live in different worlds, except for such *rapprochements* as were recently begun by such psychologists as Mowrer, looking at the Freudian super-ego from a new angle, and Gorsuch, in personality measurement, attempting to assess the moral level of a community on a quantitative scale.

This hesitation of religion and psychology to get mutually too involved is a justifiable caution and realism on the part of well-educated men before the immense complexity of the issues. But psychology is beginning to study 'values' more and more and to make of that vague term something better understood, as we have seen, in terms of attitudes developing within the self-sentiment and super-ego structures. It is now becoming possible to measure by objective, non-questionnaire means the degree to which an individual is developing these structures, and to take stock, also by scientific observations, of what the development of a religious sentiment means for behaviour.

The nature of the personality of the sheer delinquent and the implied remedial steps for personality reformation have been briefly discussed above (page 220), as well as the nature of the seemingly irremediable psychopath (as Cleckley has described him in *The Blot upon the Brain*.) But although the lost sheep deserves the first attention, yet perhaps we should also get concerned, as psychologists, about the state of personality and motivation in those far more numerous persons, not actually delinquent, who contribute less to society than they might. One can envisage morale surveys as well as mental health surveys; but, like the latter, they will also have to be liberally multi-dimensional, for there are many ways in which a society may be hindered by an individual or helped to richer spiritual living. The exploration of these many mansions is a task for the serious social psychologist.

Finally, after showing what personality knowledge can do to help prediction and therapy with others, let us ask what its value may be to the healthy and intelligently self-directing individual himself. Self-knowledge has been held up as an ideal by philosophers, and more prosaically considered 'a first step to self-improvement' by practical people. But how little is done even by psychologists to help the ordinary healthy person to understand just what his capacities and limits and unused potentials may be on major personality and ability factors! At best such a person may have a conviction that he is one side of the middle on this and that – and even this may be wrong. The writer treasures an amusing recollection of a member of a Rotary Club group whose members had recently taken some tests. A gentleman who had just discovered himself to be below average on the emotional stability factor, *C*, arose and pounded the table and loudly asserted that he knew himself to be well above average in emotional control!

Actually, no studies leading to any comprehensive conclusions have yet been carried out to find what the long-term effect may be of being given substantial and clear information about one's status on psychological tests. To know one is below average, for

TABLE 30

Technical and popular labels for personality factors A to Q_1

Low score description	Factor		Factor	High score description
Reserved (Sizothymia)	*A*−	vs	*A*+	Outgoing (Affectothymia)
Less intelligent (Low 'g')	*B*−	vs	*B*+	More intelligent (High 'g')
Emotional (Low ego strength)	*C*−	vs	*C*+	Stable (High ego strength)
Humble (Submissiveness)	*E*−	vs	*E*+	Assertive (Dominance)
Sober (Desurgency)	*F*−	vs	*F*+	Happy-go-lucky (Surgency)
Expedient (Low super-ego)	*G*−	vs	*G*+	Conscientious (High super-ego)
Shy (Threctia)	*H*−	vs	*H*+	Venturesome (Parmia)
Tough-minded (Harria)	*I*−	vs	*I*+	Tender-minded (Premsia)
Trusting (Alaxia)	*L*−	vs	*L*+	Suspicious (Protension)
Practical (Praxernia)	*M*−	vs	*M*+	Imaginative (Autia)
Forthright (Artlessness)	*N*−	vs	*N*+	Shrewd (Shrewdness)
Placid (Assurance)	*O*−	vs	*O*+	Apprehensive (Guilt-proneness)
Conservative (Conservatism)	Q_1−	vs	Q_1+	Experimenting (Radicalism)
Group-tied (Group adherence)	Q_2−	vs	Q_2+	Self-sufficient (Self-sufficiency)
Casual (Low integration)	Q_3−	vs	Q_3+	Controlled (High self-concept)
Relaxed (Low ergic tension)	Q_4−	vs	Q_4+	Tense (Ergic tension)

example, on an intelligence test may not be very helpful; but most personality factors have good qualities at both poles, as the profile sheet labels on the 16 P.F., for example, in Table 30, remind one. And even if a trait is 'awkward' the 'law of coercion to the bio-social mean' suggests that the effect on most people will be to help them to moderate or, at least, be more sophisticated about, the traits in which they are more extreme. To the averagely well-balanced person, more exact information about his mental capacities and shortcomings should be at least as helpful as knowing the results of a physical examination, while at best it could be the basis for real development and coordination of his resources.

However, for anyone to 'help himself' from the results of personality measurement tests, it is first necessary that he understand the nature of psychological measurements, as well as something about the analysis of personality structure and its roots in heredity and environment – a goal towards which this book has been aimed. Apart from any such practical aim this brief discourse may also have given a glimpse of the intricacy and delicacy of the concepts towards which science has to move in considering personality. A scientist looks at an apple and sees an array of spinning electrons, locked into shape by atomic and molecular forces. He looks at a personality and sees a still more amazing interplay of forces, following a still more awe-inspiring set of mathematical equations. Matter has indeed woven itself here into sheer movement and form – a complex creative eddy mysteriously able to appear and disappear. And while the older sciences are reaching out into space, to claim the fruits of the original thinking of Galileo and Gauss, Newton and Faraday, and Einstein, the scientists of psychology are peering into a hyperspace. In this multi-dimensional world, into which we have taken at any rate a passing glance, the great discoveries of psychological mathematics remain to be made.

Glossary

Adjustment path analysis: A standard framework for analysing a person's attempts at adjustment in terms of basic alternative paths which can be followed.

Adjustment process analysis: A means of investigating and expressing personality learning by the frequency of following certain adjustment paths and by their effect upon personality factors in a matrix multiplication design.

Affective psychoses: 'Functional' insanities showing exaggerated mood: manic-depressive disorders.

Affectothymia ($A+$): A source trait influencing outgoing, warm-hearted, easy-going, participating behaviour. (See *Affective psychoses*.)

Aids: The development of systems of cognitive ability to cope, through the discovery of some particular response formula which is successful and generates many associated performances.

Assortativeness: The principle whereby like tends to choose like in marriage selection.

Autia ($M+$): A trait of general tendency to be autistic, i.e. to perceive reality falsely as in accord with one's wishes. Also wrapped up in inner imaginative developments, bohemian, careless of practicalities.

Behaviour therapy: Form of psychotherapy in which the emphasis is on changing behaviour by immediate reward or conditioning.

Behavioural equation: A linear equation in which each trait entering into the behaviour to be predicted is given the value for the given person and is multiplied by a situational index or behavioural index which is common to all people in that situation and shows how much the trait enters into the behaviour.

Behavioural index: See *Loading*.

Behavioural situation indices: The values, which are factor loadings, usually written b or s in the behavioural specification equation, which show how much a given source trait is involved in that specific situation and response.

Bivariate experiment: A form of design in which only two variables are measured at once, one of them commonly being manipulated and called the independent variable. (Sometimes called the univariate method.) This may be called the classical, traditional experimental design in contrast with the multivariate experiment.

Chemotherapy: The treatment of mental disorders by drugs and bio-chemicals.

Chiasms: Choice points in dynamic adjustment, sometimes called 'dynamic crossroads', where emotional expression is changed.

Comention, U.I. 20: A source trait in objective traits characterized by agreeing with the group, showing emotional responsiveness and activity.

Common trait: A trait which can be measured for all people by the same battery and on which they differ in degree rather than in form.

Complex: In Freudian theory, an idea which has been repressed and dissociated from the rest of a person's mind, but continues to act from the unconscious, producing symptomatic behaviour.

Confluence learning: That learning in which an individual acquires a piece of behaviour simultaneously satisfying to two different ergic or general dynamic goals.

Consistency: The extent to which a test is consistent with itself. See *Reliability*.

Conspective test: A test in which different experimenters will arrive at the same score for a given response by the subject.

Correlation coefficient: An index widely used in psychology and social sciences to show the degree of association of scores of two kinds in a group. If there is perfect agreement, it is $+1$ and if there is a perfect inverse relationship, it is -1. A value of zero shows that the relation between the two things is purely chance.

Correlation matrix: A triangular or square arrangement of cells which gives the correlation between all possible pairings among the variables (e.g. test scores, etc.) studied.

Cortertia, U.I. 22: The factor of cortical alertness and arousal, in objective tests, such as reaction time, flicker fusion speed, etc.

Covert anxiety: That part of anxiety which is measured by question-naire items in which the individual is not particularly aware that they are signs of anxiety and which indicate that he may not himself be aware of the level of his anxiety.

Criterion: The 'outside' behaviour or concept which a psychological test sets out to measure.

Crystallized general ability: A general factor, largely in a type of abilities learned at school, representing the effect of past application of fluid intelligence, and amount and intensity of schooling; it appears in such tests as vocabulary and numerical ability measures.

Desurgency ($F-$): A trait of sober, prudent, serious and taciturn behaviour.

Dominance ($E+$): A source trait shown in assertive, independent, confident, and stubborn behaviour.

Dynamic lattice: The tracing of the subsidiation of attitudes, one to another, ending in the satisfaction of a number of primary ergic goals.

Ego Strength. ($C+$): A source trait showing itself in good emotional stability and capacity to cope with emotional difficulties.

Ego Weakness ($C-$): That pole of the C trait which manifests itself in emotional instability and being easily upset and moody.

Emergents: Things which appear in a combination of things which could not be predicted from knowing them separately.

Erg: An innate source of reactivity, such as is often described as a drive, directed to a certain goal and accompanied by a certain quality, but established by factor analysis of many motivational manifestations.

Ergic Tension (Q_4+): As a personality source trait this is interpreted as the total aroused unexpressed drive tension (from ergic sources). It covers tense, driven, over-active behaviour.

Exuberance: The name given to a trait, in objective tests, indexed as U.I. 21 and showing itself in high fluency, rapid decision, spontaneity, etc.

Exvia–Invia, U.I. 32: A factorially established broad dimension within the area of behaviour popularly referred to as extraversion–introversion. The precise core concept within extraversion–introversion.

Factor: An underlying influence responsible for part of the variability of a number of behavioural manifestations. Therefore, an influence in behaviour which is relatively independent of other influences and of a unitary nature.

Factor score: Quantitative estimate of a person's or group of persons' endowment on a factor-dimension, computed from their scores on a weighted combination of the test variables loading that factor.

Fluid general ability: That form of general intelligence which is largely innate and which adapts itself to all kinds of material, regardless of previous experience with it.

Function fluctuation: The extent to which a trait tends to vary from occasion to occasion.

G–Z Questionnaire: A personality questionnaire constructed by Guilford and Zimmerman. It differs from the Sixteen Personality Factor Questionnaire in having its factors orthogonal and, therefore, not at maximum simple structure and correspondence to natural functional unities.

General Inhibition, U.I. 17: A factor connected with a tendency to be generally cautious and timid, in many diverse objective tests.

Goal-path learning: A form of reward learning in which the individual continues to reach the same goal but by more effective means.

Guilt-Proneness (*O*+): A source trait distinct from super-ego strength but predisposing to guilt-prone, depressive, apprehensive behaviour.

Harria: The opposite pole (*I*−) of Premsia, and characterized by realism, toughness, and self-reliance (acronym for hard realism).

Homogeneity: The extent to which the parts of a test test the same thing. Sometimes erroneously called reliability.

Humour Test of Personality: An I.P.A.T. test in which the individual indicates which jokes he finds funny, and which has been shown to be diagnostic of about ten personality factors.

Hyperplane: The set of variables whose loadings on a factor are not significantly different from zero. In rotation for simple structure, the factor is placed at right angles to the hyperplane, which, when visually plotted, forms an ellipse or disk in factor space.

Hyperspace: Space of more than three dimensions, as in the mathematician's imaginary use of extra coordinates.

Individual test: A test which can be administered to only one person at a time.

Inhibition, U.I. 17: A factor of general timidity or inhibition showing itself in restriction of all kinds of behaviour.

Instrument factor: A false factor, i.e. not a real personality factor, which sometimes appears when many behaviours are measured by one kind of instrument and which is peculiar to the instrument.

Integrated motivation component: That component in motivation for a given course of action of which the person is fully aware and which is integrated with his conscious intentions and skills.

Integration learning: Learning consisting of a re-arrangement of satisfactions among a number of conflicting, independent drives.

L-data: Life record data, i.e. scores, e.g. frequency scores, on behaviour in the natural life situation, as distinct from a test.

Leptosomatic: Of lean, narrow body build.

Libido: In Freudian terms, the general mental energy deriving from sexual drive, both in its object-attached and its narcissistic form.

Loading: A value varying between $+1$ and -1 which is obtained from factor analysis and shows the extent to which increases in the strength of a factor bring about increases in the dependent behaviour score.

Master Index (M.I.) Number: A number indexing a particular objective test variable (score) and retained constant from study to study, thus enabling ready identification of this variable. For example, M.I. 104, M.I. 582, etc., in which each number refers to a different variable. Several different variables may be scored and indexed from the same test. Compare with *U.I.* or *Universal Index Number* which performs a similar indexing function for factors.

Matrix multiplication: A matrix is a box of many cells with numbers in each which describe some object, pattern or set of vectors. Mathematics has specific rules for multiplying one matrix by another.

Misperception test: A test in which the person's deviation from the norm in perception is used as a measurement of his personality.

M.M.P.I.: The Minnesota Multiphasic Personality Inventory by Hathaway and McKinley, which is a questionnaire for recognizing surface traits or syndromes of an abnormal nature.

Mobilization-vs-Regression (U.I. 23) in the Universal Index: A source trait visible as a pattern in objective tests and characterized at one pole by ability to mobilize one's skills quickly and at the other by general regression of interest and control.

Modality of trait: Traits fall into three modalities, cognitive or ability traits, temperament or stylistic traits, and dynamic or motivational traits.

Modulator factor: A factor which is brought into action as a temporary state in a person, such as a role or a mood, by some ambient stimulus which provokes the state and affects all subsequent behaviour for a while.

Motivational component: One of some seven factors found among manifestations of motivation strength, which may vary independently of the other components in motivation for a given course of action.

Motivational distortion scale: A scale introduced to determine the amount of faking or sabotage which goes on in answering a questionnaire or psychological test.

Multiple Abstract Variance Analysis (M.A.V.A.) Design: A research design for discovering relative proportions of environmental *vs* hereditary determination for personality traits (*Nature–nurture ratio*).

Multivariate experiment: An experimental design in which many variables are allowed to vary simultaneously, and in which all possible relations among them are worked out.

Music Preference Test of Personality: A long-playing record in which the person responds 'like' or 'dislike' to music, and from which measures on about twelve personality factors can be made.

Nature–nurture ratio: The ratio expressing the percentages contributed in a given social and racial group, respectively by heredity and by environmental differences, to the observed interpersonal variability in a trait.

Objective tests: A term to distinguish from questionnaires those tests in which the individual actually acts – instead of describing his acts – and has his performance measured without being aware what traits are being measured.

Overt anxiety (as in the I.P.A.T. Anxiety Scale): That part of anxiety of which the individual is aware and ready to speak. Compare *Covert anxiety*.

P-technique: A factor analytic design which measures a single person on the same set of variables repeatedly over a number of different occasions. Correlations between the variables are computed over these occasions as entries, then factor analysed. P-technique and incremental factor analysis are the two main methods for determining dimensions of personality change-over-time (or states).

Parmia ($H+$): A title derived as an acronym from 'parasympathetic immunity to threat' believed theoretically to underly the behaviour of boldness, spontaneity, and insusceptibility to inhibition found in $H+$.

Pattern similarity coefficient: A coefficient summarized as r_p which indicates the degree of similarity between the personality profiles of two people or of one person and the ideal pattern for an occupation, etc., and which varies from $+1$ to -1 like a correlation coefficient.

Personality sphere: The totality of human behaviour from which personality is inferred.

Picture Frustration Test: A test in which a number of frustrating situations are shown in pictures and the individual is asked to indicate the most likely response.

Praxernia (M—): The opposite of *autia*; a pattern of practical, careful, conventional behaviour.

Premsia (I+): An acronym to designate the theoretical source (protected emotional sensitivity) of the tender-minded, dependent, sensitive behaviour in this behaviour pattern.

Profile: As used in this book, the scores of a person or group of persons on each of a set of distinct traits or factors. The order in which traits are listed is not prescribed, but a matter of convenience.

Projection: As *true* projection, the reading into another of repressed tendencies in oneself, but loosely used in 'projective' misperception, which may arise from naïve projection.

Protension (L+): A source trait of self-opinionated, sceptical, jealous, and suspicious behaviour, designated in its more abnormal forms as paranoid, but essentially an inner tension accompanied by strong tendencies to *projection* from which, too, the name is derived.

Psychometry: That branch of psychology which is concerned with mental measurements of all kinds and the mathematics which goes therewith.

Psychosis: A form of mental disorder different from neurosis, in which the individual loses contact with reality and needs hospitalization for his own protection and that of others. Among the chief functional psychoses are schizophrenia and manic-depressive disorders.

Q-data: Evidence on personality from self-evaluative, introspective report, as in the consulting room or filling out a questionnaire.

Q'-technique: A method in which one correlates people over tests (instead of conversely as in *R-technique*) to see how alike they are. It is not a method of factor analysis (as in Q-technique) but only of searching for clusters of people as shown by the correlations.

R-technique: Ordinary factor analysis in which tests are given to people and correlated over people.

Reflexology: A system of laws in the field of learning experiment, in which a simple reflex connexion, such as might be due to a neurological reflex arc, is supposed to exist between the stimulus and the response.

Regression coefficient: A statistical device for making the best possible prediction of score on one variable, from knowledge of score on another variable. Not to be confused with regression as a clinical concept or as a factor-dimension.

Reliability coefficient: The correlation of a second administration of the test with its first administration, when the interval is too short for the persons being measured actually to have changed. It is a measure of the test's ability to measure what it measures in a consistent fashion.

Reward learning (or operant conditioning): Learning new paths or responses towards a goal, under the influence of the 'law of effect', i.e. the tendency of rewarded behaviours to be remembered.

Rorschach Test: A test consisting of ten cards showing symmetrical ink blots variously coloured to which the patient responds by giving associative descriptions.

Rosenzweig Picture Frustration Test: A test in which the subject chooses suitable responses to depicted frustrating situations.

Schizophrenia: The most common of the insanities, in which the individual shows a split between his emotional and cognitive life, with bizarre ideas, withdrawal of contact from people, and hallucinations.

Second-order or higher-order factors: Factors of wider influence obtained by correlating factors themselves and factor-analysing them. Thus factors among factors.

Self-sentiment: The sentiment structure centred upon the individual's conception of himself and his desire to maintain this self-concept, in the eyes of himself and others, intact and acceptable.

Sentiment: A set of attitudes the strength of which has become correlated through their being all learnt by contact with a particular social institution, e.g. a sentiment to school, to home, to country.

Situational index: See *Loading*.

Sizothymia (A−): The opposite end of the affectothymia dimension, characterized by reserved, cool, detached behaviour.

Source trait: A factor-dimension, stressing the proposition that variations in value along it are determined by a single, unitary influence or source. Contrast with *Surface trait*.

Specification equation: See *Behavioural equation*.

States: A form of psychological factor to be distinguished from traits. States cover dynamic conditions, fatigue, etc., and are factors found by study of longitudinal change.

Stens: Units in a standard ten scale, in which ten score points are used to cover the population range in fixed and equal standard deviation intervals, extending from $2\frac{1}{2}$ standard deviations above the mean (sten 10). The mean is fixed at 5·5 stens. In this book, questionnaire raw scores are usually converted to stens, when intending to use them normatively (to compare obtained values with population values).

Super-ego Strength (G+): A source trait governing conscientious, persevering, unselfish behaviour and impelling the individual to duty as conceived by his culture.

Surface trait: A set of personality characteristics which are correlated but do not form a factor, hence are believed to be determined by more than one influence or source. Contrast with *Source trait*.

Surgency (*F+*): A source trait of happy-go-lucky, heedless, gay, uninhibited, and enthusiastic behaviour.

T-data: Evidence on personality from objective tests, i.e. tests in which the subject performs without awareness of that on which he is actually being scored. Therefore 'unfakeable' tests.

T.A.T.: The Thematic Apperception Test. Invented by Henry Murray. It consists of 'unstructured pictures' which the subject is asked to explain in his own words.

Test: A portable, standardized situation to which the subject willingly responds and which is scored either conspectively or otherwise.

Test sophistication: The gain or change in a test score due to past familiarity with that test or type of test.

Threctia (*H−*): The opposite of *parmia*, and expressing itself in shyness and high responsiveness to threat.

Thurstone Primary Abilities Test: A test of such primary abilities as vocabulary, or verbal ability, numerical ability, spatial ability, memory, etc.

Trait: A unitary configuration in behaviour such that when one part is present in a certain degree, we can infer that a person will show the other parts in a certain degree.

Transferability coefficient: A correlation showing how much a test measures with one kind of subject the same thing that it measures with other kinds of subjects.

Transference neuroses: A name given by Freud to neuroses in which libido seems to be transferred to manifestations of anxiety.

Type or species type: A particular constellation of scores on factors or other variables which occurs with high frequency in the population, relative to other possible combinations.

U.I. or Universal Index: A scheme of indexing of factors proposed to make exact reference to factors possible despite different interpretative names used by different investigators. U.I. 1–U.I. 15 are abilities, as defined by French, and U.I. 16–U.I. 35 are personality factors.

Unintegrated motivation component: That component in a person's motivation for a given course of action which has poor reality contact and manifests itself mainly through 'I wish' expressions.

Unique trait: A trait the pattern and possession of which is peculiar to one individual.

Validity coefficient: A coefficient expressing the extent to which a test measures what it is supposed to measure. This may be a concrete validity against a particular concrete performance, or a concept validity against a psychological concept.

Variance: The magnitude of variability of a score. Technically, $\dfrac{\overset{N}{\underset{o}{\Sigma}} d^2}{N}$ where d is the deviation of each person from the mean and there are N persons.

Subject Index

Name Index

Italicized page numbers refer to the 'Further Reading' references at the end of the various chapters.